Systematic Analysis in Dispute Resolution

Systematic Analysis in Dispute Resolution

Edited by Stuart S. Nagel
and Miriam K. Mills

Q

Quorum Books
New York • Westport, Connecticut • London

Library of Congress Cataloging-in-Publication Data

Systematic analysis in dispute resolution / edited by Stuart S. Nagel
and Miriam K. Mills
    p. cm.
   Includes bibliographical references and index.
   ISBN 0-89930-623-3 (alk. paper)
   1. Dispute resolution (Law)—United States. 2. Dispute resolution
(Law)   I. Nagel, Stuart S.   II. Mills, Miriam K.
KF9084.S97 1991
347.73′9—dc20
[347.3079]   90-22125

British Library Cataloguing in Publication Data is available.

Library of Congress Catalog Card Number: 90-22125
ISBN: 0-89930-623-3

First published in 1991

Quorum Books, One Madison Avenue, New York, NY 10010
An imprint of Greenwood Publishing Group, Inc.

Printed in the United States of America

The paper used in this book complies with the
Permanent Paper Standard issued by the National
Information Standards Organization (Z39.48–1984).

10 9 8 7 6 5 4 3 2 1

Dedicated to understanding and resolving disputes in families,
neighborhoods, courts, legislatures, and the global arena

Contents

Tables and Figures

TABLES

FIGURES

Introduction

Since the title of this book is *Systematic Analysis in Dispute Resolution*, the introduction should logically begin with definitions of dispute resolution and systematic analysis. Dispute resolution refers to various methods for settling disagreements among individuals or groups; systematic analysis refers to bringing about or explaining settlements to disputes by analyzing the goals of each side, the alternatives available to each side, and how each side perceives the relations among the goals and alternatives.

The methods for resolving disputes can be classified in various ways. One way is in terms of the extent to which the disputants win or lose. In this regard, solutions to disputes can be classified as follows:

1. Super-optimum solutions, in which all sides come out ahead of their initial best expectations.

2. Pareto optimum solutions, in which nobody comes out worse off and at least one side comes out better off. (This is not a very favorable solution compared to a super-optimum solution.)

3. A win-lose solution, where what one side wins the other side loses. The net effect is zero when losses are subtracted from gains. This is the typical litigation dispute when one ignores the litigation costs.

4. A lose-lose solution, where both sides are worse off than they were before the dispute began. This may often be the typical litigation dispute, or close to it, when one includes litigation costs. These costs are often so high that the so-called winner is also a loser. This is also often the case in labor-management disputes that result in a strike, and even more so in international disputes that result in war.

5. The so-called win-win solution, which at first glance sounds like a solution where everybody comes out ahead. What it typically refers to, however, is an illusion, since the parties are only coming out ahead relative to their worst expectations. In this sense, the plaintiff is a winner no matter what the settlement because the plaintiff could have won nothing if liability had been rejected at trial. Likewise, the defendant could have lost everything the plaintiff was asking for if liability had been established at trial. The parties are only fooling themselves in the same sense that someone who is obviously a loser tells himself he won because he could have done worse.

Another common way of classifying dispute resolutions is in terms of whether there is a third party present. In this sense, adjudication, arbitration, and mediation are forms of three-party dispute resolution, while negotiation is two-party dispute resolution. Adjudication involves a court or administrative agency that resolves disputes, usually in a win-lose way. Arbitration tends to involve an ad hoc third party that is hired or obtained for the immediate dispute, but that also tends to operate from a win-lose perspective. A mediator is usually ad hoc, but seeks to have both sides arrive at mutually beneficial settlements that could be win-win, pareto optimum, or even super-optimum, but not win-lose or lose-lose. The distinction between three- and two-party dispute resolution may be undesirable because it encourages two-party negotiation to go for a win-lose solution. It is possible when two negotiators are present for one or both of them to have a mediation perspective in the sense of seeking to truly bring about a super-optimum or pareto optimum solution.

Yet another way of classifying dispute resolutions is in terms of the substance or subject matter. This can include such categories as disputes involving family members, neighbors, merchants-consumer, management-labor, litigation or rule-applying, legislation or rule-making, and foreign countries. These categories are especially meaningful if one is trying to show the broad applicability of dispute resolution methods that involve super-optimum solutions, a mediation perspective, and the systematic analysis that is associated with decision-aiding software. That helps explain why the chapters in this book are organized in terms of those substance application categories.

Like dispute resolution, systematic analysis can be classified in various ways. One way relates to whether the analysis is accompanied by decision-aiding software. Such software can facilitate super-optimum solutions by enabling one to work with many goals simultaneously. Decision-aiding software makes it relatively easy to experiment with changes in goals, alternatives, relations, constraints, weights, and other inputs until one is satisfied that a solution has been reached in which all sides come out ahead of their best expectations simultaneously.

If decision-aiding software is used as part of systematic analysis, it can be classified in various ways:

1. Decision-tree software for making decisions under conditions of risk such as whether to go to trial or accept a settlement. A decision tree is usually pictured as a tree on

its side with branches and sub-branches. The branches generally represent alternative possibilities that depend on the occurence or nonoccurrence of probabilistic events.

2. Linear-programming software for allocating money, time, people, or other scarce resources to activities, places, tasks, or other objects to which the resources are to be allocated. In terms of form rather than function, linear-programming involves maximizing or minimizing an objective function or algebraic expression subject to constraints (generally in the form of inequalities).

3. Spreadsheet-based software in which the alternatives tend to be on the rows, criteria on the columns, relations in the cells, overall scores for each alternative in a column at the far right, and a capability for determining what it would take to bring a second- or other-place alternative up to first place.

4. Rule-based software that contains a set of rules for dealing with a narrow or broad field of law. The user gives the computer a set of facts, and the computer applies the rules to the facts in order to determine which alternative decision is likely to be made. Such software is sometimes referred to as artificial intelligence (AI) or expert systems, but the other forms of decision-aiding software also have characteristics associated with AI and expert systems.

5. Decision-aiding software that focuses on a specific field of dispute resolution (in contrast to the above software, which cuts across all subjects). Litigation is the dispute resolution field in which specialized decision-aiding software seems to be developing most rapidly.

This book is especially oriented toward super-optimum solutions, although not all the chapters fit into this category. In terms of processes, the book as a whole is oriented toward mediation more than the other dispute-resolution processes. On subject matters, it treats family, neighborhood, litigation, policy-making, and international disputes. The book finds value in the use of decision-aiding software to achieve super-optimum settlements, especially software that is spreadsheet-based. Although the book emphasizes these categories, it does provide a variety of perspectives across diverse disciplines, countries, and orientations.

This book emphasizes resolving disputes in individual cases, although the parties could be individuals, business firms, labor unions, or countries. The key characteristic is developing a settlement in specific cases as contrasted to developing broad principles or precedents that cut across cases. Both kinds of dispute resolution are important. It would be inefficient to concentrate only on case-by-case resolution if changing the substantive or procedural rules could resolve many cases simultaneously. Likewise, it would be undesirable to develop elaborate cross-cutting rules with poor procedures for implementing them in specific cases. The counterpart to this book emphasizing resolving policy-making controversies is entitled *Legal Process Controversies and Super-Optimum Solutions* (Quorum Books, 1992).

The subject of dispute resolution is becoming more important partly due to the more formal ways in which people in urban and industrial societies resolve disputes. It is also becoming more important as the quantity and seriousness of disputes grow. These changes make the subject more challenging. It is hoped that this book will rise to the challenge by showing how systematic analysis and dispute resolution can aid in resolving disputes that relate to families, neighborhoods, litigation, policy-making, and foreign countries.

This book owes its existence to the editors' good fortune in meeting a wide variety of people involved in dispute resolution, partly through the Society for Professionals in Dispute Resolution, the American Arbitration Association, the American Bar Association, and the Law and Society Association. The book especially owes its existence to Eric Valentine from Quorum Books of the Greenwood Publishing Group. He has been foresightful in publishing the counterpart to this book, *Multi-Criteria Methods in Dispute Resolution: With Software Applications* (Quorum, 1990). Other essential people include Jack Cooley, who is an outstanding mediator-arbitrator in Chicago, and Joyce Nagel, who has the patience of a mediator-arbitrator to put up with all the work involved in producing this and numerous other books.

PART I

Classifying Disputes

CHAPTER 1

Broadening the Applicability of Multi-Criteria Dispute Resolution

STUART S. NAGEL

One purpose of this chapter is to discuss the broad nature of multi-criteria dispute resolution, rather than focus on the litigation and legal policy disputes that are usually emphasized. Another purpose is to compare different types of dispute resolution, including negotiation, mediation, arbitration, and adjudication.

Still further broadening involves using more generic concepts and expanding the bilateral dispute resolution to include more parties. The most important broadening, however, is thinking more explicitly about resolving disputes in terms of solutions whereby all sides come out ahead of their best expectations. This kind of thinking can apply to disputes that relate to families, labor-management, merchants-consumers, neighborhoods, government regulation, business firms, government agencies, foreign countries, litigation, or the liberal-conservative public policy adoption controversy.

GENERAL CONCEPTS AND CLASSIFICATIONS

The best way to organize this chapter is in terms of two dimensions. One dimension relates to processes and the other to subjects. Negotiation, mediation, arbitration, and adjudication are the four basic processes; subjects include the family, the neighborhood, the consumer, the workplace, litigation and legal policy disputes, and the international arena. Within each of the subject areas we could talk about the four ways of resolving disputes. This process could get redundant, however, since we would be saying repeatedly how mediation is relevant to reconciling the parties and to enabling them to achieve their goals beyond their initial best expectations.

Types of Dispute Resolution

In *negotiation*, one side is probably going to win and the other side is going to lose. The loser is likely to be bitter. The winner may feel guilty or disrespectful to the loser. In general, the results are likely to be increased friction.

In *mediation* (especially super-optimum mediation), there is a good possibility of the problems being resolved to the point where new problems have to occur in order to have a dispute, rather than a reviving of the old dispute.

In *arbitration* there is also a winner and a loser. The decision is more accepted than in a negotiation situation because it comes from the outside. We could lump arbitration and adjudication together since they both have the imposing of a winner and a loser from the outside. It does not make much difference whether the outsider is an official judge or an ad hoc arbitrator.

Adjudication refers to dispute resolution by professional judges who generally work full-time at judging as contrasted to part-time mediators or arbitrators who may have other occupations. Adjudication especially differs from mediation because it tends to emphasize deciding who is right and who is wrong, whereas mediation seeks to bring the parties together and emphasizes compromise. Adjudication differs from arbitration in that it tends to rely more on past recorded cases than on customary procedures, and more on codified rules than on uncodified common sense.

Having disputes resolved by a professional third party has been an important advance in the development of world civilization over the parties resorting to violent resolution or tactics in which the winner is determined by might or power, rather than the rule of objectively administered law. It is, however, ironic (or maybe part of normal world progress) that we now seem to be at a stage where what was considered such an advance in the past is now being substantially improved upon by the mediation perspective. This perspective emphasizes everyone coming out ahead. It also emphasizes preventive action. It is in conformity with a quality of life in which resources are not so scarce, and there is continual economic growth. This kind of expansion facilitates mutually beneficial solutions, even super-optimum solutions, where all sides come out ahead of their best expectations.[1]

Subject Matter

1. *Family* disputes may involve child custody, child support, or property settlement. Multiple criteria are common in divorce settlements. A family dispute may involve a marriage counseling rather than a divorce counseling situation. Marriage counseling may address problems that have to do with alcoholism or other vices, disagreement over how money is to be spent, or how children are to be reared.

2. A *workplace* dispute could involve an employer and either a single employee or a group of employees disagreeing over wages, working conditions, time set aside for lunch or breaks, or starting/ending time.

3. A *consumer* dispute could involve the quality of a product. One firm, for example, may contend that it was expecting to receive a certain quality level for one thousand items that it bought and the level was not met. The seller claims that it was operating with the understanding that the quality level was a 4, rather than a 5.

4. A *neighborhood* dispute could involve two neighbors who are unhappy with each other because one makes more noise than the other can tolerate.

5. *Regulatory* disputes.

6. Disputes between *business firms*.

7. Disputes between *government agencies*.

8. *International* disputes, like the U.S.–Soviet arms control issue.

9. *Litigation*, such as product liability cases.

10. *Legal policy* development may involve legal services for the poor. We could also add any legal policy problem that involves a super-optimum solution.[2]

Basic Concepts

The concept of *settlement* applies regardless of the kind of dispute. The concept of *trial* is strictly a litigation concept. Instead of talking about a trial, we can talk about the nonsettlement method of resolution, which could be a strike, a war, or a duel. Normally it is more extreme than settling. Yet going to trial may be better than settling if the settlement offer is unsatisfactory. In terms of the nonsettlement method, we can talk about the best-case scenario, the worst-case scenario, and the expected value.

Disputes often involve more than two sides. We can talk about the perspective of side, 1, 2, or 3. With three sides, presumably each side collects from the other two. If two of the three sides join together, then it is really only two sides with a coalition on one or the other side.

The best expectation of a given side is expressed in the initial offer or demands. For bargaining purposes, the initial position each side takes tends to demand more than they expect to wind up with. The disputants reason that by taking such a starting position, they can then make concessions as necessary to bring about a beneficial agreement.

All this material is relevant to the more specifically focused problem of litigation mediation and to the more broadly based problem of mediating any kind of dispute. These concepts can facilitate litigation settlements or other kinds of settlements. The multi-criteria aspects are especially helpful when the settlement involves a package arrangement with one side giving on a number of matters that are not so important to it, but are important to the other side. It is the multi-criteria aspect that is most important. The other concepts are basically visual or conceptual aids that enable the parties to see more clearly how the multi-criteria package is in their best interests.

Super-optimum means best—not just in the sense of being better than the worst possibility, but better than the best expectations of all sides. Best does not mean the best possible trial outcome, but the best expectations of each side, as indicated by their initial positions.

THE APPLICATION OF DISPUTE RESOLUTION

Family Disputes

Typically more than one process of dispute resolution will be used for a given couple. A failed mediation may end up in litigation, for example. On the other hand, although one party may file a contested divorce case, there is often a negotiated settlement well before the case gets to court. By this time there is virtually no chance of reconciliation. However, the selection of the process for resolving the remaining issues may have an effect on the future dealings between the parties. The choice of dispute resolution methods forms a continuum between the less structured procedure of negotiation to the most formal adjudicative mechanism.

Negotiation

Negotiation between a husband and wife is fine when it works, but there is usually too much ego involvement for either side to be willing to come to what an outsider would consider a reasonable agreement. The more emotional involvement there is, the more there is need for a third party. If the husband suggests a course of action, the wife is likely to react negatively. If a third party suggests the same course of action, the suggestion may receive a more positive reaction.

Negotiation eventually resolves about 90 percent of divorce disputes, but does not necessarily result in reconciliation. Few couples can put aside the emotional investment they have made during the marriage to deal with the necessary practical consequences of the end of their relationship. In fact, attorneys negotiate most divorce settlements. A negotiated settlement has an advantage in that it reflects what the couple thinks is reasonable in their particular case. In effect, then, the parties make their own law, although the court must usually approve the final settlement.

Litigation

At the opposite extreme is going to court. The typical judge is not interested in a reconciliation, but simply in determining who is right. That person wins, and the other side loses, causing a great deal of antagonism.

Litigation occurs when the parties are unable to resolve their marital problems without the direct intervention of the legal system. Some litigation, particularly in jurisdictions that consider evidence of fault in awarding the divorce or in determining whether support is appropriate, involves the judge's deciding which of the spouses is right (or least at fault). Another frequent type of litigation involves children. Here the judge must decide not which spouse is right, but which arrangement will be in the child's best interest. A third type of litigation involves the division of what was once joint property into two "equitable" or, in some states, "equal" shares. Each of these quite different types of proceedings features the application of societal norms to the private dispute, the relative formality of the process, and the necessary involvement of attorneys. As in most trial contexts, several computer software packages may be useful to the litigators and their clients. These include spreadsheet programs used to show the present values of annuities or closely held corporations. There are also decision-analysis programs, designed to simplify decisions about whether trial or settlement is the most desirable alternative.

Arbitration

The arbitrator has the advantage of not being so legalistic, being more informal, being available on short notice, and especially of being able to keep things quiet. The arbitrator, like the judge, however, is primarily concerned with deciding who is right.

Arbitration is generally inappropriate until after the final divorce decree, because of the societal interests in the marriage status and especially because of the desire to discover what is best for the children. In some states law commissioners, not judges, hear the initial case. The commissioner's reports are then reviewed by a court of law, which must make the ultimate decisions. Some states have enforced arbitration clauses for such matters as choice of college or what to do if there is change in the tax laws, which the parties agree to in a written contract. Clauses requiring arbitration are not upheld if they involve matters of custody or visitation. Unless the arbitration is "final-offer arbitration," the arbitrator probably will not have to choose between the offers made by the divorced spouses. The arbitrator can make any award deemed reasonable.

Mediation

The mediator has the same advantage as the arbitrator as far as informality and quietness, but not the disadvantage of having to think in terms of a right-wrong dichotomy. The mediator can try to find right on both sides and work out a settlement that can (if done well) be better than the best expectations of either side. One might argue that computer-aided mediation is inappropriate in an emotional family dispute. Yet such mediation might be even more appropriate than in a mercenary dispute. The use of a computer can calm things down, make things better organized, and encourage rational thought.

Mediation is a popular dispute resolution process in family law cases, and has even been made mandatory in some states. Like arbitration, it is a less formal procedure than litigation and involves the activities of a neutral third party. The goal of the family mediator, however, is to help the parties reach agreement without imposition of outside norms. Often the experienced mediator can help the parties create solutions that neither had thought of individually. Some mediators also try to help the divorcing couple develop the communications skills that were lacking during their marriage. This therapeutic mediation may be especially appropriate if there must be a continuing relationship because of the presence of minor children.

Some family mediators use computer software to help the divorcing couple focus on the financial alternatives available to them. The mediator may supply draft separation agreements typed on a word processor so that both spouses can immediately see the effect of changes. Decision-aiding software can be helpful in deciding among alternative arrangements for custody, property settlement, child support, or other issues.

Dispute Resolution in Interactions

Table 1.1 shows how dispute resolution may be applied to seven types of interaction. One of the areas that is not included is regulatory disputes, a relatively new field of dispute resolution. It generally involves administrative agencies with quasi-judicial power, such as the traditional economic regulatory agencies like the National Labor Relations Board, the Securities and Exchange Commission, the Federal Trade Commission, the Federal Communications Commission, the National Maritime Board, the Interstate Commerce Commission, and the Federal Power Commission. It also includes more recent administrative agencies that are social rather than economic in nature, such as the Equal Employment Opportunity Commission, the Environmental Protection Agency, the Occupational Safety and Health Administration, and the Product Safety Commission. These agencies are making more use of negotiated settlements in both adjudications and in rule-making proceedings. These agencies were originally founded partly to reduce delay in the judicial and legislative process, but they have become bogged down in layers of procedures. They are now welcoming alternative dispute resolution as a means of achieving both delay reduction and better-quality results.

A second area that is relatively new is disputes between government agencies, particularly in matters of intergovernment relations. Disputes might be between the federal government and a state, a state and one of its cities, two states, two cities, a city and a county, or any combination of the above. Often the mediator is a government entity at a higher level, such as a state agency trying to resolve a dispute between cities. A mediator could be a government entity at the same level, such as a third city helping to resolve a dispute between two other cities. As in any kind of dispute resolution, one does not need a third entity in order to have a mediation orientation. Any of the disputants or all of them could in effect convert traditional negotiation into mediation by seeking to arrive at a truly mutually beneficial solution, rather than a solution where one side wins and the other side loses.

Disputes between business firms are the third area not treated in Table 1.1. Disputes between business firms are mainly consumer disputes in the sense that one business firm is a seller and the other is a buyer. This is a very different kind of dispute than the kinds of disputes covered under the consumer dispute category, which mainly involve retail stores and individual buyers. These two

Table 1.1
Dispute Resolution in Interactions

TYPES OF DISPUTE RESOLUTION	FORMS OF INTERACTION						
	Family	Neighborhood	Consumer	Workplace	Litigation	Legal Policy Disputes	International
Negotiation							
Mediation							
Arbitration							
Adjudication							
Examples	Divorce Settlement	Noise	Quality of Product	Wages	Product Liability	Legal Services for Poor	U.S.-USSR Arms Control

kinds of consumer disputes raise an interesting equity question. If the individual buyer is cheated by a retail store, the individual buyer may have to wait months to obtain justice in a traditional courtroom or small claims court, assuming the consumer pursues the matter through the legal process. On the other hand, the business firm as a consumer may arrange to hire a judge as part of the modern commercial arbitration process.

At first glance, this practice might seem unfair, and perhaps should be a stimulus to some kind of restrictive legislation. At second glance, commercial arbitration may be socially desirable. It provides the following benefits to the public, especially poor plaintiffs:

1. The business buyer and the business seller relieve the taxpayer of the burden of having to support litigation at the public expense if they hire a judge at their own expense.

2. Commercial arbitration relieves the judicial process of time-consuming cases, which enables the courts to hear cases of poor plaintiffs sooner.

3. The commercial arbitration system sometimes leads to socially useful, innovative ideas because it is not so constrained by outdated legalistic precedents.

4. Commercial arbitration is likely to lead to preventive action that can benefit poor consumers indirectly and serve as a precedent.

5. Most important, commercial arbitration often leads to thinking more in terms of win-win solutions instead of the win-lose solutions of the adversary system. This could revolutionize thinking about the allocation of scarce societal resources in general. It could help move us toward the idea that the best way to do things for either poor people or rich people is to expand the total pie, rather than take from the rich and give to the poor by way of progressive taxes or a revolution, or take from the poor and give to the rich by way of exploitation and repression.[3]

BEYOND BILATERAL INTERACTION

Family disputes can include divorce settlement, child custody, child support, a dispute among children over how they are going to provide for their aged parents, a dispute between aged parents as to how they are going to provide for their children, or a dispute between parents and a daughter or a son over whom their child is proposing to marry. Any kind of intrafamily dispute or dispute among relatives would be relevant. It does not have to be a legalistic divorce case.

The classic *neighborhood dispute* occurs when people complain about noise or the neighbor's dog. Broader concerns might be over blacks, Asians, or poor whites moving in, or a crime problem. A neighborhood dispute could be a problem of how to deal with the streets getting flooded in the rain, or not getting cleared in winter. A neighborhood dispute readily broadens beyond people who share a boundary into government, society, or community concerns.

The typical legalistic *consumer dispute* occurs when somebody buys something, it does not work, and they complain. Or the merchant could complain that the buyer has not paid. Broader consumer disputes involve consumers getting together collectively. They could do so by way of a class action. A group of black consumers might organize to picket a store that does not hire blacks. A class action could involve people who have been cheated by the same seller, as in a baby photo deal. A single consumer does not make much of an impact on a seller's behavior. A single consumer does not have the time or money to bring a big lawsuit. These disputes could be mediated to the best interests of the legitimate seller and the consumers. Mediation is not appropriate when dealing with a single dishonest seller. It could be used, however, in the case of a company that sells cars and gets a lot of complaints from people that something is not working properly. The object in the latter case is not to put company employees in jail, but to work out some kind of arrangement whereby the buyers get their cars in good working shape and the company does not suffer great damage to its image.

The typical *workplace dispute* may be a complaint about a worker taking too long for a lunch break or not getting a wage increase that was promised. Bigger disputes involve collective bargaining, where perhaps one thousand employees bargain with their employer about working conditions, wages, and other matters. Such disputes could lend themselves to computer-aided mediation.

Broadening a dispute by getting more people involved is important. But it is also important to get people to see that certain kinds of disputes might be appropriate for a mediator. A family example might be where the parents want to disown their Protestant child for marrying a Catholic. A mediator could perhaps handle this highly emotional dispute so everybody goes away shaking hands, instead of never talking to each other again. Applying mediation to any kind of dispute is a broadening process. This is why it is referred to as alternative dispute resolution. Broadening can involve the number of people, the specific kinds of disputes, and super-optimum solutions where everyone comes out ahead of their best expectations.[4]

SUPER-OPTIMIZATION

Family Disputes

A typical legal services agency case involves a family dispute and a super-optimum solution.

1. The immediate beneficiary is the woman who gets a divorce so that she can marry a more responsible husband.
2. The new husband is a beneficiary.
3. The former husband is freed of some responsibilities, generally by virtue of the new husband taking over some aspects of supporting his ex-wife and children.
4. The children are better off with a new father as opposed to having no father or a father who may be violent, alcoholic, or have some other undesirable characteristic.

5. The taxpayer is better off because the mother and her children are now off welfare. It is a clear cause-and-effect relation since none of the divorces handled by the Legal Services are provided unless they are either for the purpose of marrying a new more responsible husband or for the purpose of getting rid of a violent previous husband.

Yet even though these divorces (which are the most common legal services case) benefit everybody, including conservative taxpayers, the whole program was strongly opposed by President Reagan and the American right wing—in spite of their professed concern about saving taxpayer money and being interested in good families.

Traditional conservatives tend to think of poor people on aid (especially Aid to Dependent Children) as being at fault for their problems and thus deserving of punishment. Providing such individuals with free legal aid—no matter how much it benefits the taxpayer and promotes family values—is considered providing some kind of benefit. It is another example of the classic impediment to adopting super-optimum solutions, namely, the willingness of some people to hurt themselves because of negative feelings toward other people. Conservatives are hurting their cause by promoting the family and saving the taxpayer money, partly because of their negative feelings toward people who receive public aid.

If legal services handled absolutely nothing but divorce cases, conservatives might be able to tolerate it. Many conservatives believe that it is not acceptable for a legal services attorney to question the constitutionality of the concept of fault in divorce. It is even worse for such an attorney to handle cases against merchants, welfare officials, other government officials, or landlords. These conservatives do not want law and order when it comes to expecting landlords, merchants, and abusive government officials to comply with the law.

Some rich and middle-class conservatives may have guilt feelings that they will not admit to. In order to lessen these guilt feelings, they consciously or subconsciously seek to put poor people in positions where they are forced to behave in criminal or semicriminal ways or are forced to remain unemployed. Then these conservatives can say how terrible poor people are. They can then feel that their negative feelings toward the poor are not something to be guilty about. If one argues that this kind of program will enable poor people to do better, it may not be a plus in the eyes of those who would like to argue that poor people are worthless and will never do well.

These are the same people who argue that poor people have no ambition and simultaneously want to take away every dollar they earn by way of a 100 percent income tax levy. The Reagan administration advocated such a negative disincentive system: every dollar that a person on welfare earned should be confiscated to reduce welfare payments.

Traditional conservatives argue that poor people like welfare and have no desire to better themselves. If a substantial percentage of women on welfare are found to be seeking divorces from violent husbands or husbands who have deserted them in order to better themselves, this is disruptive to the conservative theory.

Therefore, to make it a self-fulfilling prophecy, conservatives deprive these women of the ability to get divorces that will enable them to get off welfare. Pathological conservatives support legislation and government activity designed to worsen the things that they claim they want to better so they can consciously or subconsciously say, "See, I told you so."

There are people on the left like this, too, although they usually do not have much influence on government policy. Subsequent to World War II in France and Italy, the Communist party frequently opposed legislation designed to reduce unemployment, arguing that the legislation was unimportant and that they wanted to hold out for really important reform. Consciously or subconsciously, they were doing things to worsen unemployment so that they could say, "See, I told you how bad a capitalistic economy would be with regard to unemployment."

Labor-Management Disputes

The super-optimum solution of having big benefits on one side and low costs on the other especially applies to resolving disputes between litigants in damage suits. For example, in the case of the Traveller's Insurance Company versus the Sanyo Electronics Company, the plaintiff demanded a minimum of $900,000 or else they would to go trial, especially since they had receipts to show they had already paid $950,000 to their insurees for fire damage. The Sanyo Electronics Company offered to pay a maximum of $300,000 or else they would go to trial, because they considered payment of more than $300,000 as an admission of negligent wrongdoing whereas less than $300,000 could be written off as a nuisance payment to avoid litigation costs. The object for a court-appointed mediator in this case (operating from a super-optimum perspective) is to come up with a settlement that would be worth more than $900,000 to the Traveller's Insurance Company and simultaneously worth less than $300,000 to the Sanyo Electronics Company.

The solution was for the Sanyo Electronics Company to supply the agents of the insurance company with computers for use in their insurance work. Sanyo also agreed to provide large television sets for use as bonuses to the insurance agents to encourage them to sell more insurance. The Japanese insurance company that Sanyo employs also agreed to give the American insurance company about $300,000 worth of claims they had against the Americans but were unenthusiastic about trying to collect. Other elements were also included in the total settlement that had a value to the Traveller's Insurance Company of more than $1 million but would cost Sanyo and its insurance company less than $200,000, mainly because all that Sanyo had to do was pull some computers and television sets out of its warehouses without having to manufacture or buy anything.

Another illustrative example involves a leading grower in the Peoria, Illinois area (which employs approximately seven hundred farm workers a year) being sued by the Migrant Legal Counsel, a legal services agency that specializes in the legal problems of migratory farm workers. The workers were suing to recover approximately $3 million in wages that had been deducted to pay for loans, rents, and other expenses without proper legal authorization. The money had actually been loaned or advanced to the workers, but the procedures designed to prevent illegal exploitation had not been followed. The grower insisted it should pay nothing since the money deducted was for loans actually made, regardless of the paperwork that followed. The best expectations of the workers in terms of net gain were low, since whatever they collected they would have to repay, with the exception of maybe about $50,000 in compensation to some of the named plaintiffs, who were fired or had quit their jobs, unless unlikely punitive damages could be obtained. The best expectations of the grower were to spend $50,000 or more going to trial and win with no liability. Thus, the objective for a mediator was to come up with a settlement that would be worth more than $50,000 to the farm workers and would simultaneously save the grower more than $50,000 in litigation costs.

The essence of the solution was that the grower agree to deposit $100,000 to begin an employee credit union. Depositing $100,000 cost the grower nothing since it was insured by the federal government and could be withdrawn after an agreed-upon time period, possibly even with interest. The $100,000, however, served as the basis for the beginning of an economic development fund that enabled the workers through real estate leveraging to obtain a mortgage for building over $500,000 worth of worker housing. The credit union also enabled them to avoid having to get advances from the grower, which generated a lot of friction as a result of alleged favoritism in giving and collecting the advances. Other elements were also involved, such as new grievance procedures and reports regarding compliance with other rules governing the working conditions of migrant laborers. The essence of the solution, though, was that both sides came out ahead of their original best expectations.[5]

Merchant-Consumer Disputes

For merchant-consumer disputes, especially at the policy level, we could draw from the legal services material. The object is to arrive at a solution where everybody comes out ahead. This is actually very common in legal services mediation. Without the legal services program as an intervener, the consumer might collect nothing, or collect something at great expense. The consumer might wind up having property confiscated illegally. The traditional resolution was either very one-sided in favor of the merchant, or was mutually hurtful in that both sides suffered from the lack of mediation. The typical legal services solution is to work out a system of smaller payments over a longer period of time. That way the merchant gets fully paid, the consumer gets to keep the furniture or car, and everybody comes out ahead.

In terms of policies, we could talk about the small loan acts, which involve fairly high interest rates. The consumer is able to borrow money without loan shark rates and pressure. The merchant is able to charge high enough rates to make lending profitable. The consumer adds to quality of life by being able to purchase a car, refrigerator, or other major items. The liberal solution would be to force rates down. However, then merchants cannot lend, they sell nothing, and they make no profit. The conservative solution would be to force rates up, but then consumers do not buy.

Neighborhood Disputes

Neighborhood disputes involving landlords and tenants are like merchant-consumer disputes except the landlord sells housing instead of cars or refrigerators. The same types of dispute resolution are applicable.

As for disputes between property owners, the classic example of a resolution that benefits everybody at the policy level is zoning to avoid what amounts to a tragedy of the commons. Zoning is a way of maximizing the greatest happiness for the greatest number, or the greatest benefits minus costs for the greatest number, but it is not a super-optimum solution. Without zoning, each property owner would seek the most profitable (but maybe the most undesirable) use of property. Eventually the market value of the neighborhood would go down. Some property owners would get out before the deterioration and come out ahead.

For example, four people on a block own property that is not zoned. One person decides to rent his property to a stable. He makes good short-term money from the rental. Soon, however, nobody wants to live on that block anymore, and property value drastically deteriorates. Zoning would allow stables only outside residential areas. If the owner sold his property to the stable at a substantial profit and moved out, then he would lose nothing as a result of the subsequent deterioration in property value.

Let us assume that at the beginning each lot is worth 100 units. One owner sells to a stable for 120 units and comes out ahead. The value of the remaining property drops to about 80 units apiece. Three people collectively lose 60 units so that one person can gain 20 units. With zoning, the net result is that nobody loses anything or they may gain through the normal appreciation of property. Zoning does not enable people to come out ahead of their best expectations. It simply prevents one person from making a substantial gain at the expense of a number of other people whose losses total more than his gain.

Disputes Between a Government Agency and a Private Firm

Both government and a private firm can easily come out ahead if the dispute is resolved through a subsidy approach rather than through a punishment approach. The punishing or fining approach may cost the government a great deal to impose. Even if the private firm wins, it may spend a great deal of money defending itself. A good example is environmental protection. It is much easier to gain compliance by providing subsidies to cover part or all of the excess cost than to fine business firms for not incurring the costs, especially if the fines are less than the costs. It is almost a super-malimum solution if the government winds up spending a lot of money to impose the fine, the private firm pays a lot of money to fight the fine, and the pollution continues while the fighting is going on and maybe continues even after the fine is paid. With an appropriate subsidy, everybody saves money and the pollution is substantially reduced.

Disputes Between Business Firms

A dispute between two business firms usually involves a buyer-seller relation. Suppose DuPont sells GM some bad upholstery or upholstery contrary to specifications. Both sides might have a fair chance of winning in court. DuPont could argue that it was GM's fault and that the specifications were not sufficiently clear. General Motors could argue that the specifications were clear but DuPont did not comply. They could spend a lot of money fighting each other. General Motors then loses what may have been a good source of upholstery. DuPont loses a good customer, and everybody winds up substantially worse off than before.

The commercial arbitration approach seeks to work out traditional compromises that are better, but not necessarily super-optimum solutions. A super-optimum solution in the business would might involve some kind of a merger of interests that go beyond the immediate sale. General Motors would perhaps like to own a company that makes auto upholstery, and thereby cut out the middleman and the profits that go to some other company. DuPont would perhaps like to own a company that makes cars, thereby having a large market for its auto upholstery. The super-optimum solution might be to work out a partial merger whereby GM buys into a spin-off of DuPont that does nothing but make auto upholstery. General Motors does not need to buy DuPont's manufacturing of kitchen cleanser or whatever else they make. Likewise, DuPont does not need to buy into whatever GM makes that does not have anything to do with auto upholstery, such as spare parts for motors. They could set up a separate company that they both own, or DuPont could buy a piece of General Motors, or General Motors could buy a piece of DuPont. The idea is to develop a merger where both companies come out ahead of their best expectations in terms of future benefits minus costs, as contrasted to merely resolving a question over whether some specifications were for one kind of fabric versus another on one specific order.

We could use the Sanyo case as an example. A super-optimum solution involved the Japanese insurance company giving some thought to the possibility of making the American insurance company its agent for marine insurance in the United States, which could have involved millions of dollars' worth of sales per year. The proposal fell through partly because it was too super-optimum and too broad to handle.

Disputes Between Government Agencies

There is a lot of talk today about cooperative federalism, the process whereby states and other government units work together. The environmental field offers good examples, such as the case of the dispute between Milwaukee and Chicago regarding how Milwaukee disposes of its garbage. There is a twenty-year history of numerous lawsuits between the attorney general of the state of Illinois and the attorney general of the state of Wisconsin. The situation has not changed substantially. Milwaukee still uses Lake Michigan for garbage disposal, thereby polluting Chicago beaches. The federal government could subsidize some kind of garbage disposal system for Milwaukee that involves landfills or incinerators. The cost to the federal government would be less than what it has cost Illinois and Wisconsin to fight each other all these years without accomplishing anything. It is not a problem of who is at fault or who is in the right. It is a problem of requiring money for a subsidy to provide for an alternative way of disposing of Milwaukee's garbage. Milwaukee is not going to stop producing garbage, and they are not going to voluntarily spend a lot of money if they have a convenient lake to put garbage in.

International Disputes

The arms control negotiations between the United States and USSR are an example of international disputes. Since starting, the negotiations have expanded to the point of being even more of a super-optimum solution than originally imagined. The arms control negotiations have been the springboard for the thaw of the cold war, which has enabled both the Soviet Union and the United States to cut back on defense expenditures and have more funds available for domestic economic development. It goes beyond the relatively small agreement regarding medium-range missiles, which constitute only about 5 percent of all the missiles. It is a bit like the United States and China getting together to play ping pong in the early 1970s, which resulted in the thawing of U.S.-China relations, far beyond anything it did for international ping pong. One of the direct after-effects of arms control negotiation is the liberalizing of the government and the economy in Eastern European countries. One, however, cannot expect such world-impact results from every dispute resolution.

It is interesting that when the arms control negotiations were going on, the liberals who were in favor of peace did not want any other controversies discussed. They feared that doing so would disrupt an arms control agreement. They wanted to exclude mention of Eastern Europe, Central America, Africa, or Asia. This is an example where pushing for a broader perspective on the negotiations did to some extent pay off—and it was conservative pushing. However, it may be no credit to the conservatives, since part of their motivation was to wreck the talks. They believed that if anything was brought up about Russia getting out of Nicaragua, Angola, or Eastern Europe, then Russia would break off the talks. Both liberals and conservatives were surprised by the results.

The negotiations illustrate that super-optimum solutions at least sometimes have a strong element of luck to them. Things can turn out to be much better than anticipated, not because they were so carefully planned. Gorbachev's attitudes were not anticipated by the CIA or the State Department. Reagan's proposal of a drastic reduction in Soviet missiles may have been designed partly to antagonize or partly to start from an exaggerated position for bargaining purposes, but Gorbachev agreed to the proposal. As a matter of hindsight, his behavior was not so bizarre or unpredictable. It reflected some good thinking on his part with regard to the need for getting money into his country's domestic economy.

Litigation Disputes

Litigation could refer to divorce, product liability, employee relations, sales, or property disputes. It usually refers, however, to personal injury matters like auto accident cases or cases such as the Dalkon Shield, the Johns Mansville asbestos case, or the Bhopal Union Carbide case. It is an important category, especially to lawyers.

Table 1.2 provides a general outline that goes beyond the Ramirez case with regard to the resolving of litigation disputes through super-optimum solutions. The conservative alternative in most damages disputes is for the defendant to win; usually meaning victory on trial for an insurance company, a manufacturer, a landlord, or an employer. The liberal alternative is for the plaintiff to win on trial since that usually means victory for an injured person, a consumer, a tenant, or an employee. The neutral or compromise position is to develop a settlement to avoid going to trial. The super-optimum solution is for the defendant to give the plaintiff insurance, manufactured products, a rent-free apartment, a better job, or something that has high value to the plaintiff, but not much variable net cost to the defendant.

There are four goals or criteria involved in deciding among the alternatives. They include benefits to the defendant, benefits to the plaintiff, costs to the defendant, and costs to the plaintiff. The defendant winning-on-trial scores well in terms of benefits to the defendant and that alternative wins on the conservative column using the conservative weights. The plaintiff winning-on-trial scores well on benefits to the plaintiff and that alternative wins on the liberal column using the liberal weights. The out-of-court settlement wins on the neutral column and comes in second on both the liberal and conservative columns. It is the alternative most likely to be chosen in the absence of the super-optimum solution because it is everybody's second choice and has acceptability for both sides.

The super-optimum solution provides benefits to the defendant by enabling the defendant to pay the plaintiff an amount of variable cost that is likely to be even less than the defendant's low starting position for bargaining purposes. The super-optimum solution also provides benefits to the plaintiff by enabling the plaintiff to receive from the defendant an amount that is likely to be even more valuable than the plaintiff's high starting position for bargaining purposes. At the same time, the alternative represents only moderate costs to the defendant and only moderate or no costs to the plaintiff. With those scores, the super-optimum solution alternative is able to easily win on both the liberal and the conservative totals using either liberal of conservative weights.

Table 1.2
Resolving Litigation Disputes Through Super-Optimum Solutions

CRITERIA / ALTERNATIVES	C GOAL Benefits to Defendant	L GOAL Benefits to Plaintiff	N GOAL -Costs to Defendant	N GOAL -Costs to Plaintiff	N TOTAL (Neutral Weights)	L TOTAL (Liberal Weights)	C TOTAL (Conservative Weights)
C ALTERNATIVE Defendant Win on Trial	5	1	2	2	20	16	24*
L ALTERNATIVE Plaintiff Wins on Trial	1	5	2	2	20	24*	16
N ALTERNATIVE Settle	2.5	2.5	3	3	22	22	22
SOS ALTERNATIVE Insurance, Products, Credit Unions, etc.	5	5	3	3	32	32**	32**

Disputes Between Liberals and Conservatives over Public Policy

The minimum wage dispute of 1989 is an example of a potential super-optimum solution in a public policy dispute. The liberals in Congress were arguing for a minimum wage of approximately $5.00 an hour. The conservatives were arguing for approximately $4.00 an hour. Let us look at this dispute hypothetically.

A traditional compromise would be $4.50 an hour. This might be greeted as a victory by liberals since it is $1.15 more than the current $3.35. It might be greeted as a victory by conservatives since it is $.50 less than what the liberals seek.

A wage of $4.50 an hour, though, could be considered a loss for both sides. It is a loss to liberals if $5.00 an hour is necessary for minimum food, shelter, clothing, and other necessities for an average family of four. The $4.50 is a loss to conservatives if $4.00 an hour is the maximum that business firms can afford to pay to minimum-wage employees; anything higher than $4.00 an hour will mean laying off workers who will thereby suffer a lack of minimum food, shelter, clothing, and other necessities.

A super-optimum solution might involve the minimum wage being raised to $5.50 an hour in terms of what each worker would receive, but simultaneously requiring each employer to pay only $3.50 an hour. The $2.00 difference would be paid by the government for every minimum-wage worker who would otherwise be unemployed either because the firm could not afford to hire the worker, or because the worker would not be sufficiently inspired to take the job at less than the increased minimum wage.

Under such an arrangement the liberals come out ahead of their initial bargaining position of $5.00 and probably ahead of their best expectations. Likewise, the conservatives come out ahead of their initial bargaining position of $4.00 and probably ahead of their best expectations.

The government and taxpayers might especially come out ahead by virtue of the money saved in terms of public aid, public housing, Medicaid, and unemployment compensation; the decreased cost of antisocial behavior associated with people who are embittered by unemployment or who resort to criminal sources of income; the increase in GNP as a result of the product these people produce and the accompanying increase in the taxes they pay; the better role models they now provide for their children and grandchildren who might otherwise be caught in a cycle of unemployment, public aid, criminal activity, and lack of productivity; and increased societal productivity.

For a business firm to be eligible to pay only $3.50 an hour, it should provide on-the-job training so workers become even more productive to the firm, the economy, and themselves. By getting off the single track of the exchange of dollars between an employer and an employee, one arrives at mutually beneficial solutions that exceed the initial best expectations of both sides. This example is summarized in Table 1.3.[6]

IMPLICATIONS

The minimum wage example may be a good note on which to end this chapter. The dispute has now been resolved. The resolution was a textbook compromise that involved splitting the difference between the relatively high amount that the Democrats advocated and the relatively low amount that the Republicans advocated. Perhaps a more mutually satisfying resolution could have been achieved by thinking more broadly than just in terms of the exchange of money. Perhaps there should have been more of an attempt to develop a multi-criteria solution that would involve a package of alternatives, some of which would favor the Democrats and some of which would favor the Republicans. Maybe it would have been impossible to develop a super-optimum solution where both sides could come out ahead of their best expectations. Unfortunately, there was no attempt to find that kind of a solution.

One might conclude from the minimum wage experience that multi-criteria dispute resolution and super-optimum solutions may be too idealistic. On the other hand, there are encouraging signs: decision-aiding software, win-win mediation, and expansionist economics. Perhaps a few years from now, debates like the minimum wage debate will involve the disputants consciously seeking mutually beneficial super-optimum solutions. It is hoped that this book will make at least a small contribution toward that kind of thinking, especially in individual disputes and broader public policy disputes.

Table 1.3
Dispute Resolution in the Public Policy Arena: The Minimum Wage

A. THE ALTERNATIVES

Alternative

1 SOS WAGE SUPP.	($4.75)	(To Workers)
2 +Substantial	($4.50)	(Liberal)
3 COMPROMISE	($4.25)	(Neutral)
4 +SLIGHT	($4.00)	(Conservative)
5 SOS WAGE SUPP.	($3.75)	(From Employers)

B. THE CRITERIA

Criterion	Meas. Unit	Liberal Weights	Neutral Weights	Conserv. Weights
1 *PAY DECENT WAGE	1-5 Scale	3.00	2.00	1.00
2 *AVOID OVERPAYMENT		1.00	2.00	3.00
3 SAVE TAXES		2.00	2.00	2.00
4 EMPLOY UNEMPLOYED		2.00	2.00	2.00
5 ON-JOB TRAINING		2.00	2.00	2.00
6 +ROLE MODELS		2.00	2.00	2.00

C. SCORES OF ALTERNATIVES ON CRITERIA

	Pay Dece	Avoid Ov	Save Tax	Employ U	On-Job T	+Role M
+SUBSTANTIAL	4.00	3.00	3.00	2.00	2.00	2.00
COMPROMISE	3.50	3.50	3.00	2.50	2.50	2.50
+SLIGHT	3.00	4.00	3.00	3.00	3.00	3.00
SOS WAGE SUPP.	5.00	5.00	4.00	4.00	4.00	4.00

D. INITIAL ANALYSES

Alternative	Liberal Combined Rawscores	Neutral Combined Rawscores	Conserv. Combined Rawscores
1 +Substantial	15.00	14.00	13.00
2 COMPROMISE	14.00	14.00	14.00
3 +SLIGHT	13.00	14.00	15.00
4 SOS WAGE SUPP.	20.00	20.00	20.00

NOTES ON HOW THE WAGE SUPPLEMENT OPERATES:

1. The minimum wage gets raised to $4.75 per hour.

2. Employers need pay only $3.75 per hour for workers who were otherwise unemployed and who are provided with on-the-job training.

3. Those workers receive a wage supplement of $1 per hour from the government, bringing their total wage up to the $4.75 per hour new minimum wage.

4. The government provides the $1 per hour supplement to the employer to cover the minimum wage as an incentive to get the employer to hire an unemployed worker and to provide on-the-job training.

5. The government provides the $1 per hour supplement to the worker to cover the minimum wage as an incentive to get the worker to accept the job and to provide the worker with a decent wage to cover necessities.

Table 1.3 (continued)

6. The government provides the $1 per hour supplement which helps both the employer and the worker partly because
   (1) It relieves the taxpayer from various welfare burdens such as Medicaid, Medicare, food stamps, unemployment compensation, public housing, aid to dependent children, social security, disability aid, etc.
   (2) It facilitates better role models thereby relieving the taxpayer of the welfare burdens of future generations.
   (3) The new employment lessens costly anti-social behavior and attitudes such as crime, drugs, vice, bitterness, and depression.
   (4) The employment adds to the gross national product, helps create jobs for others, and adds to the tax base.

NOTES ON THE GENERAL ANALYSIS:

1. The alternatives can be generalized into the four basic alternatives of liberal, neutral, conservative, and super-optimum alternatives.

2. The dollar amounts of $4.75, $4.50, $4.25, $4.00, and $3.75 are approximations partly to facilitate easy arithmetic. They do, however, approximate the actual minimum wage amounts over which liberals and conservatives are arguing in Congress as of 1989.

3. Liberals and conservatives both place a positive weight on paying a decent wage and avoiding overpayment. They differ, however, in the relative weights which they are likely to assign to those two key criteria, as indicated in Section B of the table.

4. The alternatives are scored on the criteria using a 1-5 scale where 5 means highly conducive to the goal, 4 means mildly conducive, 3 means neither conducive nor adverse, 2 means mildly adverse, and 1 means highly adverse to the goal.

5. Liberals and conservatives tend to be roughly in agreement on the scores relating the alternatives to the criteria even though they disagree on the relative importance of the key criteria.

6. The combined raw scores are determined by adding the weighted relation scores together. For example, a substantial increase receives 15 points in the liberal total by adding (3 times 4) to (1 times 3). For the sake of simplicity in this introductory analysis, only the two key criteria are used of paying a decent wage and avoiding overpayment.

7. The wage supplement comes out so far ahead of the second-place alternative on each of the three totals that the only way the second-place alternative could be a winner is (1) if one or more of the goals were to be given a negative weight, or (2) if one or more of the relation scores were to go above 5, below 1, or otherwise be unreasonable.

A better hope on which to commence is not so much in terms of the potential impact of this book. Just as one does not need to have a third party mediator to have a mediation orientation in bilateral disputes, likewise one does not need to have a book or books in order to think along the lines of arriving at super-optimum solutions, where all sides come out ahead of their best expectations. It does require thinking more broadly than the traditional single track of exchanging money, or one side giving and the other side taking. It requires thinking along the lines of multiple goals, multiple alternatives, and multiple relations between goals and alternatives in order to choose the best alternative, combination, or allocation, with best being defined as better than each side's initial best expectations.

APPENDIX: APPLYING SUPER-OPTIMIZING TO THE PERSIAN GULF CRISIS

Except for the updated section at the end, the following was written the day after Iraq invaded Kuwait.

August 3, 1990

Possible Solution

One interesting (possibly even super-optimum) solution to the Persian Gulf crisis is for the United States, the Arab countries, or even a larger grouping of countries to suggest that if Iraq will withdraw from Kuwait, then Israel will withdraw from the occupied territories (see Table 1.4).

Table 1.4
A Possible SOS Solution to the Persian Gulf Crisis

CRITERIA ALTERNATIVES	L GOAL Avoid Casualties	C GOAL Avoid Yielding to Agression	C GOAL Keep Oil Flowing	N TOTAL (Neutral Weights)	L TOTAL (Liberal Weights)	C TOTAL (Conservative Weights)
C ALTERNATIVE Military Action	1	4	4	18	11	25*
L ALTERNATIVE Diplomatic Action	5	2	2	18	19*	17
N ALTERNATIVE Compromise (Both)	3	3	3	18	18	18
S ALTERNATIVE Acceptable Linkage & Sanctions	5	4	4	26	23**	29**

NOTE: See Table 1.3 for how the totals are calculated. One star means this is the winning alternative among the conservative, liberal, and neutral alternatives. Two stars mean this is the winning alternative after adding the SOS alternative.

Incentives to Comply

If Saddam Hussein refused to go along with this solution, then he would not be looked upon favorably by other Arabs. By his merely withdrawing from a place where he does not have a legal right to be, he could enable the Palestinians to get statehood. If Saddam Hussein agreed to the deal, he would look good by helping the Arab world and the Palestinians, and at the same time save face by not being forced out.

If Israel refused to withdraw from the occupied territories, then they would look bad by jeopardizing the peace of the whole world. Israel retains this land to which it has no legal right, and to which it has never really claimed a legal right. While there are some people in Israel who refer to those territories as being a part of Israel, even they are reluctant to say so because it would mean that the people who live there should have the same rights as all Israelis. If Israel agreed to the proposed solution, they would be favorably looked upon by the world for helping maintain peace in the Middle East.

Big Benefits and Low Costs to Each Side

This kind of trade-off does not exactly fit the seven ways of arriving at SOS solutions. But it does represent big benefits to one side with low costs to the other.

Iraq would not suffer major out-of-pocket costs by withdrawing from Kuwait. One could say they might suffer opportunity costs in the sense that if they stay there, they might absorb Kuwait's oil. That seems unlikely, though, as President Bush has said he will not tolerate Iraq using Kuwait's oil, and he could enforce that without military action simply by boycotting and establishing a blockade to prevent Iraq from exporting the oil.

Israel would not suffer any cost. In fact, they would save money by getting rid of the expense they are suffering as a result of trying to keep the occupied territories under their control.

By agreeing to the trade-off, Iraq would benefit in the eyes of the Arab world and the world in general. Israel would also benefit in the eyes of the world in general and have an opportunity to somewhat redeem itself. The world would benefit by defusing the situation and thereby preventing military action that could result in a huge loss of life. The world would also benefit in the sense that once the oil begins flowing again, it will be good for the world economy.

Dispute Resolution without Direct Negotiation

This is an example of dispute resolution between Israel and Iraq that would not involve any negotiation between those two countries. Israel could give up the occupied territories and Iraq could simultaneously give up Kuwait, without having any interaction between the two countries. Non-interaction should be to their mutual liking since they are not on speaking terms with each other, and they would lose face by even offering to negotiate.

January 9, 1991

Possible Solution

It looks more and more possible that the suggested solution can be reached. The EEC is coming out strongly in favor of it, led by the French. But Britain does not support the plan. Iraq wants a linkage conference before a withdrawal. The United States wants withdrawal before a linkage conference. The logical compromise, which would also be an SOS, would be for both to occur simultaneously, a plan that France's Prime Minister François Mitterrand advocates.

Should the compromise be agreed on, both sides could consider themselves as having won. The United States can say it did not yield on linkage before the withdrawal, and Iraq can say it did not withdraw before getting linkage. They can console themselves in the traditional way by saying that they came out ahead of their worst expectations, or at least out ahead of what the other side wanted.

Interferences

Simultaneous withdrawal from Kuwait with the start-up of linkage negotiations may be the rational way to go in terms of everyone coming out ahead of their best initial expectations, but that may not be what will happen because of the various kinds of factors that interfere with adopting or implementing SOS solutions.

One such factor involves the image of the leaders. Bush does not want to be perceived as a "wimp," and has forged ahead with a military build-up to show that he is a tough guy. Saddam Hussein is called a vicious butcher. Both will want to give the impression that without the display of macho bravado the simultaneous conference cannot have occurred, just to prove that being tough is the way to go.

Setting ultimatums can always interfere with arriving at super-optimum solutions. Super-optimum solutions may take more time to develop than ordinary solutions. If one sets an ultimatum for a point in time and does not allow sufficient time for it to develop, then that can clearly mess up its adoption and implementation. The U.N. passed a resolution that Iraq must leave by January 15, 1991 or the use of force would be condoned. In that context it is important to emphasize that although Bush's policy is not to be pushed hastily into a war, the deadline means that he will be ready, willing, and able to go to war on January 15, but that he does not *have* to if he does not want to. He can also use the claim of new information, such as grasping at any sign of not wanting to be invaded that Saddam Hussein sends out, or does not send out.

Things can also get messed up by third parties even if the main parties of Iraq and the United States are approaching an SOS or a traditional compromise. Israel might be the most likely to disrupt things, although they have maintained a low profile. But Israel could be deliberately provoked by an extremist Palestinian group that *wants* to see a war that will involve Iraq attacking Israel, either because the group is so extremist that they would rather be dead than not have their sovereignty, or simply because they think that such a war will lead to obtaining sovereignty.

January 17, 1991

The Possibilities for a Conference

The possibility of the conference for withdrawal SOS has increased. If the United States agrees to a conference at this point it will not be due to threats or a defeat. Agreement to the conference could be possible because it would be considered a positive move, rather than because bargaining power had been somehow lost or decreased.

The possibility of Saddam Hussein going along with his SOS has also increased. He was always in favor of the conference idea and had indicated that he would be willing to withdraw if it were guaranteed. It is important for Saddam's ego, if one is willing to allow him to preserve his ego, for him to be able to say he got something out of his efforts. The something would be the conference idea, even though it is an idea proposed by many others. Thus he has indicated more of a willingness to negotiate. When one side says the other side is not willing to make concessions, as the United States has done, that generally means the other side is quite willing to make concessions, but their concessions are deemed unacceptable.

Obtaining Israel's Participation

On the procedures being to Israel's liking, the demands may be unreasonable. Israel, as in the past, might stipulate that no PLO representatives can attend, although they could be a part of the delegations from other countries, such as Jordan, Syria, Iraq, or even Egypt and north African countries. Thus the PLO could possibly wind up with even more representation than if they were directly represented.

The possibility of giving up land for peace must be a possibility. It can not be ruled out. It is also not a matter of giving up what might be considered Israeli land, but giving up an occupied territory. The conservative party of Israel claims that most of the occupied territory belongs to Israel by virtue of being Biblical Sumeria and Judea. That might be open to negotiation and it could be conceded that Israel does own it. But that does not mean Israel can not trade some of it for peace.

A Camp David for the Middle East

What could be done on the super-optimum solution with regard to the conference that might occur includes the following:

1. The extreme conservative alternative from the American and Israeli viewpoint, would be to expel Palestine from the West Bank and give it all to Israel.
2. The liberals would seek to establish an independent sovereign state called Palestine which would be a member of the U.N.

3. The neutral position would be for some kind on stringent restrictions on the foreign policy of a new sovereign state, or would provide that it is to be some kind of a U.N. trust territory.

4. A Camp David-type settlement could be reached where Israel gets tremendous foreign aid benefits from the United States in return for relinquishing the occupied territories, as does the PLO and Egypt. Everyone thereby comes out ahead, including the United States. The United States benefits by no longer having to worry about a war in the Middle East, which is highly expensive. It could mean a reduction in the military aid to Israel. There could also be a reduction in military aid to Saudi Arabia and other Arab countries. The United States thereby saves a lot of money and potential casualties that might otherwise occur.

Comparisons with Vietnam

Factors that put the U.S. policy of leaning toward the use of force to remove Iraq in a more favorable light include (1) an enemy who is an imperialistic bully and a homefront dictator, (2) more world backing, (3) no jungles to hide in, and (4) no Soviet or Chinese intervention.

But there are also factors that are reminiscent of the Vietnam conflict. There is the religious issue; in Vietnam it was Buddhist against Christians, especially Catholics. In the Persian Gulf it is Moslems against Christians and Jews. There is also the same dedicated nationalism on the side of the underdog to save their country, but no such spirit on the side of the United States. And both have anti-colonial elements trying to throw out a foreign invader, namely the United States. The United States claims to be there by invitation.

The factors that have put U.S. policy in a less favorable light include (1) early anti-war activism, (2) potential embarrassment and demoralization for the United States from the possibility of not being able to defeat a foe that seems weaker than North Vietnam even though the United States has much greater fire power, (3) availability of crippling economic sanctions that were not adequately used, (4) availability of the conference alternative that has not been adequately used, and (5) possible negative association with Israel, although that has not yet substantially occurred.

Miscellaneous Ideas on the Persian Gulf

If this turns into another Vietnam, then the right wing will say the war was lost because nuclear weapons were not used, just as they said Vietnam was lost because the fire power used against Iraq was not used against North Vietnam.

If it takes months and high casualties to win the war, the United States will have gained a Pyrrhic victory at best. If somebody 20 feet tall weighing 1,000 pounds succeeds in beating up a 2-foot tall person weighing 10 pounds, but the giant is blinded and loses both arms and both legs, most outsiders would say that it was not much of a victory.

One thing the government has learned from the Vietnam war is to make no promises that the war will be over in the near future. Nobody is saying anything about a light at the end of the tunnel. Instead they keep cautioning that things may take longer than anticipated. Even the cautioning may be an underestimate of how long things may take.

The length of the war might have been much shorter if the embargo had been allowed to continue longer so as to exhaust Iraq's supplies. While their supply level was reasonably up, Iraq was probably in a relatively desirable position to be attacked.

It has been suggested that the increased money spent on the Persian Gulf crisis by the U.S. government, which is amounting to more than a billion dollars a day, is good for the U.S. economy by stimulating spending and jobs. That may be true in the very short run, but for the long haul of international competitiveness, the United States needs to invest in technological development, such as retooling the procedures involved in manufacturing automobiles, steel, textiles, chemicals, and other important industries. Not having those funds available for that purpose may substantially wipe out any technological growth that might have otherwise occurred. As a result, Japan and Germany, who are spending so little in the Persian Gulf war, may turn out to be the big economic winners and the United States the big economic loser. The sooner the Persian Gulf war is over, possibly through an SOS conference, the sooner the United States can move forward in getting its technology and economy updated and more competitive.

It looks as if the Iraq strategy is to allow the United States to completely dominate the skies. They are offering no serious resistance. Their planes are being kept underground, or being flown north away from the battle areas. Their strategy seems to be to wait for the land war where their technology and their willingness to die can outdo the Americans who have a similar land technology and less willingness to die. It is also safer to be in an underground bunker than it is to be out moving above ground in the open desert. Bush would be acting politically smarter by holding back on sending in the troops to do any kind of rooting out until months from now or better yet until a settlement is reached.

So far the fatalities on the U.S. side are slight. The may even be slight on the Iraqi side, or at least not horrendous since the United States is sensitive to the bully image of slaughtering civilians. The key point is that there is still time to resolve matters before there really are some heavy fatalities on both sides. That is where the SOS solution might especially come in.[7]

NOTES

1. On the basic types of dispute resolution, see Stephen Goldberg, Eric Green, and Frank Sanders, eds., *Dispute Resolution* (Boston: Little, Brown, 1985), 17–310; Ford Foundation, *New Approaches to Conflict Resolution* (New York: Ford Foundation, 1978); and Lewis Mayers, *The American Legal System: The Administration of Justice in the United States by Judicial, Administrative, Military, and Arbitral Tribunals* (New York: Harper,

1955). The Goldberg book refers to the primary dispute resolution processes as negotiation, mediation, adjudication, and hybrid processes. The hybrid processes include arbitrators who mediate, minitrials, rent-a-judge, summary jury trial, expert fact-finding, ombudsmen, settlement special masters, and integrated processes.

For books on each of the four basic forms of dispute resolution, see Howard Raiffa, *The Art and Science of Negotiation: How to Resolve Conflicts and Get the Best out of Bargaining* (Cambridge: Harvard University Press, 1982); Christopher Moore, *The Mediation Process: Practical Strategies for Resolving Conflict* (San Francisco: Jossey-Bass, 1986); Robert Coulson, *Business Arbitration: What You Need to Know* (New York: American Arbitration Association, 1987); and Samuel Mermin, *Law and the Legal System: An Introduction* (Boston: Little, Brown, 1982) (on adjudication).

2. On the subject matters to which alternative forms of dispute resolution can be applied, see Goldberg, Green, and Sanders, *Dispute Resolution*, pp. 311–482. The book classifies disputes as family, neighborhood, intrainstitutional, consumer, environmental, intergovernmental, and international. Also see Jay Folberg and Alison Taylor, *Mediation: A Comprehensive Guide to Resolving Conflicts Without Litigation* (San Francisco: Jossey-Bass, 1984). The Folberg–Taylor subject matters include family, housing, schools, police, workplace, minority relations, and environment.

3. The author thanks Margaret Brinig of the George Mason University Law School for her helpfulness in suggesting how the four kinds of dispute resolution can apply to family disputes.

4. On broadening the applicability of bilateral interaction with or without a third party dispute resolver, see William Ury, Jeanne Brett, and Stephen Goldberg, *Getting Disputes Resolved: Designing Systems to Cut the Costs of Conflict* (San Francisco: Jossey-Bass, 1989); and Kenneth Kressel and Dean Pruitt, eds., *Mediation Research: The Process and Effectiveness of Third-Party Intervention* (San Francisco: Jossey-Bass, 1989).

5. See Chapter 15 in Stuart Nagel and Miriam Mills' *Multi-Criteria Methods in Alternative Dispute Resolution* (New York: Quorum, 1990) for further details on this case and an analysis of the case from a broadening perspective. This perspective sees the problems as going beyond the immediate back-wages dispute to the need for upgrading the skills and job opportunities of farm laborers and the technology and profitability of farms that presently employ such labor.

6. On super-optimizing dispute resolution and related concepts, see Lawrence Susskind and Jeffrey Cruikshank, *Breaking the Impasse: Consensual Approaches to Resolving Public Disputes* (New York: Basic, 1987); and Roger Fisher and William Ury, *Getting to Yes: Negotiating Agreement Without Giving In* (New York: Houghton-Mifflin, 1981). For related ideas applied to international negotiations and public policy, see William Ury, *Beyond the Hotline: How Crisis Control Can Prevent Nuclear War* (New York: Houghton-Mifflin, 1985); Miriam Mills, ed., *Conflict Resolution and Public Policy* (Westport, Conn.: Greenwood, 1990); and James Laue, ed., *Using Mediation to Shape Public Policy* (San Francisco: Jossey-Bass, 1988).

7. As a matter of April, 1991, hindsight, one can say that the Persian Gulf War teaches at least that American foreign policy is better off seeking to export the Bill of Rights, rather than supporting repressive regimes. There probably never would have been a Persian Gulf War and its current undesirable aftermath if it had not been for the support of the United States (1) for the Shah of Iran, whose repressive regime brought the Ayatollah Khomeini into power, (2) for Saddam Hussein to fight against Khomeini, (3) for the feudalistic emir of Kuwait and the king of Saudi Arabia to fight against Hussein and possibly their own people, and (4) for re-supporting Hussein to keep the pro-Iranian Shiite Moslems and the anti-Turkey Kurds in line. Countries that respect civil liberties turn out to be our best trading partners and allies.

CHAPTER 2

A Typological Approach to Multi-Criteria Conflict Analysis

RON JANSSEN
AND PETER NIJKAMP

In the 1970s and early 1980s, an avalanche of multi-criteria methods took place, so that today there is a wide variety of multi-criteria decision methods. These methods are used not only in the context of conventional project and plan evaluation (see, e.g., Nijkamp, 1980; Rietveld, 1980; Voogd, 1983), but also as an operational framework for conflict analysis (see, e.g., Despontin, et al., 1984; Janssen and Hafkamp, 1986; Isard and Smith, 1982; Janssen, 1990).

The following factors have contributed to the increasing popularity of these methods:

- the impossibility of including intangible and/or incommensurable effects in conventional evaluation methods (like cost-benefit and cost-effectiveness analysis)
- the conflictual nature of modern planning problems so that, instead of a single decision-maker, various (often multilevel) formal and informal decision agencies determine a final choice in a participatory context
- the shift from conventional "one-shot" decision-making to institutional and procedural decision-making with a variety of strategic and opportunistic policy aspects
- the desire in modern decision-making not to be confronted with a single, unambiguous, and (sometimes) forced solution, but with a spectrum of open feasible solutions, each having its own merits

Despite the large number of (simple and sophisticated) multi-criteria decision methods that are currently available, there is still surprisingly little insight into the conditions under which these methods can best be applied. Therefore, the present chapter will especially focus on the question of which multi-criteria method is suitable for which class of conflict analysis.

The latter question has been dealt with in a systematic way by Isard and Smith (1982, Chap. 9) in their thorough treatment of conflict analysis. These authors not only describe a large number of conflict management procedures, but also present a typology of conflicts as well as a way to match these conflicts with conflict management procedures.

In the context of environmental management procedures this question has also been treated by Janssen and Nijkamp (1985a, 1985b), who used a typological approach to classify multi-criteria decision methods on the basis of the features of activities causing environmental pollution, the specific environmental effects of these activities, and the institutional planning and policy structure of the environmental problem at hand. By including problem and procedure characteristics in large matrices a classification and sequential selection of multi-criteria methods could be completed.

The present chapter will draw on the latter approach and, in so doing, present a general conceptual typology of multi-criteria decision methods. This typology is again based on a stimulus-response approach to conflict analysis and differs from the Isard–Smith approach in the manner depicted (schematically) in Figures 2.1 and 2.2.

The approach adopted by Isard and Smith (1982) is operational and to some extent superior for selecting the best method from all given methods taken into consideration. Our approach is more problem-oriented than method-oriented. It has some advantages, however, if new methods need to be developed, or existing methods need to be modified.

A TYPOLOGY OF CONFLICT MANAGEMENT PROBLEMS

The typology presented here is primarily developed for decisions to be made by various kinds of government decision-makers, but it may in principle also be useful for decisions to be made in the private sector. Conflict management

Figure 2.1
Isard–Smith Methodology for Method Selection

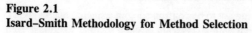
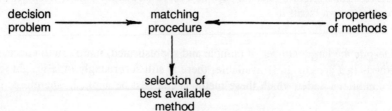

Figure 2.2
Janssen–Nijkamp Methodology for Method Selection

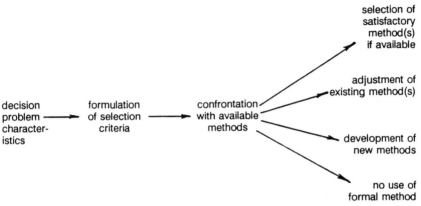

problems can be characterized according to two dimensions: the activity profile and the decision profile.

The Activity Profile

The activity profile can be characterized by two aspects: the type of activity, and the type of effects caused by the activity. For example, a conflict-generating activity (being a stimulus in the form of a public decision) may be a project (e.g., the construction of a bridge), a plan (e.g., a physical plan for urban renewal), or some form of public regulation by a government (e.g., the establishment of environmental standards). There are numerous ways to classify the effects of such activities. Effects can be differentiated according to their temporal, spatial, and other characteristics. An effect may be unique, repetitive, continuous short-term, or continuous long-term. It may also be stationary or mobile, and/or within or outside the boundaries of the decision unit involved. The effect may be equally or unequally distributed over the parties involved. An effect may be compensable (i.e., the gains of the winners are sufficient to compensate the losers) or noncompensable. Finally, an effect may or may not be submitted to formal standards.

The Decision Profile

Decision profile characteristics can be subdivided into the solution space and the decision space. The solution space comprises the alternatives set and information features. For example, the alternatives set may be composed of one, few, or many alternatives, or it may be a continuous set. Information available regarding the conflict problem may be quantitative, qualitative, or mixed. It may also be certain, uncertain with a known probability distribution, or uncertain with an unknown probability distribution. Finally, information may be limited or extensive, agreed- or not agreed-upon. The decision space comprises institutional characteristics, characteristics of decision-makers, characteristics of required decision result (e.g., efficiency), and available means for the decision-making process.

In terms of institutional characteristics, for example, the decision may be based on one or multiple objectives; may involve two, three, or more parties; and may include one or more decision levels. The decision procedure can be hierarchical or participatory and may be influenced by external interest groups. Finally, a distinction can be made between routine and nonroutine decisions. In terms of characteristics of decision-makers, they can have an analytical or heuristic attitude, can display optimizing or satisficing behaviour, can be short- or long-term oriented, and can be risk-lovers or risk-averters.

An Example: The Markerwaard Project

As a more concrete illustration, Table 2.1 gives the activity and decision profiles that can be used to characterize a major decision problem in the Netherlands—the potential land reclamation project of the so-called Markerwaard. This highly controversial project involves the reclamation of the 410 km^2 from the Ysselmeer, a lake in the heart of the Netherlands (see Figure 2.3).

Five alternative policy choices have been distinguished in our example: two "dry" alternatives and three "wet" alternatives (no polder). The final decision will be taken by the Dutch government. There are at least four ministries strongly involved in this decision: the Ministry of Transport and Waterworks, the Ministry of Finance, the Ministry of Agriculture, and the Ministry of the Environment. At least one minister (Transport and Waterworks) has publicly stated a strong preference for land reclamation. Furthermore a large number of external interest groups (farmers, environmental groups) try to influence the decision.

SELECTION OF A CONFLICT MANAGEMENT METHOD

In this section, the set of conflict problem characteristics mentioned above are translated into explicit criteria for selecting conflict management methods (see also Lichfield, et al., 1985; Voogd, 1983; Janssen, 1984). By evaluating the set of available methods against these criteria, more insight is obtained into the relative usefulness of different multi-criteria decision methods for the given conflict problem.

Selection criteria are divided into first- and second-order criteria (see Duckstein, et al., 1981). First-order criteria are mandatory binary criteria for the selection of a method; if a multi-criteria method does not comply with all first-order criteria relevant to a certain problem, this method cannot be applied to this problem. Second-order criteria are, by contrast, not a priori mandatory for the selection of a method. It is important to find a multi-criteria method that complies with as many second-order criteria as possible.

Table 2.1
The Markerwaard Reclamation Project

Reclamation Markerwaard	activity		
X X	unique repetitive	TIME	EFFECTS
X X	continuous short-term continuous long-term		
X X	stationary mobile	SPATIAL	
 X	cross-boundary within boundary		
 X	equal distribution unequal distribution	OTHER	
 X	compensable non-compensable		
 X	formal standards non-formal standards		
 X 	one alternative few alternatives many alternatives continuous	ALTERNATIVE SET	SOLUTION SPACE
  X	quantitative quantitative mixed	INFORMATION	
X X X	certain uncertain (prob. known) uncertain (prob. not known)		
 X	limited extensive		
 X	agreed on not agreed on		
 X	one objective multi-objective	INSTITUTIONAL	DECISION SPACE
 X	two parties three parties or more		
X 	one decision-level multi-level decision		
X X	participatory hierarchical interest groups		
 X	routine non-routine	DECISION MAKERS	
X X	analytical heuristic		
 X	optimizing behaviour satisficing behaviour		
 X	short-term oriented long-term oriented		
X 	risk-averter risk-lover		
X 	one optimal alternative set acceptable alternatives ranking of alternatives	GOAL	
X X X X	expertise time money computer	MEANS	

Figure 2.3
The Markerwaard Project

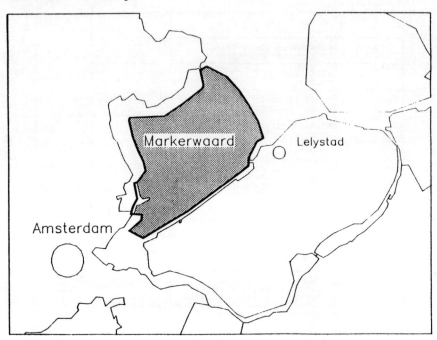

In general, only a few criteria will in practice be absolutely essential (mandatory) for any given conflict situation. On the other hand, some selection criteria can be claimed to be relevant to all conflict management problems:

1. the principles and assumptions of the method must be explicable to decision-makers
2. the method must produce results that are understandable to the decision-makers
3. costs of application of the method should be in balance with the benefits resulting from an improved decision

Most selection criteria, however, are linked to specific characteristics of conflict management problems. This means that methods can only be judged in relation to the problem that they are intended to solve. As an illustration, we present the selection criteria which are relevant for the Markerwaard decision problem in Table 2.2. These criteria can be used to evaluate the usefulness of a series of conflict management methods to this problem.

If a method in its basic form complies with a certain criterion, this is indicated by an x. If it is possible to adjust or extend a method in such a way that it may (in principle) comply with a certain criterion, this is indicated by an o. The first nine criteria are first-order criteria; they are followed by four second-order criteria.

Table 2.2
Selection Criteria for the Markerwaard Decision

Selection criteria	The method is based on a continuous decision function	The method is based on a decision function for discrete choices	The method is able to handle quantitative information an efficient way	The method is able to handle qualitative or mixed information in an efficient way	The method is able to process uncertain information	The method produces immediate results	The method produces efficient solutions	The method gives insight into the distribution of effects over the interested parties	The method leads to converging solutions	The method is able to produce compromise solutions	The method allows for the introduction of constraints	The method maximizes the chance on the best results	The method minimizes the chance on the worst results
Reclamation of Markerwaard		x		x	x			x		x	x		x
Conflict management methods													
1. concordance analysis		x	x	x	x	o	x	o	o	x	o	x	x
2. frequency method		x		x	o	o	x	o	o	x	o	x	x
3. lexicographic ranking		x		x	o	o	o	o	o	x		x	x
4. permutation method		x		x	x	o	x	o	o	o	o	x	x
5. eigenvalue method		x		x	o	o	o	o	o	o		o	o
6. regime method		x		x	x	x	x	o	x	x	x	x	x
7. multidimensional scaling		x		x	x	x	x	o	x	x	x	x	x
8. metagame method		x		x	o		o	x	o	o	o		
9. mixed data method		x		x	x	x	x	o	x	x	x	x	x
10. trichotomic choice		x		x	o		o	o	o	o			
11. score card method		x		x	o	o	o	x	o	o		o	o
12. key issue matrix		x		x	o	o	o	x	o	o		o	o
13. Delphi procedure	x	x	o	x	x			o	x	x	x	o	x
14. postponement of decision	x	x	o	x	o			o	o		o		x

Table 2.2 confronts a selection of twelve multi-criteria decision methods and two procedural methods (the Delphi technique and postponement of decisions) with the characteristics of our Markerwaard conflict. An examination of this table leads to the following conclusions:

First, as far as the first-order selection criteria is concerned, it is easily seen that all fourteen methods may in principle be used for this planning problem. There is, however, no method that is in all cases directly applicable. The concordance analysis, the permutation method, the regime method, the multidimensional scaling method, the metagame method, the mixed data method, the score card method, the key issue matrix, and the Delphi technique are apparently slightly superior to the remaining methods.

Second, the second-order conditions lead to more straightforward results, as there are methods that are in agreement with all criteria, while others are not. Again there is no single method that can be directly applied, but there are some methods that can in principle be employed in all cases. These methods are concordance analysis, the frequency method, the regime method, the mixed data method, and the Delphi technique. Depending on the relative weights attached to each of the second-order criteria, one may make a selection of an appropriate conflict analysis method for the planning problem at hand.

In the policy practice of the decision problem on the reclamation of the Markerwaard, a much used—and definitely not always the worst—conflict management procedure was chosen, namely, postponing the decision. This delay of the decision was mainly for financial reasons, but also because of insufficient reliable information.

NOTE

This paper was originally published in *Conflict Management and Peace Science*, vol. 8 no. 2. Reprinted by permission.

REFERENCES

Despontin, M., P. Nijkamp, and J. Spronk, eds. (1984). *Macro-Economic Planning with Conflicting Goals*. Berlin: Springer Verlag.

Duckstein, L., I. Bogardi, and M. E. Gerishon. (1981). "Multi-Objective Decision-Making: Model Choice." *IIASA Working Paper*, Laxenburg, Austria.

Isard, W., and C. Smith. (1982). *Conflict Analysis and Practical Conflict Management Procedures*. Cambridge, Mass.: Ballinger.

Janssen, R. (1984). *Evaluatiemethoden ten behoeve van het Milieu-beleid en-beheer*. Amsterdam: Free University, Economic and Social Institute.

———. (1990). "DEFINITE: A System to Support the Decision Making Process." In S. S. Nagel, ed., *Decision Aiding Software and Decision Analysis*. Cambridge: Cambridge University Press.

Janssen, R., and W. Hafkamp. (1986). "A Decision Support System for Conflict Analysis." *Annals of Regional Science* 20, no. 3: 67–85.

Janssen, R., and P. Nijkamp. (1985a). "A Multiple Criteria Evaluation Typology of Environmental Management Problems." In Y. Haimes and V. Chankong, eds., *Decision-Making with Multiple Objectives*. Berlin: Springer Verlag, pp. 495–514.

——— . (1985b). "Environmental Policy Analysis: Which Method for Which Problem?" *Revue d'Economie Régionale et Urbaine* 18, no. 5: 839–55.

Lichfield, N., P. Kettle, and M. Whitbread. (1985). *Evaluation in the Planning Process*. Oxford: Pergamon.

Nijkamp, P. (1980). *Environmental Policy Analysis*. New York: Wiley.

Nijkamp, P., R. Rietveld, and H. Voogd. (1990). *Multicriteria Evaluation in Physical Planning*. Amsterdam: North Holland.

Voogd, H. (1983). *Multicriteria Evaluation for Urban and Regional Planning*. London: Pion.

PART II

Family and Neighborhood Disputes

CHAPTER 3

Dispute Resolution Education, Training, and Critical Issues for Criminal Justice Professionals

MARIA R. VOLPE

Throughout American society, increasing attention is being given to alternative means of dispute resolution (ADR), including negotiation, conciliation, mediation, fact-finding, arbitration, minitrial, rent-a-judge, and ombudsmen (Marks, et al., 1984; Goldberg, et al., 1985; Salem, 1985; McKay, 1985). These developments coincide with the widespread concern about the nature of adversarial handling of a wide range of matters in a variety of contexts. In the case of criminal matters, a small sampling of some of the innovative uses of ADR approaches includes varied state legislation that has been passed introducing new dispute resolution processes, particularly mediation in community situations (ABA, 1990b); hundreds of dispute resolution programs that have been started to process diverse criminal and civil disputes that might otherwise be sent to the courts (ABA, 1990a); other community-based dispute resolution programs that have been established to provide victim/offender mediation at different stages of the criminal justice process, including pretrial diversion, between conviction and adjudication, between sentencing and disposition, or after sentencing (Umbreit, 1986); and diverse dispute resolution coursework and programs in educational institutions, particularly law schools (Crohn, 1985; Volpe, 1985; Sander, 1984).

Of what significance are these developments to criminal justice professionals, particularly with respect to their education and training in dispute resolution? Any changes in the processing of disputes will have a considerable impact on professionals working in the criminal justice system, including police, prosecuting and defense attorneys, judges, and probation, parole, and correction officers. Of all of the ADR processes gaining national attention, mediation, perhaps, poses the most innovative and challenging set of problems for criminal justice professionals.

Although mediation is not new for some of them, its development is creating a need for criminal justice professionals to gain some formal and systematic understanding of this process as it relates to their everyday work.

There are essentially two uses of the mediation process for criminal justice professionals. They can choose to refer cases to dispute resolution centers that provide mediation services, or use mediation skills and techniques as an intervention strategy when they process cases. This chapter will address some of the concerns raised by mediation for criminal justice professionals, bearing in mind the diverse roles that different sectors have to play.

CRIMINAL JUSTICE WORLDVIEW: ADVERSARIAL ORIENTATION

The criminal justice system reflects the premises central to the American legal system. One of the basic premises of this system is that business is to be conducted within the framework of an adversarial approach. This means that professionals are essentially expected to work in a variety of milieus that requires them to take positions opposed to disputants.

It is not surprising, then, that virtually all preparation for criminal justice system professionals reflects this premise. It produces and consistently reinforces adversarial thinking and behavior. Police, for instance, are socialized to see others as potential adversaries, both individually and collectively. Police work is such that any action implies the existence of potential adversaries, resulting in situations where officers are constrained to testify in court against given individuals.

Legally trained criminal justice professionals who attended law school—prosecuting and defense attorneys and judges—are generally trained to maintain control over clients, protect rights, and present cases to a third party for a decision. Although these criminal justice practitioners often negotiate in their daily work, the essential stance remains adversarial.

While the recommended education for parole and probation officers is often in one of the "helping" professions such as social work or counseling, actual on-the-job training inevitably prepares them for the same adversarial system that defines their role. Although the formal educational background of correction officers is less clearly defined, once employed as correction officers they too are socialized to perform in an adversarial system. Job orientation and socialization in correctional facilities place them in opposition to inmates and sustain a culture of hostility.

Adversarial worldviews allocate individuals to categories defined by the overall legal system. Solutions are imposed based on understood rules, both explicit and implicit. The legal system, in consequence, rewards professionals whose behavior is congruent with this pervasive win-lose approach. Its internal structure demands that this be the case.

DISPUTE RESOLUTION
AND CRIMINAL JUSTICE PROFESSIONALS

In recent years, the dispute-processing landscape has been changing. Dramatic changes have been underway in a number of areas that have had an impact on the way in which criminal justice work is done. For example, in New York State, the criminal procedure law has been amended so that criminal cases can in certain circumstances be adjourned in contemplation of dismissal to local dispute centers (Chap. 847, Laws of 1981). While this legislation initially diverted only less serious cases, since November 1, 1986, selected felonies are also being remanded.[1] In addition, New York State has new legislation that requires parents filing PINS (persons in need of supervision) petitions against their children to turn to diversionary programs offering diverse social services, of which mediation is one (Chap. 813, Laws of 1985).

Legislation such as that mentioned above cannot go unnoticed by criminal justice system professionals. Depending on the legislation and the programmatic efforts built around it, they may be expected or even required to screen for, refer to, or utilize community-based dispute resolution programs in lieu of traditional court processes. In some instances, they may be asked to mediate cases themselves.

Criminal justice professionals receiving widest exposure to mediation efforts are those coming from a legal background. For instance, former Chief Justice Burger has urged lawyers "to serve as healers of social conflict" (1982: 274), something that would involve a considerable shift in philosophy. The American Bar Association and local bar associations have established committees to work on ADR processes. Law schools throughout the country have developed coursework and training programs in mediation. The National Institute for Dispute Resolution (NIDR) has also been instrumental in advancing mediation education and training in law schools by offering varied incentives for law faculty to develop suitable resource materials and by sponsoring conferences (NIDR, n.d.).

The other group of criminal justice professionals most associated with mediation are police. In many instances, police intervention work with disputants is characterized as police mediation. More recently, efforts have been made to enlist the support of police to refer selected criminal cases to dispute resolution centers. In New York City, for example, a police operations order was issued in 1986 encouraging police officers to send disputants with an ongoing relationship involved in selected misdemeanors to local dispute resolution centers as an alternative to issuing summonses or making arrests.[2]

In some instances, probation officers have been familiarized with mediation efforts through victim-offender mediation programs (Umbreit, 1985a: 99–106; Umbreit, 1985b) and PINS mediation such as that in New York State. For parole and correctional officers, exposure to mediation has been more restricted (Cole and Silbert, 1984: 317–19). An example of the use of mediation in corrections is the Post-Conviction Victim/Offender Mediation Program developed by the

Oklahoma Department of Corrections, which provides victims with an opportunity to give input in the sentencing of convicted persons.

MEDIATION

Certainly mediation is not new to our society or the criminal justice system. What is unique about its current status is its developing institutionalization and the accompanying adjustments that this process requires.

Mediation is generally understood to be a relatively short-term, structured, goal-oriented, participatory intervention process engaged in voluntarily by the participants, who presumably agree to work with a neutral, trained third party to reach an agreed-upon outcome in an informal, private fashion (Folberg and Taylor, 1984; Moore, 1986). A major premise of the mediation process is that the parties themselves will control the decision-making; the mediator does not impose a decision on them as does an arbitrator or judge (Cooley, 1986).

Mediation work varies with the style and skill of the mediator, the context within which the mediation is conducted, past relationships between the parties involved, their negotiating styles, and the nature of the issue mediated. Generally, however, mediation does involve face-to-face sessions with the parties. Whether the mediator meets separately with the individual parties depends on some of the identified variables. Regardless of the format used, mediators generally ensure confidentiality unless circumstances outside the mediation process dictate otherwise.

While the activities engaged in by a mediator have been variously defined (Folberg and Taylor, 1984: 7–9; Moore, 1986: 13–19), certain activities are recognizable in virtually all mediation situations: the mediator works with the parties to gather relevant information, frame the issues, isolate points of agreement and disagreement, generate alternatives, and consider compromises for possible future agreement.

Mediation can be seen as an extension of a negotiation process that has broken down between the parties. Consequently, a mediator should be thoroughly knowledgeable about negotiation skills and techniques (Raiffa, 1982: 108–9). In addition, there are other roles a mediator may be required to assume, depending on circumstances. Stulberg (1981: 91–94) suggests that the following are particularly important: catalyst, educator, resource expander, bearer of bad news, agent of reality, and, sometimes not least, scapegoat.

Mediation does not focus on blame, that is, who is right and who is wrong. It is, rather, a future-oriented process. The understanding of underlying issues and the past is relevant only insofar as it helps the parties to get beyond the impasse and develop a solution, which will involve restructuring their relationship to some degree.

Any mediator recognizes the necessity for collaboration between the individuals involved in a dispute, the importance for these individuals to respect each other, and flexibility and creativity in reaching outcomes. What mediation offers criminal justice professionals, therefore, is an opportunity to foster interaction between the disputants themselves and to let the disputants attempt to resolve their own differences. As an alternative to an externally imposed decision at any level such as arrest or adjudication, disputants can be placed in a position of controlling their own agendas through work with a third party (either a criminal justice professional or some other qualified neutral) to reach a mutually satisfactory agreement. This can be achieved either by referring a case to a local dispute center, if one is available, or by employing mediation skills when handling a case.

MEDIATION EDUCATION AND TRAINING

Although mediation has experienced rapid growth in recent years, widespread training and education in mediation are still relatively new and uneven at the present time. This is complicated by the fact that mediators do not currently have to comply with any uniform standards for training or practice. Furthermore, a curriculum of suitable theoretical, substantive, and skills knowledge is only beginning to emerge.

Despite this unsettled picture, it is widely acknowledged that central to all mediation work is an understanding of the negotiation process. It is true that familiarity with negotiations is much more common than with mediation and that some formal training in negotiation processes has in fact been in existence for years.

However, negotiation training has not been conducted widely for criminal justice professionals. For the police, generally, negotiation training has been limited to specialized teams, particularly those handling hostage negotiations or domestic violence cases (Bard, 1973, 1975). Widespread training in negotiation for all police officers working in other settings has not been typical.

For lawyers, negotiation is often viewed as at the heart of all legal work (Bellow and Moulton, 1981). Yet historically it has not been a highly visible area of study for these professionals (Williams, 1983: v).

What should the content of mediation training be for criminal justice professionals? Ultimately, and because mediation is dissimilar to their traditionally defined role activities, these professionals need to learn how to facilitate discussion between parties in order to let them work through their differences. Generally, mediation training should consist of a sound basis in conceptual knowledge (e.g., theories of conflict and conflict intervention and management) as well as experiential learning situations involving simulations, videotaping, discussion, and critique. The training should focus particularly on developing and enhancing skills in listening, communication, problem-solving, and critical thinking. It should enable the criminal justice professional to demonstrate sensitivity and understanding toward disputants in developing an ability to facilitate communication between them. Finally, criminal justice professionals should be made aware of legal and ethical considerations involved in the mediation of criminal cases.

MEDIATION AND CRIMINAL JUSTICE PROFESSIONALS: EMERGING CRITICAL ISSUES

As an informal, imprecise intervention process that often occurs in private settings, mediation raises numerous issues for professionals working in the criminal justice system. Unlike mediation of disputes in other settings, the mediation of criminal cases is distinguished not only by the strong values about due process rights but also sentiments about punishing individuals who violate criminal laws.

This section highlights some of the issues and questions of particular importance to those involved in the mediation of criminal cases. Due to the newness of the more pervasive use of mediation and the limited research, the queries are much more extensive than the knowledge base at the present time.

Is a second-class system of criminal justice being institutionalized? The kind of justice meted out when criminal cases are mediated has been the object of much discussion and debate (Abel, 1982; Christian, 1986; Rosenberg, 1981). A major concern is whether a second-class system of criminal justice is created when rules of law or procedure are relaxed, nonlawyers are used as mediators, and disputants are not represented.

The informal, private nature of mediation does not lend itself to traditional protection of strong American values such as due process rights associated with the ideal justice system. By privatizing dispute-processing and removing disputes from public scrutiny, the potential for injustices may go unnoticed. This possibility has been viewed as particularly harmful to powerless and disadvantaged defendants who could be deprived of their constitutional rights.

Is mediation of criminal cases old wine in new bottles? For many in the criminal justice system, the question arises regarding how different mediation is from other efforts that have been undertaken to handle criminal cases informally, such as plea bargaining. The following questions begin to surface: Does mediation allow for the faster disposition of criminal cases? If the processing of the cases through mediation takes as long as some of the other processes, what does this mean for mediation and the criminal justice system?

When is the mediation of criminal cases appropriate? Ground rules for establishing which criminal cases should be mediated are fairly nebulous. Mediation has been generally encouraged for misdemeanor cases (ABA, 1990a) where individuals have an ongoing relationship. It has also been strongly discouraged in instances involving violence, particularly domestic violence (Lerman, 1984). Despite these concerns, there has been considerable experimentation with the mediation of many types of criminal disputes, including felonies and those involving violence (Bethel and Singer, 1982).

Given the discretion allowed by criminal procedure laws, criminal justice professionals are often caught in the middle, particularly when it comes to deciding when the use of mediation is appropriate.

Does the mediation of criminal cases expand the net? Some concern has been expressed regarding the availability of a readily available process such as mediation that allows for additional cases to be processed through informal intervention mechanisms that might not otherwise have been processed through court-connected forums (Abel, 1982).

What do volunteer mediators mean for the criminal justice system? Who should be resolving disputes in the criminal justice system? What are the reasons for using volunteers? The answers to these questions vary depending on who is answering them. In fact, most of the community dispute resolution programs use volunteer mediators to handle cases that would otherwise have been handled by the courts (ABA, 1990a). These volunteers are not required to have a legal background. One of the challenges for criminal justice professionals is to work with a new group of practitioners that may have little or no understanding of the legal system.

The use of volunteers is often seen as a cost-effective measure to reduce the court calendar congestion. It has also been seen as an effort to empower members of the community. Regardless, the use of volunteers stresses a nonlegalistic approach to the resolution of disputes and raises questions about what kind of preparation they should have.

What does mediation do to the image of the criminal justice system? Mediation can be seen as a soft or even inappropriate approach by criminal justice professionals. For example, police who define their job as one that is designed for action and based on a concept of authority and an authoritative preference may have difficulty with a process that restricts any decision-making. Prosecutors who refer cases to mediation may likewise feel that they are not doing what is expected of them. Riskin and Westbrook (1987: 241; see also Galanter, 1986) point out that "not everyone believes judicial mediation is good." And in the correctional setting, Cole and Silbert (1984: 318) note that "mediators are often confronted by officials claiming that rules and regulations make it impossible to mediate particular cases. Additionally, in dealing with both inmates and staff, the mediator frequently must be able to understand and to communicate issues of constitutional law."

The use of mediation is not consistent with traditional adversarial thinking without some modification of attitudes. Umbreit (1985c: 204) notes that "some within the criminal and juvenile justice system continue to strongly believe one cannot work with victims and offenders simultaneously, since their interests are diametrically opposed. The growing nationwide network of programs providing victim offender reconciliation services, however, presents important evidence to the contrary."

In addition, the justice system's effectiveness is often measured in terms of recidivism. One of the concerns raised by mediation of criminal cases is whether individuals are deterred from committing other offenses in the future. For those who feel strongly that prosecution of such cases deters recidivism, mediation is seen as soft and even inappropriate.

Why is the mediation of criminal cases resisted? Resistance to the widespread use of mediation for criminal cases is likely to surface for many reasons (Millhauser, 1987; Volpe and Bahn, 1987; Salazar, 1986), not least of which is the traditional culture of the criminal justice system that thematizes an adversarial orientation. Mediation clearly departs from this perspective. While the legal system is governed by rules of evidence and procedure and is operated in public, mediation allows for the disputants to participate in the process by exploring underlying causes, expressing their sentiments, discussing their needs, and generating creative solutions to their differences in an informal private setting. In light of this, some concern may emerge over the violation of strong American values such as due process rights.

In a recent article about lawyers and mediation, Riskin (1982: 41; see also Salazar, 1986) commented that "the future of mediation in this country rests heavily upon the attitudes and involvement of the legal profession." Lawyers are the gatekeepers of dispute resolution. When individuals have disagreements they are most likely to seek legal advice on how to proceed. Hence, if attorneys are not inclined to be supportive of mediation, they are not as likely to refer clients to use such processes.

In addition, despite the widespread interest in alternative ways of resolving disputes, the public in general does not seem to seek out mediation programs. Merry and Silbey (1984) found that by the time disputants turn to a third party, they are not interested in intervention efforts that ask them to work directly with disputants to reach their own outcomes for several reasons. They may want vindication, protection of rights, and/or an advocate to prove that the other party was wrong.

In sum, when individuals call the police or seek legal assistance, they have certain expectations. This is equally true of the public's expectations of judges. In American and other Western societies, legal authorities are expected to make decisions rather than work with the parties to achieve given agreements. Hence, mediation may be perceived by the public as destroying their notion of what a criminal justice system should be offering.

The increasing popularity of the use of mediation in the criminal justice system has provided criminal justice professionals with numerous challenges associated with acquiring the requisite knowledge and skills in order to use it. The structural situation of different sectors of the criminal justice system, and corresponding cultural attitudes, are highly variable. Educational requirements for recruitment into different sectors are also variable, as are the sophistication and length of job-training. There are in addition other background variables that need to be considered when introducing mediation training. These include rural/small town/urban differences in social experience, class status, and the like. Training programs need to be as sensitive to these questions as they are to the general issue of the underlying adversarial culture of the criminal justice system—at whatever level it is expressed.

There is a great deal to be learned from the emerging developments toward less adversarial handling of criminal disputes. There are also many challenging issues that need to be looked at more carefully. Clearly, research studies are needed to help answer the who, what, when, where, and whys of the mediation of criminal cases.

NOTES

1. Felony cases cannot be referred to a dispute center if they are class A felonies, violent felonies as defined in Sect. 70.02 of the Penal Law, drug offenses as defined by Art. 220 of the Penal Law, or felonies for which a defendant would be convicted as a second felony offender, a second violent felony offender, a persistent violent felony offender, or a persistent felony offender. See Art. 215, New York State Penal Law.

2. The following misdemeanors and violations can be sent to mediation: assault, third degree; menacing; reckless endangerment, second degree; reckless endangerment of property; criminal mischief, fourth degree; aggravated harassment, second degree; harassment; disorderly conduct; trespass; criminal trespass, second and third degree. The operations order states that "complainants will not be referred to such a Center as a substitute for arrest in the following situations: (a) When the officer determines there is probable cause to believe that a crime has been committed and the complainant refuses to accept mediation referral, OR (b) When the officer determines that there is probable cause to believe that a violation has been committed in his presence and the complainant refuses to accept mediation referral."

REFERENCES

Abel, R. (1982). "The Contradictions of Informal Justice." *The Politics of Informal Justice* 1: 267–320.

American Bar Association (ABA). (1990a). *Dispute Resolution Program Directory 1990.* Washington, D.C.: ABA Standing Committee on Dispute Resolution.

—— (1990b). *Legislation on Dispute Resolution: Federal and State Laws and Initiatives Pertaining to ADR.* Washington, D.C.: ABA Standing Committee on Dispute Resolution.

Bard, M. (1973). *Family Crisis Intervention: From Concept to Implementation.* Washington, D.C.: U.S. Department of Justice.

——. (1975). *The Function of the Police in Crisis Intervention and Conflict Management.* Washington, D.C.: U.S. Department of Justice, Law Enforcement Assistance Administration, National Institute of Law Enforcement and Criminal Justice.

Bellow, G., and B. Moulton. (1981). *The Lawyering Process.* New York: Foundation.

Bethel, C., and L. Singer. (1982). "Mediation: A New Remedy for Cases of Domestic Violence." *Vermont Law Review* 15–32.

Burger, W. (1982). "Isn't There a Better Way?" *ABA Journal* 68: 274–77.

Christian, T. (1986). "Community Dispute Resolution: First Class Process or Second Class Justice?" *NYU Review of Law and Social Change* 14: 771–83.

Cole, G. F., and J. E. Silbert. (1984). " Alternative Dispute Resolution Mechanisms for Prisoner Grievances." *Justice System Journal* 9: 306–24.

Cooley, J. (1986). "Arbitration vs. Mediation—Explaining the Differences." *Judicature* 69: 263–69.

Crohn, M. (1985). "Dispute Resolution in Higher Education." *Negotiation Journal* 1: 301–5.

Folberg, J., and A. Taylor. (1984). *Mediation: A Comprehensive Guide to Resolving Conflicts Without Litigation.* San Francisco: Jossey-Bass.

Galanter, M. (1986). "The Emergence of Judge as a Mediator in Civil Cases." *Judicature* 69: 257–62.

Goldberg, S., E. Green, and F. Sander. (1985). *Dispute Resolution*. Boston: Little, Brown.

Lerman, L. (1984). "Mediation of Wife Abuse Cases: The Adverse Impact of Informal Dispute Resolution on Women." *Harvard Women's Law Journal* 7: 57–113.

McKay, R. (1985). "The Many Uses of Alternative Dispute Resolution." *Arbitration Journal* 40: 12–16.

Marks, J., E. Johnson, and P. Szanton. (1984). *Dispute Resolution in America: Processes in Evolution*. Washington, D.C.: National Institute for Dispute Resolution.

Merry, S., and S. Silbey. (1984). "What Do Plaintiffs Want? Reexamining the Concept of Dispute." *Justice System Journal* 9: 151–78.

Millhauser, M. (1987). "The Unspoken Resistance to Alternative Dispute Resolution." *Negotiation Journal* 3: 29–35.

Moore, C. (1986). *The Mediation Process: Practical Strategies for Resolving Conflict*. San Francisco: Jossey-Bass.

National Institute for Dispute Resolution (NIDR). (n.d.). *Progress Report*. Washington, D.C.

Raiffa, H. (1982). *The Art and Science of Negotiation*. Cambridge: Harvard University Press.

Riskin, L. (1982). "Mediation and Lawyers." *Ohio State Law Journal* 43: 29–60.

Riskin, L., and J. Westbrook. (1987). *Dispute Resolution and Lawyers*. St. Paul, Minn.: West.

Rosenberg, M. (1981). "Second Class Justice." *Windsor Yearbook of Access to Justice* 1: 294–302.

Salazar, O. (1986). "Resistance to Mediation within the Legal Profession." In J. Palenski and H. Launer, eds. *Mediation: Contexts and Challenges*. Springfield, Ill.: Thomas, pp. 125–36.

Salem, R. (1985). "The Alternative Dispute Resolution Movement: An Overview." *Arbitration Journal* 40: 3–11.

Sander, F. (1984). "Alternative Dispute Resolution in the Law School Curriculum: Opportunities and Obstacles." *Journal of Legal Education* 34: 229–36.

Stulberg, J. (1981). "The Theory and Practice of Mediation: A Reply to Professor Susskind." *Vermont Law Review* 6: 85–117.

Umbreit, M. (1985a). *Crime and Reconciliation: Creative Options for Victims and Offenders*. Nashville: Abingdon.

————. (1985b) *Victim Offender Mediation: Conflict Resolution and Restitution*. Ind.: PACT Institute of Justice.

————. (1985c) "Victim Offender Mediation and Judicial Leadership." *Judicature* 69: 202–4.

————. (1986). "Victim Offender Mediation: A National Survey." *Federal Probation* 50: 53–56.

Volpe, M. (1985). "ADR: The Emergence of a New Educational Landscape." *NIJ Reports* 14.

Volpe, M., and C. Bahn (1987). "Resistance to Mediation: Understanding and Handling It." *Negotiation Journal* 3: 297–305.

Williams, G. (1983). *Legal Negotiation and Settlement*. St. Paul, Minn.: West.

CHAPTER 4

Options for Dispute Resolution in the Public Decision Processes on Urban Land Development

DAVID J. ALLOR

The emergence of urban land use planning in the early decades of the present century can be characterized as an extended battle for the recognition of interests. The recurrent conflict took two forms: (1) disputes over damages to individual interests in land, often called "nuisance"; and (2) disputes over the use of public power to restrain individual interests in service to the public interest. A nuisance was an unreasonable interference with the quiet use and enjoyment of land. Such disputes were not so much resolved by the contending neighbors as externally decided by a planning commission, city council, board of zoning appeals, or civil court. As informal processes for resolution of such disputes among neighbors failed, land use decisions were increasingly transformed into formal processes, absorbing various characteristics of legislative, administrative, and judicial processes.

These influences are reflected in the adoption of *Robert's Rules of Order* (1876, rev. 1915) by planning commissions to guide decision processes. In practice, however, this text is extraordinarily cumbersome for deliberative bodies and tends to reinforce the conception of contending parties. Its primary function is to assure order within partisan legislative debate. Its decision processes focus upon majority rule, rather than substantive agreement. Not only then are there "sides" to the questions, but also "winners" and "losers" in the outcome.

More recently, courts have required that planning commissions produce findings in support of their decisions. Consequently, decision processes have been bent toward a judicial character. Decision processes are more formally structured to require:

- giving of formal and constructive notice
- identification of applicants, proponents, and opponents

- swearing-in of persons wishing to testify
- cross-examination of persons testifying
- certification of the documentary record of proceedings
- transmission of binding decision

While such procedures certainly have the intention of producing a complete, objective, and coherent record of decision, they also reinforce the conception of public decision-making as an arena of contention, where parties win or lose but rarely agree.

As the present century enters its last decade, there is some indication that public decision processes are turning toward models of mediation. The formalized tradition of confrontation in public decision-making processes has borne bitter fruit for many of the parties. In land use planning decisions, as in other contentious arenas (as marital and child custody disputes, public utility rate disputes, and international military conflict), mediation techniques are now seen as offering the possibility of better fruits. The present chapter seeks to specify critical points at which mediation techniques can be incorporated into public decisions on urban land use. These techniques can preserve the legal character of these processes, increase their administrative efficiency, and promote social consensus.

ACTOR, PROCESS, AND ARENA

Academic and professional literature on negotiation and mediation of public disputes presents a broad array of actor roles, process variations, and interaction settings. Actors are usually identified in reference to their attitudes, interests, and formal role. Here the approaches range from applied social-psychology (Filey, 1975; Fisher and Ury, 1981) to applied political science-public administration (Barry, 1965; Huelsberg and Lincoln, 1985) and to planning-public policy (Forester, 1987; Rabinovitz, 1989). A more generalized orientation focuses on process construction and performance (Susskind and Madigan, 1984; Minnery, 1985; Moore, 1987a; Moore, 1987b; Carpenter and Kennedy, 1988). These actors execute processes in varied arenas. While mediation techniques are being incorporated into both legislative and administrative settings (Minnery, 1985; Huelsberg and Lincoln, 1985; Richman, et al., 1986; Forester, 1987), increasing attention is focused upon mediation of disputes directly lodged with or indirectly appealed to the courts (Susskind and Madigan, 1984; Folberg and Taylor, 1984; Gabbard and Clark, 1988). All of these considerations must be integrated if the actors are to have equitable opportunity to express their interests, to explore alternatives, and to share in the resolution.

SUBSTANTIVE FOCI

Much of the discussion regarding mediation in urban land use disputes have three foci: local, public, and intergovernmental. The first of these is the constructive management of citizen participation processes in local disputes. Because past losers are embittered, they often enter the next debate with rigid positions. It is very difficult to move these participants toward conceiving and offering mutually acceptable options (Bidol, et al., 1986; Moore and Carlson, 1984; Sacarto, 1985; Susskind and Cruikshank, 1987; Fulton, 1989). While land use disputes between neighbors are often socially divisive, impassioned opposition is more clearly manifested in the second of the substantive foci: the public use.

Conventionally labeled a LULU (a "Locally-Unwanted-Land-Use") or a NIMBY (a "Not-in My-Back-Yard" use), such development proposals as group homes, convention centers, and solid waste dumps stir deep public opposition (O'Hare, et al., 1983; Lake, 1987) and reinforce a crisis orientation in public participation processes. These disputes, however, can quickly transcend local opposition, moving the debate into intergovernmental arenas. Environmental disputes are the most common of the intergovernmental disputes. Assessments of environmental impacts often carry local development proposals to the level of regional dispute, entangling local, state, and federal governments (Bacow and Wheeler, 1984; Meeks, 1985; Agranoff, 1986; Richman, et al., 1986; Herrman 1987). While much of the writing on mediation focuses on such "extraordinary," "sensitive," or "cataclysmic" issues, this chapter explores options for the generalized incorporation of mediation techniques into the everyday decision processes on urban land development.

RATIONALE FOR MEDIATION OF LAND USE DISPUTES

The application of mediation techniques to public decision processes on urban land use (both as initial development and as redevelopment) is justified on both conceptual and pragmatic grounds. Public decision processes have several of the critical conceptual attributes for mediation:

1. a multiplicity of perceptions, interests, and expectations, which are differentially held by
2. a multiplicity of actors, who are or will be embedded in
3. an ongoing relationship, which will have
4. both short- and long-term consequences, which will in turn affect
5. the perceptions, interests, and expectations of both the initial and new actors, and hence will require
6. a continuing decision process

As a practical matter, recurrent land use disputes adversely affect the social, economic, and political integration of the community. With increasing frequency, decisions of planning commissions, municipal councils, and boards of zoning appeals are being appealed to the courts. Such appeals frustrate the effective implementation of land use public policy and stall specific land development.

Planning commissions, local legislatures, and municipal administrators are coming to favor the incorporation of mediation techniques into decision processes, as continuing community conflict impedes objective deliberation, engenders political stalemate, and yields administrative impotence. Many such court appeals do not address a question of law. They more commonly reflect a failure of social and political institutions to secure a resolution. Where there is no constitutional or statutory question, where there is no violation of due process, and where a legislative action or administrative decision is not unreasonable, the courts are very reluctant to rule on a land use dispute. Here, local courts are turning toward "court-annexed" options of voluntary or mandated referral to mediation. Such options are seen not only as constructive in outcome but also as effective in clearing court dockets of unnecessary litigation.

OPTIONS FOR MEDIATION IN PUBLIC
DECISION PROCESSES

Public decision processes on land use are incorporated into local government through a number of state constitution and statute provisions and municipal charter and ordinance provisions. These provide both the legal shell and formal process for land use decision-making. Commission by-laws, adopted plans, and development policies more fully enclose decision processes as local social convention. The discussion that follows presents several options for the incorporation of mediation techniques into a generalized public decision-making process on land use. These options are arrayed in Figure 4.1, where the mediation options are inserted in uppercase type, while the conventional process appears in upper/lowercase type.

There are seven options. The first two (prepetition review and staff hearing) are administrative in character and rest largely upon the availability of professional staff. The second two (planning commission working session and committee of council working session) are quasi-legislative in character. A fifth (mediation by mayor/city manager) is once again administrative in character. The final two options (voluntary referral to mediation and mandated referral to mediation) are quasi-judicial in character.

For clarity of reference, it is best to discuss each of these options in relation to the flow of a conventional decision process. That process generally begins with a development proposal. Such proposals vary from rough ideas to fully detailed *pro formas*, including design drawings, market studies, and financing packages. These proposals must be converted into adopted application format as a proposal submittal. Where the proposals are likely to be controversial, the option for prepetition review can be inserted.

A prepetition review is a formal informational meeting, requiring public notice. Planning commission staff act only as moderators and reporters. Such a review permits the voluntary accommodation of proposal and objections before the proposal becomes cast in stone and the opponents' political wills are hardened.

Figure 4.1
Options for Mediation in Land Use Decision-Making

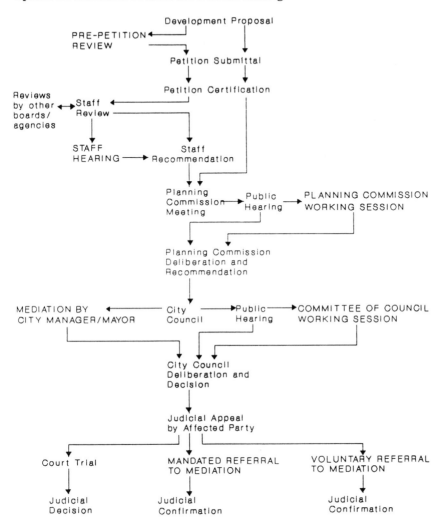

Following petition submittal and certification of completeness, a staff review is generally initiated. This review may include both in-house research and referral to other commissions and agencies for information and critical comment. Once the staff review is completed, but prior to formulation of a staff recommendation, a staff hearing option can be inserted.

A staff hearing is a formal, informational, and deliberative meeting of all interested and potentially affected parties, which requires public notice. Following presentation of the staff report, additional information is solicited. Here, however, the designated staff act as more than moderators. They serve as mediators, such that the proposal may be amended to reflect agreement among affected parties. Such mediation contributes to the comprehensiveness of the final staff report and permits a more specific staff recommendation. It is important to note that, while the designated staff function as mediators among the interested parties, they are not agents of the planning commission. Whatever the outcome of the staff hearing, the planning commission reserves the power to accept, amend, or reject the recommendation.

Prior to a decision by a planning commission, a public hearing must be called on the petition. Where neither the prepetition review nor the staff hearing option have been created, the public hearing is the first opportunity for interested and affected parties to speak. Because the record of the public hearing is often long, complex, and acrimonious, it may be appropriate to insert a planning commission working session option at this point in the process.

A planning commission working session is an open, nondeliberative session for which notice is given. The petition is presented and reviewed in light of the public hearing record. While individual members of the planning commission may request information and clarification, no action may be taken. Members of the planning commission can suggest revisions in accord with public policy and seek to accommodate developer, interested party, and community concerns. The full public hearing record, as well as the information volunteered in the working session, must be included in the later deliberative session of the planning commission.

Following deliberation and decision by the planning commission, its recommendation is forwarded to the city council. The council must call a public hearing on the petition. In that the public hearing record is often longer, more complex, and more acrimonious, the council may wish to insert a committee of council working session option at this point in the process.

An open, possibly deliberative session of council members for which public notice is given is parallel to the planning commission working session, except that the petition may have become more "politicized" as the members of the council are free to express positions. Only in the case of political stalemate, where there is high uncertainty of consequences, might politically divided parties seek a functionally mediated resolution. Where such a working session has not secured a resolution, the municipal council may seek another option prior to forcing itself to decision. This option is the referral to mayor/city manager.

This is a less open, less formal mediation technique, perhaps centered in separate caucuses among contending groups. Here, the mayor or city manager, as the chief municipal officer, can bring the "weight of the office" to bear upon the parties. A mayor's efforts may be seen as less than neutral, possibly influenced by interest or constituency pressure. While a city manager may be seen as more objective, rising from professional training, the city manager may have limited discretion in mediation when seen as an "employee" of the city council.

Assuming that none of the above options have worked to reconcile differences, the city council would be forced into a decision. The petition is now so heavily politicized that mediation within council chambers is impossible. Nevertheless, some decision is made, which any of the dissatisfied parties could appeal to the court. At this point two court-annexed options exist for mediation: voluntary referral to mediation or mandatory referral to mediation.

In some states, judges can offer the option of voluntary referral to mediation. Such a court-annexed option generally includes a list of court-recognized mediation masters, the selection of which all parties must agree to. If the master is successful, the contending parties would agree to a resolution, the judge would confirm the agreement, and the lawsuit(s) would be withdrawn. If mediation fails, the court would decide.

In other states, judges can direct a lawsuit to mediated settlement. Under such an option, masters are appointed by the court to conduct mediation processes in a formal manner. The power of such an option is contingent, however. If the contending parties fail to come to an agreement, the court-appointed mediator is then empowered to impose a settlement by arbitration, which the presiding judge would then confirm.

These seven options do not guarantee amicable settlement of disputes on land use. They do promote a more inclusive decision process, a more dispassionate argument on merits and consequences, and a more creative conceptualization of acceptable resolutions.

BREADTH OF APPLICATION

The incorporation of mediation techniques into public decision processes on land use is most easily accomplished in regard to master plan formulation and adoption, public capital improvements programming, and zoning. Mediation techniques are equally applicable to Euclidean and performance-based ordinances and would facilitate decisions related to special site plan review, planned unit development, and conditional use permits. These same techniques are applicable to subdivision regulations (sometimes called platting regulations), except that the range of discretion is narrower when tied to questions of public health and safety. There is one serious limitation upon the incorporation of these techniques. A board of zoning appeals, as a quasi-judicial body, deciding only issues of "hardship" generated by the strict application of a zoning ordinance, has very limited discretion. Decision processes focused upon the technical determination of hardship and the granting of the minimal variance are less open to mediation techniques.

LEGAL CONSTRUCTION, EFFECTIVENESS, AND SOCIAL ACCEPTANCE

The ability to incorporate and sustain mediation techniques in urban land use decision processes rests upon three sets of considerations. First is their legal construction. In some states, mediation techniques may require amendment to state enabling legislation, followed by amendment to local ordinance. In other states, mediation techniques may be adopted directly by local ordinance under general home-rule provisions or by charter provisions. The second consideration is the effectiveness of administration. Effectiveness of mediation techniques depends upon the articulation of procedures that meet due process and reasonableness requirements. For all of the above options, training, selection, assignment, and evaluation of mediators are critical to effectiveness. Third and finally, the effectiveness of mediation techniques cannot be sustained if the members of the community do not find such techniques more appropriate than conventional processes. While it is not necessary that each party of a land use conflict "gets all they want," the processes now incorporating mediation techniques much be seen as "fair" in distributional effects and "contributory" to the long-term social integration of the community.

NOTE

An earlier version of this chapter "Alternatives to Confrontation: Options for Dispute Resolution in the Public Decision Processes on Urban Land Development," was presented at the American Planning Association National Conference, Atlanta, Georgia, May 1989.

REFERENCES

Agranoff, R. J. (1986). *Intergovernmental Management*. Albany: State University of New York Press.

Bacow, L., and M. Wheeler. (1984). *Environmental Dispute Resolution*. New York: Plenum.

Barry, Brian. (1965). *Political Argument*. London: Routledge and Kegan Paul.

Bidol, P., et al. (1986). *Alternative Environmental Conflict Management: A Citizen's Manual*. Ann Arbor: University of Michigan, Environmental Conflict Project.

Carpenter, S. L., and W. J. D. Kennedy. (1988). *Managing Public Dispute: A Practical Guide to Handling Conflict and Reaching Agreements*. San Francisco: Jossey-Bass.

Filey, A. C. (1975). *Interpersonal Conflict Resolution*. Glenview, Ill.: Scott, Foresman.

Fisher, R., and W. Ury. (1981). *Getting to Yes: Negotiating Agreement Without Giving In*. New York: Penguin.

Folberg, J., and A. Taylor. (1984). *Mediation: A Comprehensive Guide to Resolving Conflicts Without Litigation*. San Francisco: Jossey-Bass.

Forester, J. (1987). "Planning in the Face of Conflict: Negotiation and Mediation Strategies in Local Land Use Regulation." *Journal of American Planning Association* 53, no. 3 (Summer): 303–14.

Fulton, W. (1989). *Reaching Consensus in Land Use Negotiations*. PAS Report No. 417. Chicago: American Planning Association.

Gabbard, A., and J. Clark. (1988). "Mediation, An Alternative to Litigation." *Current Municipal Problems* 15 (Summer): 49–53.

Herrman, M. S. (1987). *Mediation in a Regional Setting*. Washington, D.C.: National Association of Regional Councils.

Huelsberg, N. A., and W. F. Lincoln, eds. (1985). *Successful Negotiating in Local Government*. Practical Management Series. Washington, D.C.: International City Management Association.

Lake, R. W., ed. (1987). *Resolving Locational Conflict*. New Brunswick, N.J.: Rutgers University Press.

Meeks, G. (1985). *Managing Environmental and Public Policy Conflicts: A Legislator's Guide*. Denver: National Conference of State Legislators.

Minnery, J. R. (1985). *Conflict Management in Urban Planning*. Brookfield, Vt.: Gower.

Moore, C. W. (1987a). *The Mediation Process: Practical Strategies for Resolving Conflict*. San Francisco: Jossey-Bass.

——— , ed. (1987b). *Practical Strategies for the Phases of Mediation*. San Francisco: Jossey-Bass.

Moore, C. W., and C. M. Carlson. (1984). *Public Decision Making: Using the Negotiated Investment Strategy*. Dayton, Ohio: Kettering Foundation.

O'Hare M., L. Bacow, and D. Sanderson. (1983). *Facility Siting and Public Opposition*. New York: Van Nostrand Reinhold.

Rabinovitz, F. F. (1989). "The Role of Negotiation in Planning, Management, and Policy Analysis."*Journal of Planning Education and Research* 8, no. 2 (Winter): 87–95.

Richman, R. (1985). "Formal Mediation in Intergovernmental Disputes: Municipal Annexation in Virginia." *Public Administration Review* (July/Aug.): 510–17.

Richman, R., et al. (1986). *Intergovernmental Mediation: Negotiations in Local Governmental Disputes*. Boulder, Colo.: Westview.

Robert, H. M. ([1915] 1971). *Robert's Rules of Order Revised*. New York: Morrow.

Sacarto, D. M. (1985). *Economic Development Conflicts: Model Programs for Dispute Resolution*. Denver: National Conference of State Legislatures.

Susskind, L. E., and J. Cruikshank. (1987). *Breaking the Impasse: Consensual Approaches to Resolving Public Disputes*. New York: Basic.

Susskind, L. E., and D. Madigan. (1984). "New Approaches to Resolving Disputes in the Public Sector." *Justice System Journal* 9, no. 2: 179–203.

PART III

Litigation Disputes

CHAPTER 5

Merging of Minds and Microcomputers: The Coming of Age of Computer-Aided Mediation of Court Cases

JOHN W. COOLEY

COMPUTER-AIDED MEDIATION

Mediation in General

Traditionally, mediation has been defined as a process in which an impartial intervenor helps disputants reach a voluntary settlement of their differences through an agreement defining their future behavior. Mediation consists of eight stages: initiation, preparation, introduction, problem statement, problem clarification, generation and evaluation of alternatives, selection of alternatives, and agreement.[1] The mediator does not impose a decision on the parties. Yet despite this lack of decision-making authority, the mediator is effective for several reasons:

1. Parties are more likely to disclose important information concerning their true settlement objectives to a mediator than to an arbitrator, judge, or other party with decision-making authority.

2. A mediator is able to work, in caucus, with each party in defining a realistic settlement range or solution, often discovering an overlap in settlement ranges or solutions that can lead to a prompt agreement.

3. By focusing on problem-solving rather than fault-assignment, a mediator keeps the parties in a settlement frame of mind rather than an adversarial one.

4. Mediation is confidential and involves virtually no risk to the parties since they cannot be bound by the mediator.

5. If the parties cannot agree, each is free to terminate the mediation. This freedom allows the parties to consider more creative solutions than are likely to emerge from an adversarial process.[2]

In short, in mediation the parties can avoid posturing and move quickly to the issues about which they disagree. Resolution occurs through collaborative problem-solving, the linchpin of which is joint decision-making. Many of these characteristics of the mediation process make it quite amenable to computer enhancement.

Mediation and the Computer

Computer-aided mediation is similar to traditional mediation, but with the added dimension of computer-enhanced thinking, problem-solving, and decision-making capability. It represents a unique partnership of human intelligence and artificial intelligence in an interactive, joint problem-solving process, having both creative and analytical elements. It has several modes of application. For example, the computer and its decision-aiding software can be used by the mediator(s) working with the parties during a mediation conference; the mediator(s) between sessions or conferences; or the parties and their counsel between sessions or conferences. The computer can be used to analyze and evaluate information and settlement opportunities generated in a prior session or conference and to develop settlement strategies and opportunities to discuss jointly at succeeding sessions or conferences.

The computer-aided mediator helps the parties develop a creative settlement arrangement that both sides recognize as being substantially better than the probabilistic value of going to trial. The parties, with the assistance of a mediator conducting joint and/or caucus sessions, work together with a user-friendly computer program that enables each party to clarify the benefits and costs of settling versus the benefits and costs of going to trial. No substantial knowledge of computers or computer-aided mediation is needed in order to be able to make constructive use of this type of procedure. Normally, a mediator can become adept at using decision-aiding software in a one- or two-day training session.

Computer-aided mediation has advantages over traditional mediation in its ability to assist parties to arrive at mutually beneficial solutions with less time and expense. It is especially capable of arriving at solutions in which each side compromises on some issues that are not so important to it, but may be quite important to the other side. It therefore facilitates solutions in which each side can come out ahead of their respective best expectations, rather than merely ahead of their worst expectations. These types of solutions are called "super-optimum" (better than win-win) solutions, and use of a computer in mediation can, in many instances, expand the window of opportunities for achieving them.

Types of Super-Optimum Solutions

Four types of super-optimum solutions are achievable through computer-aided mediation:[3]

Solution that achieves a super-optimal goal. A super-optimal goal is one that is far higher than is traditionally considered to be the best attainable. An example would be doing better than zero percent unemployment by simultaneously eliminating or reducing traditional unemployment and greatly increasing job opportunities for those who are willing and able to work more, but were formerly considered outside the laborforce or formerly considered fully employed.

Solution that resolves public policy disputes. This solution satisfies liberals and conservatives in a policy dispute so that both liberals and conservatives consider the solution to be better than their original best expectations.

Solution that resolves adjudicative or rule-applying controversies. This solution satisfies disputants in a way that is better than their best expectations. An example would be where a plaintiff demands $900,000, the defendant refuses to pay more than $300,000, and they agree that the defendant will turn over merchandise worth more than $1 million to the plaintiff, but whose variable cost to produce is worth less than $200,000 to the defendant.

Solution that enables all sides in a dispute to add substantially to their original net worth. An example would be when the defendant agrees to give the plaintiff a franchise for selling the defendant's products and the franchise brings in a net of $1 million each year, with $500,000 a year for the plaintiff and $500,000 a year for the defendant. This type of expanded sum solution would still be met if the total net worth of all participants substantially increased, even if the net worth of some of the participants slightly decreased, provided that the decrease did not cause those participants to go below a minimum level of satisfaction.

The goal of achieving super-optimum solutions through computer-aided mediation takes into account, if at all possible, the interests of affected outsiders. Thus, normally a solution reached through computer-aided mediation should not only be optimum in one or more of the above four ways, but should also enable affected outsiders who are not parties to the dispute or the negotiations to come out ahead as well. An agreement that greatly benefits the immediate parties to a dispute, but at the substantial expense of others, could not reasonably qualify as a super-optimum solution.

Functions of Decision-Aiding Software in Computer-Aided Mediation

Decision-aiding software, if properly selected and employed, can assist the mediator and the parties in mediation stages 4 (problem statement), 5 (problem clarification), 6 (generation and evaluation of alternatives), 7 (selection of alternatives), and 8 (agreement) by:[4]

1. making predictions as to the probability or magnitude of events occurring, such as winning at trial and the level of damages;
2. choosing among alternative approaches to presenting evidence, negotiating, mediating, or choosing among other alternative courses of action;
3. allocating time, people, money, or other scarce resources to activities, places, or other people;

4. determining what it would take to bring a second-place alternative (like accepting a settlement) up to the desirability level of a first-place alternative (like going to trial);

5. developing and analyzing a number of criteria or components in a package settlement so that each side yields on items that are not so important to it but are important to the other side;

6. dealing with nonmonetary goals;

7. dealing with missing information on future events by converting questions of the likely probability, benefits, or costs of a choice into questions as to whether they are above or below computer-calculated threshold, break-even, or critical values;

8. dealing with conflicting constraints where, for example, there are various minimum demands that add to more than the maximum available; and

9. solving other problems involving predicting, choosing, allocating, what-if analyses, packaging criteria, multidimensional goals, missing information, conflicting constraints, or the need for simplicity amid the complexities of dispute situations.

Depending on the specific decision-aiding software selected, other functions may be available to assist in dispute resolution.

Decision-Aiding Software

Below is a list of software that can be used separately or in combination in resolving disputes through computer-aided mediation:[5]

1. *Decision tree software:* Arborist, Supertree, Clarence, Ondine, StrataTree, and RiskCalc[6]

2. *Linear programming and related software:* Erikson-Hall, Lee-Shim, IFPS, Holden-Day, LP Master, Burns-Austin, LP Professional, and Vino-Gino-Lindo[7]

3. *Statistical Software:* StatPal, Hall-Adelman, ABC, Stata, EpiStat, PsychoStats, Crosstats, Chao, SPSS, SAS, BDM, StatFast, StatPac[8]

4. *Spreadsheet Software* (especially if based on Lotus 1-2-3): Best Choice, What's Best, 1-2-Tree, Minitab, 1-2-3 Breakeven, PG Lotus, and GoalSeeker[9]

5. *Rule-Based Software for Prediction or Prescribing Decisions:* Teknowledge, Expert87, ExSys, ESCA-DSS, MicroExpert, Ashton-Tate, and Texas Instruments[10]

6. *Miscellaneous Multi-Criteria Decision-Making Software (MCDM):* Lightyear, Confidence, Factor, Decision Analyst, Expert Choice, Prefcalc, DecAid Electre, Policy PC, P/G%, DecisionMaker, Decision, P-G Plato, Seriatim, Decision Making, Decide, Pairs, MASS, MOLP, MAUD, and MIDAS[11]

7. *Substantive Legal Software:* Determining Damages, Legal Analytics, SettleMate, In-Valve, Comprowise, TaxCalc, Aardvark, TaxMan, and Meldman[12]

8. *Alternative Generating Software:* Idea Generator, Brainstormer, Trigger[13]

Software Used in Computer-Aided
Mediation of Federal Court Cases

Using a software program in mediation usually involves the following steps:[14]

1. Listing the alternatives from which a choice needs to be made, or to which an allocation needs to be made.

2. Listing the criteria or goals that one wants to achieve and their relative importance.

3. Scoring each alternative on each criterion with as precise or as rough a relation score as is available.

4. Converting the scores into part/whole percentages or other scores that can show the relative relations of the alternatives on each criterion.

5. Aggregating the relative scores for each alternative across the criteria in order to arrive at an overall score or allocation coefficient for each alternative.

6. Drawing a conclusion as to which alternative or combination is best.

7. Changing the alternatives, criteria, relations, and other inputs to see how such changes affect the conclusion.

The computer program is divided into five parts or options, covering the following areas:[15]

1. Accessing, creating, or deleting a datafile of information relevant to resolving a decision problem.

2. Inserting or changing the inputs regarding the alternatives, goals, relations, and so on.

3. The initial results based on the alternatives, goals, and relations.

4. The post facto analyses, which include threshold analysis and convergence analysis.

5. A provision for saving and storing data for future reference.

The post facto analyses are especially useful in dispute resolution in that they identify what the weights or relation-scores should be. Threshold analysis is one option whereby the computer shows what it would take in changing the goals-weights or the relation scores to bring the second-place alternative up to first place or any alternative up to any other alternative. Convergence analysis is another option whereby the computer shows at what level the weight for a goal becomes high enough to produce results that are quite close to the results that would occur if that goal were the only goal.

COMPUTER-AIDED MEDIATION IN
A FEDERAL COURT CASE

Background

In late 1985, a Chicago area restaurant and several business establishments occupying the same building filed a lawsuit in the United States District Court for the Northern District of Illinois, Eastern Division, against a Japanese electronic equipment manufacturer and its U.S. affiliate.[16] The gist of the dispute was that a cassette tape player manufactured and distributed by the defendants allegedly started a fire that caused substantial damage to the plaintiffs' business premises and their contents. The case was assigned to Judge Marvin E. Aspen. The complaint consisted of four counts. The first count alleged the defendants' liability on the ground of strict liability in tort; the second count, on negligent manufacture or design of the tape player; the third count, *res ipsa loquitur* (literally, "the thing speaks for itself"; in law, a mode of proving negligence in which the plaintiff must show that the accident was one that would not normally happen without negligence); the fourth count, on a contract theory premised on a claim of the warranty of merchantability implied by law in §2-314 of the Uniform Commercial Code. The defendants moved to dismiss counts 3 and 4 of the complaint. Aspen declined to dismiss count 4 (relating to warranty of merchantability). He ordered count 3 dismissed, not for the reasons addressed by defendants, but rather because he found count 3 to be a subset of count 2. Although he dismissed count 3, Aspen noted that the plaintiffs were free to develop their *res ipsa loquitur* theory under count 2. Thus, for all practical purposes, the complaint was left intact.

In April 1987, the parties agreed to Aspen's suggestion that a special master be appointed for the limited purpose of attempting to mediate a resolution of the case. Aspen appointed Stuart Nagel and myself as special masters to co-mediate the dispute using computer-aided mediation.

Nagel and I, with the assistance of computer expert Paul Bernstein, conducted two full-day and two half-day mediation conferences with the parties during the summer and fall of 1987. Initially, Bernstein's involvement was deemed necessary because of the geographic location of the mediators, parties, and their counsel, and the prospect that portions of the computer-aided mediation might be conducted by use of phone modems (several of the participants were remotely located).

Plaintiffs

Major American Insurance Co.	Chicago, Illinois
Counsel	Chicago, Illinois

Defendants

Major Japanese Insurance Co.	Japan
Major Japanese Electronics Co.	Japan
Principal U.S. counsel	New York City
Local counsel	Chicago, Illinois

Mediators

Stuart Nagel	Champaign, Illinois
John Cooley	Evanston, Illinois
Paul Bernstein	Chicago, Illinois

Although, as events unfolded, computer-aided mediation was not conducted remotely by use of modems, two members of the mediation team (Cooley and Bernstein) did use modems to communicate settlement ideas and strategies during the course of the mediation. Needless to say, the opportunities presented by this case have set the stage for expanded experimentation with remotely conducted computer-aided mediations in the future.

First Mediation Conference

The first mediation conference was held in early June 1987 in a vacant grand jury room in the United States Courthouse in Chicago, an unlikely but workable site for a mediation conference. The conference lasted approximately six hours. Present were the court-appointed mediators and Bernstein, two Chicago-based counsel on behalf of the plaintiff insurance company, and a New York-based and local Chicago counsel on behalf of the defendant Japanese insurance and electronic companies.

I initiated the session by introducing myself, Nagel, and Bernstein, and then described the mediation process generally. None of the four lawyers had previously experienced private mediation and only one of them (one of plaintiffs' counsel) was familiar with a microcomputer and its functioning.

Nagel explained, generally, the functioning of the microcomputer and the P/G% software. During part of the demonstration, he ran through a sample dispute resolution problem and had the lawyers get ''hands-on'' experience with the computer. The equipment used during the mediation included a microcomputer with a small incorporated monitor and keyboard; an overhead projector; and a flat electronic device for placement on the overhead projector to project a large videoscreen image on the wall. After this introduction to the computer and the software, the mediators conducted a joint session with counsel to get an understanding of each side's perception of the case and to determine the status of any settlement negotiations. The rest of the morning was spent in caucus with the defendants' counsel. The afternoon session was spent with the plaintiffs' counsel. In the caucus sessions, the mediators, working with counsel at the microcomputer, determined each side's view as to alternatives, criteria, weights, and data needed to solve the problem. After these sessions, it was clear to the mediators that:

- Each side most probably had an unrealistically high expectation of victory.
- Each side believed that it would cost relatively little, monetarily, to proceed with trial (although these beliefs might have been exaggerated posturing efforts).
- The defendants were withholding information that, if disclosed, might precipitate settlement.
- The defendant electronics manufacturer's engineering pride was at stake.
- Each side desired to avoid going to trial and possibly litigating an appeal.
- Each side desired to avoid the risk of losing.

- Each side desired to settle.
- The plaintiffs would be compensated sooner if the case settled.
- The defendant electronics manufacturer feared adverse publicity, loss of business, and perhaps forced recall of products.
- The plaintiffs could prove actual damages in excess of $900,000 but would accept $700,000 to settle the case; the defendants were willing to pay $90,000 to settle the case.

In a final joint session of the first day's conference, nonmonetary elements of a settlement were discussed generally, and counsel agreed to meet again to discuss some creative options for resolving the case.

First Interim Analysis and Collaboration

Between the first and second conferences, the mediators analyzed the information obtained from the first conference and shared thoughts about the development of a super-optimum solution. Nagel prepared a 20-page postconference computer analysis and summary of the ideas developed at the first meeting and distributed it to the mediation team and counsel for the parties. Interspersed in this document were copies of computer printouts of nonconfidential information showing the parties' perceptions regarding probabilities of victory, costs of proceeding to trial, cost of settling the case, expected damages, and so on. This document also contained some of Nagel's random thoughts about possible nonmonetary elements of a settlement package.

Nagel also distributed to the mediation team a second 18-page document containing: (1) the alternatives, criteria, and data from the plaintiffs' perspective followed by an initial analysis and threshold analysis; (2) similar information from the defendants' perspective including the criterion related to engineering pride; (3) a liability analysis of criteria relating to combustibility, circuit-breaking, and prior occurrences, which yielded a probability of liability of approximately .37 or about 1 in 3; and (4) a damage analysis of possible damage findings that predicted recoverable damages of approximately $756,000 if the case proceeded to trial. Some of the implications of this analysis were that the plaintiffs should be pleased to settle for less than their original demand in view of the low predicted probability of liability being found. Similarly, the defendants should be pleased to settle for more than their original offering in view of the high predicted damages. On the matter of the pride criterion, going to trial was not that much better than settling, especially settling under a nondisclosure [to the public] arrangement. Going to trial could mean a damaging loss, but also bad publicity even if there was a victory. Moreover, if the plaintiffs could recognize the need to lower their original demand, and the defendants could recognize the need to raise their original offer, then a mutually agreeable settlement should be reached. Such a settlement would be especially desirable if it involved a transfer from the defendant manufacturing company and insurance company to the plaintiff restaurant and insurance company—something that would have relatively low cost to the defendants, but relatively high value to the plaintiffs.

During the hiatus between the first and second conferences, this author suggested several settlement strategies to the mediation team. They included: (1) encouraging the parties to develop creative solutions and complimenting them when they offered suggested solutions; (2) encouraging the parties to look at the lawsuit not as a problem, but rather as an opportunity for a mutually advantageous business deal; (3) keeping the issue of an allegedly defective product out of the discussion by emphasizing that the electronics company was really a bystander watching the development and formation of a business transaction between two insurance companies which, if agreement was to be reached, had to protect the interests of the electronics company; (4) reframing the situation by showing the parties that the combustibility issue brought the insurance companies together and that the lawyers could help those companies "make music together" by orchestrating a holistic solution; (5) concentrating on things that the defendant insurance company had (or had access to) that the plaintiff insurance company needed.

These "things" perhaps held little value to the defendant insurance company but could be of great or even inestimable value to the plaintiff insurance company; or, the comparative worth of the things could mean more to the plaintiff insurance company. For example, real property in Japan or the United States; computers; accounts receivable; business contacts; payment of claims; and insurance business (reinsurance; special lines; excess liability; and so on). It was also suggested that the word "no" should not be used until all ideas were stated and fully discussed. Additionally, it was pointed out that the electronics company eventually had to come to grips with the fact that the risks of its going to trial were enormous, in terms of the deluge of claims that might follow; the possible forced recall of millions of products; the possible tarnishing of its engineering reputation; the potential loss of millions of dollars worth of sales; and that the risk of ultimate harm to the defendant electronics company was much higher than any risk the plaintiffs had in going to trial. I also suggested that the mediation team develop other information relative to the monetary and nonmonetary aspects of settlement, including other settlement formulas; the exchange rate of the dollar versus the yen; the effect (or status of) any government embargo on Japanese products; the tax consequences of any trade of products (electronics or insurance); and types of products that the electronics company manufactures.

The mediation team members agreed that the second conference should focus on developing nonmonetary elements of a settlement formula toward achieving a super-optimum solution.

Second Mediation Conference

The second mediation conference was held in early July 1987. Since the consensus of the mediators was that the second conference should be a creative experience, this author agreed to make a short presentation on creative problem-solving and lateral thinking at the beginning of the session.

In introducing this topic, several points were stressed. Computer-aided mediation relies, in large part, on the creative efforts of participants for its effectiveness. These participants must be willing to adopt a mindset for creative problem-solving. In negotiating a super-optimum solution, the principles of "getting to yes" (Roger Fisher and William Ury) are important considerations (i.e., separating people from the problem; focusing on interests, not positions; inventing options for mutual gain; and insisting on objective criteria). The settling of a case is a joint problem-solving effort. The parties own the problem and the process, and they will also own the solution, while the mediators protect the process and help make it work. The challenge for the parties and their counsel is not to determine who is right or wrong, but rather to create a solution yielding mutual benefits.

The ground rules suggested for the second conference included: (a) the assignment of fault would not be allowed; (b) the lawsuit would be viewed as an opportunity for mutual gain, as if corporate lawyers were putting together a business deal; (c) discussion should revolve around the needs and interests (not rights and duties) of the parties; (d) the word "no" is taboo: all ideas are welcome, judgment will be suspended, and evaluation of ideas will be deferred.

The lawyers were surprisingly receptive to these unusual parameters and ground rules. It was as if they welcomed the opportunity to think freely and to be creative.

Next, I described the differences between vertical and lateral thinking and the importance of each in the problem-solving process.[17] I explained that in that day's session, mostly lateral (innovative, intuitive) thinking would be employed and that we would reserve vertical (analytical, logical) thinking for the evaluation and selection stages of the settlement process. Lateral thinking was defined as insight restructuring. Several methods of lateral thinking, including brainstorming, thought reversal, analogy, and fractionation, were briefly described.

Counsel for the parties then participated in four short exercises to give them a "feel" for thinking laterally in solving problems before focusing on the actual problem—the settlement of the lawsuit. These exercises involved solving four problems, described in Figures 5.1 through 5.4.[18]

After these exercises were completed, the mediation team conducted brainstorming sessions with counsel for each side in separate caucuses. The enthusiasm for creativity demonstrated by counsel in these sessions was truly remarkable. Several possible nonmonetary components of a possible settlement package were suggested by counsel. In a final joint session of the day, the mediation team reconvened the attorneys to discuss some of the ideas generated in the caucuses. After discussion, counsel agreed that they wished to explore more extensively the following settlement formulas: the transfer of electronics products from the defendant electronics company to the plaintiff insurance company (the possibility of the plaintiffs' counsel being compensated, at least in part, by computer products received by the plaintiff insurance company was also considered; ethical implications were discussed); the transfer of insurance claims from the defendant Japanese

Figure 5.1
Exercise 1

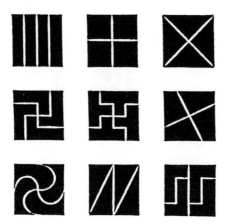

Notes: The lawyers were asked to determine how many ways a square could be divided into four
equal pieces. They worked individually on this problem. After two or three minutes, they
were finished. The most ways determined by any one lawyer was 6. They were surprised
and somewhat embarrassed when told that the correct answer to the problem was ''an infinite
number of ways.'' A few of the infinite number of ways are shown above. The point of this
exercise was to teach the lawyers not to think narrowly about the number of alternative settlement solutions to the lawsuit. The number of potential solutions was limited only by the restrictions they placed, consciously or unconsciously, on their imaginations and power of thinking.

insurance company to the American insurance company (these claims would be
worth as much as three times more to the American insurance company than to
the Japanese insurance company); and the transfer of cash by the defendants.
Because of the conversion rate, the Japanese would have to advance fewer yen
than usual to meet the plaintiffs' needs. The plaintiffs' counsel insisted that the
final settlement package would have to contain some cash element. One reason
for this was that one or more of the plaintiffs had been insured by other insurance
companies and had not been fully reimbursed for their losses.

Much of the discussion in the final joint session focused on the first option.
Attorneys for the American insurance company were interested in knowing the
products manufactured by the Japanese electronics company, the suggested retail
sales price of such products in dollars, and the number of products that the Japanese
electronics company would be willing to transfer. They could then advise their
American insurance company client as to the relative value it would be receiving
on that aspect of the settlement. The defense counsel did not have that information available, but they suggested that another meeting be set up at which Japanese
client representatives would be present (along with a representative of the

Figure 5.2
Exercise 2

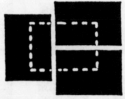

Notes: In the second exercise, the problem involved arranging four business cards on the table so that each business card was touching three others. This was a group or collaborative problem-solving exercise requiring both plaintiff and defense counsel to work together toward a solution. This problem is quite difficult for some people because they *assume* that all the cards have to lie in the same plane. The solution is for three cards to lie touching each other on the table with the fourth card raised and placed on top of the three cards. As soon as one breaks free from the "same plane" *assumption* and realizes that there is no rule preventing movement into the third dimension, the problem is solved. One of the lawyers in the group was not stymied by the "same plane" assumption and saw the solution to the problem. He and the group were complimented on their creativity. The point of this exercise was to demonstrate that effective problem-solving (even in a lawsuit) requires one to be free to move into new dimensions, to be wary of false assumptions regarding alternative solutions, and to avoid cliche patterns of thinking.

American insurance company) to discuss the feasibility of a transfer of electronics products and the other elements of a possible settlement package. Counsel agreed to meet again at a mutually convenient date.

Second Interim Analysis and Collaboration

Between the second the third mediation conferences, the members of the mediation team again shared thoughts about the progress of the settlement and future settlement strategies. Shortly after the second mediation conference, Bernstein communicated with me via computer modem, and I responded similarly. This telecommunication option permitted us to maintain a continuing dialogue in writing that was available practically instantaneously on our computer videoscreens. If ideas came to us at any time during the day or night, we could insert the information, typing the date and time, and the other person could review the new material at his leisure and respond, if appropriate. This greatly facilitated communication between Bernstein and me at the time because we were engaged in various projects and found it difficult to contact each other by conventional telephone. Appearing below is an example of one message Bernstein transmitted to me through the computer conference network. The hard copy print-out read as follows:

I inquire as to the fluctuating value of the Japanese YEN as a factor in trying to mediate and thereby settle this pending matter. Assume the following:

Figure 5.3
Exercise 3

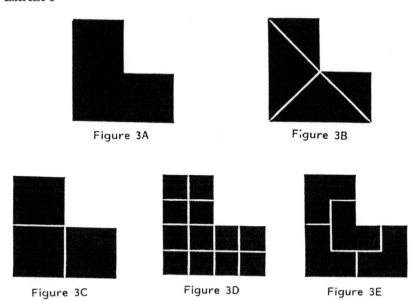

Figure 3A   Figure 3B

Figure 3C   Figure 3D   Figure 3E

Notes: Next the lawyers were given a paper on which appeared a geometrical "L" shape. The problem was to divide the shape into four pieces identical in size, shape, and area. Again, the adversaries collaborated in an attempt to solve the problem. A solution (Fig. 3B) was proposed, but it soon became evident that, although the figure was divided into four pieces, the solution did not satisfy the criteria of identity of size, shape, and area of the pieces. The lawyers struggled with the problem, but were unable to solve it in the time allotted. I then noted that to solve a problem, oftentimes it is necessary to break it down into smaller parts or elements (to fractionate) and try to see alternative configurations. The steps in solving this problem appear successively in Figs. 3C, 3D, and 3E. A correct solution is Fig. 3E and consists of four small "L"-shaped pieces, of identical size, shape, and area. The point of this exercise was to demonstrate that the settlement ultimately designed for the lawsuit might consist of several component elements, derived untraditionally, yet fully satisfying all criteria (the needs and interests of all the parties).

1. Value of dollar when loss brought to attention of Japanese insurance carrier: 300 yen = $1.00

2. Value of dollar today: 150 yen = $1.00

3. Reserve set up by insurance company at time of loss in yen: 270,000 yen

4. Reserve set up by insurance company at time of loss in $: 270,000 yen /300 = $90,000.00

5. Assume insurance company were to renew offer of 270,000 yen. That would = $180,000.00

A counterargument by the Japanese insurance company is that differences in value of the U.S. dollar should NOT inure to the benefit of the plaintiff and is a day to day risk of insurance companies. That would be negative thinking. The idea is to convince the carrier

Figure 5.4
Exercise 4

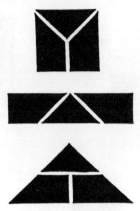

Notes: The fourth exercise was probably the most difficult. The problem was to divide a triangle into three parts in such a way that the parts could be put together again to form a rectangle or square. The difficulty of the problem stems from missing information. The problem statement fails to specify the shape of the triangle. Counsel worked on this problem individually, and then collaboratively, without success. To solve the problem quickly, one must recognize that it is much easier to start with a square instead of with a triangle (which was the suggested starting point). There can be no doubt about the shape of a square, whereas the shape of a triangle (and to a lesser extent, of a rectangle) is variable. Since the three parts must fit together again to form a square, one can solve the problem by dividing a square into three parts that can be put together again to produce a rectangle or triangle. The purpose of this exercise was to demonstrate the effect of missing information in reaching a settlement solution and the significance of one's entry point into the information available to design a settlement. It also demonstrated the power of thought reversal as a trial-and-error method for identifying a possible settlement element or for uncovering an obscured route or avenue for achieving agreement.

that this fortunate turn in the value of the $ from their point of view should be taken advantage of and that the plaintiff is interested in $ only. Further, the value of the $ may rise and the advantage that exists today for the defendant will, or could, quickly go away. This alone, depending on time frames and points of view, could immediately double the offer in $ and get us substantially along the way to settlement.

Another modem communication from Bernstein read as follows:

One of the areas we have discussed is exchanging something of value, other than yen or $, between the defendants and plaintiffs. One of the plaintiffs is [an American insurance company]. [It] has a policy, I am told, of having its agents and brokers purchase IBM PCs for their use in their homes and offices so as to better communicate with the insurance company. My broker had to purchase a PC and the price she paid, in my opinion, was no bargain.

[The Japanese electronics company] is, I believe, in the computer business. The mark-up on computers is 3 to 1 or 4 to 1. Assume almost anyone can get a PC at 25 percent off list price, so let's use 3 to 1.

An excellent PC with a 20 meg hard disk (no printer) can be purchased today for about $1,000. That would mean a cost to the manufacturer (ignoring tariffs, etc.) landed in the United States of about $350.00. 100 PCs could be given to the plaintiffs (value of U.S. $100,000) for a cost to the defendants of U.S. $35,000, and at today's exchange rates, that would be much less YEN than in the past and probably in the future.

Given the nature of trading companies in Japan and the close working relationship of Japanese banks and the Japanese government in business, it may be quite possible to arrange this type of "exchange" of values. However, I would submit that such a proposition could best be discussed via teleconferencing with a Japanese interpreter involved, if necessary, so that the Japanese insurance carrier can participate quickly and in a meaningful way.

Comments?

During the interim between conferences, Nagel prepared a 20-page revision of the computer-aided perspectives of the parties presented in his prior interim memoranda and distributed it to Bernstein and myself. Unlike the first interim memoranda, this revision included a computer analysis of the nontraditional settlement options in addition to the traditional payment-of-money option. Part of Nagel's analysis appears below (the appendices that he refers to contain computer printout data and are not reproduced here).

I. The Revised Plaintiffs' Perspective
  A. The New Criteria
     [The appendix] adds four new criteria. They are:
     1. The transfer of a large quantity of computers from [the Japanese electronics company] to [the American insurance company]. . . . [T]hese computers are tentatively valued at $700,000 from the plaintiffs' perspective. They are valued much less than that from the defendants' perspective, which will be discussed shortly.
     2. The transfer of some insurance claims from the [Japanese insurance company] to the [American insurance company]. These are claims that the [Japanese insurance company] has mainly against Americans, which the [American insurance company] can more easily collect. According to [the appendix], those insurance claims are worth $300,000 to the [American insurance company] although substantially less to the [Japanese insurance company]. These are only tentative illustrative figures, although reasonably realistic.
     3. Some cash moving from the defendant to the plaintiff to compensate those individual plaintiffs whose damages are not fully covered by insurance. . . . [D]efendants can now buy dollars very cheaply to give to the plaintiffs. Those dollars can buy a lot on the American market, even if they cannot buy so much on the Japanese market. . . . [There] should be an incentive for the defendants to want to settle as soon as possible before the value of the dollar goes up as it is predicted to do.
     4. A structured settlement moving from the [Japanese insurance company] to the individual plaintiffs. This would be the equivalent of an annuity whereby the plaintiffs would receive so many dollars per year upon reaching a certain age. Such

an arrangement may be highly valuable to the individual plaintiffs, but not so costly to an insurance company. . . . The structured settlement idea was not discussed at the [last mediation conference]. It is given a value from the plaintiffs' perspective of $100,000 according to [the appendix].

B. The New Results

1. The next thing to notice in Appendix 1 with regard to the revised plaintiffs' perspective is what happens with that new information when it comes to deciding whether to settle or go to trial. . . . With the information above and the previous estimates of the damages on trial and the probability of victory, the value of settling is over a million dollars, and the value of going to trial is less than $300,000. The figures, . . . to be more exact, are $1,099,000 for settling under the above circumstances, and only $290,000 for going to trial.

2. The settlement figure comes from adding $700,000 for the value of the computers to the plaintiffs, $300,000 for the value of the insurance claims, and $100,000 for the value of the structured settlement. That is a total of $1,100,000. From that figure one deducts $1,000 for the settlement costs figured at $100 per hour according to page B2 and 10 hours according to page B6 or .01 of 1000 hours.

3. Where does the $290,000 expected value of going to trial come from? Page B7 shows that the minimum damages that the plaintiffs expect from going to trial is $600,000. The minimum probability of victory from the plaintiffs' perspective is about .50. The expected value of those damages is thus $300,000. From the $300,000 one needs to subtract $10,000 for litigation costs, figured at $100 an hour for 100 hours or .10 of $1,000.

4. To further clarify what a desirable settlement this is from the plaintiffs' perspective, one can look at the threshold analysis. . . . That analysis shows what it would take to bring going to trial, which is the second-place alternative, up to a tie with settling, which is the first-place alternative. The three key variables are the probability of victory, the amount of damages, and the value of the three or four products that the defendants have to offer.

   (1) The analysis shows that the probability of victory would have to rise from .50 to 1.848 in order to make going to trial as desirable as accepting the settlement. It is, of course, impossible for a probability to rise any higher than 1.00 and quite difficult for it to rise that high.

   (2) The minimum damages would have to rise from $600,000 to well over $2,000,000 to make going to trial as desirable as accepting settlement. That is quite unlikely when all the plaintiffs are suing for is about $900,000 at the most and there are no grounds for punitive damages.

   (3) The market value of the computers, the insurance claims, or the structured settlement would have to become substantially less than zero in order to lower the settlement down to the low level of the expected value of going to trial.

II. The Revised Defendants' Perspective

A. The New Criteria

The new data from the defendants' perspective are as follows:

1. The giving of $700,000 worth of computers by [the defendant electronics company] is worth only about $200,000 to [it] in terms of the incremental variable cost to produce those computers as contrasted to the fixed costs that [the defendant

electronics company] has to pay for rent, capital, and fixed salaries. The 7 to 2 ratio is an estimate but probably roughly realistic.

2. The insurance claims that [the American insurance company] might consider to be worth about $300,000, the [Japanese insurance company] might consider to be worth only $100,000.

3. Again we are tentatively leaving out the exchange of dollars although even dollars may be worth less to [the Japanese electronics and insurance companies] than they are to [the American insurance company] and the individual plaintiffs, especially at the present time.

4. The structured settlement that may be worth about $100,000 to the individual plaintiffs may only be worth $25,000 in terms of the missed opportunities from tied up capital in order to provide for the promised annuity.

B. The New Results

1. With that information, how much will settling cost the defendants as contrasted to going to trial? . . . The cost of settling, given these figures, is only $326,500, whereas the cost of going to trial is expected to be $330,000.

2. The cost of settling could be made a lot lower and still be appealing to the plaintiffs as will be discussed in a moment. At this point one might clarify where the $326,500 came from. It comes from adding the $200,000 for the variable cost of the computers, the $100,000 for what [the Japanese insurance company] would be willing to sell the insurance claims, and the $25,000 evaluation on the annuity or structured settlement. That adds up to $325,000. The additional $1,500 comes from noting that the settlement costs would involve $150 an hour, . . . and 10 hours, . . . [in the appendix].

3. The $330,000 cost for going to trial comes from figuring the worst damages at $900,000. . . . That $900,000 has to be discounted or multiplied by a worst probability of victory from the defendants' perspective of .20. . . . If we multiply $900,000 by .20 we get $180,000. That figure we need to add to litigation costs that had previously been estimated at 1,000 hours at $150 an hour for a total of $150,000, which brings the $180,000 cost or payout up to $330,000.

The Third Mediation Conference

Because of conflicting schedules of the attorneys, mediators, and the Japanese businesspeople who would be traveling from Japan, the third mediation conference could not be held until the end of August. The conference was held at the plaintiffs' counsel's law firm. Present at the conference were all those persons who participated in the previous conference plus one executive each from the American insurance company, the Japanese insurance company, and the Japanese electronics company. Fortunately, the Japanese representatives could speak and understand English. I initiated the conference by giving a brief explanation of the mediation process for the benefit of the newcomers. I also summarized the results of the progress of the two previous settlement conferences, and suggested that the subject matter of concern in the third mediation conference would be to refine some of the ideas that originated in the other two conferences. Nagel then explained, for the benefit of the new participants, what role the computer played in the mediation and in developing the analyses as we proceeded through the process. The mediation team then conducted separate caucuses with the attorneys for each side and their respective client representatives to explore the feasibility of some of the nonmonetary aspects of settlement. After these caucuses, the mediation team conducted a final joint session. In that session, it became clear that of the several nonmonetary settlement elements available, the parties were most interested in pursuing the possibility of a transfer of television and computer products from the defendant electronics company to the plaintiff insurance company. The other nonmonetary elements would still be considered, but they were thought to be of secondary interest. The parties agreed to one more mediation conference to try to work out the details of the transfer of electronics products. The Japanese executives agreed to provide the plaintiffs' counsel with information on types and retail prices of the computer and television products prior to the next meeting.

Interim Developments

Two weeks after the third mediation conference, the defense counsel sent the plaintiffs' counsel information regarding types and retail prices of computer and television products manufactured by the Japanese electronics company. Due to several considerations, the fourth settlement conference was scheduled to be held in the U.S. Courthouse. Through telephone conferences, the parties made clear to the mediation team that if settlement was not reached during the fourth conference the case should be immediately set for trial by Judge Aspen. Thus, if the fourth conference were held in the courthouse, Aspen could be asked right there to set a trial date if settlement had not been reached. On the other hand, if the parties were close to settlement, perhaps Aspen's involvement could help conclude it. Also, the plaintiffs' counsel's law firm was in the process of relocating and it would be impossible to meet in their conference room. Finally, the mediation team felt that it would be beneficial to the settlement process if the last scheduled mediation conference were held on neutral turf. Aspen was notified of the time and place of the fourth conference and of the possible need for his assistance.

Because of schedule conflicts, neither Nagel nor Bernstein were able to attend the fourth mediation conference. Alternate dates were suggested to counsel for the parties, but because they were intent on either settling the case or going immediately to trial, they wanted to go ahead with the conference with only one mediator present. The attorneys' professional schedules also interfered with setting a different conference date.

Fourth Mediation Conference

The fourth mediation conference was held in Aspen's witness room located on the same floor as his chambers in the U.S. Courthouse in Chicago. Present at the conference were myself, two counsel for each side, and an executive of the plaintiff insurance company. At the beginning of the conference, counsel for the plaintiffs stated that the plaintiffs were no longer interested in pursuing non-monetary aspects of the settlement. It was not made exactly clear why the super-optimum settlement possibilities were being abandoned, but it would be safe to surmise that the plaintiffs, at that point, favored the quick solution that a cash settlement would provide. The defendants' counsel also seemed to desire closure on the matter, either through a cash settlement or trial. They also believed that a nontraditional settlement in this instance (particularly the product transfer) would require a detailed legal analysis of the tax and regulatory trade ramifications, which their clients did not particularly desire to undertake. Each side wished to pursue settlement based on a discussion of the merits of their cases and for a cash amount. Therefore, I conducted a traditional mediated settlement conference.

At the joint session, each side told their stories and expressed the amount they believed was appropriate for settlement. The plaintiffs wanted $700,000; the defendants were willing to pay $90,000. Each were willing to move from those figures. In separate caucuses, I asked questions that required each side to "reality test." I asked them to enumerate both the strengths and weaknesses of their cases. They were quite candid in expressing the weaknesses of their cases. This candor allowed me to create doubt about their original dollar positions. For example, the plaintiffs admitted that one of the fire investigators contradicted another fire investigator about the tape deck being the cause of the fire and that testimony could be quite damaging before a jury at trial. The defendants' counsel disclosed that it had subjected the electronics component at issue to a scientific test that replicated the circumstances under which the component had allegedly caught fire. The test proved that the component could not have caused the fire. The defendants' counsel had a videotape of this product test and intended to introduce it at trial and totally surprise the plaintiffs' counsel. The defendants' counsel said that the videotape had not been produced in discovery because the plaintiffs had filed no discovery request seeking the results of product tests. I pointed out to the defense counsel that if the mediation was not successful, the trial would begin within in the next few weeks. Disclosure of the videotape was as important to the settlement negotiations as it would be to a jury at trial. After a private caucus, the defense counsel authorized me to disclose the existence of the product-test videotape.

In a subsequent caucus with the plaintiffs' counsel, I disclosed the existence of the videotape. They acknowledged that the videotape could definitely have an impact on how they would value the case. They also asked me what I thought a fair settlement value for the case would be. I responded that I would share my thoughts about a reasonable settlement range only as a last resort, if both parties requested it, and during a joint session. The plaintiffs' counsel asked me to hold a joint session and pose the question to the defense counsel regarding their suggestion that I share my view as to a reasonable settlement value or range for the case.

A joint session was held and I explained that the plaintiffs' counsel had requested a mediator's value opinion because this, in their view, was to be the last mediation conference. The defense counsel agreed that a mediator's value opinion would be helpful. I reviewed the strengths and weaknesses of both plaintiffs' and defendants' cases. It was clear that each side had approximately a 50-50 chance of winning if they went to trial, not taking into account the product-test videotape. Considering the probabilities of victory of the plaintiffs, the potentially damaging evidence of the product-test videotape, and the previous damage analyses of Nagel, I suggested that a reasonable settlement range might be $375,000 to $400,000. The plaintiffs' and defense counsel acknowledged that this range would be presented to their respective clients for serious consideration. Counsel for both sides agreed that Aspen should be invited to the meeting. They wanted to advise him personally as to the status of the settlement and have his input as to the reasonableness of the settlement range, since he had conducted settlement conferences previously. They also wanted him to set a firm trial date to keep the pressure on the settlement process. Aspen joined the meeting, confirmed the reasonableness of the settlement range, and gave a firm trial date. Within a few days, counsel informed me that the case settled for $375,000.

Although the defendants had to pay more to the plaintiffs ($375,000) than the cost of the proposed super-optimum settlement ($326,500), because of the monetary exchange rate and the likelihood that they had placed an amount on reserve to cover settlement in the case early in the court proceedings, their actual payout was probably much less in terms of value lost. On the other hand, the plaintiffs settled for perhaps more than two times less than the value they could have derived from the super-optimum settlement.

If asked, the lawyers involved in this computer-aided mediation would probably say that the computer and decision-aiding software benefited them little in reaching settlement. On the other hand, the mediators would contend that the computer aided them in analyzing information, determining reasonable settlement ranges, and developing proposals for super-optimum solutions that, at least indirectly, benefited the parties and their counsel. This experience suggests that computer-aided mediation might well be a very useful tool in resolving many types of court cases, or aspects of them.

COMPUTER-AIDED MEDIATION IN OTHER TYPES OF COURT CASES

A number of general observations about computer-aided mediation can be made:

1. Cases that appear to have a damage remedy only (i.e., a distributive solution) may in fact have many nonmonetary aspects conducive to an integrative super-optimum solution.
2. Participants are able to acclimate to using a computer rather quickly.
3. Attorneys welcome opportunities to be creative.
4. Simple exercises in creative thinking and collaboration, conducted early in the mediation process, enhance the creative productivity of mediation participants.

5. The computer analyses can be quite beneficial to mediators between mediation conferences.

6. Computer telecommunication can assist mediators between conferences.

7. Court-ordered deadlines (setting trial dates, etc.) and judicial interest in the settlement progress facilitates the work of computer-aided mediators.

These general observations suggest that further experimentation and evaluation of computer-aided mediation should be undertaken by state and federal trial and appellate courts around the country. Courts desiring to experiment with computer-aided mediation must consider how to train computer-aided mediators, and how to select cases for processing by computer-aided mediators.

Training Computer-Aided Mediators

Because computer-aided mediation is a new concept, the availability of training is somewhat limited. However, Nagel presents periodic workshops in conjunction with the American Law Institute—American Bar Association (ALI–ABA) Committee on Continuing Professional Education and with continuing legal education organizations around the country.[19] He conducts one- or two-day workshops for persons with prior training and/or experience in mediation. Lawyers, judges, and nonlawyers may participate. Primary features of the workshops are: (1) limited class size (normally up to 40 participants); (2) participants work in small groups at a microcomputer, or each participant is assigned to a microcomputer; and (3) training incorporates a step-by-step hands-on familiarization with the computer and decision-aiding software. No prior knowledge of computers or decision-aiding software is necessary. A typical agenda for a one-day workshop follows.

The First Morning: *Hands-on Demonstration*. Procedures involved in creating a computerized datafile consisting of: (1) alternatives being considered; (2) goals to be achieved; and (3) relations among alternatives and goals in choosing the best alternative or combination. *Practical Exercise*. Participants engage in resolution of a simple problem using decision-aiding software.

The First Afternoon: Hands-on Demonstration. Procedures involved in dealing with decision-making situations that have multiple goals, missing information, scarce resources, conflicting constraints, and the need to simplify complex situations. *Practical Exercise*. Participants divide into groups for a simulated mediation exercise requiring the application of more advanced computer techniques covered earlier in the afternoon.

A typical agenda for a two-day workshop would incorporate the agenda for the one-day workshop with additional demonstrations and practical exercises occurring on the second day.

The Second Morning: Hands-on Demonstration. Procedures involved in using spreadsheet software for handling problems that involve predictions, risk, sequencing, or group decision-making. *Practical Exercise*. Participants engage in mediation exercise requiring application of computer techniques covered earlier in the morning.

The Second Afternoon: Practical Exercises. Participants engage in two practical exercises of a more complex nature, designed to integrate the learning of the two-day workshop and to provide each participant with the opportunity to mediate (or co-mediate) in a "real life" dispute situation.

In addition to the "Best Choice" software, participants in workshops also receive copies of books by Nagel on the subjects of legal decision-making and microcomputers and of application of microcomputers to dispute resolution.

Criteria for Selecting Court Cases for Computer-Aided Mediation Treatment

The criteria used by courts to select cases for computer-aided mediation treatment are not substantially different from those used by courts generally to select cases for traditional mediation treatment. There are no hard and fast selection rules. Practically every case on a court's docket is suitable for computer-aided mediation, but some general screening considerations might be as follows:[20]

1. a certain category (or categories) of case(s) that tend(s) to overload a court's docket
2. parties and counsel are agreeable to participate in the computer-aided mediation process
3. parties will have to maintain a direct or indirect relationship after the resolution of a dispute (e.g., manufacturer and distributor; child custody situation)
4. sufficient discovery has occurred in the case to make settlement discussions meaningful
5. parties desire to settle the matter promptly
6. parties desire to minimize litigation costs
7. parties desire a remedy that the court is not capable of providing (e.g. renegotiating a business contract)
8. parties wish to avoid establishing a judicial precedent or a judgment that may have a preclusive effect
9. parties or their lawyers have difficulty initiating negotiations with the other side, or the parties are deadlocked in negotiations
10. parties or their lawyers lack effective negotiation skills
11. parties have differing appraisal of the facts of a case
12. voluntary compliance with a result is particularly desirable
13. parties or their counsel are stubborn, but rational
14. situations involving requests for damages *and* nonmonetary relief; of second priority are cases involving damage relief only or nonmonetary relief only
15. parties have differing assessments of the law and are interested in using the case-prediction capabilities of the decision-aiding software
16. resolution requires complex trade-offs
17. parties want the matter settled confidentially

Computer-aided mediation may be contraindicated in these situations:[21]

1. a party cannot effectively represent its best interests and will not be represented by counsel at the mediation sessions
2. parties have a history of acting in bad faith in negotiations
3. a party seeks to establish legal precedent or a judgment with preclusive effect
4. significant parties are unwilling to mediate
5. parties are business competitors in highly concentrated markets and mediated settlement could be viewed as price-fixing or some other violation of antitrust laws
6. a party is threatening to press criminal charges
7. one or more parties stand to gain from a strategy of delay
8. more formal discovery is needed to give a party necessary information before settlement can be achieved
9. parties have rigid assessments of the law applicable in the case and desire the court to decide who is right and who is wrong, legally

These indications and contraindications for the use of computer-aided mediation are not intended to be exhaustive or inclusive. Neither are they intended to be prescriptive or preclusive. They are simply general considerations to be taken into account when deciding whether to select a case or cases for computer-aided mediation. It may well be that in any specific situation, a case that on the surface may appear to be contraindicated for computer-aided mediation may in fact be quite suitable for the process. An overriding consideration in any particular situation is that all parties and counsel agree to participate meaningfully in the process.

Although mediators perform various tasks and functions during the traditional mediation process, their primary role is to facilitate collaborative problem-solving. The essence of collaborative problem-solving is joint decision-making by the parties. If joint decision-making is the goal of the mediation process, then mediators must understand the principles of effective thinking, problem-solving, and decision-making. The computer and decision-aiding software is the next logical step in helping mediators help parties to reach appropriate, effective, and durable joint decisions (agreements) either in a dispute or transactional context. This is *not* to say that the microcomputer and its program is better than the mind or vice versa. It *is* to say, however, that the microcomputer and the mind each has capabilities that complement one another and enhance the opportunities for optimal and even super-optimal joint decision-making.

The merging of minds and microcomputers in the resolution of court cases is an inevitable consequence of the confluence of two current societal conditions: (1) unprecedented advances in computer technology and computer aids to problem-solving and decision-making; and (2) the unprecedented interest of lawyers, judges, and laypersons in alternative methods of resolving litigated disputes. There is no question that computer-aided mediation is still an infant. The challenge is to share in this infant's upbringing and to watch it develop, mature, and come of age as we enter the twenty-first century.[22]

NOTES

1. J. Cooley, "Arbitration versus Mediation: Explaining the Differences," *Judicature* 69 (1986): 263, 266. See also N. Rogers and R. Salem, *A Student's Guide to Mediation and the Law* (New York: Matthew Bender, 1987).

2. B. Muldoon, "Responding to the Liability Crisis: The Systematic Use of Alternative Dispute Resolution to Reduce the Expense and Delay of Litigation" (unpublished paper prepared for submission to the Illinois General Assembly by RESOLVE Dispute Management, Chicago, Ill., 1986), pp. 8–9.

3. S. Nagel, "What Are Super-Optimum Solutions?" (working paper, 1989).

4. S. Nagel, "Announcing the Availability of Computer-Aided Mediation" (working paper, 1989).

5. S. Nagel, "Decision-Aiding Software and the Law" (draft of working paper, Mar. 1988).

6. For an analysis of decision trees applied to law, see M. Raker, "The Application of Decision Analysis and Computer Modeling to the Settlement of Complex Litigation," *Symposium on Computer Models and Modeling for Negotiation Management* (MIT, 1987).

7. A comparative analysis of linear programming and related packages can be found in R. Sharda, "Mathematical Programming Software for Microcomputers," in S. Gass, ed., *Impacts of Microcomputers on Operations Research* (New York: North Holland, 1986).

8. For an analysis of statistics packages, see D. Lezotte, "Statistical Software for Microcomputers," in ibid.

9. For an analysis of some aspects of decision-aiding spreadsheet software see D. Bammi and L. Padelford, "Using Spreadsheets for Decision Analysis," in ibid. See also S. Nagel, "Using Spreadsheets to Choose among Alternatives," *Ashton-Tate Quarterly* (1988).

10. A comparative review of rule-based expert systems software appears in C. Grafton and A. Permaloff, "Expert System Development Programs and Their Alternatives," *Social Science Microcomputer Review* 4 (1986): 165–80. Rule-based software that is specifically related to legal rules include Judith, DataLex, Rubric, Hypo, Lex, Default, Oblog-2, Esplex, and LexVision. Many law-related programs are described in *Proceedings of the First International Conference on Artificial Intelligence and Law* (Northeastern University, 1987).

11. For comparisons of MCDM software, see P. Humphreys and A. Wisudha, *Methods and Tools for Structuring and Analyzing Decision Problems* (London School of Economics and Political Science, 1987); B. Radcliff, "Multi-Criteria Decision Making: A Survey of Software," *Social Science Microcomputer Review* 4 (1986): 38–55. Some of the MCDM software fits into more than one category, such as Best Choice or P/G%, which can perform the functions of six categories, although it is mainly classified as spreadsheet-based software.

12. Settlemate, for example, uses jury verdict information as its data base and is used as an aid in determining reasonable settlement values of personal injury lawsuits.

13. Statistical software can also be used for generating relations, such as regression coefficients or average scores of an alternative on a criterion.

14. See S. Nagel and C. Barczak "Can Computers Aid the Dispute Resolution Process?" *Judicature* 71 (1988): 253.

15. Ibid.
16. The parties or counsel in the case are not identified because of their request of anonymity.
17. See J. Cooley, *Appellate Advocacy Manual* (Deerfield, Ill.: Callaghan, 1989), pp. 37–42.
18. These problems appear in ibid., pp. 135–37, 160–62, 172–75, 212–14, 219. They are based on problems appearing in E. de Bono, *Lateral Thinking: Creativity Step by Step* (New York: Harper and Row, 1970).
19. Nagel also conducts computer-aided mediation training for court systems on an ad hoc basis. He can be contacted at the Department of Political Science, University of Illinois, 361 Lincoln Hall, 702 South Wright Street, Urbana, IL 61801.
20. See generally Rogers and Salem, *Student's Guide*, pp. 41–51.
21. Ibid., pp. 51–59.
22. For other materials on computer-aided dispute resolution, see Nagel and Barczyk, "Can Computers Aid the Dispute Resolution Process?" S. Nagel and M. Mills, "Microcomputers P/G% and Dispute Resolution," *Ohio State Journal on Dispute Resolution* 2 (1987): 187–221; S. Nagel, "Computer-Aided Negotiation," *Attorney's Computer Report* 4 (Nov. 1986): 11–14; S. Nagel, *Decision-Aiding Software and Legal Decisionmaking: A Guide to Skills and Application Throughout the Law* (New York: Greenwood-Quorum, 1989); S. Nagel, *Applying Microcomputers to Dispute Resolution* (Champaign, Ill.: Decision Aids, 1988).

REFERENCES

Bammi, D., and L. Padelford. (1986). "Using Spreadsheets for Decision Analysis." In S. Gass, ed., *Impacts of Microcomputers on Operations Research*. New York: North Holland.
Cooley, J. (1986). "Arbitration vs. Mediation: Explaining the Differences." *Judicature* 69: 263.
———. (1989). *Appellate Advocacy Manual*. Deerfield: Callaghan.
———. (1990). "Mediation, Conflict Frames, SOS, Split Brains, Creativity, and Joke Design: Resolving the Incongruities." Draft of working paper.
de Bono, E. (1970). *Lateral Thinking: Creativity Step by Step*. New York: Harper & Row.
Grafton, C., and A. Permaloff. (1986). "Expert System Development Programs and Their Alternatives." *Social Science Microcomputer Review* 4: 165–80.
Humphreys, P., and A. Wisudha. (1987). *Methods and Tools for Structuring and Analyzing Decision Problems*. London: London School of Economics.
Lezotte, D. (1986). "Statistical Software for Microcomputers." In S. Gass, ed., *Impacts of Microcomputers on Operations Research*. New York: North Holland.
Nagel, S. (1986). "Computer-Aided Negotiation." *Attorneys Computer Report* 4 (Nov.): 11–14.
———. (1988). "Decision-Aiding Software and the Law." Draft of working paper.
———. (1988). "Using Spreadsheets to Choose among Alternatives," *Ashton-Tate Quarterly*.
———. (1989). *Decision-Aiding Software and Legal Decisionmaking: A Guide to Skills and Application Throughout the Law*. New York: Quorum.
———. (1989). "What Are Super-Optimum Solutions?" Working paper.

Nagel S., and C. Barczak. (1988). "Can Computers Aid the Dispute Resolution Process?" *Judicature* 71: 253.

Nagel, S., and M. Mills. (1989). "Microcomputers P/G% and Dispute Resolution." *Ohio State Journal on Dispute Resolution* 2: 187–221.

Radcliff, B. (1986). "Multi-Criteria Decision Making: A Survey of Software." *Social Science Microcomputer Review* 4: 38–55.

Raker, M. (1987). "The Application of Decision Analysis and Computer Modeling to the Settlement of Complex Litigation." *Symposium on Computer Models and Modeling for Negotiation Management*, Massachusetts Institute of Technology.

Rogers, N. and R. Salem. (1987). *A Student's Guide to Mediation and the Law.* New York: Matthew Bender.

Sharda, R. (1986). "Mathematical Programming Software for Microcomputers." In S. Gass, ed., *Impacts of Microcomputers on Operations Research.* New York: North Holland.

CHAPTER 6

Legal Rules, Bargaining, and Transactions Costs: The Case of Divorce

MARGARET F. BRINIG
AND MICHAEL V. ALEXEEV

For almost ten years, legal commentators have been aware of the possibility of applying economic bargaining principles to the problems of negotiations at the time of divorce.[1] Although some cases and journal articles have mentioned the Mnookin and Kornhauser article suggesting that custodial time and financial assets might be exchanged,[2] attempts to apply the analysis have been confined to description. No one has attempted an empirical study to see if there really are trade-offs between custodial time and marital assets at the time of divorce, and there has been no formal model describing the process.[3] Furthermore, there has been no analytical discussion of what happens when the legal rules change,[4] either in terms of the outcomes of bargaining or in terms of the transactions costs of the process. On the other hand, there has been much attention devoted to the plight of single women with children in the era of no-fault divorce.[5]

This chapter will attempt to fill the gap in the existing literature by examining the bargaining process that resolves the issues involved in divorce in the overwhelming majority of cases.[6] It will investigate the jurisprudential consequences of such a system in terms of "result" versus "rule equality,"[7] and will discuss the effects of changes in the law on the resulting allocations and the extent that the parties use the court system. The authors' results suggest that trading does exist, and that changes in rules regarding grounds for divorce, alimony, property, and child custody affect not only the results reached, but also the procedures and transactions costs involved in reaching them.

There is undoubtedly a significant amount of bargaining between the divorcing spouses that occurs before the legal proceedings.[8] In fact, the legal agreement that becomes a court decree is nearly always merely a ratification of the settlement reached by the spouses.[9] However, this bargaining, like all such exchanges, is affected by the existing legal statutes and precedents.[10] The spouses' expectations about the likely outcome if the judge intervenes provide the alternative to continuing to bargain for a better outcome.[11] Further, the likely legal alternative, set by state statutes and the less precise information about local judges' practices, serves as a benchmark[12] that each spouse uses to determine the extent of concessions to the other spouse.[13]

For these reasons the outcomes of the bargaining between the spouses depend on the particular state divorce laws as well as what the spouses want or their partners think they want.[14] For settlement purposes, the most important laws include the statutory preference for child custody arrangements (e.g., "joint-custody"[15] as opposed to a presumption that the "primary caretaker" before separation,[16] usually the mother, is the best custodian following divorce), grounds for divorce (a fault and no-fault combination[17] versus no-fault alone), the prevailing rationale for alimony (support of a dependent former spouse,[18] or temporary payments for rehabilitative purposes),[19] and the property regime (equitable division[20] or the division of community property[21]).

In this chapter, we will investigate these issues both theoretically and empirically. The theoretical discussion applies the simple bargaining model of F. Y. Edgeworth to illustrate the bargaining in Wisconsin, a state where the court outcomes are determinate.[22] Following this, the effect of uncertainty of litigated outcomes is discussed in the context of Virginia marital settlements. The contrasting approaches are followed by a discussion of the effect on transactions costs as legal rules vary from the parties' desired outcomes. Both parts of the theoretical model are illustrated by an empirical study of divorce cases in two jurisdictions.

The data for statistical testing of the theoretical propositions come from Fairfax County in Virginia (where more than 4,500 cases were analyzed) and Waukesha County in Wisconsin (with more than 3,500 cases).[23] Both counties are suburban communities that are parts of metropolitan areas. However, Virginia permits fault to be considered both for divorce and as a bar to spousal support;[24] Wisconsin courts do not even admit evidence of fault. In Virginia, neither spouse has a statutory advantage in seeking custody, although the spouse who has been the primary caretaker before separation gets custody in most cases.[25] In Wisconsin, there is a presumption of joint custody.[26] Virginia allocates marital property based upon several equitable factors, while Wisconsin, a community property state, presumptively divides it evenly.

We have collected information on the wealth of each household before the divorce, on the shares of that wealth received by each spouse in the final divorce decree, on the custody arrangements and visitation rights of the noncustodial parents, and on the issues actually litigated by the spouses in court. Using relatively simple statistical analysis, we relate the shares of custodial time and wealth received by husband and wife in the two jurisdictions, and contrast the amount of transactions costs required to reach these outcomes. Not surprisingly, we find that regardless of the legal rule, the outcomes of child custody are very similar. In terms of outcomes, the difference appears in the share of wealth received by the divorcing wife, or in her ability to receive long-term spousal support. In terms of the use of the court system, the data reveal that, paradoxically, the closer the legal rules approach what the parties want, the more likely the parties are to resort to courts rather than to resolve the issues through the bargaining process.

DETERMINATE OUTCOME MODEL (WISCONSIN)

The bargaining in Wisconsin between the two spouses over the divorce agreement can be analyzed with the help of the Edgeworth box diagram. Suppose that the preferences of each spouse over the wealth-custody space can be described by smooth convex utility indifference curves. If either of the spouses decides to litigate, then the court will determine the details of the divorce agreement. In other words, no bargaining between the spouses has to take place in order for either of them to obtain the court-determined outcome. In this sense, the predicted outcome of the litigation provides an endowment point for the bargaining process (see Figure 6.1).[27] Let us assume that each of the spouses is aware of the likely outcome of litigation.[28] Unless the endowment point lies on the contract curve,[29] both spouses can be made better off as a result of bargaining. Given the endowment point, the data on the actual divorce agreements achieved without litigation can provide us with some interesting information on the preferences of the spouses.

In Wisconsin, because of the presumption of joint custody and the presumption of even allocation of marital property, each spouse can normally obtain a 50-50 split of custody and property without entering into predivorce bargaining with the other spouse. In the context of an Edgeworth box diagram, this implies that the endowment point is located exactly in the center of the box. The Wisconsin data indicate, however, that the most common outcome of the divorce agreements is located far from the middle of the box. A wife receives (on average) 76.6 percent share of the custody while maintaining the 50 percent of the marital property[30] that she would receive in court. The bulk of the individual outcomes is clustered in the right half of the Edgeworth box (see Figure 6.2). Presumably, the observed outcomes lie in the core of the bargaining game between the husband and the wife. The indifference curves of the spouses must be consistent with the position of the core. A set of such indifference curves is shown in Figure 6.2. Notice that given the endowment point E and typical outcome A, a wife's indifference curve through E must be steep at that point while a husband's indifference curve through the endowment point must be flat, or, more likely, positively sloped. In other words, in the region close to the endowment point, wives tend to have a high marginal rate of substitution (MRS) of property for custody, while for the husbands this MRS is negative.[31]

The fact that the actual outcomes of bargaining lie away from the endowment point suggests that both spouses would prefer to avoid costs associated with obtaining a court-ordered division of child custody and property, so that there is

Figure 6.1
Property versus Custody

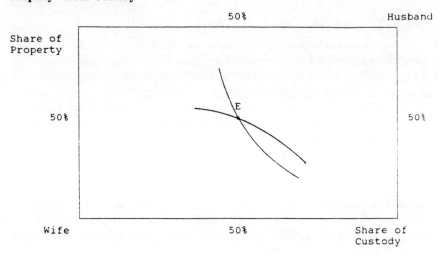

50%   Husband

Share of
Property

50%   50%

Wife   50%   Share of
                                       Custody

Figure 6.2
Property versus Custody Reconsidered

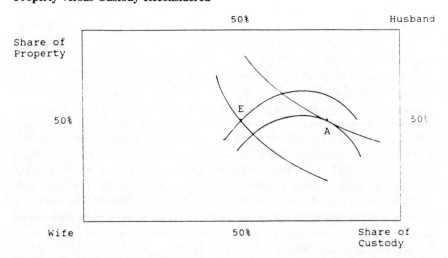

50%   Husband

Share of
Property

50%   50%

Wife   50%   Share of
                                       Custody

an incentive for negotiations outside of the courtroom.[32] These costs include the cost of litigation itself.[33] In addition to the considerable cash outlay that a trial requires,[34] there is a substantial body of social science literature that suggests that the adversary process, particularly if protracted or requiring the child's participation, is itself harmful to the child.[35] Thus, even if the wife achieves a "win" outcome in court, the net magnitude of her gains, assuming that she has the child's interests at heart, is less than the total custody plus dollar figure she receives.[36]

Thus the costs of litigation and the determinant nature of the outcome are likely to result in relatively few cases of divorce litigation, reducing transactions costs of divorce proceedings. In some cases, however, the divergence between the individual spouses' preferences and the endowment may force one of the spouses to accept a much more inferior bargaining outcome compared with the situation where the endowment is less "gender neutral."[37]

In this regard it is instructive to compare the situations in Wisconsin and Virginia. In Virginia child custody is usually awarded to the primary caretaker (who will be the wife in most cases) and the marital property is allocated according to a number of equitable factors.[38] If the outcomes in Virginia courts were determinate, the framework of the Edgeworth box model would imply that the endowment point would be located in the right half of the box. Point A may serve as a good approximation. The typical outcomes of the bargaining process between the spouses would provide only a slightly lower share of child custody to the wife and award her a significantly greater share of marital property. Assuming that the preferences of the wives and the husbands are similar, whether they reside in Wisconsin or in Virginia, the core solutions in both states should belong to the same contract curve. It should be clear at this point that, given the preferences implied by the relative location of points A and E and the husband's preferences over the relevant range, the Virginia divorce statutes and precedents are more favorable to the husbands than the laws in Wisconsin with respect to the spouses' position in the informal bargaining process between the spouses.[39]

INDETERMINATE OUTCOME: THE EFFECT OF UNCERTAINTY OF LITIGATION OUTCOME ON PRIVATE NEGOTIATIONS

Due to the higher uncertainty of the outcomes of litigation in Virginia, the Edgeworth Box description oversimplifies the true situation. The litigation outcome is much less predictable in Virginia than it is in Wisconsin because of the presence of fault grounds for divorce, the effect of fault on alimony, and the use of equitable factors in determining the percentage of property that each spouse will receive. (It is also possible that the custody issue itself is indeterminate, as the statute suggests. Practically speaking, however, courts have awarded primary custody to the wife in all but a negligible number of cases.[40]) In contrast, Wisconsin does not even admit evidence of fault, and the statutes require that marital property be divided equally.

In order to explain the outcomes of voluntary negotiations in Virginia, we must therefore model the risk associated with litigation.[41]

Note that while a typical outcome of litigation in Virginia is favorable to a wife (unlike in Wisconsin, where she would end up with far less custody than most women want), the "downside risk" of litigation for a Virginia wife is relatively high.[42] On the other hand, the occurrence of an outcome that is significantly better than the typical outcome for a wife is extremely unlikely in Virginia. Of course, the wife's share of child custody may be increased from the high percentage the court would normally award her, but normally wives would want to assure some participation of the husband in the upbringing of children even after the divorce. This may be because the wives feel participation is better for children, or because the wives want some time for themselves, to get tasks done that cannot be completed with children around (recreate, pursue hobbies, or begin new relationships).[43] The corollary of this is that the husband may not experience a "downside risk" that deviates substantially from his expected court outcome, since the probability of catastrophic financial loss or no visitation with the child is very low.[44] In what follows we will assume that the wife could either obtain a typical outcome or end up with a considerably worse outcome.

Suppose a wife is an expected utility maximizer. Let us denote the outcome of the voluntary negotiations by A, the typical outcome of litigation by E,[45] and the "disastrous" (from the wife's point of view) litigation outcome by D.[46] Then the worst voluntary agreement the wife is willing to make (A*) is such that

$$U_w(A^*) = pU_w(E) + (1 - p)U_w(D) \qquad (1)$$

where p is the probability of a typical court outcome E and U_w is the wife's utility associated with various outcomes. Since $U_w(E) > U_w(D)$, it is evident from (1) that the lower p is, the lower U(A*) has to be. Also, $U_w(A^*)$ is lower the lower $U_w(D)$ is. Therefore, as long as $U_w(D)$ is low enough and p is low enough, U(A*) may be considerably worse than $U_w(E)$.

Notice that this argument does not depend on the degree of risk aversion[47] of the wife's utility function.[48] Other things being equal, the more risk-averse the wife is, the lower $U_w(A^*)$ is.

Of course, the outcome of the voluntary negotiations does not have to be the minimum acceptable to a wife. Given that the worst outcome of negotiations acceptable to a husband is A' and that the utility of that outcome is[49]

$$U_h(A') = pU_h(E) + (1-p)U_h(D), \qquad (2)$$

the out-of-court agreement should satisfy $U_w(A) \geq U_w(A^*)$, and $U_h(A) \geq U_h(A')$. Other things being equal, however, the lower $U_w(A^*)$, the lower $U_w(A)$ would be.

The above provides a theoretical explanation, in terms of expected utility maximization, of why Virginia wives may be willing to settle for less custody and property[50] than they might achieve had they litigated in court. There are less rigorous alternatives that provide the same result. One possibility is that women and their attorneys may not have known what courts were granting women in the first few years of equitable distribution in Virginia.[51] It is not very likely that attorneys specializing in domestic relations or those with well-to-do clients would be ignorant of the published appellate decisions or of those from the various circuit courts in northern Virginia. Nor did they probably feel that this information would be unimportant to their clients, so that they would not disclose it. As a group, it is unlikely that lawyers would prefer to generate increased fees through the more costly litigation process, both because of ethical considerations and the importance of reputation (goodwill) for the health of their practice. It is possible that the women misunderstood their attorneys,[52] or that they misperceived the variance in the litigated outcomes, so that their subjective probability of loss was higher than the actual probability.[53]

A second group of explanations relates to the curvature of husbands' and wives' utility functions. One such explanation, favored by several legal writers, is that women as a group are more risk-averse than their husbands.[54] This may be true, but would not be easy to prove. What is more likely is that there is a difference in men's and women's preferences, particularly those involving child custody.[55] To lose custody of a child, even if there is only a small chance of such loss, may represent such a catastrophic loss that women are unwilling, despite risk neutrality, to take the gamble.[56]

THE EFFECT OF RULES ON LITIGATION STRATEGIES

One interesting question posed by our research is what type of legal rules might cause couples to prefer to settle their differences through negotiation rather than litigation.[57] The immediate reaction might be that if the legal system provided alternatives (or "distortions," as one attorney called them[58]) that the parties found acceptable, they would be inclined to settle rather than to waste time through litigation that would be costly and eventually end up with nearly the same result. This, however, is the opposite of what our data revealed. The reason for this apparent paradox is that the litigation alternative becomes credible only if the predicted legal result closely approximates what the parties really want. A father in Virginia, for example, can threaten a custody battle by asking for it in divorce pleadings or by filing motions even though he does not truly want custody and probably would not get more than generous visitation rights if he went to court.[59] (This was the result in some cases where the wife eventually received primary custody, but only a token alimony and less than half the property.) If his wife very much wants custody, she may be inclined to settle for less in terms of child or spousal support to avoid the possibility of losing substantial time with the children.[60] (see Table 6.1). The Wisconsin father does not want to go to court because he actually does not want equal custody with his wife, which is what the law presumes is in the best interests of the children. The wife does not threaten

Table 6.1
Property and Alimony Shares

Wisconsin
Without Litigation

Overall	50% (48)	
Custody Percentage	Mean Property(Med.)	Alimony
Awards		
50%	48%	
70(5)	67%	
90%	55%	

Virginia
Without Litigation

Overall	40% (43)	
50%	44% (44)	33%
70%(0)		
90%	45%	50%

With Litigation

50%(W filed 50%)	40(46)%	9%
70%(2; W filed 2)	74%	33%
90%(W filed 78%)	56(52)%	29%

---

litigation because, although she may get an equal share of the marital resources, she may very well get less than primary custody of the children.

A more generalized prediction, then, would be that if the parties' endowment points (anticipated results of litigation) closely approximate solutions readily acceptable to both, there should be frequent resorts to the court system and relatively high transactions costs in reaching settlement outcomes. These high transactions costs may continue after the final decree.[61] The additional friction between the parties may result in an unwillingness to meet the agreed-upon conditions of facilitating visitation or paying child or spousal support. Conversely, if the endowment point (or anticipated judicial outcome) bears very little relationship to what the parties really want, they are more likely to be forced to resolve their disputes themselves. They are, in effect, cast upon their own resources, for the threat of litigation is not credible. There should be lower transactions costs in such states both before and after trial. (To the extent, however, that divorced women with primary custody are actually impoverished, there will be increased public costs in the form of public assistance and other social services.[62])

Since the Wisconsin endowment point lies farther from the negotiated outcomes than does the endowment point in Virginia, one would expect to observe divorce cases litigated more often in Virginia. Our data support this conclusion (see Table 6.2). Thus, 5 percent of the cases in our Wisconsin subsample versus 20 percent for Virginia went to trial. In addition, some motions filed during the preliminary proceedings can serve as threats of taking the case to litigation. Such threats would be much more credible in situations where the difference between the negotiated outcomes and the endowments is relatively minor. We would expect the threats of litigation to be more credible in Virginia and, therefore, to see more pretrial motions filed in Virginia than in Wisconsin. Again our data support this conjecture. Pretrial motions were filed in 20 percent of our cases in Virginia compared with only 5.5 percent of the cases in Wisconsin.

MOTIONS PRACTICE IN DOMESTIC RELATIONS

Domestic relations cases in some ways are very typical of civil litigation in general. At the beginning, each attorney has only the testimony of the client. There may be immediate problems that will require court action. Where a spouse needs money to pay for immediate living or trial expenses, the attorney will seek support

Table 6.2
Comparative Litigation

State	Virginia	Wisconsin
Litigate	21.45	9.27
Pendente Lite	18.41	4.78
Motions	19.76	5.53
Trial	10.13	5.38
Issue of Fault	13.34	0.29
Issue of Support	18.07	5.38
Issue of Custody	13.18	4.04
Issue of Property	16.79	4.78

pendente lite (pending litigation).[63] There also may be a motion for an award of temporary custody. Either of these will be treated as a serious step by both attorneys, and will require preparation time and anywhere from a few moments to several days in court time. A *pendente lite* award will establish the duty of the obligor to support the needy spouse, and also will set a precedent for the amount of support needed that may greatly influence the trial court. A temporary custody award may be determinative of the outcome at trial, since the stability of the child's situation will be important in determining what is in the child's "best interests."[64] Less often, there may be such motions as an injunction to keep one spouse from harassing the other, or to freeze a joint bank account. Besides the obvious purposes for such actions, this type of proceeding suggests the client's willingness to resort to the court system (threat behavior).[65] A motion of this type probably would not exist in isolation, but would appear among a greater group of motions.

Once the statutory period (usually a year in both states) has passed, one or the other spouse will file the complaint for divorce or dissolution. The other spouse may answer (admitting or denying the allegations of the complaint, asking for divorce him or herself, or asserting legal defenses), may indicate that the attorney will appear on the client's behalf, or may do nothing, letting the matter proceed by default. At this point there may be various procedural devices designed to simplify litigation.

The most common will be some type of motion for discovery. This may take the form of written interrogatories, or questions, which may be about anything "relevant."[66] The parties may seek the production of documents such as business records or psychiatric or psychological reports. The attorney may seek a deposition, or oral questioning of a witness before a court reporter, with both counsel present. Any of these activities, while it theoretically resolves or narrows some of the issues before trial,[67] also may be designed to exhaust the resources of the other side (like gambler's ruin).[68]

In some cases, but probably not any of those studied, there may be motions to change venue (seek a different, more appropriate court), for continuances (delays of various types), or to relieve the attorney (who no longer wishes to take the case). Any of the former would be threat-type behavior.

Changes in legal rules affect not only the income distributions of parties negotiating divorce settlements, but also their transactions costs. As the legal rules move away from what the parties want to agree to anyway, they become more and more likely to settle disputes, with the help of their attorneys, without resort to the formal judicial process. Our results suggest that allowing fault to have an effect on financial allocations at divorce may not only "imprison" some women in unfortunate situations,[69] but may also impair their bargaining position upon divorce.

NOTES

1. Robert Mnookin and Lewis Kornhauser, "Bargaining in the Shadow of the Law: The Case of Divorce," *Yale Law Journal* 88 (1979): 950.

2. See, e.g. Garska v. McCoy, 278 S.E.2d 357 (W. Va. 1981); Jon Elster, "Solomonic Judgments: Against the Best Interest of the Child," *University of Chicago Law Review* 1, no. 5 (1987); Jerry McCant, "The Cultural Contradiction of Fathers as Nonparents," *Family Law Quarterly* 21 (1987): 127, 137.

3. There are formal models describing the difference between bilateral and unilateral no-fault divorce. See Elizabeth Peters, "Marriage and Divorce: Informational Constraints and Private Contracts," *American Economic Review* 76 (1986): 437. For pretrial strategic behavior, including divorce cases, see Robert Cooter, Stephen Marks, and Robert Mnookin, "Bargaining in the Shadow of the Law: A Testable Model of Strategic Behavior," *Journal of Legal Studies* 11. (1982): 225.

4. In the style of Ronald Coase, "The Problem of Social Cost," *Journal of Law and Economics* 3 (1960).

5. See, e.g., Lenore Weitzman, *The Divorce Revolution* (New York: Free Press, 1985); Lenore Weitzman, "The Economics of Divorce: Social and Economic Consequences of Property, Alimony and Child Support Awards," *UCLA Law Review* 28 (1981): 1181; Heather Wishik, "Economics of Divorce, An Exploratory Study," *Family Law Quarterly* 20 (1986): 79; Robert McGraw, Gloria Sterin, and Joseph Davis, "A Case Study in Divorce Law Reform and Its Aftermath," *Journal of Family Law* 20 (1981–82): 443; Herma Hill Kay, "Equality and Differences: A Perspective on No-Fault and Its Aftermath," *University of Cincinnati Law Review* 56 (1987): 1149.

6. See, e.g., Cooter, Marks, and Mnookin, "Strategic Behavior", pp. 243–44 (20 percent); McCant, "Cultural Contradiction," pp. 127, 137.

7. The term comes from Martha Fineman, "Implementing Equality: Ideology, Contradiction and Social Change: A Study of Rhetoric and Results in the Regulation of the Consequences of Divorce," *Wisconsin Law Review* (1983): 789, 791. See also Herma Hill Kay, "An Appraisal of California's No-Fault Divorce Law," *California Law Review* 75 (1987): 291, 309; Weitzman, *Divorce Revolution*, pp. 16–41.

8. See, e.g. Mnookin and Kornhauser, "Bargaining in the Shadow of the Law"; Cooter, Marks, and Mnookin, "Strategic Behavior"; John Murray, "Improving Parent-Child Relationships within the Divorced Family: A Call for Legal Reform," *University of Michigan Journal of Law Reform* 19 (1986): 563, 588; Marygold S. Melli, Howard S. Erlanger, and Elizabeth Chambliss, "The Process of Negotiation. An Exploratory Investigation in the Context of No-Fault Divorce," *Wisconsin Law Review* 40 (1988): 1133, 1142 (stating that parties went to trial in only 32 out of 249 cases studied).

9. Mnookin, "Divorce Bargaining: The Limits of Private Ordering," *University of Michigan Journal of Law Reform* 18, no. 4 (1985): 1015; Melli, Erlanger, and Chambliss, "Process of Negotiations," p. 1142.

10. This is the point of Mnookin and Kornhauser, "Bargaining in the Shadow of the Law"; and Mnookin "Divorce Bargaining," p. 1024.

11. Murray, "Improving Relationships," p. 588; Cooter, Marks, and Mnookin, "Strategic Behavior."

12. Elster ("Solomonic Judgments," p. 33) calls the likely outcome a "baseline."

13. Murray, "Improving Relationships," p. 589.

14. Mnookin ("Divorce Bargaining," pp. 1025–26) discusses the difference between a person's subjective probabilities and the actual chances of varying outcomes.

15. See, e.g., Va. Code § 20-107.2, defining joint custody as either: (1) joint legal custody, where both parents retain joint responsibility for the care and control of the child and joint authority to make decisions concerning the child even though the child's primary residence may be with only one parent; or (2) joint physical custody, where both parents share physical and custodial care of the child, or (3) any combination of joint legal and joint physical custody that the court deems to be in the best interest of the child.

16. For favorable comments involving the primary caretaker presumption, see Garska v. McCoy, 278 S.E.2d 357 (W. Va. 981); Robert Cochran, "The Search for Guidance in Determining the Best Interests of the Child at Divorce: Reconciling the Primary Caretaker and Joint Custody Preferences," *University of Richmond Law Review* 20 (1985); Elster, "Solomonic Judgments," p. 11; David Chambers, "Rethinking the Substantive Rules for Custody Disputes in Divorce," *Michigan Law Review* 83 (1984): 477, 493.

17. An example of this is Virginia's divorce statute (Va. Code § 20–91), which provides for divorces based on the fault grounds of adultery, cruelty, desertion, imprisonment and confinement for a felony, and the no-fault ground of living separate and apart for six months (no children, property settlement agreement) or one year (children, with property settlement agreement). Wisconsin's divorce statute provides simply for dissolution based upon irretrievable breakdown of the marriage (Wis. Stat. Ann. § 767.17).

18. See, e.g., Eaton v. Davis, 176 Va. 330, 338, 10 S.E.2d 893, 897 (1940), quoted favorably in Newport v. Newport, 219 Va. 48, 245 S.E.2d 134 (1978): "It stems from the common-law right of the wife to support by her husband, which right, unless the wife by her own misconduct forfeits it, continues to exist even after they cease to live together."

19. See, e.g., Wis. Stat. Ann. § 767.26, providing for maintenance for a limited or indefinite length of time after considering, among other things, the "time and expense necessary to acquire sufficient education or training to enable the party to find appropriate employment."

20. See, e.g., Va. Code § 20-107.3, setting forth 11 factors the court must consider before making a marital property allocation.

21. Wis. Stat. Ann. § 767.255 provides that the "court shall presume that all other property is to be divided equally between the parties," although this may be altered after consideration of 12 factors.

22. This is the language of Mnookin, "Divorce Bargaining."

23. Even though many cases were analyzed in each jurisdiction, only 114 in Wisconsin and 98 in Virginia had all the information we needed, had final divorces, and had minor children.

24. This statute (Va. Code § 20-107.1) was amended in 1988 so that only adultery acts as a bar, and even then the judge may award alimony if not to do so would constitute manifest injustice, based upon the respective degrees of fault during the marriage and the relative economic circumstances of the parties.

25. See, e.g., McCreery v. McCreery, 218 Va. 352, 237 S.E.2d 167 (1977) (where the husband had been a "very nurturing parent" willing to place the welfare of the children above all else); and Peple v. Peple, 5 Va. App.414, 423, 364 S.E.2d 232 (1988) (where the father had become an "exceptionally attentive parent, actively involved in the physical, mental and religious guidance of the child," while the mother, "while a loving and fit parent, was more occupied by her employment and not able to provide the same quality of care").

26. This statute was amended in 1988 so that the court may only award joint legal custody if in the child's best interests, and either the parents agree to it or one parent seeks it and the judge finds that both parents are capable and that there are no conditions that would substantially interfere with the exercise of joint legal custody. There is still a presumption that a child is entitled to periods of physical placement (visitation) with both parents unless it would endanger a child's physical, mental, or emotional health. A number of factors must be considered when making this determination.

27. This is comparable to the analysis of Cooter, Marks, and Mnookin (trial outcome).

28. Cooter, Marks, and Mnookin say spouses will be aware of this outcome because if their lawyers made unrealistic predictions about one case, they would adjust in a Bayesian method once confronted with the unexpected solution.

29. Or the collection of points, where each party's exchange rate of money/child custody is equal.

30. This is a mean; the median figure is 48 percent.

31. MRS is defined as the slope of the indifference curve.

32. This is consistent with Cooter, Marks, and Mnookin (undesirable outcome).

33. Mnookin, "Divorce Bargaining," p. 1026; Chambers, "Rethinking," p. 559.

34. See, e.g., Melli, "Process of Negotiation," pp. 1155–56.

35. For citations, see Elster, "Solomonic Judgments," pp. 3, 24; Chambers, "Rethinking," pp. 479, 505, n. 88; Cochran, "Search for Guidance," nn. 76, 98–99; and Judith Wallerstein and Joan Kelly, *Surviving the Breakup* (New York: Basic Books, 1980).

36. See e.g., Mnookin, "Child Custody Adjudication: Judicial Functions in the Face of Indeterminancy," *Law and Contemporary Problems* 39 (1975): 226; Elster, "Solomonic Judgments", p. 24.

37. This in fact may be the reason for Weitzman's findings of low awards to wives in California. See Cochran, "Search for Guidance," n. 75.

38. Although alimony was awarded in some cases to Virginia spouses, since in many cases the income levels of the wife and husband were not known, we did not take the figures into account in making our calculations.

39. This observation is consistent with Kay and Fineman's findings regarding enactment of no-fault legislation in California and Wisconsin, and Mnookin, "Divorce Bargaining," p. 1025. Robert Mnookin, in "Child Custody Adjudication," p. 225, suggests that the husband might even concede custody were there a specific maternal preference rule.

40. Nationally, in 1981 wives got custody in 90 percent of all litigated cases (Gerald Silver and Myrna Silver, *Weekend Fathers* [Los Angeles: Stratford Press, 1981] p. 54).

41. Cooter, Marks, and Mnookin do this for the problem of deciding whether to negotiate or to go to trial, assuming there is only one good rather than two (pp. 229–31).

42. See John Murray, "Understanding Competing Theories of Negotiation," *Negotiation Journal* (1986): 179, 184.

43. These suggestions are made by Elster, "Solomonic Judgments," p. 4; Chambers, "Rethinking," p. 557.

44. No visitation would occur only if he was shown to be unfit. See, e.g., Kern v. Lindsey, 182 Va. 775, 30 S.E.2d 707 (1944) (although the father for some years paid little attention to his son); Doe v. Doe, 222 Va. 736, 284 S.E.2d 799 (1981) (otherwise fit mother allowed to keep visiting child although she was involved in a lesbian relationship).

45. The actual endowment point was determined by reading all the reported cases (trial and appellate) involving equitable distribution that were decided in Virginia during the

period 1983–87, noting the percentages of property received by Virginia wives. In none of these cases where minor children were involved did the husband receive more than "substantial visitation" (90 percent custody given to the wife). Homes were uniformly divided. Women received somewhere between 15 and 40 percent of their husbands' pensions, business property, and securities.

46. Compare the model of Mnookin, "Child Custody Adjudication," p. 256, n. 155, where he models outcomes of decisions in terms of their effect on the child.

47. Risk aversion refers to the ratio of the second derivative of the utility function to its first derivative, and has to do with willingness to settle for less than the expected utility of a gamble in order to avoid the chance of a bad outcome. See, e.g., Milton Friedman and L. J. Savage, "The Utility Analysis of Choices Involving Risk," *Journal of Political Economy* 46 (1948): 279.

48. Risk aversion of wives is assumed by Mnookin, "Divorce Bargaining," p. 1025; Melli, Erlanger, and Chambliss, "Process of Negotiation," p. 1154.

49. Notice that presumably $U_h(E) < U_h(D)$, or at least that the husband may pretend that this is the case in order to make his threat of litigation credible. In other words, he would prefer the outcome disastrous to his wife (he gets primary custody) to the usual court outcome of "liberal visitation." Mnookin, "Divorce Bargaining," p. 1032, Mnookin and Kornhauser, "Bargaining in the Shadow of the Law," p. 972 n. 15; Chambers, "Rethinking," p. 567; and Elster, "Solomonic Judgments," p. 19, suggest that there may be strategic misrepresentation of preferences. Elster quotes Judge Richard Neely, "The Hidden Cost of Divorce; Barter in the Court," *New Republic* 13 (Feb. 10, 1986).

50. Virginia women on average settled for 74.8 percent of the custodial time and about 45 percent of the property. The difference between the average of the wife's share of marital property in Wisconsin and in Virginia is statistically significant at the 3 percent level.

51. See, e.g., Murray, "Improving Relationships," p. 589.

52. Mnookin ("Child Custody Adjudication," p. 253) suggests that this is not impossible, given the indeterminate nature of child custody decisions. His suppositions are complemented, to some extent, by the verbal findings of Austin Sarat and William Felstiner, "Lawyers and Legal Consciousness: Law Talk in the Divorce Lawyer's Office," *Yale Law Journal* 98 (1989): 1663. The authors indicate that while clients may understand their attorneys, they may be urged toward settlement because of a distrust in he validity of the legal proceedings: "Clients are introduced to a chaotic 'anti-system' in which they cannot rely on the technical proficiency, or good faith, of judges and rival lawyers and which have no hope of understanding on their own" (pp. 1665, 1669, n. 39).

53. See Mnookin, "Divorce Bargaining" p. 1026.

54. See n. 44.

55. See, e.g., Nancy Chodorow, *The Reproduction of Mothering* (Berkeley, Calif.: Univ. of California Press, 1978), pp. 205–9; Chambers, "Rethinking," pp. 533–37.

56. Elster, ("Solomonic Judgments," p. 2) suggests that this may because of bonding, social pressures, and so forth. See also Chambers, "Rethinking," p. 516; Cochran, "Search for Guidance," n. 12.

57. This follows the discussion in Cooter, Marks, and Mnookin.

58. Murray, "Improving Relationships," p. 589.

59. This is because he would be getting close to what he wanted if the court did order visitation. See Chambers, "Rethinking," p. 568.

60. Cochran ("Search for Guidance," nn. 8–86) suggests how devastating this may be.

61. See Chambers, "Rethinking," p. 569. Until 1988, Virginia had one of the worst child support collection records in the nation. The *Washington Post* (Aug. 28, 1989, p. A12) states that in 1986, Virginia collected less child support per family than any state in the Union except Oklahoma. By 1989, Virginia ranked 16th nationally.

62. Weitzman, *Divorce Revolution*, pp. 15–41, 339; Mary O'Connell, "Alimony after No-Fault: A Practice in Search of a Theory," *New England Law Review* 23 (1988): 437, 440–41.

63. See, e.g., Va. Code § 20-103.

64. This is one of the most important findings of Anna Freud Goldstein and Albert Solnit, *Beyond the Best Interests of the Child* (New York: Free Press, 1973).

65. See, e.g., Frank Flegal, "Discovery Abuse: Causes, Effects and Reform," *Review of Litigation* 3 (1982).

66. See, e.g., Va. Rule 4:1(B) (5), which requires that questions seek relevant information. Types of discovery are provided in Va. Rule 4:1(a).

67. Richard Posner, "An Economic Approach to Legal Procedure in Judicial Administration," *Journal of Legal Studies* 2 (1973): 399, 435.

68. Flegal, "Discovery Abuse," pp. 27–28.

69. This is one of the claims made by Jana Singer in "Divorce Reform and Gender Justice," *North Carolina Law Review* 67 (1989): 1103–1111. Singer suggests that alimony should be awarded on a partnership rationale to spouses after lengthy marriages.

PART IV
Policy-Making Disputes

CHAPTER 7

Reducing Risk Conflict by Regulatory Negotiation: A Preliminary Evaluation

MARK E. RUSHEFSKY

The movements of the interested parties—familiar groups from the debates over acid rain, toxic air pollution, and dozens of other issues—are so predictable and formalized, they can almost be choreographed as a dance.

Environmentalists take two steps forward, projecting disastrous consequences if particular industrial practices continue. Industry representatives take two steps backward, conjuring up horrible hardships for society and enormous economic costs if these practices, the consequences of which they minimize, are curtailed. The most that's needed, they say, is more study.

Meanwhile, scientists stand in the middle, reluctant to leap boldly in either direction because of the uncertainties connected with complex physical phenomena. Congress and federal agencies form a ring around the other dancers, proposing their own solutions, discrediting the others' proposals and generally trading insults and gibes.[1]

In 1982, the Administrative Conference of the United States (ACUS) recommended that federal regulatory agencies use a process of rule-making that would supplement normal administrative procedures, a process that we will call regulatory negotiation. By mid-1986, four formal such negotiations had been conducted by three different agencies: two by the Environmental Protection Agency (EPA) and one each by the Federal Aviation Administration (FAA), and the Occupational Safety and Health Administration (OSHA). A fifth such negotiation is underway within EPA. There have also been a number of informal voluntary negotiations at the federal level without agency participation, known as policy dialogues. Similar negotiations have taken place at the state level. Finally, a small number of interest groups have recommended changes in the Federal Insecticide,

Fungicide, and Rodenticide Act (FIFRA), through what may be called legislative negotiation. By 1986, a number of evaluations of regulatory negotiation have been published of the four completed negotiations[2] (some evaluations including policy dialogues) and ACUS has issued a subsequent recommendation.[3] Thus, there is considerable activity surrounding regulatory negotiation.

The purpose of this chapter is to review the experience with regulatory negotiation, based on published reports, comparing the promise of negotiation with the hopes of those who wrote about it in the early and mid-1980s. My particular interest is in controversies involving risk to public health, such as the benzene standard considered by OSHA. These controversies, as I have written elsewhere,[4] are difficult to resolve because the standards and the more generic issues (such as cancer policy) are based on an uncertain technical or scientific basis. While these issues are, on the surface, technical, they are in reality more fundamental, involving value judgments. In some cases the kinds of issues those writing about negotiated rule-making suggest may not be good candidates. The value differences contribute to the lengthy and unsatisfactory administrative proceedings that regulatory negotiation seeks to avoid. How well does negotiation live up to its potential for resolving risk disputes?[5]

First, some definitions are necessary. *Environmental dispute resolution* is the generic label for "a variety of approaches that allow the parties to meet face to face in an effort to reach a mutually acceptable resolution of issues in a dispute or potentially controversial situation."[6] There are three types of environmental dispute resolution processes. *Site-specific disputes* concern "a specific natural resource such as a river, lake, or island or a site that was defined by its proposed use."[7] A *policy dialogue* involves "an area designated by political boundaries such as a city, county, state, or the nation as a whole or it involves a type of natural resource that occurs in many locations, such as rivers."[8] *Regulatory negotiation* "is a term that refers to use of negotiation in any decisionmaking process by an administrative agency." An institutionalized form of regulatory negotiation is *negotiated rulemaking*, "a specific application of regulatory negotiation, referring to the use of negotiation in the decisionmaking process associated with rulemaking."[9] Finally, because this chapter focuses on risk policy issues, *risk* is defined as "the probability and severity of adverse effects."[10] Severity of a risk is a function of the number of people exposed and the magnitude of the exposure.

THE BACKGROUND OF NEGOTIATION

Negotiation occurs, of course, when the various sides in a dispute get together to resolve their differences. There are many examples of negotiation in our society: labor contracts, out-of-court settlements, arms control, and trade negotiations. With regulatory negotiation, or the somewhat stricter negotiated rule-making, an agency is considering a rule. In normal administrative proceedings, the agency would publish a preliminary version of the rule in the *Federal Register*, invite comments, consider those comments, and then publish a final version of the rule. In adjudicatory proceedings, an agency would hold a hearing and then decide an issue, say on possibly banning or restricting the use of a substance. Hybrid or informal rule-making involves both types of procedures. In any event, the normal process (based on a judicial, adversarial model) is generally a lengthy one that may polarize parties by forcing them to extreme positions. Many of the rules have been subsequently contested in court; one estimate is that 80 percent of EPA's rules have been challenged.[11] Thus a search was on for an alternative that, if no less lengthy, would be less divisive.

Regulatory negotiation emanated from two separate streams, one inside and the other outside the federal government. The federal stream began with the tenure of John Dunlop, secretary of labor during the Ford administration. Dunlop, an economist with considerable experience in labor negotiations, was looking for alternatives to the traditional administrative processes (based on the legal model) to handle highly controversial issues such as those OSHA was addressing. He wrote a paper that was widely distributed suggesting that those involved in disputes should be more involved in resolving them. According to Perritt, Dunlop also attempted to start negotiations to develop a health standard for coke oven emissions. Dunlop began liaison efforts with the academic community; and Phil Harter, a staffer with ACUS, worked with OSHA on negotiation. Dunlop's successor continued the effort, including sponsoring research. The Department of Labor (DOL) also provided seed money for the negotiation project at Harvard. The first executive director of that project was William Drayton, later associate administrator of EPA during the Carter administration. "Thus were seeds planted at the Administrative Conference, Department of Labor and at EPA for the negotiated rulemaking idea."[12]

The second, parallel stream, consisted of efforts at state and local levels, beginning in the mid-1970s, to mediate environmental disputes (thus creating the category of environmental dispute resolution).[13] Here the different parties to a dispute, say over construction in a marshland, would get together, often with a convener/facilitator.[14] Some of this work was facilitated by the Conservation Foundation (as well as other negotiation centers and institutes around the country), particularly with national issues. The Conservation Foundation publishes a newsletter, *Resolve*, reporting various dispute resolution efforts. In addition, it has convened a number of policy dialogues, and has begun holding annual dispute resolution conferences.

By the time of the Reagan administration, there was considerable impetus for regulatory negotiation as an alternative to traditional rule-making. In 1980, two Senate committees held joint hearings on the subject.[15] The hearings focused on the success of two privately sponsored policy dialogues, the National Coal Policy Project and the Toxic Substances Dialogue Group. There were also several bills introduced in the early 1980s that would make negotiations an integral part of regulatory procedure; the bills never made it out of committee.[16] Putting the imprimatur of the Reagan administration on the effort was a speech before ACUS by Vice-President Bush in 1981 in which he urged ACUS to explore this alter-native.[17] Regulatory negotiation fit in well with the Reagan emphasis on regulatory reform, including the use of voluntary standards. What could be more voluntary than having the interested parties produce a consensus on a rule? On October 26, 1982, OMB issued Circular A-119 encouraging agencies to use voluntary standards.[18]

In January 1982, Philip Harter, the ACUS staffer who had worked with OSHA, presented a report to ACUS, later published in the *Georgetown Law Review*, reviewing the experience with regulatory practices and previous negotiations, and looking at the various conditions that facilitate successful negotiations.[19] This was followed by a March 1982 ACUS draft resolution recommending regulatory negotiations.[20] There was also some private literature on the subject, such as the 1980 law review article by Susskind and Weinstein.[21] After Perritt's evaluation of the four negotiated regulations,[22] ACUS issued a supplemental recommenda-tion for agencies, including the suggestion that the agency itself participate in the negotiations.[23] Based on the evaluation of the four completed negotiations, EPA seems to have had the greatest success because of its institutional involve-ment (an office to promote negotiated regulation) and its genuine enthusiasm for the process.[24] By contrast, OSHA did not participate in the benzene negotiations and may have possibly undermined them. In the informal version of regulatory negotiation, policy dialogues, agency participation is not a necessary requirement.

THE THEORY OF REGULATORY NEGOTIATION

The procedures suggested in this recommendation provide a mechanism by which the benefits of negotiation could be achieved while providing appropriate safeguards to en-sure that affected interests have the opportunity to participate, that a rule is within the discretion delegated by Congress, and that it is not arbitrary or capricious. The premise of the recommendation is that the use of negotiation and mediation can, in appropriate cases, result in rules that are developed in less time and at less cost than under traditional rule-making procedures. Such rules would likely be more acceptable to affected interests because of their participation in the negotiations.[25]

Harter, in his 1982 report to ACUS, suggested nine criteria for successful negotiations. The most important criterion is that all of the interested parties have some incentive to negotiate, what Perritt calls BANTA (best alternative to negotiated agreement).[26] The BANTA concept has two related dimensions. Perritt stated that parties look at what an agency will do in the absence of negotia-tion. Harter suggested that each party has some variant of power over the pro-cess that the other parties, including the regulatory agency, must consider. The forms of power include bargaining strength (such as political clout or strong factual argument) and the ability to impede a decision or invoke an alternative decision.[27] Industry groups tend to have political clout. Environmental-consumer-labor groups may be able to forestall a decision or threaten litigation.

In addition, the various parties to a dispute have a range of options in achieving their goals. These include using the legislative arena, regulatory agencies, the courts, or even a decision not to do anything (stalemate). A choice of options is dependent upon a group's power, resources, and a cost-benefit analysis of one option over another.[28] The notion of countervailing power is vital. A party lacking some form of countervailing power is at the mercy of stronger groups.

Successful negotiations usually include a limited number of parties.[29] This limited number of parties is both a strength and a weakness. A small group can more easily negotiate, but those interests left out may contest this result.[30] The limited number of parties is the basis for looking at regulatory negotiation as "corporatist" in nature.[31] We talk about industry, or labor, or environmental interests, recognizing that there may well be intrainterest conflicts (say, large businesses versus small). The epitome of the limited number of interests was the policy dialogue on inadvertent polychlorinated biphenyl (PCB) spills, which involved only three groups.

The issue should be mature, a concrete question on which the agency is ready to issue a rule. Related to this is the criterion that the decision be inevitable: if the groups do not negotiate a recommendation, then the agency will issue a rule through traditional processes.[32] The issue should be a non-zero-sum game, or a win-win situation: every party should be better off than if it had not participated. Otherwise, there would be no reason to participate.[33] There should be multiple issues, so that there is something to trade. Research should not dictate a result; although research (and information in general) is important, there generally should be no fundamental research needed that would settle issues. Finally, the agreement should be implemented; the agency should use the agreement, and therefore may (but not necessarily) be part of the negotiations. The final criterion set forth by Harter is that fundamental values of the various groups cannot be negotiated. For example,

it seems unlikely that OSHA, the unions, and industry could initially agree through negotiations on the extent to which OSHA must, or may, consider costs in setting occupational health standards. Once the fundamental questions get resolved, the parties may then use them as a basis for negotiating agreements on individual regulations.[34]

In the traditional administrative process, the tendency is for the parties to act as adversaries, presenting worst-case scenarios and moving toward extremes. Not all interests are considered and some groups with political clout may have a strong advantage. In addition, during the Reagan administration, EPA in particular held private sessions with industry groups (*ex parte* contacts) as part of the administration's regulatory relief program.[35] There is also considerable evidence that similar sessions were held between industry and the Office of Management and Budget.[36] Negotiations should include all parties to a dispute (or at least representatives of all parties) under conditions in which each interest has some political power. With such a result, the expectation is that a rule recommended by the negotiation panel and adopted by an agency will have greater acceptance than one adopted through more traditional procedures.

BEGINNING THE PROCESS

In February 1983, EPA published a notice in the *Federal Register* that it was going to experiment with regulatory negotiations and invited nomination of possible candidate rules.[37] EPA assigned the negotiation project to a staff bureau. There was some reluctance to nominate rules, especially on the part of environmental groups.[38] A potential candidate for negotiation had to be in the "middle range" of development—"neither near to final promulgation or years from initial proposal."[39] EPA considered and rejected 16 candidates for negotiation for three reasons: timing (i.e. a rule that was not in this middle range of development), too many interests or unsettled issues, and complex generic issues rather than a distinct regulation.[40] One rule investigated in great detail was the disposal of low-level radioactive wastes (LLW). It was considered a good candidate, but environmentalists raised some objections about the process and some of the controversial data, and the Nuclear Regulatory Commission (NRC) was concerned that any EPA actions would slow down state waste disposal efforts. The negotiation over the rule also did not have the support of higher EPA officials.[41]

The EPA process for selecting rules is described by Fiorino and Kirtz.[42] EPA, in its 1983 *Federal Register* notice, requested recommendations of candidates for negotiation. In addition, the agency, acting as convener of negotiations, contacted a number of organizations and asked for nominations. Fifty were suggested and evaluated by the criteria mentioned above. A convener then explored the interest of the responsible EPA program office. If the interest was there then the convener engaged in a broad conflict assessment. He sent letters to potential parties asking if they were interested in participating, and also contacting them directly. A final notice was published after the assessments describing the proposal, process, and participants, and inviting comment.

EPA agreed on two rules that were successfully negotiated, one suggested by Natural Resources Defense Council (NRDC) lawyer David Doniger. This rule focused on nonconformance penalties for emissions from heavy-duty vehicles. The participants in the negotiations included 13 manufacturers, five trade groups, one environmental group, three state groups, EPA, and an observer from the Office of Management and Budget (OMB). The second rule, also suggested by an environmental group, concerned emergency exemptions from FIFRA. This proposed rule directly touched upon public health risk issues, "including such items as how EPA should consider risk, how residues should be evaluated, and how to deal with chemicals for which there is inadequate data."[43] The participants were somewhat more varied than in the nonconformance penalties group: there were four environmental groups, four state organizations, four user groups, seven trade groups, two federal agencies (the Department of Agriculture and EPA), and an OMB observer. Both sets of negotiations were conducted in 1984–85 and in each case EPA accepted the rule. There was limited comment after EPA published the preliminary version of the rule, demonstrating that the consensus produced by the negotiating groups was generally accepted. In 1986, EPA began a third negotiation, this time on protection for farm workers using pesticides.

Two other agencies have experimented with negotiation. The Federal Aviation Administration (FAA) within the Department of Transportation successfully negotiated a rule on flight and duty time. The Occupational Safety and Health Administration (OSHA) attempted a negotiation on the regulation of benzene, a long-standing issue that was the subject of an important Supreme Court decision overturning OSHA's original standard.[44] This was less successful; no rule was recommended, nor has OSHA issued one. The benzene negotiations, even more so than EPA's emergency exemptions rule, involved fundamental values and uncertain science. Perritt observes:

Negotiations proceeded for a little more than a year, producing agreement in principle on a standard, which the parties did not report to OSHA because they could not agree on certain substantive details and because changes in the political climate and dissension within represented interests and those similarly situated made agreement too risky for the participants. . . .

Though one of the reasons negotiations were adjourned without agreement was the expectation that OSHA would promulgate a standard unilaterally, no such standard emerged more than a year after the negotiations ended.[45]

There was, according to Gusman and Harter, disagreement over the benzene risk assessment. The negotiating panel was unable to resolve this issue (extent of low dose exposure) and instead focused on the risk management issue—"what should be done in response to risk, whatever its magnitude."[46] This is a rather intriguing model of handling risk controversy issues: sidestep risk assessment and concentrate on risk management or acceptable risk. We see here a pragmatic attempt to deal with risk as a "two-stage process," perhaps one way to avoid the normal protractedness of risk controversies. OSHA did not participate in the negotiations, but did submit a draft standard for permissible exposure levels. Perritt retrospectively concludes that benzene was not a good candidate for negotiations.[47] OSHA has negotiated other rules prior to the 1980s' efforts. In the 1970s, OSHA adopted a rule on coke oven emissions agreed upon by the agency, industry, and labor. Limited negotiations also occurred on the cotton dust standard between industry and labor, without OSHA participation. This seems to be an example of a policy dialogue. Perritt points out that the cotton dust agreement was important because it showed that negotiations can be used on controversial issues. Finally, in 1985, OSHA announced that it wanted to use negotiations for MDA (4,4'-Methylenedianiline), an adhesive that has been identified as a potential human carcinogen.[48] Thus again, we see that a risk issue is at stake.

Apart from the negotiations discussed above, four completed (though one of those unsuccessful), one underway, and one proposed, there have been a number of policy dialogues over the last several years, generally informal negotiations among the interest groups without agency participation. In several cases, the negotiations have recommended a rule to the agency, which the agency has accepted.

There are a number of differences between policy dialogues and the more formal negotiated rule-making, differences that point to some problems with the former, but also imply areas where policy dialogues might be successful.[49] The most basic difference between the two forms of regulatory negotiation is, of course, that negotiated rule-making is sponsored by an agency, whereas policy dialogues are privately sponsored (say by the Conservation Foundation) and sometimes occur without any sponsorship at all. From this fundamental distinction flow other differences. Because an agency is not a direct party to the negotiations, the result of a policy dialogue (apart from better communication) is a recommendation, rather than a decision. Thus, how and whether the recommendation will be implemented is a problem.[50] Funding is also a consideration, a serious one for environmental groups in particular. EPA provided some funding for its three negotiated rule efforts. But in a policy dialogue, funding is more difficult to come by. One last difference between the two forms concerns the openness of meetings. Negotiated rule-making is subject to the Federal Advisory Committee Act (FACA), and meetings of the panels are open, as are the announcements of the rules, selection of participants, and so on. Policy dialogues, on the other hand, are informal and subject to no such restrictions.

These differences also create potential advantages for policy dialogues, chiefly flexibility. With negotiated rule-making, there is a rule on an agency's regulatory agenda, which limits the issues and creates time pressures.[51] Policy dialogues may cover a wide range of issues, not necessarily on an agency's agenda, and can extend over a period of time. Of course, the absence of a deadline or other pressure may reduce the necessity for groups to resolve differences and produce a concensus.

Perhaps the best example of the benefits of policy dialogues concerns the inadvertent release of PCBs. EPA considered and rejected the issue for negotiations on the grounds that it was too complex. In mid-1982, the Chemical Manufacturers Association, the Natural Resources Defense Council, and the Environmental Defense Fund began negotiating on a rule to be presented to EPA. Not only was the agency not involved in the negotiations, but the negotiations took place without the auspices of anyone. A consensus among the three groups was reached and presented to EPA. EPA agreed to use the proposal as the basis for its regulation and in December 1983 published a proposed rule, based on the consensus.[52] A second example is the ongoing Toxic Substances Dialogue Group, meeting under the auspices of the Conservation Foundation. The group, again made up of industry, state, and public interest groups, recommended a procedure to EPA for overseeing new chemicals. There is also an Agricultural Chemicals Dialogue Group that has been meeting for some time. Other dialogue groups have focused on state issues, including hazardous waste, groundwater, coal-mining, and herbicide use.[53]

LEGISLATIVE NEGOTIATION

Related to regulatory negotiation, certainly the policy dialogue version of it, is the virtually unprecedented legislative negotiations over amendments to the Federal Insecticide, Fungicide, and Rodenticide Act (FIFRA). The FIFRA negotiations are important to look at in the context of regulatory negotiation, first because they represent one of the few attempts at legislative negotiation, and second, because they raise many of the same issues as regulatory negotiation (e.g., adequate representation of interests and resolution of controversial issues).

FIFRA was passed in 1972 (as an amendment to earlier pesticide legislation) and amended in 1978. As Stanfield points out,[54] the act had changed from a focus on consumer protection to environmental safety and public health. The major negotiators were unhappy with the act, particularly the trade group, the National Agricultural Chemicals Association (NACA). NACA wanted a bill that would reform and extend manufacturers' patents. Environmentalists were concerned that parts of the bill dealing with updating pesticide registration and banning or restricting hazardous uses of pesticides were inadequate. NACA had several motivations to negotiate: the delay in FIFRA reform caused by environmentalists who linked the patent issue with deadlines for health and safety testing;[55] some court defeats over pesticide regulations; and some bad press for the industry, like the pesticide ethylene dibromide (EDB). The motivation of the two parties was thus similar to those involved in policy dialogues and negotiated rule-making. Neither side could push a bill through Congress (the House passed a bill in 1982, but the Senate never held hearings) and the two sides began negotiations. On one side was NACA; on the other side was a coalition of environmental, labor, and consumer groups. Farmer groups and smaller manufacturers were not included in the negotiations.

There were 14 points of negotiation, reinforcing the Perritt and Harter notion that there has to be a number of bargaining issues. Most of the issues were noncontroversial; several were highly contentious ("reregistration of old pesticides, reforming the registration cancellation process, providing public access to test data and remedying groundwater contamination").[56] The groundwater contamination issue was the only one not agreed upon. Stanfield concludes that the agreement was due to environmentalists' political leverage rather than to "reasoned consensus."[57] As an example of the controversies, consider the process for re-evaluating old chemicals. EPA used a two-stage process that combined elements of adjudication and rule-making. EPA wanted to change to a rule-making process, but NACA liked adjudication, so the hybrid process remained in the proposal. For groundwater contamination by pesticides, the group agreed on a statement calling it a problem, a step forward as far as the coalition is concerned. NACA has also agreed to share test data on pesticides with the coalition, a major advance.

One of the issues the FIFRA negotiations raises is that of outside parties. In this case, EPA and OMB are outside parties, as they are with policy dialogues. EPA wanted a reformed FIFRA, while OMB preferred the status quo. Because neither side was a party to the negotiations, and because the negotiations were legislative rather than regulatory, both agencies had minimal input on the final outcome. There were other interests that were not part of the negotiations: smaller manufacturers and farmer groups. The major question is who pays for reregistration, an issue, Stanfield writes, that is caught up "with a long-standing internal industry struggle over patent rights and the use of test data."[58] NACA agreed to pay the reregistration fee, but this would put smaller manufacturers at a disadvantage (costs would increase). Farmers want the pesticides but are also concerned about costs. There are other issues involved in the FIFRA negotiations, but this gives some idea of the complexity of the issue. The FIFRA revision was finally passed in the autumn of 1988, but most of the controversial provisions, such as groundwater contamination, were left out.

CONCLUSION

Perritt believes that negotiation has proven effective in certain circumstances:

What will "work" in a particular case depends on the substantive issues, the perception of the agency's position by affected parties, past relationships among the parties, the authority of party representatives in the negotiations, the negotiating style of the representatives, the number and divergence of views among individual units within each constituency represented, and the skill of agency personnel mediators.[59]

Regulatory negotiations raise a number of issues, some procedural, others substantive. Most of the procedural issues are easily dealt with; with policy dialogues, the formal procedural questions are virtually irrelevant. For example, formal negotiations require a charter under the Federal Advisory Committee Act (FACA).[60] A second problem relates to delegation.[61] Congress delegates authority to agencies to issue rules that have the power of law. The agency is politically responsible to Congress and the president. But with regulatory negotiation, agencies are further delegating authority to private groups. In the case of policy dialogues, the agency is not even a party to the negotiations. Because policy dialogues negotiate only a recommendation and the agency will still issue a proposed rule for comment and consideration, this does not appear to be a problem. In the case of negotiated rule-making, where the agency is an integral party to the negotiation, the product is a decision, a proposed rule. But that proposed rule still must go through normal administrative processes. That the rules agreed upon have not been challenged indicates that a genuine consensus exists as long as interested parties are represented.

Perhaps the most interesting administrative issue is the role of the Office of Management and Budget. Under Executive Order 12291, issued by President Reagan in February 1981, OMB was given a major role to play in developing regulations. Under that executive order, agencies considering major rules must subject those rules to cost-benefit analyses, subject to OMB oversight. There has been some question about whether OMB has used executive order to delay regulations.[62] In any event, the cost-benefit analysis comes before a proposed regulation can be published in the *Federal Register*. A subsequent executive order in 1985 gave OMB the power to work with the agency at the stage where it is considering writing the regulation. The purpose of the executive order is to centralize the writing of regulations in the White House. [63]

The issue here is OMB participation in negotiated rule-making. And that role has varied:

Some agencies and commentators question the appropriateness of OMB participation, argu-ing that it is the agency's responsibility to obtain OMB concurrence in any proposed regula-tion. The whole point of negotiations, however, is to get *all* the interests likely to influence the substance of a regulation to communicate directly with each other. Under Executive Order 12291 . . . OMB has a major role to play. Evidence from the benzene negotiations suggests strongly that Industry's position was determined in significant part by what it thought OMB would do with a unilateral OSHA proposal. Such perceptions should be tested and taken into account in the negotiations themselves, rather than outside. The FAA and EPA experiences show that OMB can express support for negotiations and can par-ticipate in various ways. At a minimum, agencies considering negotiated rulemaking in a particular proceeding should have a clear strategy for obtaining OMB support and for involving OMB as negotiations proceed. This may be accomplished using facilitators/ mediators as intermediaries. [64]

Again, in the case of policy dialogues, the OMB role is not a central concern, for neither OMB nor the agency participates in the negotiations. This is a possi-ble disadvantage of policy dialogues versus negotiated rule-making.

There are also substantive issues raised by negotiations. We have the Harter criteria that seem to predict which issues are suitable for negotiations and which are not. For example, after the negotiations, benzene did not seem to be a good candidate after all. This may be because benzene is an old issue, with a long history of regulation, litigation, and hardened positions. The proposed negotiations over MDA may avoid the benzene problem because it is of more recent concern. [65]

The benzene, MDA, and cotton dust cases do raise important questions. While the subjects of the three successful negotiations are important within themselves, they do not raise the level of argument and disputation as do more controversial issues. Consider, for example, two types of related controversial issues. One was the banning of EDB on fruits by EPA. Here is a specific issue, an adjudicatory process, that might make good use of negotiations, whether through formal or informal negotiation. [66] The related issue is the more generic question of cancer policy, dealing with risk assessment. We have, with EDB as an example, or the banning of the herbicide 2,4,5-T, a series of questions that frequently recur. Because there are numerous issues involved, there is the possibility of trade-offs. Because the issues are unlikely to be resolved scientifically, then a political resolu-tion is necessary, which is essentially the basis for regulatory negotiation. [67]

There have been some attempts to deal with these difficult and technically com-plex issues. During the early 1980s, there was an attempt by the New York

Academy of Sciences, funded by EPA, to adopt negotiation for the resolution of scientific disputes. The project, unfortunately, failed.[68] But such risk issues may be and have been dealt with on the state and local levels. For example, as part of deregulation at EPA, states select sites for hazardous waste disposal; EPA has encouraged and facilitated negotiation in several cases.[69] One intriguing example is the disposal of dioxin by incineration ("trash-to energy plants") in New York City. In this instance, scientists disagreed about the nature of the risk but through negotiation of the different views were able to agree on what the risk was.[70] This is an excellent model of how risk disputes might work. And in fact, there is some basis for such a model in the risk perception literature. Apparently, we do not accept risk in the abstract (such as OSHA's or EPA's cancer policy), but evaluate risks in specific instances.[71] Regulatory negotiation thus seems quite appropriate for risk disputes such as benzene, cotton dust, and MDA.

Where do we go from here? First, we need to recognize that negotiated rule-making is in its infancy, an experiment. Thus it bears watching. Second, there has not been sufficient work done on the attitudes and expectations of the participants in regulatory negotiating and policy dialogues. For example, there is some evidence that environmental/consumer interests at the federal level are less than enthusiastic about regulatory negotiation. We might ask how the outcome of negotiation compares with initial expectations. Third, we know in considerable detail how the individual negotiated rule-makings began, but less about policy dialogues. For example, how and why did the interest groups that participated in the PCB dialogue group come together, especially since the dialogue was not sponsored by either the agency or a third party? Fourth, there are a series of implementation issues that can be raised. Bingham (1981) discusses implementation at some length, but limits her analysis to site-specific disputes. We might also want to call upon the theoretical literature on implementation in political science and public administration to analyze this area. Fifth, Susskind (1986) and Bingham (1981) look at negotiation at the state and local levels. How does negotiation differ at the various government levels?

Finally, how do the various forms of environmental dispute resolution (the generic term for all these activities) deal with risk issues? Susskind (1986) briefly mentions the "trash-to-energy" case in New York City, but provides little detail. Perritt's (1985) comprehensive review of the four federal negotiated regulations is particularly skimpy on the EPA negotiations. Bingham (1981) considers them in the context of implementation issues. Gusman and Harter (1986) are the only ones who explicitly examine environmental dispute resolution as it concerns public health issues. What is needed is more detailed case studies on the handling of the substantive risk issues. Regulatory negotiation is a promising alternative mechanism (to traditional administrative procedure) for handling controversies, but it is still in its infancy. Based on these early analyses, regulatory negotiation—or environmental dispute resolution to use its more generic name—holds out the promise to reduce, although not eliminate, the kinds of problems that can be described as a "dance of environmental controversy."[72]

NOTES

1. Rochelle L. Stanfield, "Environmental Focus: Ozone Two-Step," *National Journal* 18 (July 12, 1986): 1750.
2. Gail Bingham, *Resolving Environmental Disputes: A Decade of Experience* (Washington, D.C.: Conservation Foundation, 1986); Daniel J. Fiorino and Chris Kirtz, "Breaking Down Walls: Negotiated Rulemaking at EPA," *Temple Environmental Law and Technology Journal* 4 (1985): 29–40; Sam Gusman and Philip J. Harter, "Mediating Solutions to Environmental Risks," *Annual Review of Public Health* 7 (1986): 193–213; Philip J. Harter, "Regulatory Negotiation: An Overview," *Dispute Resolution Forum* (Jan. 1986): 3–4, 11–14; Henry H. Perritt, Jr., "Analysis of Four Negotiated Rulemaking Efforts," *Administrative Conference of the United States: Final Report*, Nov. 15, 1985, ACUS Contract No. AC8501007; and Henry H. Perritt, Jr., "Negotiated Rulemaking in Practice," *Journal of Policy Analysis and Management* 5 (Spring 1986): 482–95.
3. Administrative Conference of the United States, "Procedures for Negotiating Proposed Regulations," Recommendation 85–5, adopted Dec. 13, 1985.
4. Mark E. Rushefsky, *Making Cancer Policy* (Albany, N.Y.: State University Press of New York, 1986).
5. Mark E. Rushefsky, "Institutional Mechanisms for Resolving Risk Controversies," in Susan G. Hadden, ed., *Risk Analysis, Institutions, and Public Policy* (Port Washington, N.Y.: Associated Faculty Press, 1984), pp. 133–49.
6. Bingham, *Resolving Environmental Disputes*, p. 5.
7. Ibid., p. 10.
8. Ibid. See Bingham for a detailed discussion of the differences between site-specific disputes and policy dialogues.
9. Perritt, "Analysis of Four Negotiated Rulemaking Efforts," p. 14.
10. William O. Lowrance, *Of Acceptable Risk* (Los Altos, Calif.: William Kaufmann, 1976), p. 94.
11. Fiorino and Kirtz, "Breaking Down Walls," p. 29.
12. Perritt, "Analysis of Four Negotiated Rulemaking Efforts," p. 26.
13. For a discussion of the second evolutionary stream of environmental dispute resolution, see Bingham, *Resolving Environmental Disputes*, pp. 13–30.
14. There are a number of mediation groups around the country, such as the Harvard Negotiation Project. The work of these groups is discussed in *Resolve*, published by the Conservation Foundation and edited by Gail Bingham.
15. U.S. Senate, Select Committee on Small Business and Subcommittee on Oversight of Government Management of the Committee on Governmental Affairs, *Hearings on Regulatory Negotiation*, Washington, D.C., U.S. Government Printing Office, 96th Congress, 2nd Session, July 29–30.
16. Three bills were proposed in 1981: H.R. 1336, the Regulatory Negotiations Commissions Act; S. 1360, the Regulatory Negotiation Act; and S. 1601, the Regulatory Mediation Act.
17. Remarks by the vice-president of the United States before the Twenty-Third Plenary Session, Administrative Conference of the United States, Washington, D.C., Dec. 10, 1981.
18. Office of Management and Budget, OMB Circular A-119, "Federal Participation in the Development and Use of Voluntary Standards," Oct. 26, 1982.
19. Philip J. Harter, "Negotiating Regulations: A Cure for the Malaise?" Technical Report, Administrative Conference of the United States, Washington, D.C., 1982.

122 Policy-Making Disputes

20. Administrative Conference of the United States, Draft Recommendation 82-A, "Procedures for Negotiating Proposed Regulations," Mar. 10, 1982.

21. Lawrence Susskind and Alan Weinstein, "Towards a Theory of Environmental Dispute Resolution," *Boston College Environmental Affairs Law Review* 9 (June 1980): 9, 311–57.

22. Perritt, "Analysis of Four Negotiated Rulemaking Efforts."

23. Administrative Conference of the United States, "Procedures for Negotiating Proposed Regulations."

24. "An Interview with Lee Thomas," *Dispute Resolution Forum* (Jan. 1986): 5–6.

25. Administrative Conference of the United States, "Procedures for Negotiating Proposed Regulations."

26. Perritt, "Analysis of Four Negotiated Rulemaking Efforts," p. 34.

27. For a discussion of different types of power available to various interest groups in regulatory proceedings, see Harter, "Negotiating Regulations," pp. 46–51.

28. Bingham (*Resolving Environmental Disputes*) mentions these different arenas of policy-making in several places. The concepts of different policy-making arenas and different types of power are integrally related. For example, environmentalists have been very successful in using litigation (judicial arena) to force policy changes in agencies. This may be one reason why environmental groups are reluctant to wholeheartedly embrace negotiation.

29. Bingham (*Resolving Environmental Disputes*, p. 99) suggests that limiting the number of parties is not a necessary condition.

30. This may be the case with the legislative negotiation over amendments to FIFRA.

31. Rushefsky, "Institutional Mechanisms for Resolving Risk Controversies," pp. 142–43.

32. Again, policy dialogues contrast with negotiated rule-making. In the latter, the issue of maturity is a vital one. In the former, maturity is not necessary. One of the goals of a policy dialogue may simply be better communication among the parties. See Bingham, *Resolving Environmental Disputes*, pp. 77–89, for a discussion of the goals of environmental dispute resolution and characteristics of policy dialogues.

33. Even this criterion is a bit tentative. Because a party might be better off with negotiations than without does not mean that the party is satisfied with the outcome. Bingham's 1986 analysis of 160 cases of environmental dispute resolution does not touch upon the satisfaction of the parties with the process. Fiorino and Kirtz ("Breaking Down Walls") report a great deal of satisfaction with the two EPA cases of negotiated rule-making, although even here there does seem to be some hesitation on the part of some parties.

34. Harter, "Negotiating Regulation," p. 57.

35. Mark E. Rushefsky, "The Misuse of Science in Governmental Decisionmaking," *Science, Technology, and Human Values* 9 (Summer, 1984)): 47–59.

36. See Martin H. Belsky, "Environmental Policy Law in the 1980's: Shifting Back the Burden of Proof," *Ecology Law Quarterly* 12 (1984): 49–52. Belsky terms the relationship between the Office of Management and Budget and industry as "cooperative regulation."

37. Environmental Protection Agency, "Regulatory Negotiation Project," *Federal Register* (Feb. 22, 1983): 7494–95.

38. The reluctance to nominate rules can also be seen in the hesitation with which environmental and labor groups endorse negotiation. This may be due to their preference

for some of the other options, such as conventional rule-making and litigation. Participation in negotiation is also expensive, in terms of money, time, and expertise, an expense that probably weighs more heavily on these groups than on trade groups. Finally, environmental and labor groups may be less willing to engage in trade-offs than industry groups (which have enthusiastically endorsed negotiation), being very uncomfortable about negotiating what they consider to be fundamental values.

39. Fiorino and Kirtz, "Breaking Down Walls," p. 31n.
40. This is based on Fiorino and Kirtz, "Breaking Down Walls," p. 31n.; and Perritt, "Analysis of Four Negotiated Rulemaking Efforts," pp. 153–56.
41. Perritt, "Analysis of Four Negotiated Rulemaking Efforts," p. 155; Fiorino and Kirtz, "Breaking Down Walls," pp. 31–32.
42. The discussion of the process of negotiation is based on Fiorino and Kirtz, "Breaking Down Walls," pp. 30–32.
43. Gusman and Harter, "Mediating Solutions to Environmental Risks," p. 310.
44. *Industrial Union Department, AFL-CIO v. American Petroleum Institute*, 448 U.S. 607 (1980). For a discussion of the Supreme Court's benzene decision and the related cotton dust decision, see Albert R. Matheny and Bruce A. Williams, "Regulation, Risk Assessment, and the Supreme Court: The Case of OSHA's Cancer Policy," *Law and Policy* 6 (Oct. 1984): 425–48.
45. Perritt, "Analysis of Four Negotiated Rulemaking Efforts," pp. 64–65.
46. Gusman and Harter, "Mediating Solutions to Environmental Risks," p. 307.
47. See Perritt, "Analysis of Four Negotiated Rulemaking Efforts," pp. 115–22 on why benzene was not a good candidate. Perritt's reasons include the complexities of the issue, and its long history of attempted resolution (which tended to harden the position of various parties). Some questions may also be raised about OSHA's sincerity in issuing a benzene standard, as demonstrated by its actions during and after the negotiation process.
48. Ibid., p. 187.
49. The following discussion is based on a telephone interview with Sam Gusman, June 26, 1986. For a discussion of policy dialogues, see Bingham, *Resolving Environmental Disputes*, pp. 77–83.
50. For a discussion of implementation problems associated with policy dialogues, see Bingham, *Resolving Environmental Disputes*, pp. 120–25. Note that in the benzene negotiated rule-making effort, OSHA was not an active participant and, it might be argued, impeded the process. Perritt and ACUS both recommended that the agency take an active role in negotiations.
51. Note the Harter criteria that an issue should be ripe and mature. With policy dialogues maturity is not necessary, although some type of pressure is required to bring the parties together and keep the process moving.
52. See issue of *Resolve* (Winter 1984).
53. See issue of *Resolve* no. 17 (Winter, 1986).
54. Rochelle L. Stanfield, "Politics of Pesticides," *National Journal* 17 (Dec. 14, 1985): 2846.
55. Philip Shabecoff, "Pesticide Law Amendments for Congress Agreed Upon," *New York Times* (Mar. 11, 1986).
56. Stanfield, "Politics of Pesticides," p. 2847.
57. Ibid.
58. Ibid.

59. Perritt, "Analysis of Four Negotiated Rulemaking Efforts," p. 241.

60. As mentioned above, EPA and OMB held informal sessions with industry on a number of rules, a procedure that appears to have violated FACA. See Erik D. Olson, "The Quiet Shift of Power: Office of Management and Budget Supervision of Environmental Protection Agency Rulemaking under Executive Order 12291," *Virginia Journal of Natural Resources Law* 4 (Fall 1984): 1–83. Negotiated rules are a distinct improvement on the informal practices of the early Reagan administration in that they include environmental, consumer, and other interests. Indeed, a fair amount of rule-making and adjudication involves negotiation. For example, the hearings over the banning of the herbicide, 2,4,5-T were suspended while EPA negotiated with industry groups, a negotiation that occurred over several years.

61. See Perritt, "Analysis of Four Negotiated Rulemaking Efforts," p. 208.

62. Dale Whittington and W. Norton Grubb, "Economic Analysis in Regulatory Decisions: The Implications of Executive Order 12291," *Science, Technology, and Human Values* 9 (Winter 1984): 63–71.

63. There is considerable controversy over OMB's role. Several congressional committees sought to limit this role, or at least control it, with some degree of success. See "Raising the Shades at OMB," *Washington Post National Weekly Edition* 3 (June 30, 1986): 33.

64. Perritt, "Analysis of Four Negotiated Rulemaking Efforts," p. 250.

65. Ibid., pp. 188–91 discusses MDA.

66. This type of issue resembles what Bingham calls site-specific disputes.

67. For a discussion of cancer policy and the issues it raises, see Rushefsky, *Making Cancer Policy.*

68. See *Resolve* (Winter 1981).

69. This is based on a telephone interview with Kathy Tyson of the regulatory management office in the Environmental Protection Agency.

70. Lawrence Susskind, "Regulatory Negotiation at the State and Local Levels," *Dispute Resolution Forum* (Jan. 1986): 6–7.

71. See Baruch Fischoff, et al., "Lay Foibles and Expert Fables in Judgments about Risk," *American Statistician* 36 (Aug. 1982): 240–55.

72. Stanfield, "Environmental Focus," p. 1750.

REFERENCES

Administrative Conference of the United States. (1985). "Procedures for Negotiating Proposed Regulations." Recommendation 85-5, adopted Dec. 13.

Amy, Douglas J. (1982). "Environmental Mediation: A New Approach to Some Old Problems." *Citizen Participation* 4 (Nov./Dec.): 10–11, 24.

"An Interview with Lee Thomas." *Dispute Resolution Forum* (Jan.): 5–6.

Bingham, Gail. (1981). "Does Negotiation Hold a Promise for Regulatory Reform?" *Resolve* 10 (Fall): 1, 3–5.

———. (1986). *Resolving Environmental Disputes: A Decade of Experience.* Washington: Conservation Foundation.

Crowfoot, Hames E. (1980). "Negotiations: An Effective Tool for Citizen Organizations?" *NRAG Papers* 3 (Fall): 24–44.

"Dialogue Group Develops New Procedure for Overseeing Certain New Chemicals." (1986). *Resolve* 17: 9.

"Dialogue Recommends Hazardous Waste Management Law for Massachusetts." (1986). *Resolve* 17: 10.

Environmental Protection Agency. "Regulatory Negotiation Project Information Kit: Executive Summary." Washington, D.C.

———. (1984). "Intent to Form Advisory Committee to Negotiate Nonconformance Penalty Regulations." *Federal Register* (Apr. 24): 17576–80.

"EPA Completes Two Negotiated Rule Makings." (1986). *Resolve* 17: 8.

Feldman, Jay. (1985). "Stalemate Broken on Pesticide Reform Amendments." *Pesticides and You* 5 (Oct.): 8.

Fiorino, Daniel J., and Chris Kirtz. (1985). "Breaking Down Walls: Negotiated Rulemaking at EPA." *Temple Environmental Law and Technology Journal* 4: 29–40.

Gusman, Sam. (1981). "Policy Dialogue." *Environmental Comment* (Nov.): 14–16.

———. (1984). "Hazardous Waste Dialogue Group Reaches Agreement." *Resolve* 16 (Jan.): 4.

Harter, Philip J. (1982). "Negotiating Regulations: A Cure for the Malaise?" Technical Report, Administrative Conference of the United States, Washington, D.C.

———. (1984). "Regulatory Negotiation: The Experience So Far." *Resolve* 16 (Jan.): 1, 5–10.

———. (1986). "Regulatory Negotiation: An Overview." *Dispute Resolution Forum* (Jan.): 3–4, 11–14.

Lake, Laura M. (1980). *Environmental Mediation: The Search for Consensus*. Boulder, Colo.: Westview.

Mosher, Lawrence. (1983). "EPA, Looking for Better Way to Settle Rules Disputes, Tries Some Mediation." *National Journal* (Mar. 5): 504–6.

"National Groundwater Policy Forum Releases Proposed Recommendations." (1986). *Resolve* 17: 11.

"New Mexico Task Force Recommends Policies for Assessing Impact of Coal Mining on Water." (1986). *Resolve* 17: 11.

Office of Management and Budget. (1982). OMB Circular A-119. "Federal Participation in the Development and Use of Voluntary Standards" (Oct. 26).

Perritt, Henry H., Jr. (1985). "Analysis of Four Negotiated Rulemaking Efforts." *Administrative Conference of the United States. Final Report*, Nov. 15, ACUS Contract No. AC8501007.

———. (1986). "Negotiated Rulemaking in Practice." *Journal of Policy Analysis and Management* 5 (Spring): 482–95.

"Regulatory Negotiation: Four Perspectives." *Dispute Resolution Forum* (Jan.): 8–11.

Remarks by the Vice-President of the United States before the Twenty-Third Plenary Session, Administrative Conference of the United States, Washington, D.C., Dec. 10, 1981.

Rushefsky, Mark E. (1984). "Institutional Mechanisms for Resolving Risk Controversies." In Susan G. Hadden, ed., *Risk Analysis, Institutions, and Public Policy*. Port Washington, N.Y.: Associated Faculty Press, pp. 133–49.

———. (1985). "Assuming the Conclusions: Risk Assessment in the Development of Cancer Policy." *Politics and the Life Sciences* 4 (Aug.): 31–66.

———. (1986). *Making Cancer Policy*. Albany: State University Press of New York.

Schneider, Keith (1986). "Who's Making the Rules?" *New York Times* (Feb. 8).

Schuck, Peter H. (1979). "Litigation, Bargaining, and Regulation." *Regulation* 3 (July/Aug.): 26–34.

Shabecoff, Philip. (1983). "Mediating, Not Suing, over the Environment." *New York Times* (May 29).

———. (1986a). "Pesticide Law Amendments for Congress Agreed Upon." *New York Times* (Mar. 11).

———. (1986b). "All Hail the Pesticide Amnesty." *New York Times* (Mar. 28).

Stanfield, Rochelle L. (1985). "Politics of Pesticides." *National Journal* 17 (Dec. 14): 2846–51.

Susskind, Lawrence. (1986). "Regulatory Negotiation at the State and Local Levels." *Dispute Resolution Forum* (Jan.): 6–7.

Susskind, Lawrence, and Alan Weinstein. (1980). "Towards a Theory of Environmental Dispute Resolution." *Boston College Environmental Affairs Law Review* 9 (June): 9, 311–57.

"Texas Legislature Adopts Dialogue-Developed Hazardous Waste Siting Process." (1986). *Resolve* 17: 10.

U. S. Congress, Senate, Select Committee on Small Business and Subcommittee on Oversight of Government Management of the Committee on Governmental Affairs. *Hearings on Regulatory Negotiation*. Washington, D.C.: Government Printing Office. 96th Congress, 2nd Session, July 29–30.

CHAPTER 8

Dimensions of Negotiated Rule-Making: Practical Constraints and Theoretical Implications

DANIEL J. FIORINO

One of the more interesting applications of alternative dispute resolution (ADR) techniques in recent years has been to administrative rule-making. In theory and practice, negotiated rule-making differs fundamentally from more typical uses of ADR techniques, including site-specific mediation, minitrials, or arbitration. Its purpose is less to resolve conflict than to formulate policy that is prospective and general in its application. The representational requirements for negotiating rules are thus far more substantial than they are in resolving more specific disputes, such as the design or siting of a treatment facility or the construction of a highway through a wetland. It is in this respect that negotiation enters the realm of political theory. Because negotiation allocates costs and benefits of government action at a societal level, it also enters the realm of economic theory and analysis. In altering the role of the agency in the rule-making process and its relations with outside groups, negotiation raises issues of administrative law. Finally, by establishing a structure for outside parties to engage in policy deliberations with government officials, negotiation raises issues of democratic process and participation.

What may be most distinctive about the application of ADR to rule-making is its very pragmatic orientation. Above all else, ADR is a form of practical problem-solving that seeks to define the sources of disagreement and, through application of a set of group process techniques, to bring affected parties toward a consensus. Regulatory negotiation reflects this orientation by establishing a process for identifying interested parties, assessing their interests, determining the issues and their negotiability, searching for common ground, and working with the parties toward consensus. Like the ADR field generally, the emphasis in negotiated rule-making has been on results, with less of a focus on theoretical issues. Considering these theoretical issues is perhaps even more important in the context of negotiating rules, however, because it is designed to be a process of general policy formulation rather than one for settling specific disputes (Bingham, 1986).

This chapter considers regulatory negotiation from several perspectives. One is the practical problem-solving perspective that has been the basis for many observers' positive assessments of the process. Negotiation applies the practical tools of ADR to the incremental, interest-group character of regulatory policy-making. On practical grounds, assessments have generally been positive. Despite these positive assessments at a practical level, there are problems that could affect parties' willingness to conduct negotiations in the future. Two possible problems are reviewed in this chapter. The discussion then turns to two important theoretical criticisms of negotiation. One stream of criticism is premised on an economic rationality argument, and the second on an argument for legal rationality. Much of this criticism relies on a comparison of negotiation with ideals of rationality, rather than with the realities of conventional rule-making. An assessment of negotiation as a democratic process—a perspective that the literature on negotiation has overlooked—will be presented. One of my purposes is to begin to correct a bias in the commentary on negotiated rule-making that tends to overlook both the practical limitations and theoretical strengths of the process.

Before turning to these issues, however, I present a brief profile of negotiation as it has been practiced at the federal level. More detailed discussions can be found in the references (Susskind and McMahon, 1985; Fiorino and Kirtz, 1985; Perritt, 1986; Harter, 1987; Hall, 1988; Fiorino, 1988).

A PROFILE OF NEGOTIATED RULE-MAKING
AT THE FEDERAL LEVEL

Negotiations conducted by EPA and other agencies exhibit three principal characteristics. First, negotiations complement but do not replace the conventional rule-making process. The process conforms to the requirements of the Administrative Procedure Act, as well as the additional provisions of the Federal Advisory Committees Act. The negotiations are designed to produce a notice of proposed rule-making that reflects a consensus of the parties, to be published for formal public comment under conventional procedures. Second, the agency participates as a party-at-interest in the negotiations. It also commits to publishing the negotiating committees's consensus as a proposed rule, so long as it is consistent with the agency's statutory authority. Third, once a negotiating committee is formally constituted, it has substantial control over its mode of operation, composition, use of resources, and the terms and timing of its dissolution. Committees establish their own protocols and are free to define key issues, establish work groups, and assign issues for study and recommendation. The negotiations typically occur in a series of two- or three-day sessions spread over four to eight months.

The most active federal agency in conducting regulatory negotiations has been the Environmental Protection Agency (EPA). This discussion focuses on EPA's experience for illustration. The result in five of EPA's seven negotiations was a consensus on all or most issues. In negotiations on emergency pesticide exemptions and standards for wood-burning stoves, the parties reached agreement on the language of the proposed rules. In the negotiations on nonconformance penalties, hazardous waste facility permit modifications, and asbestos in schools, the parties achieved a consensus on all or most of the issues, with a number of limitations on the agreements in the asbestos rule. The committee as a whole did not reach consensus on the underground injection rule, because the five parties representing environmental interests could not accept the other committee members' position regarding migration of hazardous waste constituents. Beyond this, however, the agency was able to use the negotiations as the basis for a rule that reflected the committee's position on most issues. The effort to negotiate protective standards for farm workers exposed to pesticides collapsed when representatives of farm workers' interests withdrew.

With a few exceptions, assessments of negotiated rule-making have been positive (Fiorino and Kirtz, 1985; Susskind and McMahon, 1985; Harter, 1987; Fiorino, 1988). In particular, these assessments stress the practical value of negotiation as a means of formulating workable rules that are acceptable to affected interests and of drawing outside parties into policy deliberations. Even when the negotiating committees have failed to reach a consensus on all issues, both participants and observers have concluded that the negotiations offer a number of advantages over the conventional rule-making process. As others have noted, this generally positive experience can obscure practical weaknesses (Funk, 1987).

NEGOTIATION FROM A PRACTICAL PERSPECTIVE

Two practical aspects of negotiation warrant attention as possible weaknesses. One is the demands that the process makes on the time and resources of participants. The second is the way the process strains an agency's internal capabilities for policy coordination, especially given the current fragmentation in rule-making authority and the growth in executive office oversight (West, 1988). The first problem affects the willingness of agencies and other parties to commit more broadly to negotiation. The second will be important in determining how widely agencies can rely on negotiation as well as the validity of negotiated rules in administrative and legal terms.

One of the practical arguments in favor of regulatory negotiation is that it saves time and money. Implied in this argument are a number of more specific expectations about the effects of the negotiating process on parties' time and resources—that the agency's data collection costs will be reduced, that progress from the proposed to the final rule will be smoother and less costly, and that the likelihood and scope of litigation will be lessened (Harter, 1982). The experience to date has borne out some but not all of these expectations.

The evidence on near-term cost savings is mixed, although there are clearer signs of longer-term savings and related benefits. EPA's own evaluation of its negotiations concluded that the process probably cannot be expected to reduce an agency's data collection costs much below what they would be in conventional rule-making (EPA, 1987). Much of the more systematic health and environmental data that an agency requires to support a rule-making would be unavailable through the negotiating process. What health and environmental effects data the parties did possess would likely not be acceptable to all the parties as the formal basis for a rule-making. The agency and the other parties do have access, however, to information of another kind—practical, problem-oriented information on what the problems in the field appear to be, on the kinds of solutions that would appear to be effective, and on the pitfalls of regulatory design and implementation that should be avoided (Fiorino, 1988: 768–88). Rather than reducing the costs of collecting certain kinds of information, negotiation appears to bring other kinds of useful information to the parties at the right time in the policy-making process.

There will be clearer evidence of resource savings in the progression from proposed to final rule and in the avoidance of substantive litigation. The logic is that if the key outside interests have been a part of the process of defining and drafting the proposed rule and agreed to its contents, there will be less need for formal comment after proposal and for an agency analysis and response to those comments in preparing the final rule-making. The EPA experience generally confirms that logic. Comments have been fewer than might have been expected, and tended to be far more supportive on lesser issues. In the woodstoves negotiation, for example, the agency's air quality office estimated that it spent half as much time and money as it normally would to conduct additional analysis and respond to public comments (EPA, 1987: 7). Although the record to date is still too sparse to allow any firm conclusions on the litigation consequences of negotiation, the evidence to date is at least encouraging. Of the five rules issued as final, asbestos in schools and underground injection control have been challenged in court.[1] There is thus some evidence that negotiation can, over the longer term, reduce the resources necessary for producing final rule.

In the near term, however, negotiation is likely to impose greater resource and time demands on the participants. Parties assume many of the burdens of data collection, analysis, issue resolution, and legal drafting that normally are carried by the agency. Negotiation is an instance where the price of influence is to assume a substantial share of the burden of policy-making.

A consistent response in followup interviews with participants is that the negotiating process made demands on their time that were well in excess of typical rule-making. The parties' capacities to absorb these demands vary. The agency will have budgeted resources for the rule-making anyway, so its total commitment is not fundamentally different. What we have found is that the negotiation process affects the configuration rather than the total of the agency's resource commitments. Negotiation requires a more concentrated effort over a limited time period. For example, a typical EPA rule-making of moderate controversy and policy significance can easily take from one to two years to move from the start of work to publication of a proposed regulation. In EPA's six completed negotiations, the period from the notice of intent to negotiation and publication of the proposed rule ranged from three to 14 months, with an average of just over ten months.

A second difference between negotiation and conventional rule-making is the demand on senior management time.[2] The agency representative at the table has the authority to make binding commitments on behalf of the administrator or secretary. With this authority comes the obligation to devote time to the negotiating sessions themselves, to discussions between meetings, and to detailed preparation of agency positions and strategies. Senior management participation in conventional rule-making is less intense and extends over a longer period of time. Even for a major regulatory action, senior managers' involvement is generally limited to review of workplans and interim products, periodic resolution of issues, and representation of policy products before the top agency leadership. To participate in a negotiation, however, the manager must play more of a project leadership than an oversight role (EPA, 1987: 10).

Industry interests are in a relatively good position to absorb the resource demands of a negotiation. Usually some degree of technical and policy analysis of regulatory proposals will be necessary, and large organizations especially will have the depth to allocate time and staff to a negotiation. Trade associations can substantially augment the resources that individual firms will dedicate to the process. Relatively greater burdens are borne by state and local representatives, and especially by environmental groups. For the latter, who may have no more than one or two full-time staff to address an issue area, the intense demands of a negotiation constitute a major time commitment that promises to be an obstacle to any broader reliance on negotiated rule-making in the future. Environmental representatives, for example, have asserted that agencies will need to devise ways of compensating them for resources expended if they expect environmental group participation in any significant number of future negotiations.

Resources are one important practical issue in assessing the feasibility of negotiated rule-making. A second is the demands of the process on the internal policy-coordinating capacities of administrative agencies. Here many of the practical and theoretical concerns with negotiation intersect. The issue is the accountability of the agency and of the government as a whole for the result reached in the negotiations. Negotiation adds a demanding and often dynamic external process of policy development to an already demanding internal process. EPA, for example, relies on an internal process of staff-level work groups, a senior-level steering committee, top-level "options selection" reviews of key regulations, and a formal concurrence system by political-level officials (EPA, 1988; McGarrity, 1985). In addition to these internal demands on policy coordination, recent expansions in executive office oversight of regulatory development stretch the agency's capacities to keep up with the pace of some negotiations, especially in the last one or two negotiating sessions, when closure on many issues comes quickly.

A particular issue in EPA's negotiations has been how to accommodate the public negotiating process with the requirement that the Office of Management and Budget's Office of Information and Regulatory Affairs (OIRA) review and (as a matter of practice) concur with all proposed and final rules. Established in Executive Order 12291, the OIRA review relies on net-benefit and cost-effectiveness criteria in evaluating agencies' rule-making proposals (Smith, 1984).[3] OIRA has been critical of negotiated rule-making on both procedural and substantive grounds. Its procedural criticism has been that the negotiating process produces a proposed rule that OIRA cannot challenge, unless it upsets the committee's consensus. The alternative has been for OIRA staff to monitor the negotiations, and for EPA negotiators to raise and obtain agreement on any positions they will take in the negotiations. OIRA's substantive criticism has been that using a consensus-based process to produce a proposed regulation is inconsistent with the net-benefits approach prescribed in the executive order.

There are other practical issues that agencies will need to face if they expand their use of negotiation: the adequacy of procedures for identifying parties that can represent affected interests, the resources available to the committees to conduct independent data-gathering and analysis, or the range of issues that the negotiating process can cope with given the typical time constraints. At this point, however, it appears that the demands on the resources of certain participants and on senior managers' time and the strains on internal policy coordination are two that are especially significant. Despite practical advantages over conventional rule-making, ADR techniques have certain practical limitations. ADR reconfigures the resources required to make regulatory policy by concentrating the effort into a fairly short time period (leading up to the proposed rule); by demanding more of outside parties, especially environmental groups and state and local officials; and by drawing more on senior managers' time. It also stretches the agency's capacity to reconcile its internal policy processes and its obligations to such agencies as OIRA with the dynamics of the negotiating process.

Whether these considerations will dampen the appeal of negotiation in the longer term is uncertain. Their most important effect may be in limiting the number of negotiations that an agency can engage in at any one time. Rather than an alternative that is broadly applicable to a range of regulatory issues, negotiation may be more feasible as a complement to conventional rule-making procedures for a select subset of issues.

NEGOTIATION FROM A THEORETICAL PERSPECTIVE

Much of the criticism of negotiated rule-making has focused on theoretical rather than practical issues. To many of its critics, negotiated rule-making challenges traditions of rationality that have become important attributes of the rule-making process. This discussion focuses on two such streams of criticism. One I will call the net-benefits or social utility argument, and the other the administrative law or agency delegation argument. The first has been a source of criticism from economic analysts, the second from administrative lawyers. Both streams of criticism reflect important themes in the contemporary regulatory process.

The proposition that regulatory decisions should maximize net benefits to society has emerged with particular force since the late 1970s. Then the rapid expansion of social regulation at the federal level and the troubled economy stressed the need to formally incorporate considerations of economic efficiency into regulatory decision-making. Net-benefit analysis defines a set of decision criteria and techniques that allow decision-makers to compare the expected social costs of regulatory decisions with their expected benefits, if possible in quantitative terms (Reich, 1985). Its origins in environmental policy-making can be traced back to the 1930s and the Flood Control Act (Andrews, 1984). In its more recent form, it represents a counterweight to the pluralist orientation of regulatory policy-making, in particular, the tendency to set standards at levels that respond to the relative political influence of different groups. It presupposes a rational analytic approach in place of the incremental mutual adjustment, or "muddling through," that has characterized American policy-making (Lindblom, 1959). Negotiated rule-making is a process of policy formulation that fits squarely within that pluralist conception (Fiorino, 1988; Wald, 1985).

The irony is that regulatory negotiation is both the product and the counterweight to two competing impulses for regulatory reform. As a procedural reform, it reflects the impulse to define better working relationships among traditional antagonists through use of ADR techniques. The conflict is with the other impulse behind the regulatory reform movement, which emphasizes rational analysis in pursuit of economic efficiency. The analytic impulse is a reaction to the very pluralist tradition that negotiated rule-making seeks to build upon.

There are several contrasts between a decision process based on negotiation and one based on net-benefits analysis. One is in the decision criteria. In negotiation, the criteria are implicit. A good decision is one that meets the needs of the parties. Participants can claim not to have achieved the best possible outcome, only one that all of them can accept as the basis for policy. It is explicitly a satisficing strategy that reflects the pragmatic orientation of ADR principles and techniques. A decision based on net-benefits analysis relies on objective, external criteria, based on utilitarian principles. It is explicitly an optimizing strategy whose purpose is to achieve the most economically efficient outcome for society.

The two kinds of decision processes also use information differently. In negotiation, information is a means to an end. The parties use information to meet the instrumental needs of the process. In a net-benefits approach, information has objective importance. We see much greater concern over methodology, validity, and replicability, because the legitimacy of the result can depend on the defensibility of the information and the analytic basis for the decision. In another source of contrasts, negotiation relies on the development of personal relationships among the parties in part as the basis for reaching agreement on the substance of a decision. A major task of the facilitator is to manage personal relationships among the participants as well as to direct their progress on the substantive issues. In a net-benefits approach, whatever personal and institutional relationships exist would be irrelevant to the decision, which in theory is based entirely on rational, analytic factors.

The second line of theoretical criticism faults negotiation on grounds of legal rationality. Like the net-benefits argument, the thrust of the criticism is that negotiation relies on group consensus as the test of good policy rather than on objective decision rules or criteria that reflect the interests of society at large. What is different is the form of the rationality that the process fails to meet. Where the net-benefits approach asserts a substantive rationality based on utilitarian principles, the administrative law approach argues for a rationality based on logical consistency and procedural symmetry.

This line of criticism is expressed in a recent analysis of EPA's woodstoves negotiation, in which the author asserts that regulatory negotiation is incompatible with the principles and values of administrative rule-making (Funk, 1987). The core of the criticism is that the negotiating process improperly (although not necessarily illegally) delegates the agency's rule-making authority to private parties. Negotiation turns administrative law "on its head" by reducing the agency to the role of a mere participant, thus denying the agency's responsibility for anything beyond accepting and carrying out the group's consensus. The legitimacy of the policy then derives from the agreement between the parties "rather than in the determination under law of the public interest" (Funk, 1987: 92). In the case of the woodstoves negotiation, the author cites a number of legal liabilities in the rule that can be attributed to the effects of the negotiating process itself. He argues, for example, that the preamble does not explain how or why decisions are made but offers only a post hoc rationalization of agreements reached; that key decisions reflect the result of negotiated compromises rather than objective determinations; and that the rule's numerical emission limits were negotiated rather than derived "solely" from the "data and methodology described in the preamble" (Funk, 1987: 89).

There is something to be said for both lines of criticism. As Lowi (1969) and others have argued over the years, pluralist policy-making carries its own substantial baggage. It can bias policy to emphasize the interests of those with access, erode the authority and even the legitimacy of government institutions, and reward narrow private interests at the expense of broad social interests. And negotiated rule-making as an institutional mechanism fits squarely within the pluralist tradition of American policy-making. Yet the net-benefits and administrative law arguments share a liability as well, in that both hold negotiated rule-making up against a rational ideal that is unattainable in practice. Instead of comparing negotiation to the facts of conventional rule-making, they match it against a fully rational ideal that exists more in economic and legal theory than in the world of practical administration.

Even if we set aside the several philosophical and methodological objections to net-benefits analysis and accept it on its own terms, it is clear that the technique is feasible and useful for only a limited set of regulatory decisions (Shrader-Frechette,

1985). These include decisions that allocate identifiable, measurable, societal costs and benefits, such as a health-based standard. Regulations that are primarily implementing mechanisms, or where the larger risk or benefit decisions have already been made in the legislature or other forum, are simply inappropriate for this kind of analysis. Nearly all of the issues that EPA has negotiated can be described as "how-to" decisions, or what can be described as "regulatory problem-solving." For these kinds of decisions, negotiation by a representative group of affected interests within a pragmatic ADR context can be an effective and analytically defensible form of policy-making.

The legal criticism should also be subject to qualification. To assert that policy conclusions are the product of bargaining rather than an objective application of policy principles to a factual situation is to miss the central characteristics of American policy-making. Bargaining is inevitable. At least in negotiation, it is conducted in the context of an explicit and public framework. Nor is it reasonable to argue that negotiation simply delegates the agency's rule-making authority to private parties. An agency enters a negotiation with the same set of legal, institutional, and political constraints that it carries into any rule-making effort. As in any other rule-making, it accepts the need to accommodate its own preferences with those of influential interests outside of the agency. The virtual certainty of litigation and the broad scope of judicial review make this accommodation a practical necessity. The agency remains accountable for the outcome. Negotiated rules are as subject to legal challenge as any other rule, as EPA's underground injection control and asbestos-in-schools rules have shown. Although some observers have argued that a lesser standard of judicial scrutiny should apply to negotiated rules, there are good arguments for maintaining the current standard (Wald, 1985). And as the underground injection and farm worker protection rules demonstrate, parties will withdraw if they find that the negotiations are not serving their policy or political interests. The agency thus remains accountable during the negotiations and in court once the final rule has been issued.

The most important lessons of the net-benefits and administrative law criticisms relate to the institutional limitations of negotiation rather than its inherent value or usefulness. The conclusion to draw from the net-benefits critique is that negotiation is poorly suited to decisions that involve fundamental social values or allocate environmental risks and benefits on a broad scale (Rabe, 1988). The lesson of the administrative law critique is that a process that sacrifices agency accountability or procedural integrity in fact or in appearance is of questionable value, whatever its practical merits. When we use it and with what procedural guarantees thus become central issues in evaluating regulatory negotiation.

The tests of economic and legal rationality define two possible bases for assessing negotiation. The next section considers a third: What can we say about negotiation as a democratic process and a forum for democratic participation in administrative policy-making?

NEGOTIATION AS A DEMOCRATIC PROCESS

Because of the emphasis of the ADR community on dispute resolution, much of the commentary has overlooked the value of negotiation and mediation as mechanisms for democratic participation in social decision-making. Yet negotiated problem-solving meets many of the criteria that contemporary democratic theorists have proposed for democratic participation (Barber, 1984; Pateman, 1970; Thompson, 1970; Bachrach, 1967; Cook and Morgan, 1971).

One democratic process criterion is that people outside of formal government positions share in decision power. Effective participation, many theorists would argue, is that in which "citizens share in governing" by having the opportunity to exercise decision authority or co-determine policy in collaboration with government officials (Thompson, 1970: 3). A second criterion is the opportunity to engage in face-to-face discussion over some period of time. Parties need to be able to engage in debate and discussion, immerse themselves in issues and information, and search for common ground. A third criterion suggested by democratic theorists is whether a process allows participants to take part in decisions on some basis of equality with administrative officials and technical experts. A process can be more effective to the extent that it allows people to determine the format, define the key issues and an approach to their resolution, acquire minimal levels of technical knowledge, and deal directly with decision-makers rather than their surrogates.

The degree to which negotiated rule-making meets these criteria is most apparent in its contrasts with conventional rule-making. Despite the relative openness of national American administration, it is a process in which the agency retains control. As the institution with delegated authority for action, the agency involves outside parties to the extent it considers appropriate, subject to minimal legal requirements. Outside participation typically occurs through the mechanisms of the public hearing, the written comment period, or through seriatim meetings with representatives of specific outside groups or interests.

Negotiation is more participatory for several reasons. First, by operating on the principle of consensus within the negotiating committee, the agency grants to all the participants a share in authority for making the decision. By definition, each party's consent is necessary for the group to achieve a consensus. So long as the result is consistent with the agency's interpretation of its statutory authority, the agency commits to adopting the committee's consensus as the basis for its proposed rule. Second, the negotiators have the opportunity to engage in policy deliberations with senior representatives of the agency and of important interest groups that make up the relevant "issue networks" in a policy area (Heclo, 1979). Such theorists as Barber, Thompson, and Pateman stress the value of discussion and debate as an element in democratic process. To these theorists, discussion has several values: it opens people's eyes to the perspectives of others; it draws interested parties into a search for common ground, leading to joint problem-solving; and it can transform, at least temporarily, relationships based on conflict into ones based on attitudes of cooperation and collective problem-solving. Parties become a part of the process, rather than outsiders whose main interest is to penetrate weaknesses in the agency's case and lay the groundwork for litigation later.

DIMENSIONS OF NEGOTIATED RULE-MAKING

Regulatory negotiation represents a complex phenomenon in contemporary American rule-making. It attempts to reconcile the procedural requirements of administrative law with the pluralist tendencies and traditions of American politics. It seeks the conflict-reducing advantages of ADR techniques as an ameliorative to the adversarial tendencies of administrative rule-making. It is corporatist in its reliance on institutional representation of social and economic interests, without conceding the requirements for openness and inclusiveness of the American administrative process. By relying on the implicit values of participants and defining agreement (within legal constraints) as the criterion of a good decision, negotiation runs directly counter to the socially optimizing tendencies of the rational analysis school of regulatory reform.

It may be that the practical case for negotiation has been overstated and the theoretical case has been incomplete. Certainly the virtues of the process are most obvious at the level of a practical analysis. It can be an effective tool for drawing traditional antagonists together for collective problem-solving. It does bring useful information to bear on issues at the appropriate time in the policy process. And it can reduce the time and expense of moving from a proposed to a final rule, and then to implementation by the affected parties. The advantages of the process at a theoretical level are less obvious. To many of its critics, making general policy through negotiation replaces the objective determination of the public good with the subjective reconciliation of narrower private interests. These criticisms have merit, but should be seen in the light of two qualifications. The first is that they hold negotiation up against models of economic and legal rationality that typically do not exist in the administrative process. The second is that we can apply and design the negotiating process to reduce or avoid the problems that the critics have identified. If we think further of negotiation as a form of democratic participation in policy-making—with its advantages of collective responsibilit for decisions, deliberation, and debate over time, and direct interaction with senio policy-makers—then a theoretical analysis can reach more positive conclusions.

In the end, our views about regulatory negotiation are determined by our conceptions of the administrative process. If one accepts the "administrator as expert" model of the administrative process, then negotiation is suspect because it compromises administrative neutrality and expertise. If one accepts the rational analysis/net-benefits model, then the flaw of the negotiating process is its inability to maximize social utility. For the traditional administrative law emphasis on logical symmetry and the development of a record of legal precedent, negotiation is too oriented toward results rather than doctrine and explicit substantive rationalization of decisions.

Conversely, negotiation is most appealing from the pluralist and practical problem-solving perspectives. If one conceives of administrative policy-making as a process of balancing the competing demands of diverse interests in society toward mutually acceptable outcomes, then negotiated rule-making is an appealing institutional solution. It is interest-group pluralism made specific, workable, and legally acceptable. ADR techniques provide a tested and pragmatic approach to meeting the process requirements of political pluralism. They are, in sum, a pragmatic set of techniques applied to the service of a pragmatic political philosophy. This may not be a match made in the economist's or lawyer's heaven, but it is a sensible approach to much of the malaise of contemporary rule-making.

NOTES

1. The asbestos-in-schools rule was challenged by the Safe Buildings Alliance, a group representing former manufacturers of asbestos building products, which claimed it would require unnecessary removal of the materials. The Court of Appeals for the D.C. Circuit upheld the rule in May 1988 (Safe Buildings Alliance v. EPA, 846 F. 2d [D.C. Cir. 1988]). The Natural Resources Defense Council challenged the "no migration" provisions of the underground injection rules in a suit filed Sept. 7, 1988, also in the Court of Appeals for the D.C. Circuit.

2. In four of EPA's seven negotiations, its representative at the negotiating table was an office director, and in the fifth it was a deputy office director. An office director is the highest career management level in the agency. The EPA representative in the other two cases was a division director and a branch chief.

3. The cite for Executive Order 12291 is *Federal Register* 46 (1981): 13193–13198.

REFERENCES

Andrews, Richard N. L. (1984). "Economics and Environmental Decisions, Past and Present." In V. Kerry Smith, ed., *Environmental Policy under Reagan's Executive Order*. Chapel Hill: University of North Carolina Press, pp. 43–85.

Bachrach, Peter. (1967). *The Theory of Democratic Elitism: A Critique*. Boston: Little, Brown.

Barber, Benjamin R. (1984). *Strong Democracy: Participatory Politics for a New Age*. Berkeley: University of California Press.

Bingham, Gail. (1986). *Resolving Environmental Disputes: A Decade of Experience*. Washington, D.C.: Conservation Foundation.

Cook, Terrence E., and Patrick M. Morgan. (1971). *Participatory Democracy*. New York: Harper and Row.

Fiorino, Daniel J. (1988). "Regulatory Negotiation as a Policy Process." *Public Administration Review* 48 (July/Aug.): 764–72.

Fiorino, Daniel J., and Chris Kirtz. (1985). "Breaking Down Walls: Regulatory Negotiation at EPA." *Temple Environmental Law and Technology Journal*. 6 (Summer): 29–40.

Funk, William. (1987). "When Smoke Gets in Your Eyes: Regulatory Negotiation and the Public Interest—EPA's Woodstove Standards." *Environmental Law* 18 (Fall): 55–98.

Hall, Lavinia. (1988). "Bending the Rules: Negotiating Rules in Administrative Agencies." *Policy Studies Journal* 16 (Spring): 533–41.

Harter, Philip J. (1982). "Negotiation Regulations: A Cure for the Malaise?" *Georgetown Law Review* 71 (Oct.): 1–118.

——. (1987). "The Role of Courts in Regulatory Negotiation—A Response to Judge Wald." *Columbia Journal of Environmental Law* 11:51–72.

Heclo, Hugh. (1979). "Issue Networks and the Executive Establishment." In Anthony King, ed., *The New American Political Establishment*. Washington, D.C.: American Enterprise Institute.

Lindblom, Charles E. (1959). "The Science of Muddling Through." *Public Administration Review* 19 (Spring): 79–88.

Lowi, Theodore J. (1969). *The End of Liberalism: Ideology, Public Policy, and the Crisis of Public Authority*. New York: W. W. Norton.

McGarrity, Thomas O. (1985). *The Role of Regulatory Analysis in Regulatory Decision Making*. Washington, D.C.: Administrative Conference of the United States.

Pateman, Carole. (1970). *Participation and Democratic Theory*. Cambridge: Cambridge University Press.

Perritt, Henry H., Jr. (1986). "Negotiated Rulemaking in Practice." *Journal of Policy Analysis and Management* 5 (Spring): 482–95.

Rabe, Barry G. (1988). "The Politics of Environmental Dispute Resolution." *Policy Studies Journal* 16 (Spring): 585–601.

Reich, Robert B. (1985). "Public Administration and Public Deliberation: An Interpretive Essay." *Yale Law Journal* 94 (June): 1617–41.

Shrader-Frechette, K. S. (1985). *Risk Analysis and Scientific Method: Methodological and Ethical Problems with Evaluating Societal Hazards*. Boston: D. Reidel.

Smith, V. Kerry. (1984). *Environmental Policy under Reagan's Executive Order*. Chapel Hill: University of North Carolina Press.

Susskind, Lawrence, and Gerard McMahon. (1985). "The Theory and Practice of Negotiated Rulemaking." *Yale Journal on Regulation* 3 (Fall): 133–65.

Thompson, Dennis F. (1970). *The Democratic Citizen: Social Science and Democratic Theory in the Twentieth Century*. Cambridge: Cambridge University Press.

U.S. Environmental Protection Agency (EPA). (1987). "An Assessment of EPA's Negotiated Rulemaking Activities." Program Evaluation Division, Dec.

——. (1988). "Regulatory Development in EPA." Office of Standards and Regulations.

Wald, Patricia. (1985). "Negotiation of Environmental Disputes: A New Role for the Courts?" *Columbia Journal of Environmental Law* 10: 1–33.

West, William F. (1988). "The Growth of Internal Conflict in Administrative Regulation." *Public Administration Review* 48 (July/Aug.): 773–82.

Zinke, Robert C. (1987). "Cost-Benefit Analysis and Administrative Legitimation." *Policy Studies Journal* 6 (Fall): 63–88.

PART V

International Disputes

CHAPTER 9

The Use of Simulation in International Negotiations

GILBERT R. WINHAM

Since 1973, the author has employed simulation exercises for the purpose of training government officers in negotiation techniques. These exercises have been held in Ottawa, Washington, D.C., Geneva (General Agreement on Tariffs and Trade), and in various locations in developing countries. The exercises have generally lasted two to three days, with participants taking roles and attempting to reach a negotiated settlement within the boundaries established by the simulation scenario. The negotiation situations established by these simulation exercises include the following: multilateral trade (tariff) negotiation; negotiation between an "authority" established by the Convention on the Law of the Sea and a consortium of mining companies; negotiation between a small developing country and two foreign multinational corporations; and a bilateral negotiation between two nations over six issues. (The simulation exercises are described briefly in the appendix.)

The simulation exercises portray realistic examples of international negotiation, which is necessary to retain the attention of professional participants. Realism also makes the exercises useful for theoretical analysis of negotiation processes. The simulation exercises portray concrete situations, and demonstrate the capacity of substantive material to shape negotiation behavior. The exercises also represent institutional factors, which are an important and largely forgotten issue in negotiation theory. In international negotiations it is relatively uncommon for the interaction to be limited to single individuals, and the Vietnam peace negotiations between Henry Kissinger and Le Duc Tho, or the Camp David negotiations involving President Jimmy Carter, President Anwar Sadat, and Prime Minister Menachen Begin are exceptions that prove the rule. Usually institutional factors in the form of large delegations, crowded agendas, conflicted domestic political processes, and the uncertain communication patterns that flow from these circumstances, are inescapable features of most international negotiations. These factors are capable of being built into a simulation exercise, which then becomes a useful instrument for teaching and analyzing the negotiation process.

The purpose of this chapter is to examine the use of simulation in international negotiation, and to report on my experience with this method. The emphasis will be placed on the use of simulation for teaching and training.

SIMULATION IN INTERNATIONAL RELATIONS AND NEGOTIATIONS

Since the 1950s, social scientists have been experimenting with various representational techniques in the study of international relations. At the core of these experiments has been the effort to distill some aspect of international behavior into a model that could serve an equivalent function for the social scientist that laboratory testing serves for the physical scientist.

One strand of this work is represented in the gaming literature, developed especially by social psychologists with some help from political scientists and economists. Games normally are an attempt to represent the structural aspects of human relationships (e.g., conflict) in a simplified and limited model, usually one in which human participants are used (Schlenker and Bonoma, 1978: 28–30). Typically, games are constructed pursuant to some theory of behavior, and are a means to test and elaborate the wider theory. For example, game theory, and particularly the prisoners dilemma (PD) game, has stimulated a great deal of laboratory-gaming on various aspects of cooperative and conflictual behavior.

Laboratory-gaming has played a critical role in the progression of scientific knowledge, because it is a bridge between abstract theory and operational analysis. This progression can be seen in the development of the "tit-for-tat" strategy for inducing cooperation. The intellectual genealogy of this important strategic concept can be traced from a seminal stage, that is, the theory of games (Von Neumann and Morgenstern, 1947), through a developmental stage, that is, laboratory-gaming (Rapoport and Chammah, 1965), to a later stage when the concept is tested against competing hypotheses and then publicized broadly (Axelrod, 1984).

Simulations differ from games in that they attempt to present a more complete picture of a policy situation. An analogy can be made to a flight simulator, which attempts to confront a user with almost all of the stimuli faced in actually flying an aircraft. Simulations of policy situations usually incorporate simplifying assumptions, and therefore do not approach realism to the degree of flight simulators. However, the important variables in a policy situation must be included in a simulation of that situation, and the relationships among the variables must be drawn accurately. If the simulation is incorrect, that is, if it is unrealistic, it will have little value either as a teaching tool or as a means for generating theory.

The most prominent example of simulation in international relations is the Inter-Nation Simulation (INS), developed by Harold Guetzkow and his colleagues in the late 1950s (Guetzkow, et al., 1963). Guetzkow defined simulation as "an operating representation of central features of reality" (p. 25), and he developed an interactive exercise that required participants to make foreign policy decisions based on conditions presented by the experimenter, or previous moves by other participants. INS was a sophisticated exercise based on a rich appreciation of existing theories of international relations (Coplin, 1966), and, in turn, was a vehicle for further theoretical development (e.g., Hermann and Hermann, 1967).

Another important development initiated around the same time was the political exercise (or POLEX), which was pioneered at the Rand Corporation and later pursued extensively by Lincoln Bloomfield and his colleagues at MIT (Bloomfield and Gearin, 1973). The purposes of the political exercise were teaching and policy-planning (or analysis), and the exercises involved role-playing with government officials in hypothetical but relatively realistic crisis situations. The exercises had a common format whereby teams of participants represented national decision-making units, but the precise roles depended on the scenario adopted for any given exercise.

POLEX was used to model many situations, from Middle East crises to regime collapse in Iran or Angola. Although the scenarios portrayed rarely occurred in the real world exactly as they did in the simulation the decision-making processes, bureaucratic interactions, and even final policy choices were "astonishingly similar to real life processes" (Bloomfield, 1984: 788) POLEX had obvious uses for the policy community, and the U.S. Defense Department has maintained organizational units responsible for political- and crisis-gaming since the 1960s.[1]

Most simulations of international relations—both of the theoretical (e.g., INS) or gaming (e.g., POLEX) varieties—involve processes of negotiation. This is probably inescapable, since international relations simulations are likely to include diplomatic intervention; and diplomacy, as Nicolson (1963: 4) reminds us, is effectively the "management of international relations by negotiation."

While early international relations simulations implicitly included negotiation processes, negotiation and simulation became explicitly linked when foreign offices began to teach negotiating skills to junior and mid-career Foreign Service Officers (FSO). In the early 1970s, the Foreign Service Institute (FSI) of the Department of State commenced a week-long Negotiating Skills Workshop which made extensive use of a one-day, bilateral negotiation simulation (Winham and Bovis, 1978, 1980). Other simulations, such as the author's Trade Negotiation Simulation, were used on an occasional basis. Similar negotiation training activity commenced at the Department of External Affairs in Canada about 1973, and again simulation was featured prominently as a training method. Negotiation training with simulation has continued to the present in both capitals. In a further development, FSI in 1982 established a Centre for Study of Foreign Affairs designed to enrich traditional FSI training. Among its activities is the task of developing simulations of various international negotiations and conflict resolution processes.

Organizations other than national governments have also developed an interest in negotiation training through simulation techniques. This is true of nongovernment organizations (NGOs). The International Peace Academy of New York and the International Ocean Institute of Malta regularly incorporate negotiation simulations in their training programs that cover security problems and ocean management, respectively. University centers specializing in negotiation also utilize simulation as a tool for training and analysis. Faculty associated with the Programme on Negotiation at Harvard Law School have developed a one-week public training program on negotiation, more than half of which consists of various simulation exercises. Similarly, faculty at Carleton University's School of International Affairs have recently prepared simulation training courses for Canadian FSOs. In sum, it appears that negotiation simulations, particularly in connection with training programs on negotiation, are a growth industry.

The interest in simulation as a tool for studying or teaching international relations appears to have receded from a high point reached in the 1960s. However, its use has accelerated in international negotiation, and there are two reasons for this. One is that negotiation is a "simulatable" experience; that is, the human interaction implicit in negotiation can be effectively represented in a laboratory setting. Many if not most negotiations entail people sitting around a table talking to each other, and this form of behavior can be modeled without need for either a complex environment (such as a large terrain for simulated military operations) or complex equipment (such as a manned space flight simulator). The second reason is that the perceived need for training in negotiation has escalated at all levels of society in recent years, and simulation is often seen as one of the most effective means of carrying out this training. As a form of human behavior, negotiation requires both applied and intellectual skills; and as a methodology, simulation is uniquely capable of providing training for both these requirements. There is a complementarity of substance and method that makes negotiation and simulation well suited to each other.[2]

SIMULATION AND NEGOTIATION TRAINING

In a useful review article, Cunningham (1984) has presented a typology of simulations used in social sciences. Cunningham defines simulation as "a device for replacing some aspect of reality for purposes of experimentation, prediction, evaluation, or learning" (p. 215). In using simulation for *experimentation*, the analyst typically creates controlled laboratory experiments that will generate or test hypotheses about decision-making processes. *Predictive* simulations are used to indicate what might happen rather than why, and are especially valuable when the goal is to understand relationships among a number of variables. *Evaluative* simulations are used to assess organizational work routines, of which a simple example might be ambulance emergency procedures. Finally, *educational* simulations have the goal of teaching participants how to use information, in addition to simply acquiring that information. In the progression from experimental to educational simulations, Cunningham suggests the emphasis shifts from finding solutions to transferring knowledge. Significantly, he argues the accurate representation of reality is critical for success in any of the types.

Of the simulations discussed earlier, INS would appear to be an example of the experimental or predictive type. The behavioral environment of INS was tightly controlled by game rules, and the moves of participants were assessed according to quantitative formulas that in turn specified the conditions for succeeding moves. The rigor introduced by the game rules and by the formulas facilitated hypothesis-testing. By comparison, POLEX would appear to a mixture of the predictive or educational simulation, with possibly some elements of experimentation in terms of generating hypothesis about decision-making processes. Negotiation simulations, for the most part, appear to be inspired by the educational purpose, but like POLEX they may have experimental or predictive uses as well.[3]

When a simulation is used for educational purposes, particularly with expert participants, the researcher's ability to use the exercise for hypothesis-testing is considerably restricted. As Bloomfield has put it, it is "necessary to avoid interfering with the suspension of disbelief essential for game purposes" (Bloomfield, 1984: 786). This means researchers are generally limited to unobtrusive forms of observation such as note-taking or possibly tape-recordings, but it rules out more active forms of observation such as periodic questionnaires or interviews.

Simulation Design

How is a negotiation simulation designed?[4] Yefimov and Komarov (1982) have suggested the following sequence of developments: concept phase, definition phase, development phase, and operation phase. In practical terms, each simulation should start with a concept of the scenario, which is the situation into which the designer wants to place the participants. To be interesting to participants, a negotiation simulation should attempt to capture the more profound elements that often divide parties in a negotiation. Examples of this might be the tension between liberalism and protectionism in a trade negotiation, or the division between private and collective rights in a negotiation over deep sea mining contracts. The scenario should also demand some action of the participants, which in a negotiation simulation will usually be a decision to accept or reject a negotiated agreement.

Once the scenario is specified in general terms, a rough hypothetical agenda should be drawn up. Agenda refers to the probable number and length of various meetings (e.g., negotiation sessions) to be included in the exercise. The agenda will usually be affected by a number of procedural considerations, such as the overall time allowed for the exercise, and whether the play is to be continuous or interrupted. The main substantive consideration is to make sure the agenda is realistic in relation to the amount of work participants must accomplish during the simulation, as well as the actions they are expected to take.

Designing participant roles is the next task. The roles should be realistic in relation to the scenario and the work to be done; each participant should insofar as possible have a defined task. The next step is to refine the scenario and to add issues that clearly invoke the interests of the negotiating parties. The issues should also raise tough, painful, and generalizable questions of principle. Included in the drafting of issues should be the instructions that parties are to receive regarding their negotiating positions. The final step is to specify the rules and procedures participants are to follow in conducting the exercise.

Realism and credibility should be emphasized at every step, particularly for exercises that will be conducted with professional participants. Realism is best assured by having a thorough substantive knowledge of the situation to be simulated, as well as sufficient knowledge of game processes to be able to simplify the situation without losing fidelity. Generally, substantive knowledge about the situation to simulated will be most important in designing the scenario and in drawing up issues to be negotiated. Procedural knowledge about simulation is important in designing the agenda, rules, and game procedures. The most difficult step is issue construction, which is plausible considering that the positions parties take on issues is the crux of most international negotiations.

One choice faced in simulation design is whether to create a static or dynamic exercise. A static simulation is one where the participants are given all the information at the outset to enable them to conclude the exercise. No further input is needed from the experimenter (i.e., control) once the simulation is put into play. A dynamic simulation is one where participants are given an initial scenario, and control then periodically inputs new and changing information to keep the exercise moving on a predetermined path. Dynamic simulations of international negotiations often entail a scenario where control plays one party in the negotiation and the participants play the other(s). Control can then direct the exercise by the responses it gives to the participants. This format is common in simulations of crisis negotiation, for it enables control to manipulate the bargaining in order to increase tension in the exercise.

Static simulations are generally more valuable for training in international negotiation than dynamic simulations. Static simulations remove the artificiality of having participants play against an impersonal and external force. In a properly crafted simulation that includes a deadline for the exercise, control should have no function other than to observe, or to answer technical, nonstrategic questions. This leaves the participants with the entirely realistic problem of arranging their own scheduling, and deciding on the priorities to apply to the work before them. How the parties handle these apparently mundane issues of procedure is often one of the most important factors in the eventual success or failure of the agreement.

The Teaching of Negotiation

Can negotiation be taught? This question is an old saw that cannot be answered here, but what can be said about simulation is that it places participants in a situation where they can experience directly the methodology of negotiation. It is interesting that participants often regard a training simulation as an equivalent of a real experience; for example, in debriefing sessions held in the GATT Trade Negotiation Simulation (TNS), participants recalling their experience with intergovernment negotiations often list the simulation as one of those experiences. It is usually assumed that something of value is taken from experience, and the fact that the simulation is apparently viewed as being on a par with real-life experiences suggests it has been useful to the participants.

One of the main advantages of using simulation to teach negotiation is that it promotes subjective understanding of negotiation processes that are difficult to convey through other methods (Foster, et al., 1980: 225). Critics of simulation often question whether students learn factual information as well through simulation exercises as they do through other more traditional methods of lectures and directed readings. While the evidence on this point is debatable, it seems clear that role-playing simulations allow the participants to gain a subjective insight into the complexities of the situation they are experiencing. The advantage of such insight was expressed by a student participant in a simulation in public administration: "In summary, I don't think I learned so much by way of facts and theory models as I learned to *think* about this kind of information. It gave me a reference against which to hold different administrative theories and models" (Foster, et al., 1980: 238). In negotiation, where the requisite skills are both intellectual and operational, the ability to think about information in relation to a particular situation is precisely what courses on negotiation should be teaching.

Experience with negotiation simulations suggest there are some aspects of negotiations that students are not likely to fully understand until they have lived through them. One example comes from the EEZ simulation, where the task for the participants is to draw up two negotiated contracts between a developing country and two foreign companies. Typically in this exercise participants underestimate the amount of time needed to complete a written agreement once a verbal agreement-in-principle has been reached. The problem is not simply a matter of miscalculating how long it takes to write things down; rather, it is that participants fail to appreciate the natural imprecision of verbal communication in comparison to the greater precision of written communication; and therefore, they fail to realize how much these differences can complicate and delay a negotiation. The important point is that this matter is not profound, and one would think it could be easily grasped from a lecture; but indeed it appears to be something that must be experienced to be thoroughly understood.

A second example of the capacity of simulation to produce subjective understanding comes from the multilateral TNS exercise. Experience with this simulation suggests that multilateral negotiation is difficult to practice, perhaps because multilateral negotiation is not as clear a concept as is often assumed. The term "multilateral" essentially means more than two parties, but this simple notion can be complicated by the fact that some parties to multilateral negotiation may not be significant players, which reduces the effective multipolarity of the situation; or

alternatively, nations engaged in ostensibly bilateral negotiations maybe so preoc-
cupied with the concerns of third parties that the negotiation is effectively widened.

From an analytical perspective, it may be more meaningful to speak of
multilateral situations in negotiation rather than multilateral negotiation per se,
with the understanding that multilateral situations could be invoked irrespective
of the number of parties actually at the table. A multilateral negotiating situation
might be roughly defined as a situation that occurs when actions one country takes
with another affects its relations with a third country, and vice versa. The important point is the concept of interrelationships. This is the point Neustadt (1970:
5) was making when he wrote in the context of analyzing Anglo-American relations: "Reality is not bilateral."

There is some evidence that "multilateral thinking" is hard to achieve in negotiation. The reason is that it calls for participants to keep track simultaneously of
the primary and secondary effects of their actions. The difficulties of doing this
have been noted by Doerner (1980: 92): "Subjects who are not accustomed to
dealing with complexity usually see only the aspired main effect of the measure,
and not the side effects which also appear." In multilateral negotiations, parties
are usually obliged to keep track of their position with third parties, while at the
same time they are dealing with other parties more important to their immediate
interests. The fact that multilateral negotiation is often a confused and pressured
affair makes it even more difficult to keep track of secondary effects, as the following example from the Trade Negotiation Simulation (TNS) will attest.

TNS is mainly a tariff negotiation among four countries, and the parties operate
on the basis of the real-life principle of most-favored nation (MFN). This means
in practice that the parties maintain only one tariff per product, and if they lower
a given tariff after negotiations with any country, they must extend to all parties
the new tariff they have accorded to the most-favored-nation.[5] This principle is
easy to understand in the classroom, but is often misunderstood in practice. It
is commonplace in TNS to find that parties have made different tariff cuts to different nations (e.g., a 10 percent cut on the tariff on footwear offered to one
nation, and a 20 percent tariff cut on the same product offered to another nation).
When this is discovered near the end of a negotiation, the effects on an evolving
multilateral agreement can be crippling. Parties are distressed to find that the
"rules" require them to give away more than they intended to, but when they
attempt to withdraw concessions previously offered, they are met with retalia-
tion in kind. The negotiation then runs a serious risk of unraveling, with ensuing
breakdown.

It is clear how the participants *should* negotiate in this situation, and indeed
this is explained to them in pregame briefings. They should negotiate with the
principle supplier of a given product, keeping track of the effects of any agreements
reached on secondary suppliers; and then negotiate with those secondary suppliers to obtain compensating benefits. But what the parties often do in practice
is to "see only the aspired main effect of the measure," as Doerner (1980: 92)
has put it. This analytical statement is remarkably similar to a comment made

by a Canadian trade negotiator in an interview taken in 1972. In assessing the Kennedy Round concluded in 1967, the officer complained that the United States had had "tunnel vision" with regard to the European Communist, and had missed the opportunity to conclude an attractive deal with Canada.

Apart from improving the subjective understanding of negotiation, simulation as a teaching technique also has some advantages in the transmission of factual information, although the benefits in this area are less clear-cut. One problem with using simulation to convey factual information is that the method is not particularly cost-effective (Jacobs and Baum, 1987: 388). Simulations require considerable research to construct, and the time requirements far exceed those for other methods, especially lectures. These disadvantages probably explain why the use of simulation is still limited in profession training programs (Jacobs and Baum, 1987: 393).

Once the start-up costs are absorbed, simulation does present some considerable advantages as a teaching method. It is argued that simulation develops different skills from classroom teaching (Brademeier and Greenblat, 1981: 316). Among these skills are especially those of being imaginative and innovative (Brewer, 1984: 805). These skills are especially important in negotiation training, since it is usually assumed that creativity—especially in a practical and institutional sense—is an important part of negotiation.

It is further argued that simulation promotes the retention of factual knowledge better than other teaching methodologies (Brademeier and Greenblat, 1984: 320). This contention is especially plausible where a simulation requires the application of a specialized body of knowledge or data. For example, in the Seabed Mining Simulation, participants are expected to draft a joint venture contract pursuant to the relevant articles of the UN Convention on the Law of the Sea. Since provisions of the convention for joint ventures are not entirely clear on all particulars, simulation participants likely come away with better understanding of the legal framework of joint ventures than they would from a conventional classroom discussion of the issue.

A second circumstance where simulation promotes knowledge retention is where a simulation requires specialized analytical techniques. An example can be seen in the EEZ simulation, where a personal computer using spreadsheet software is used to calculate alternative future cost-sharing arrangements between the country and the two foreign companies. It seems probable that the participants develop a more penetrating appreciation of spreadsheet analysis when confronted with its use in a practical and even urgent situation than they would have from a classroom demonstration of the technique.[6]

CONCLUSION

One of the most useful aspects of simulation for training is that it demonstrates problems faced in the real world of negotiation (Brooker, 1983: 152–53). One such problem is the "nonrational" element. Negotiations between governments are institutionally complex; they often proceed in the absence of adequate information and analysis; and they have complicated and often ineffective communication patterns.

Clausewitz (1976) observed similar phenomena in the conduct of war, and described these phenomena with the memorable phrase, "the fog of war." A similar term could also describe many international negotiations. What is especially needed in teaching and researching negotiation processes is to appreciate the nonrational aspects of real negotiations, and simulation is a good methodology for addressing this issue.

Simulations that faithfully model real negotiations have the capacity to bring nonrational factors into the laboratory where they can be closely observed. There is apparently some intellectual resistance to doing this, however. For example, Bracken (1984: 798) has noted that when large-scale political military games are played within the U.S. government, the inevitable problems that arise with coordination and communication are usually seen as defects of the game. As a result, there is a tendency to use smaller, more controlled games where organizational dynamics are unlikely to intrude or where information exchanges are unlikely to get fouled up. Bracken argues the smaller games lack the capacity to explore the institutional or organizational behaviors associated with conflict management, which are "the most poorly understood part of deterrence" (p. 799).

In the same manner, the negotiation simulations described here address some of the less understood aspects of negotiation theory. These include especially the impact (intended or otherwise) of organizational structure on communication; the process of establishing negotiating priorities within and between parties; the effect of intraparty communication (and transmission of instructions) on relations between negotiators and their governments; the effect of bureaucratic politics; and the evaluation of final offers. Because simulation is an inexact methodology, it is unlikely it will lead to rigorous testing of propositions about negotiation behavior. However, it is the most successful means for training individuals in some of the important but less analyzed aspects of negotiation behavior.

APPENDIX: DESCRIPTION OF FOUR NEGOTIATION SIMULATION EXERCISES

Trade Negotiation Simulation (TNS)

Description: The TNS is a four-country trade negotiation over 30 products. The purpose is to achieve a reciprocal agreement reducing tariffs and other restrictions on these products. Each country is represented by a home government and a negotiating team (NT).

Use: The TNS can be conducted in two to four days. Personnel can range from 13 to 25. Documentation includes a 60 page scenario (including trade tables) and additional material specifying instructions, communication rules, and so on. The exercise has been conducted twice (1974–75) for Canadian FSOs at the Department of External Affairs; five times (1975–78) for U.S. FSOs at the Foreign

Service Institute, and 16 times (1980–) for government officers from developing countries in the Commercial Policy Course at the GATT, Geneva.

Seabed Mining Joint Venture Simulation (Seabed)

Description: The Seabed Simulation represents a negotiation between an "Authority" set up under the UN Convention on the Law of the Sea and a consortium of private mining companies. The purpose is to negotiate a contract for minerals exploration in the Area controlled by the Authority, pursuant to Annex III of the Convention. The broader task is to establish a mutually beneficial regime between the Authority, which represents a wide range of national views on the role of private capital in seabed development; and the consortium, which possesses technology needed to exploit seabed minerals.

Use: The Seabed Simulation takes about three days and requires 11 participants, 8 on the Authority and 3 on the consortium. Documentation includes a 10 page scenario and individual scoresheets; additional bibliographic references are recommended. The exercise has been conducted five times (1981–85) in Ocean Mining Courses organized by the International Ocean Institute (IOI), Malta; and once (1982) with national delegates to the Eleventh Session of the UN Conference on the Law of the Sea.

Exclusive Economic Zone Management Simulation (EEZ)

Description: The EEZ Simulation represents two simultaneous negotiations between a developing country and two foreign multinational corporations (a petroleum company and a fishing company). The purpose is to conclude an offshore oil exploration agreement with the former, and a joint fishing agreement with the latter. The country is represented by a Prime Minister, Cabinet, and two negotiating teams. The companies are represented by a single team each. The exercise requires participants to consider alternative courses of national development, and to operationalize the concept of technology transfer in a practical contract. A PC with spreadsheet software is used to project alternative cost-sharing regimes.

Use: The EEZ Simulation takes about three days and has identified roles for 22 participants; 10 Cabinet members, and 3 individuals for each of 4 negotiating teams. Five roles can be added or subtracted as needed. Documentation includes a 9 page scenario and individual scoresheets. The exercise has been conducted in IOI Ocean Management training courses six times (1983–89) at Dalhousie University, and in IOI regional training courses in Trinidad, Tanzania, China and Malaysia. Participants have been government officers from developing countries with responsibilities in the area of marine management.

Foreign Service Institute "Slobbovia" Negotiation (Slobbovia)

Description: The Slobbovia Simulation represents a negotiation between two countries over six issues. Each country is represented by an Inter-governmental Team (IGT) and a Negotiating Team (NT), and communications are restricted between these groups. Participants are given individual role scoresheets which permit individual assessment of different outcomes on issues. The exercise represents the difficulties that bureaucratic politics and incomplete communications present in international negotiation.

Use: The Simulation is conducted in one day. It requires 16 participants, 4 for each IGT and NT. Documentation includes a 5 page scenario and individual scoresheets. The exercise is included as an appendix in Winham and Bovis (1978). It has been conducted frequently in negotiation training courses at FSI since 1972.

NOTES

1. Such as the Studies, Analysis and Gaming Agency (SAGA), which reports to the U.S. Joint Chiefs of Staffs.

2. There is a similar complementarity between simulation and business decision-making, resulting in increasing use of simulations in business schools. See Faria (1987).

3. Exceptions to this generalization would include an all-computerized diplomatic game (Bensen, 1961); an interactive man-machine collective bargaining game (Murphy, et al., 1982); and even the author's Trade Negotiation Simulation, which in its original form was designed to be played by paid subjects (graduate students) for heuristic and predictive purposes.

4. Simulation here refers to a role-playing exercise with human subjects.

5. This principle has application beyond commercial negotiation, and especially to the negotiation of collective goods. For example, when nations reach agreement to limit arms or to reduce environmental pollution, it is possible that benefits from the agreements will be realized by nations not party to the agreement.

6. A further effect of the computer was to reduce the political and psychological component in the simulation, and to increase the economic and technical component. The development of a computer model of seabed mining had a similar effect on negotiation behavior at the UN Conference on the Law of the Sea.

REFERENCES

Axelrod, Robert M. (1984). *The Evolution of Cooperation*. New York: Basic Books.
Bloomfield, Lincoln P. (1984). "Reflections on Gaming." *Orbis* 27:4, 783–90.
Bloomfield, Lincoln P., and Cornelius J. Gearin. (1973). "Games Foreign Policy Experts Play: The Political Exercise Comes of Age." *Orbis* 16:4, 1008–31.
Bracken, Paul. (1984). "Deterrence Gaming and Game Theory." *Orbis* 27:4, 790–802.
Brademeier, Mary E., and Cathy Stein Greenblat. (1981). "The Educational Effectiveness of Simulation Games: A Synthesis of Findings." *Simulation and Games* 12:3, 307–32.

Brewer, Garry D. (1984). "Child of Neglect: Crisis Gaming for Politics and War."
    Orbis 27:4, 803–12.
Brooker, Russell G. (1983). "Elections and Governmental Responsibility: Exploring a
    Normative Problem with Simulations." *Simulation and Games* 14:2, 139–54.
Clausewitz, Carl. (1832, 1976). *On War.* Edited and translated by Michael Howard and
    Peter Paret. Princeton, N. J.: Princeton University Press.
Coplin, William D. (1966). "Inter-Nation Simulation and Contemporary Theories of
    International Relations." *American Political Science Review* 60:3, 562–78.
Cunningham, J. Barton. (1984). "Assumptions Underlying the Use of Different Types
    of Simulations." *Simulation and Games* 15:2, 213–34.
Doerner, Dietrich. (1980). "On the Difficulties People Have in Dealing with Complex-
    ity." *Simulation and Games* 11:1, 87–106.
Druckman, Daniel. (1971). "Understanding the Operation of Complex Social Systems:
    Some Uses of Simulation Design." *Simulation and Games* 2:2, 173–95.
Faria, A. J. (1987). "A Survey of the Use of Business Games in Academia and
    Business." *Simulation and Games* 18:2, 207–24.
Foster, John L., Allan C. Lachman, and Ronald M. Mason. (1980). "Verstehen, Cogni-
    tion and the Impact of Political Simulations: It is Not as Simple as It Seems."
    Simulation and Games 11:2, 223–41.
Guetzkow, Harold, et al. (1963). *Simulation in International Relations: Developments
    for Research and Teaching.* Englewood Cliffs, N. J.: Prentice-Hall, Inc.
Hermann, Charles F., and Margaret G. Hermann. (1967). "An Attempt to Simulate
    the Outbreak of World War I." *American Political Science Review* 61:2, 400–16.
Jacobs, Ronald L., and Maryanne Baum. (1987). "Simulation and Games in Training
    and Development." *Simulation and Games* 18:3, 385–94.
Mahoney, Robert, and Daniel Druckman. (1975). "Simulation, Experimentation and
    Context: Dimensions of Design and Inference." *Simulation and Games* 6:3,
    235–70.
Nicolson, Sir Harold. (1963). *Diplomacy. 3d. ed.* London: Oxford University Press.
Rapoport, Anatol, and Albert M. Chammah. (1965). *Prisoner's Dilemma: Study in Con-
    flict and Cooperation.* Ann Arbor, MI: University of Michigan Press.
Schlenker, Barry R., and Thomas V. Bonoma. (1978). "Fun and Games: The Validity
    of Games for the Study of Conflict." *Journal of Conflict Resolution* 22:1, 7–38.
Sergeev, V. N., V. P. Akimov, V. B. Lukov and P. B. Parshin. (1989). "Interdepen-
    dence in a Crisis Situation: Simulating the Caribbean Crises." Paper presented
    at the Annual Meeting of the International Studies Association, London, March
    28–April 1, 1989.
Von Neumann, John, and Oskar Morgenstern. (1947). *Theory of Games and Economic
    Behaviour.* 2d ed. Princeton, N. J.: Princeton University Press.
Winham, Gilbert R. (1986). *International Trade and the Tokyo Round Negotiation.*
    Princeton, N. J.: Princeton University Press.
Winham, Gilbert R. (1977). "Complexity in International Negotiation." In Daniel
    Druckman, ed., *Negotiations: Social-Psychological Perspectives.* Beverly Hills:
    Sage, 347–66.
Winham, Gilbert R., and H. Eugene Bovis. (1978). "Agreement and Breakdown in
    Negotiation: Report on a State Department Training Simulation." *Journal of Peace
    Research* 15:4, 285–303.

Winham, Gilbert R., and H. Eugene Bovis. (1979). "Distribution of Benefits in Negotiation: Report on a State Department Training Simulation." *Journal of Conflict Resolution* 23:3, 408–24.

Yefimov, Vladimir M., and Vladimir F. Komarov. (1982). "Developing Management Simulation Games." *Simulation and Games* 13:2, 145–63.

CHAPTER 10

The Cambodian Peace Process: An Options Analysis

MICHAEL HAAS

On September 26, 1989, the army of the Socialist Republic of Vietnam marched home from Cambodia, completing a decade-long assignment to defend the government in Phnom Penh from the possibility that the Khmer Rouge might return to power. The purpose of this chapter is to determine how the government of the United States decided on a new policy in light of this fundamental change in the situation.

CAMBODIA: ASIA'S LEBANON

War has visited Cambodia for much of its history.[1] French colonial rule was established in the nineteenth century. During most of World War II Vichy France was nominally in charge. When Nazi control over France ended, Japan moved in, but soon Anglo-French forces evicted the Japanese army from Indochina, and France sought to reestablish colonial rule. Prince Norodom Sihanouk, originally installed by Vichy France, was able to obtain independence from France in 1953, but he was the victim of a coup in 1970. Lon Nol, his premier, ousted him but remained in office for only five years.

In 1975, just before Saigon fell into the hands of North Vietnam, Pol Pot's genocidal Khmer Rouge seized control of Phnom Penh from Lon Nol's regime. Encouraged by China, the new Cambodian regime attacked Vietnam as soon as it came to power. Although at least thirty-thousand Vietnamese died from Khmer Rouge attacks from 1975 to 1978, Hanoi tried to settle its dispute with Cambodia peacefully. After Phnom Penh refused to negotiate, Beijing refused to mediate, and the United Nations failed to act on Hanoi's complaint about a breach of the peace, members of Vietnam's army entered Cambodia in late 1978 along with Cambodian refugees in order to end the genocidal rule of the Khmer Rouge. Encountering little resistance, the invading forces set up a new government in Phnom Penh, known as the People's Republic of Kampuchea (PRK).

During 1979, supporters of all three previous Cambodian regimes regrouped inside Thailand, where they were aided militarily by China. Bangkok, in turn, was supported by its allies in the Association of South East Asian Nations (ASEAN)—Indonesia, Malaysia, the Philippines, and Singapore.[2] Although Vietnam hoped to leave Cambodia to the Cambodians, the externally supplied resistance was stronger than the PRK army, so Hanoi's army stayed on.[3] It took a decade to build a PRK army from a population devastated by the Khmer Rouge holocaust. When Vietnam decided that the new army was capable of defending the regime, its forces departed, leaving the insurgent armies of Pol Pot and the noncommunist resistance (NCR) to do battle with the government in Phnom Penh. The NCR consisted of Prince Sihanouk's supporters and the Kampuchean People's National Liberation Front (KPNLF), led by Sihanouk's former prime minister Son Sann.

U.S. POLICY TOWARD CAMBODIA

The Khmer Rouge was a small band of less than one thousand dissidents up to 1969, when President Richard Nixon secretly bombed Cambodia to cut supplies to the Vietnam war. After Sihanouk was swept from power in a coup in 1970, the new Cambodian president Lon Nol allied with the United States. Pol Pot's Khmer Rouge quickly increased its strength tenfold. According to Sihanouk, the United States "created" the Khmer Rouge by installing the unpopular Lon Nol government.

After the Khmer Rouge came to power in 1975, they were responsible for deaths of at least one million of their own people while preparing to attack Vietnam. Due to the genocide taking place in Cambodia, Senator George McGovern urged in mid-1978 that an international force drive Pol Pot from power, but the State Department rejected the idea out of hand. Instead, Vietnam did the job.

U.S. National Security Adviser Zbigniew Brzezinski claims credit for having persuaded China to provide military aid to revive the Khmer Rouge in 1979. U.S. delegates lobbied to enable the Khmer Rouge to retain control of the Cambodian seat at the UN in 1979, although Pol Pot was living in Thailand and the PRK controlled most of Cambodia. U.S. lobbying for the Khmer Rouge continued in 1980 and 1981.

U.S. humanitarian food aid to Cambodia, due to a famine in 1979, went to both the PRK and the displaced Cambodians in camps along the Thai border. The food enabled soldiers of the Khmer Rouge to stay alive.

In 1979 Sihanouk called for an international conference on Cambodia. Although Senator Edward Kennedy was in favor, Brzezinski vetoed the idea. The United States has never issued a peace plan for Cambodia but instead has backed the plans of other countries.

In 1980, Ray Cline of President-elect Ronald Reagan's transition team visited the Khmer Rouge to establish contact. By 1981 secret Central Intelligence Agency armaments flowed from Washington to the Cambodian resistance. As the aid went to third parties, such as Singapore and Thailand, there was no way to prevent these arms from reaching the Khmer Rouge. Sihanouk has described the noncommunist allies of the Khmer Rouge as "smugglers and bandits."

In 1982 U.S. diplomats persuaded Sihanouk to join in a coalition with the Khmer Rouge. Son Sann, Sihanouk's one-time premier, also joined. The coalition was then touted as Cambodia's representative in the UN, although the Khmer Rouge headed the delegation.

In 1985 Congress voted overt aid to Cambodia's noncommunist resistance, but an amount far smaller than China supplied to the Khmer Rouge. There was never any U.S. policy to have the noncommunist resistance eliminate the Khmer Rouge from Cambodia.

The Paris Conference on Cambodia convened in mid-1989, ostensibly to draft a peace treaty. Beforehand, U.S. government officials, including Vice President Dan Quayle, stated that a Khmer Rouge role in a future Cambodia would be unacceptable. During the conference, however, State Department diplomats lobbied for an interim government that would include the Khmer Rouge; this was the Khmer Rouge's peace plan. When Sihanouk objected, the State Department stuck to the Khmer Rouge proposal.

After the conference, the State Department blamed Vietnam for blocking a treaty. Hanoi's foreign minister Nguyen Co Thach was at fault, according to Assistant Secretary of State Richard Solomon, because he did not pressure Hun Sen to lay out a red carpet, welcoming Pol Pot to participate as a fully legitimized partner in an interim government.

U.S. military aid flowed to the resistance in Cambodia after the Paris conference. As the Khmer Rouge claimed that there was a military structure to coordinate military operations with the noncommunist resistance forces, the United States was again aiding allies that were working for a military solution that might bring Pol Pot back to power.[4]

THE CAMBODIAN PEACE PROCESS

Although Sihanouk called for an international conference on Cambodia in 1979, he was regarded as a "finished man." Hanoi was eager to negotiate, but China and Thailand were intent on a military solution. When Vietnam nearly achieved a victory in 1985 by crushing the Cambodian resistance militarily, negotiations were pursued. Three levels of negotiation emerged: intra-Cambodia, regional, and international.[5]

The first breakthrough was Sihanouk's decision to meet Hun Sen, who became PRK prime minister in 1984. They met in December 1987 and January 1988 in France. Next, a regional dialogue of the four Cambodian factions, the six ASEAN states,[6] Laos, and Vietnam convened at Jakarta in July 1988. In November

Sihanouk and Hun Sen met with Son Sann at Paris. The Khmer Rouge sent a representative to make the negotiations quadripartite in December. In February 1989 the Jakarta regional meeting resumed. Intra-Cambodian discussions without the Khmer Rouge continued in May at Jakarta. An international conference was held in mid-1989 at Paris; the countries involved were those in the regional dialogue plus the five permanent members of the UN Security Council, along with Australia, Canada, India, and Zimbabwe (the latter as head of the Nonaligned Movement). The United Nations also had a delegation, headed by the Secretary-General.

All these efforts made some progress but fell short of bringing peace. Then, after Vietnamese troops marched out of Cambodia at the end of September 1989, the Cambodian civil war resumed, leaving the Khmer Rouge in a position to return to power if it could overcome the untested army of Hun Sen's regime. Since U.S. policy in Indochina was premised on ending Vietnamese aggression in Cambodia, Hanoi's departure left Washington in need of a policy reassessment. Most countries were in a similar boat, compelled to examine their priorities regarding Cambodia.

DECISION-MAKING CRITERIA

Most foreign policy decisions apply four criteria: feasibility, security, prosperity, and prestige. Each criterion has subcriteria (see Table 10.1).

The criterion of *feasibility* usually rates very high in relation to standards of judgment. Decision-makers rarely adopt unattainable policies. Feasibility could be defined in two ways. Technical feasibility means the probability that a policy can in fact be implemented. In the case of Cambodia, technical feasibility has rarely been at issue, although U.S. policies have rarely achieved desired objectives,

Table 10.1
Decision-Making Criteria in Foreign Policy Decisions

MAIN CRITERION	SUBCRITERIA
feasibility	technical feasibility
	policy feasibility
security	probability of officeholding
	enhance power in the region
	support for allies
	reduce superpower conflict
prosperity	raise living standards
	build socialism/stop Communism
prestige	appear altruistic
	appear peaceloving
	gain respect for leadership

a point to which we return later. Policy feasibility refers to the extent to which B accepts A's policy toward B. The second type of feasibility is the key element in regard to Cambodian peace initiatives, so we will use it in our analysis. Some policies are more likely to gain acceptance than others, so we can rate each peace plan accordingly.

Security also has a high rating in foreign policy decision-making. Several forms of security need to be differentiated. One consideration is the probability of office-holding: decision-makers need to know whether decisions jeopardize their domestic positions as leaders. A second element, the impact on a country's power in the region, assesses how a decision relates to the external power position of a state vis-à-vis other countries in the geographic area. Weaker countries must also determine whether their decisions please stronger alliance partners, so support for allies is yet another security consideration. Reduction of superpower conflict also plays a security role: contending elephants have a habit of trampling the grass beneath them.

Prosperity usually ranks below security. Leaders tend not to starve until their governments are toppled. The primary prosperity goal is usually to raise living standards for a country, but this can include profits from sales of military supplies as well as economic development for consumers. When the world was divided into capitalist and socialist countries, a second prosperity criterion for the latter countries was to build socialism. The other side of the coin was to stop communism, which threatens the existence of the capitalist system.

Prestige criteria are the least important, although most governments prefer to sell themselves in terms of the moral values they promote. One prestige factor is whether a policy makes a leader appear altruistic. A second prestige yardstick is whether a country or a leader is seen as peace-loving. Governments go to war on behalf of ideals, so the two criteria are not identical. A third aspect of prestige is whether a policy enhances a country's respect as a leader; for superpowers, this includes the extent to which they support bloc followers when the latter are in need.

POLICY ALTERNATIVES FOR PEACE IN CAMBODIA

Several alternative policies for peace in Cambodia vied for acceptance after Vietnamese troops left Cambodia in late September 1989 (see Table 10.2). Most countries tried to maintain earlier positions, even though these stances were out of date and needed to be reevaluated.

The default policy is usually to do nothing. One reason for a do-nothing policy is to postpone a decision until options became more clear or the situation becomes more urgent. A second possibility is to ignore the issue. Either option in regard to Cambodia in October 1989 translated into allowing the various Cambodian factions to fight to the finish.

Commitment of troops was the default option for the Cambodians, however reluctantly in the case of the Phnom Penh government. This alternative, formally abandoned by Vietnam, quietly reemerged. Hanoi could rely on the dual

Table 10.2
Cambodian Peace Plans, October 1989

NATURE OF PLAN	SUPPORTERS
do nothing	all but those below
encapsulation	Chatichai, Vietnam
back Khmer Rouge	China, Khmer Rouge
back ASEAN	ASEAN, USA
back Sihanouk and the NCR	NCR, Sihanouk, USA
back Hun Sen regime	Hun Sen regime, USSR, Vietnam
quiet diplomacy	Australia
mediation	Thailand, UN
conference diplomacy	France, Indonesia
coercive diplomacy	USA
interim government	China, Khmer Rouge, NCR, Sihanouk, USA
interim council	Hun Sen regime, USSR, Vietnam
commit troops	Cambodian factions, Vietnam
file genocide case with ICJ	one member of Congress

justification of self-defense and ridding the world of a genocidal regime again, but enthusiasm for returning to Cambodia was substantially below what it was when Vietnam entered Cambodia in 1978. The French army's chief of staff mused in due course whether he would have to send back a French army in order to annihilate the Khmer Rouge.

Sending arms to allies reappeared as an alternative. As the noncommunist resistance was allied with Pol Pot, most Western countries hesitated to support the NCR. At the urging of ASEAN, the United States, and perhaps Britain, sent military aid to the NCR, since China was unashamed of arms shipments to Pol Pot, and the Soviet Union and Vietnam sent weapons to Phnom Penh. The alternatives, thus, were to back the Khmer Rouge, back Sihanouk and the NCR, or back the Hun Sen regime. Backing ASEAN at this stage meant sending arms to the NCR so that the noncommunists would survive in case of a bloodbath between the other two armies.

The opposite of arming allies was encapsulation, whereby non-Cambodian parties would shut off aid to their allies in the civil war. Secretary of State James Baker and former Soviet Foreign Minister Eduard Shevardnadze agreed before Paris to encapsulate the conflict, but China refused to follow suit. Vietnam preferred to leave Cambodia to the Cambodians, although military advisers were doubtless present in October 1989 so that Battambang would not fall to Pol Pot. Encapsulation was the aim of Thailand's prime minister Chatichai Choonhavan and Indonesian leaders.

Partition became an option. If negotiations failed and the four parties were to achieve a military stalemate once again, the model of divided Cyprus loomed as potentially relevant. One part of the country could be called Eastern Cambodia, the rest Western Cambodia. Although proposed by Hun Sen as a temporary modality for facilitating a cease-fire, this option was deemed unacceptable on a permanent basis by the principal countries and factions involved. Cambodians did not want to further weaken their country in comparison with neighboring Thailand and Vietnam. Accordingly, we exclude this option from our analysis.

Various forms of diplomacy emerged as the main nonmilitary response to advance the peace process. Thailand's Chatichai sought to mediate, but he ended up accepting the policies of Phnom Penh, whereupon he could sell his proposals neither to China nor to the United States. The UN Secretary-General's office was ready to mediate but less actively. Quiet diplomacy was pursued by Australia, which sent Deputy Foreign Minister Michael Costello on a mission of shuttle diplomacy in the region in December 1989. The conference diplomacy option of France (to reconvene the Paris conference) and Indonesia (to reconvene a regional dialogue) was on hold until an agreement became possible.

Coercive diplomacy lingered as an option. Having sought to apply sanctions against Cambodia and Vietnam since 1975, Secretary of State Baker thought that refusing to normalize relations with Hanoi would force Vietnamese leaders to extract new concessions from Phnom Penh. The rest of the world, however, regarded the U.S. position as too extreme, and sanctions were lifted from Cambodia and Vietnam by Australia, Britain, Canada, France, Japan, New Zealand, and some Western European countries after policy reviews.

The content of diplomatic negotiations focused on a method to achieve an interim rule of Cambodia after a cease-fire and disarmament of the warring factions so that "free and fair" elections could be held to select leaders of a new government that would rule by popular consent rather than force. The option favored by Hanoi, Moscow, and Phnom Penh was an interim council, composed of all four warring factions, that would organize elections within three to six months. The alternative favored by China and the Khmer Rouge was an interim government in which the four Cambodian factions would have veto power over each other; Baker backed this option at Paris.

The option of legal condemnation of Pol Pot's genocide remained. No party was willing to take this step, although at least one member of Congress urged the establishment of a special international tribunal to put the Pol Pot clique on trial.[7] The practical implication of this proposal was to disqualify the Pol Pot clique from any role in a negotiated settlement.

POLICY CRITERIA OF THE UNITED STATES

We now begin our estimates of importance of the criteria brought to bear on each policy alternative by President George Bush (see Table 10.3). Policy feasibility was very high, since Bush did not want the United States to appear impotent or inept in order to maintain world leadership. Bush had to assess the potential acceptability of any policy around the world before proceeding.

Table 10.3
Bush Administration's Options Matrix for Cambodia

CRITERIA FOR EVALUATION	WEIGHTS	OPTIONS[a]											
		BA	BS	PV	KR	IG	EC	WC	QD	BH	IC	DN	CT
Policy feasibility	V-High	E[b]	E	U	E	P	P	P	P	E	P	P	U
Officeholding	High	F	F	E	P	F	F	P	P	U	U	P	U
Increase power	V-High	F	?	G	V	F	P	P	F	U	P	U	P
Reduce super-power conflict	High	?	P	P	P	P	E	F	P	E	E	E	U
Support allies	High	E	F	P	P	F	P	F	P	U	P	U	P
Raise living standards	High	?	F	P	P	P	P	F	P	P	P	P	F
Stop Communism	Medium	E	F	V	F	F	P	P	P	U	P	U	F
Appear altruistic	Low	F	F	F	P	G	F	F	G	U	P	U	P
Appear peace-loving	Low	F	F	G	P	G	F	F	G	U	P	P	U
Assume leadership role	Low	F	P	G	P	F	P	F	G	U	P	U	F
SCORE		6.2[c]	4.7[c]	4.3	4.2	3.5	3.4	3.0	3.0	2.8	2.7	2.0	1.9
RANK		1	2	3	4	5	6	7.5	7.5	9	10	11	12

[a] Options Code:
BA = back ASEAN
BS = back Sihanouk/NCR
PV = pressure Vietnam
KR = back Khmer Rouge secretly
IG = interim quadripartite government
EC = encapsulate conflict
WC = refer genocide case to World Court
QD = quiet diplomacy
BH = back Hun Sen regime
IC = interim council
DN = do nothing
ST = commit troops

[b] Assessment Code:
E = excellent
V = very good
G = good
F = fair
P = poor
U = unacceptable

[c] Average of range of scores

Among security goals, probability of office-holding was of moderate concern. Bush hoped to be reelected in 1992, but Cambodia was not his foremost consideration. He had two more years to serve, and Southeast Asia was of low salience to the U.S. public. Bush wanted to maximize U.S. power in the region, consistent with the role of a superpower; this evidently meant containing the influence of Vietnam. Reducing superpower conflict became a higher principle of foreign policy for Bush than it was for his predecessor, Ronald Reagan.

Bush believed that he had a mandate to raise living standards for the American people, but he left this task to the private sector. Defense contractors were among the Republican interests best served by weapons shipments to the NCR.

The Bush administration believed that communism was withering away, so the program to stop communism was seen as a relatively passive waiting game. Investments in Indochina to make a buck were of little consequence to corporate interests that supported Bush.

In regard to prestige, support for allies was of high priority; the days of Reagan's unilateralism were fading. The United States had treaty commitments with the Philippines and Thailand. There was close cooperation with Singapore, but on an informal basis. Washington also maintained a strategic relationship with China, which Bush did not want to jeopardize. Bush wanted the United States to be perceived as altruistic, but had not yet proclaimed precisely what ideals he was pursuing in foreign policy. All U.S. presidents want to appear peace-loving. Bush administration statements on Cambodia, however, suggested that geostrategic concerns were more important than peace in Southeast Asia. Bush took almost no action to implement his inaugural pledge to put the war in Vietnam behind the nation. Bush dodged a leadership role in regard to Cambodia and Vietnam, as these subjects evoked strong yet polarized emotions in the American public.

The Democratic majority in Congress had different criteria weights (see Table 10.4). Although it avoided articulating foolish proposals, it had a somewhat lesser need to attend to questions of policy feasibility, since its policies would only be tested after their acceptance by the executive branch.

Security was more important to the Democrats. Probability of office-holding was a crucial consideration. Democrats had only been in the White House for four of the previous twenty-two years; there was a need to trip up Bush whenever possible. Democrats wanted to maximize U.S. power in Southeast Asia, too, but they saw China in a more threatening light than Bush. Democrats in Congress preferred to take active steps to reduce superpower conflict: they saw the beginning of an end to the cold war, and they welcomed this development more than such Republican hawks as Defense Secretary William Cheney.

Concerning prosperity, Democrats professed to be more eager to raise living standards for ordinary citizens than Republicans. Democrats received support from certain U.S. corporations that wanted to cash in on the potential profitability of investment in Vietnam before Europe and Japan sewed up most opportunities from an industrious workforce that accepts wages of $100 per month. The Democratic majority in Congress sought to stop communism as much as the Republicans,

Table 10.4
Congressional Democrats' Options Matrix for Cambodia

CRITERIA FOR EVALUATION	WEIGHTS	OPTIONS[a]											
		BA	EC	QD	WC	QC	BH	BS	PV	KR	CT	DN	IG
Policy feasibility	High	E	E	F	V	P	E	E	U	E	U	P	U
Officeholding	V-High	G	P	P	F	F	P	P	G	U	U	P	U
Increase power	V-High	G	P	F	P	F	P	P	F	P	U	U	P
Reduce super-power conflict	V-High	P	E	P	G	E	E	P	P	U	F	P	P
Support allies	Medium	E	F	P	P	P	P	P	P	U	P	U	P
Raise living standards	V-High	F	P	F	P	F	P	P	P	P	P	P	P
Stop Communism	Medium	F	P	P	G	P	P	P	P	U	P	P	P
Appear altruistic	V-High	G	V	E	E	F	P	P	P	U	U	U	U
Appear peace-loving	V-High	G	V	E	G	F	F	P	F	U	U	U	U
Assume leadership role	V-High	G	V	E	G	F	P	P	P	U	P	U	U
SCORE		5.8	5.7	5.3	5.2	4.2	3.8	2.7	2.7	1.3	1.2	1.0	0.9
RANK		1	2	3	4	5	6	7.5	7.5	9	10	11	12

[a]For key to symbols, see Table 10.3.

but favored the carrot, including diplomatic normalization and trade, rather than the stick.

There was also divergence in prestige criteria. Democrats were suspicious of such U.S. "friends" as the late Philippine president Ferdinand Marcos, so they were less keen on supporting allies. The party of Woodrow Wilson believed strongly, in the words of the former professor and president, that "America is the first idealist nation." Democrats not only wanted the world to perceive the United States as idealistic but also as peace-loving, differing from hawks that tended to guide the Republican party. Democrats, finally, were more interventionist; they wanted the United States to gain respect by assuming a leadership role.

U.S. POLICY ASSESSMENTS ON CAMBODIA

Democrats were in control of the pursestrings of the executive branch, so they could veto an active policy. As critics of the resulting passivity of the Bush administration toward Cambodia, they relied on congressional hearings and media dissemination. The result quite often was checkmated policy.

The decision-aiding software to be used below is *Decision Pad*. Although it has a simple algorithm that transforms qualitative judgments into numerical ranks and makes arithmetic computation, an interesting feature is that one can derive a composite rating of several judges.[8] Through our analysis below we may be able to find a consensus between Democrats and Republicans on Cambodia that was unexpected in the fall of 1989.

Commenting briefly on each option (Tables 10.3 and 10.4), we can see that the do nothing option was largely unavailable to a superpower, a term used to refer to a country with global interests. Both Bush and the Democrats found this option unacceptable to achieve the various goals that they were pursuing in foreign affairs.

Vietnam, by pledging to withdraw all military personnel in 1989, made the encapsulation option viable. China and the Soviet Union remained the major external suppliers, each premising their policies on the determination of the other to continue aid. This policy had few advantages for the Bush administration except for its contribution toward a superpower detente, because the largest factions in Cambodia were controlled by communist parties. For Democrats, encapsulation had a strong idealistic component; if feasible, it would be consistent with the Wilsonian principle of self-determination.

There was no open pro-Khmer Rouge policy from the Bush administration, but it demonstrated no interest in tracking down how U.S. aid to NCR leaked to the Khmer Rouge, as widely reported in the past. The Republicans, in short, appeared to have made a secret Faustian pact with the Khmer Rouge in order to enhance U.S. power. For the Democrats, this was morally unthinkable.

A pro-ASEAN policy was the official bipartisan position toward Cambodia since 1979. While the Thai prime minister sought to encapsulate the conflict by working to bring the parties to the bargaining table again, the Thai military continued to derive commissions on resales of arms to the Cambodian resistance, so ASEAN policy was ambiguous. The Bush administration no longer referred to ASEAN. Democratic policy-makers were still more pro-ASEAN, as the organization appeared to promote a peace process more than a military stalemate.

The pro-Sihanouk/NCR position taken by the Bush administration at Paris was also based on a bipartisan consensus. The prince's reputation, however, was marred as pro-Khmer Rouge early in the conference; later he switched to take an anti-Khmer Rouge stand, and then he returned to the land of Tiananmen Square. While Democratic congressional representative Chet Atkins called upon Sihanouk to break from the Khmer Rouge, the Bush administration did not know where the prince stood. In short, the prince's U.S. support evaporated. If he returned to rule in Cambodia, he was not expected to overpower his rivals, which had their own independent power bases.

The pro-Hun Sen position was unacceptable in the United States. The regime was set up in the wake of Vietnam's effort to annihilate the Khmer Rouge all the way to the Thai border. Some Western observers believed that no Cambodian leader qualified as ideal, but that Hun Sen was the lesser evil, since his record demonstrated that he was the most pragmatic of the various contenders, but this was not an official Democratic view in October 1989.

The United States took few diplomatic initiatives in regard to Cambodia. Baker's quiet diplomacy, which aided the Khmer Rouge more than the other factions by continuing to have the Thai military maintain the covert flow of weapons to the resistance, was greeted with little enthusiasm. The Democrats wanted diplomacy in order to enhance U.S. prestige, but they advanced no agenda for negotiation. For the same reason an offer to mediate was left to others; mediation is most successful when parties perceive a mediator to be unbiased. Washington could not credibly call for a conference, since it could not play a neutral role in the chair for a meeting on Cambodia. Democrats preferred diplomacy, but Congress is constitutionally prohibited from such activity. The mediation and conference options, thus, were unavailable, and there was no clarion call for quiet diplomacy.

Coercive diplomacy is a distinctive feature of U.S. foreign policy. In the case of Cambodia, it had taken the form of pressuring Vietnam by a refusal to normalize relations and a trade embargo; the same sanctions were applied to the Hun Sen government as well. Toughness toward Vietnam was still popular in American domestic politics for Republicans, so Baker withheld normalization of U.S.-Vietnam relations in order to force Vietnam to get Phnom Penh to agree to the Khmer Rouge peace plan. Hanoi's leverage declined, however, when Vietnamese troops withdrew from Cambodia at the end of September. Democrats noted that for a decade Washington informed Hanoi that the principal obstacle to normalization was the presence of its troops in Cambodia. After September 26, however, normalization was contingent upon an active role by Vietnam in promoting a peace settlement in which the Khmer Rouge would be allowed to return to a role in the Phnom Penh government. The message seemed to be that Bush's administration would continue to impose ever newer conditions indefinitely. As this would support worst-case scenarios of hardliners in Hanoi, Democrats believed that continued pressuring of Vietnam would boomerang: Vietnam would never accept the Khmer Rouge, and extremists would prevail over reformers in the Politburo. At the same time, the voters would punish Democrats who argued for lifting sanctions from Vietnam.

The Bush administration backed the Sino-Khmer Rouge plan for a one-year quadripartite interim government presented by Sihanouk in Paris. The State Department continued to support a Khmer Rouge presence in a transitional regime. Democrats believed that the Khmer Rouge would never abandon genocidal practices and thus did not deserve any role in a future Cambodia.

Baker rejected Hun Sen's interim council plan in Paris. A three-month election campaign was viewed as too short to be fair. Bush did not want to be seen as the president who "lost Cambodia" through "appeasement" of Vietnam. The Democrats would have pursued a compromise, based on the idea of the council with a UN interim government, in order to appear more peace-loving.

Sending troops was out of the question for the United States. Americans would riot in the streets if the government ordered them to return to die in Southeast Asia.

Bringing a genocide case against the Khmer Rouge at the International Court of Justice was not on the agenda for consideration by the Bush administration. U.S. delegates in Paris nodded while the Khmer Rouge argued that international law is not clear on the definition of "genocide." At least one member of Congress, however, envisioned a court decision that would serve to exclude perpetrators of genocide from a role in the future of Cambodia.

Based on our assumptions about criterion weights and assessments of how well each of the proposed policies would achieve the ten basic foreign policy goals, we find that support for ASEAN was everyone's best option, as it did the least damage to U.S. interests. But that was not the policy of the Bush administration because there was no clear ASEAN position to back. Bush's second choice, supporting Sihanouk, was also useful politically to pretend that the U.S. government had a policy toward Cambodia. But the ASEAN and Sihanouk figleaves over the U.S. nonpolicy toward Cambodia had fallen off. In all nakedness the public increasingly could see a punitive policy toward Vietnam and continued support for the Khmer Rouge (see Table 10.3).

The five favorite policies of the Bush administration differed from the ranking of options by the congressional Democrats. Backing ASEAN was the Democrats' best policy as well (see Table 10.4), but the reason was different: Thailand was seeking to mediate the conflict on terms less favorable to the Khmer Rouge. The next two options for the Democrats were encapsulation and quiet diplomacy. At ranks 4 and 5 were putting the Khmer Rouge on trial before the International Court of Justice (ICJ) and the Hun Sen peace plan as the basis for a comprehensive settlement.

Both parties agreed that a do-nothing policy was unacceptable, and they vowed not to send U.S. soldiers to Cambodia. The failure to converge at ranks 2 to 5 indicated a fundamental bipartisan division.

Using the composite method of *Decision Pad*, the resolution of the partisan conflict was unexpected (see Table 10.5). The bipartisan consensus was to support ASEAN. Just as Thailand could embrace contradictory diplomatic and military actions relating to Cambodia, so could the United States. But, to quiet the Democrats, the analysis reveals that the Bush administration would have to engage in quiet diplomacy in order to bring about an encapsulation of the Cambodian conflict, as these two options emerged in positions 2 and 3 in the composite analysis. A threat to submit Pol Pot's case before the World Court was the fourth most popular option by Democrats and Republicans combined. Continued sanctions against Vietnam ranked fifth, with the Hun Sen and Khmer Rouge peace plans left behind.

The above analysis was completed in early October 1989 for delivery at a conference in mid-November. U.S. policy toward Cambodia was in a shambles during October after congressional hearings on the conduct of U.S. diplomats at the Paris conference. By the time I gave my paper, U.S. policy had changed. The "Baker initiative" emerged. Baker announced that the United States was prepared to stop sending aid to the Cambodian resistance, provided China, the Soviet Union, and Vietnam would do likewise. The Soviet Union had already agreed to this policy in July, on the eve of the Paris conference. Vietnam's troop withdrawal indicated its acceptance. But China quickly nixed the idea again. Baker was back to square one, while at least having the satisfaction of appeasing his domestic critics by appearing to advance a more reasonable policy.

Word soon leaked out that U.S. secret aid had been resumed. Hun Sen displayed recently captured American-made weapons, which had never been seen before in Phnom Penh. Congress responded by cutting off military aid.

There was a further nuance to the Baker initiative involving quiet diplomacy. During the fall Baker was trying to obtain consent to the idea of a fourth level of dialogue on Cambodia—the Perm Five. Launched at the suggestion of the UN Secretary-General in 1985 as a way to advance the Afghanistan peace process, the Perm Five was a forum in which the five permanent members of the UN Security Council had discussions on major world problems on an as-needed basis. As China thought that the Hun Sen government would collapse when Vietnamese troops left Cambodia, Beijing failed to respond to Baker's proposal to place Cambodia on the agenda of the Perm Five. When a stalemate on the battlefield emerged by the end of 1989, China agreed to go ahead, and the first Perm Five meeting on Cambodia convened at New York in January 1990.

The Perm Five met in January, February, and March, initially pretending to make progress, thereby aiding Baker's effort to place the figleaf back over his nonpolicy toward Cambodia. The regional dialogue, renamed the Informal Meeting on Cambodia (IMC), resumed at Jakarta in February. IMC came near to an agreement on a UN transitional role for the country but left other disputes for later discussion.

In February bitter congressional hearings forced Baker to give up the quadripartite interim government option, hoping to sever the apparent umbilical cord between

Table 10.5
Composite U.S. Options Matrix for Cambodia

CRITERIA FOR EVALUATION	WEIGHTS	OPTIONS[a]											
		BA	EC	QD	WC	PV	BS	IC	BH	KR	IG	DN	CT
Policy feasibility	High	E	G	P	F	U	E	P	E	E	U	P	U
Officeholding	High	F	P	P	P	V	P	P	U	U	P	P	U
Increase power	V-High	F	P	F	P	F	P	P	U	F	P	U	U
Reduce super-power conflict	High	P	E	P	F	P	P	E	E	U	P	G	P
Support allies	Low	E	P	P	P	P	P	P	U	U	P	U	P
Raise living standards	High	F	P	P	P	P	P	P	P	P	P	P	P
Stop Communism	V-Low	G	P	P	F	F	P	P	U	P	P	U	P
Appear altruistic	Low	F	G	V	G	P	P	P	U	U	P	U	U
Appear peace-loving	Low	F	G	V	F	F	P	P	P	U	P	U	U
Assume leadership role	Low	F	F	V	F	F	P	P	U	U	P	U	P
SCORE		5.1	4.2	3.8	3.3	2.9	2.9	2.9	2.7	2.0	1.8	1.3	.9
RANK		1	2	3.5	3.5	5	6.5	6.5	8	9	10	11	12

[a]For key to symbols, see Table 10.3.

Washington and the Khmer Rouge. Baker then endorsed the idea of "free and fair" elections so that the Khmer Rouge could run as a party, with a few hundred non-Khmer-speaking UN personnel to provide security in thousands of villages, but pooh-poohed the problem of Khmer Rouge voter intimidation.

Meanwhile, Australia, Canada, Japan, New Zealand, and Western European countries broke with Washington by reinstituting aid programs to Cambodia and Vietnam. Then came increased investment and trade.

During March Chatichai threatened to close the camps on the Thai-Cambodian border that the resistance forces had used as a recruiting ground and furlough site for their armies over the previous decade. In April, when Thai Deputy Prime Minister Chaovalit Yongchaiyut arranged for cease-fire pledges from all four factional leaders, Japanese Prime Minister Toshiki Kaifu invited the four to resume the intra-Cambodian dialogue at Tokyo in early June.

When the four Cambodian factions met in Tokyo, all but the Khmer Rouge agreed to form a Supreme National Council (SNC) as a transitional body. When the Khmer Rouge appeared to hold out for a military solution, Bush overruled NSC Adviser Brent Scowcroft's hardline policy toward Cambodia and accepted Bakers' twofold proposal—to drop the tripartite resistance coalition and to recognize the SNC as the representative of Cambodia at the UN as well as to negotiate with Vietnam. Baker and Bush wanted to accelerate the peace process. In August the Perm Five agreed to the outlines of a text for a UN transitional body for Cambodia, and in September the four Cambodian factions held the first SNC meeting at Bangkok but adjourned *sine die* in a dispute over who would chair the body. In November the Perm Five met at Jakarta and Paris to adopt a comprehensive agreement for a UN body for Cambodia. In December the SNC met; chaired by France. The resistance accepted the Perm Five plan, but Hun Sen wanted more concrete assurances on the non-return of the Khmer Rouge. The year 1990 ended with an impasse.

Our options analysis, thus, predicted the subsequent course of events, notably Baker's quiet diplomacy at a time when there was no report of his secret efforts on behalf of the Perm Five process. Democratic options displaced Bush administration figleaves for nonpolicy when events and hearings embarrassed Baker. Because the newer U.S. policies were in accord with goals held by both Democrats and Republicans, the agenda of the congressional Democrats was advanced.

As I write these lines at the end of 1990, the Cambodian peace process continues. It is a few steps closer to ending the war. Whereas the Bush and Reagan administrations failed to develop foreign policy through bipartisan consultation for over a decade, Congress and other countries around the world were more democratic in deliberating foreign policies. The U.S. government finally reached policy conclusions that were realistic and reasonable.

NOTES

1. For further background on the war in Cambodia, see Elizabeth Becker, *The War after the War* (New York: Simon and Schuster, 1986); Nayan Chanda, *Brother Enemy* (New York: Simon and Schuster, 1986). These sources are summarized in Chap. 1 of my *Genocide by Proxy* (New York: Praeger, 1991).

2. ASEAN's original members were Indonesia, Malaysia, the Philippines, Singapore, and Thailand.

3. "Vietnamese Says Army Will Stay in Cambodia Till Regime Is Firm," *New York Times*, Nov. 7, 1979, p. A-5.

4. For more details on U.S. policies toward Cambodia, see William Shawcross, *Sideshow* (New York: Simon and Schuster, 1979); Haas, *Beyond the Killing Fields*, Chap. 6, 15, 24.

5. Accounts of the current Cambodian peace process are in Elizabeth Becker, "The Progress of Peace in Cambodia," *Current History* 88 (Apr. 1989): 169ff.; Nayan Chanda, "Civil War in Cambodia?" *Foreign Policy* 76 (Fall 1989): 26–43; Haas, *Beyond the Killing Fields*, Chaps. 11, 20.

6. Brunei, joined ASEAN in 1984.

7. *Decision Pad* (Menlo Park: Apian Software, 1988).

8. He is representative Jim Leach. See Hurst Hannum, "International Law and the Cambodian Genocide: The Sounds of Silence," *Human Rights Quarterly* 11 (Feb. 1989): 82–138.

PART VI

Improving Systematic Analysis with Math and Decision-Aiding Software

CHAPTER 11

Decision-Aiding Software and Alternative Dispute Resolution

LINDA M. V. LISK

If the plaintiff in a civil case demands $100,000 and the defendant is only offering a $10,000 settlement, how can each simultaneously get benefits exceeding their initial best expectations? If a prosecutor estimates that a five-year prison sentence is the maximum for a criminal case, and the defendant's best realistic outcome seems to be a one-year prison term, what result will guarantee that both the prosecutor and the defendant will realize more than their initial best estimates?[1] The answer lies in decision-aiding software and creative lawyering. Attorneys can utilize certain microcomputer software, such as Policy/Goal Percentaging (P/G%),[2] to enhance negotiations so that seemingly impossible optimizing solutions can be determined and evaluated with greater ease. Answers to the above questions and others concerning decision-aiding software, including legal and ethical considerations, will be explored in this chapter. Also, an actual case will be used to explain and evaluate the P/G% program.

The P/G% program is an expert system, meaning that the instructions the computer executes are substantially the same as the thought process or decision-making process of a human expert in the field.[3] Therefore, an understanding of this thought process is necessary in evaluating the software.

The overall goal envisioned for use of this software is aiding in creating super-optimum or win-plus solutions as opposed to win-loss or win-win approaches. Litigation outcomes are generally perceived as being win-loss situations, where for one party to gain the other party must give up something. A traditional negotiating approach is to compromise or split the difference between the plaintiff's and defendant's expectations. This solution, although sometimes referred to as win-win or pareto-optimum,[4] actually only ensures that each side gets something rather than losing if going to trial. The P/G% program can aid the user in creating a win-plus solution, whereby both parties exceed their initial best expectations by expanding the single bargaining criterion, such as money damages, to multi-criteria. Formulating such a settlement involves the defendant offering some criteria to which it assigns a low value, but to which the plaintiff assigns a high value.[5]

A simple civil case illustrates the different goals. The traditional approaches to negotiation would result in compromising the plaintiff's expectation of $700,000 and the defendant's estimate of $350,000 by averaging the positions, reaching approximately $500,000.[6] Thus the plaintiff receives some damages and the defendant is not required to pay the initial plaintiff's demand—a win-win approach. A win-plus result can be achieved by exploring criteria that the plaintiff values more than the defendant does. For instance, if the defendant is a manufacturer, then the defendant's products could be transferred to the plaintiff, such as an electronics manufacturer offering a plaintiff insurance company a computer package. The plaintiff may value the package at the market price of $800,000 and use the products in an employee incentive plan, while the cost to the defendant may be less than $350,000. If the defendant is an insurance company, a win-plus agreement could be based on the defendant issuing an annuity to the plaintiff for $10,000 payable yearly for life beginning at age 65. The plaintiff may value the annuity settlement as more valuable than the initial demand of $100,000, if the plaintiff lives to age 85, $200,000 will be accumulated. The defendant insurance company can invest the $20,000 it initially offered until the plaintiff reaches age 65.[7] Other possibilities for super-optimum solutions include performance agreements,[8] lifetime use certificates for the defendant's products or services,[9] or institutional reform that benefits both parties.[10]

An example from criminal law is the option of joining the military service as an alternative to incarceration. The prosecutor may feel such a settlement saves taxpayers' money both on trial and incarceration costs. The defendant may benefit by avoiding jail, receiving training, and gaining pride in serving the country.[11] Policy considerations arise, however, when a negotiated super-optimum solution results in the deterrent purposes of criminal remedies being avoided. Nagel explains:

[W]e probably do not want defendants to go away from negotiations in criminal cases feeling that they have achieved something greater than their best expectations. Doing so could have an adverse effect on the higher goal of decreasing crime, even if it is in accordance with the lower goal of facilitating out-of-court settlements.[12]

GENERAL BENEFITS IN ALTERNATE DISPUTE RESOLUTION

Obviously some of these alternatives have previously been utilized without the aid of computers. What, then, are the benefits of using decision-aiding software?

Also, not all cases would seem to lend themselves to multi-criteria analysis, such as when the defendant in a civil case is an individual rather than an insurance company or a manufacturer. Are there any benefits to using P/G% in such cases?

Decision-aiding software has numerous benefits for mediation.[13] Utilizing the program requires attorneys and their clients to make what was an implicit decision-making process more explicit. Attorneys naturally assess alternatives and their values without the aid of computers. A decision-aiding program forces this analysis to be more methodical. Also, the program allows evaluation of several criteria with different valuations to be compared simultaneously, which is more difficult without computer matrix use.

The P/G% program is flexible enough to facilitate both process dispute resolution and subject-matter dispute resolution. Process dispute resolution involves deciding among available processes of dispute resolution, such as mediation, arbitration, and adjudication. Another process application is deciding between settlement or trial for a specific case. Subject-matter dispute resolution refers to the alternative outcomes of the specific dispute,[14] such as whether the defendant should agree to pay money damages or to transfer products to the plaintiff.

STEPS IN P/G% UTILIZATION

A simple process dispute resolution example of comparing adjudication, arbitration, and mediation will illustrate the P/G% process step by step.

STEP 1

1. Determine the initial alternatives, the criteria, and the relations the alternatives and the criteria in light of each side's values and perceptions. The P/G% input-format facilitates clarification of those dispute parameters.[15]

The alternatives are: (1) adjudication with a judge who can issue an order that is subject to review; (2) arbitration with a party-chosen decider who can issue a binding order; or (3) mediation by a party-chosen mediator without binding power. The criteria used in this example to evelute the alternatives are: (1) avoiding delay in resolving the dispute; (2) the finality or binding effect; (3) a mutually beneficial solution as opposed to a win-lose solution; and (4) the ability for one side to initiate or compel the other party into a dispute resolution process without the other side's consent. The relations among the alternatives and the criteria are measured on a scale of 1 to 3, where 1 is unfavorable, 2 is neutral, and 3 is favorable. (See Table 11.1 for the relations.) Adjudication scores unfavorably to delay reduction, whereas arbitration and mediation score mildly favorably. On finality, arbitration is best, adjudication neutral, and mediation worst. Mediation scores favorably on finding a mutually beneficial solution, however, followed by arbitration, then adjudication. On initiating an action without another's consent, adjudication is most favorable, mediation is unfavorable, and arbitration is between the two. The weight of the criteria can be specified to account for

Table 11.1
Alternative Methods of Dispute Resolution

A. HOW THE THREE ALTERNATIVES SCORE ON FOUR CRITERIA

Alternative	Delay	Finality	Mutual B	Initiate	Combined Rawscore
1 Adjudication	1.00	2.00	1.00	3.00	7.00
2 Arbitration	2.50	3.00	2.00	2.00	9.50
3 Mediation	2.50	1.00	3.00	1.00	7.50

B. COMPARING ADJUDICATION WITH ARBITRATION

	Ajudication	Arbitration	Weight
Delay	3.50	0.00	-0.667
Finality	4.50	0.50	-1.500
Mutual Benefit	3.50	-0.50	-1.500
Initiate-Consent	5.50	-0.50	3.500

C. COMPARING ARBITRATION WITH MEDIATION

	Arbitration	Mediation	Weight
Delay	0.50	4.50	??
FInality	1.00	3.00	-0.000
Mutual Benefit	0.00	5.00	3.000
Initiate-Consent	0.00	3.00	-1.000

D. COMPARING ADJUDICATION WITH MEDIATION

	Adjudication	Mediation	Weight
Delay	1.50	2.00	0.667
Finality	2.50	0.50	1.500
Mutual Benefit	1.50	2.50	0.750
Initiate-Consent	3.50	0.50	1.250

Source: Adapted from "Multi-Criteria Methods," p. 149.

their relative importance. A negative weight is used to indicate a cost. If all criteria in this example are given equal weights of 1, arbitration receives the highest overall score. This score is calculated by multiplying the criteria value by the weight for each criterion and summing these products of each alternative. So the arbitration score of 9.5 is reached by simply adding across the row of arbitration scores since the weight is 1 for all criteria. Since the arbitration score is highest, arbitration rather than adjudication or mediation initially is the best choice.[16]

STEP 2

2. Determine what it would take each side to convince the other side. The threshold, break-even, or tie-causing analysis of the P/G% program facilitates that determination.[17]

The threshold analysis compares two of the alternatives and calculates what change in each criterion or its weight, if it were the only change made, would cause a tie score between those alternatives. In our example, a threshold analysis of adjudication and arbitration indicates that if the weight of initiating an action without the other's consent is increased from 1.0 to 3.5, and all the other original values remain, then the overall value of adjudication would match that of arbitration. The other threshold analysis scores are interpreted as meaningless or practically impossible since they are outside the 1–3 range. Similar threshold analysis is shown for arbitration versus mediation, and for adjudication versus mediation.[18]

Additional steps in the P/G% process are not directly applicable to this general example, but they are listed here and may be illustrated in later examples.

STEPS 3–7

3. Experiment with a variety of additional alternatives, as contrasted to the original deadlock alternatives. Look especially for new alternatives that could be endorsed by both sides more strongly than their original first choices.

4. Try changing the alternatives by subtracting some, by consolidating two or more, or by subdividing some. Try doing the same things with the criteria.

5. Try changing the criterion weights, or try averaging the alternatives in light of the different sets of weights the conflicting that disputants have.

6. Try working with reasonable minimum and/or maximum constraints on the criteria and/or the alternatives to see what difference that makes.

7. Try changing some of the relation scores and maybe the measurement units on which the scores are based.[19]

NEIGHBORHOOD DISPUTE EXAMPLE: PROCESS DECISION WITH VARIATIONS

Another example involving a property dispute between a plaintiff who recently purchased property adjacent to the defendant landowner's property shows how specific facts fit into the P/G% program. The example will illustrate the steps listed above and give a software user's perspective. The relevant facts are that plaintiff purchased the house and lot adjacent to the defendant's property without obtaining title insurance or surveying the property. A dispute as to the boundary lines of the newly purchased property arose when the plaintiff asked the defendant to move his utility meter off her property. The plaintiff subsequently surveyed the property, which confirmed her belief that the three- to four-foot strip in question was hers. The defendant disputed the property boundary and had evidence supporting an adverse possession claim on the four-foot area. The parties could not reach an informal agreement, but are considering some form of mediation before resorting to trial.

The P/G% program has several attributes that can aid in resolving such a dispute. In such a situation, the program can be used by one party to evaluate possibilities and probable outcomes. Another use for the decision-aiding program, however, is to present a numerical representation of the alternatives and note how any change in the data affects these alternatives. When used during mediation, both the plaintiff's and defendant's perspectives should be considered. In many mediations, relevant criteria may by necessity be measured in different units. For example, damages can generally easily be valued in currency, whereas important subjective factors, such as the finality of a dispute process, are easier to measure on a numerical 1–3 scale. P/G% computes results through a percentaging method to allow simultaneous comparisons of criteria measured in different scales.[20]

Initially a file must be set up for the data through the P/G% File Management option by simple menu selection and typing in the file name. The first step is to determine the alternatives, the criteria, and weights, and input this data through the Data Management option. The relevant alternatives are litigation or mediation on the process level shown in Table 11.2. From the plaintiff's perspective the criteria are the cost of litigation (10 hours × $85/hour), the possible benefits from litigation (2 on a 1–5 scale) weighted by the probability of gaining these benefits (assume 100% chance), costs of settling (2 hours × $75/hour), benefits of settling (4 on a 1–5 scale) weighted by the estimated probability of gaining those benefits (100%), maintaining a good relationship with the neighbor (on a 1–5 scale, trial is 2 and settlement is 4), and reaching a final agreement (on a 1–5 scale, trial is 2 and settlement is 1). (See Tables 11.3 and 11.4.) Then the Primary Analysis menu option is selected, producing Table 11.5 showing that settling is better than litigating. Table 11.6 shows the intermediate computations to reach the Primary Analysis results. The part/whole percentages in Table 11.7 are calculated by assigning a percentage amount of each criterion to the alternatives. These percentages are then multiplied by the weights assigned to the criteria

The threshold or tie-causing evaluation is next performed by selecting the appropriate menu option and selecting which alternatives to compare. Here settling and litigating are compared to see what value each criterion and its weight would have to become to obtain a tie between litigating and settling. Table 11.8 shows the results. Interpreting the data involves discarding statistically impractical and unrealistic numbers to reach meaningful results. Here, trial costs and benefits are irrelevant for settlement analysis, as are settlement costs and benefits for litigation analysis. Percentages that are negative or exceed 1.00, that is, 100 percent,

Table 11.2
Alternatives

| Alternative | Budgets | |
	Minimum	Actual
1 SETTLE	0.00	0.00
2 LITIGATE	0.00	0.00

Table 11.3
Criteria

Criterion	Measuring Unit	Weight
TRIAL COSTS	$/HR	-.85
TRIAL BENEFITS	1-5	1.00
SETTLE COSTS	$/HR	-.75
SETTLE BENEFITS	1-5	1.00
GOOD NEIGHBOR	1-5	1.00
FINALITY	1-5	1.00

Table 11.4
Relation Scores

	Alternative/Criteria Scoring					
	Trial Cost	Trial Benefits	Settle Cost	Settle Benefits	Good Neighbor	Finality
SETTLE	0.00	0.00	2.00	4.00	4.00	2.00
LITIGATE	10.00	2.00	0.00	0.00	2.00	4.00

Table 11.5
Total Scores

Alternative	Combined W P/W	%
1 SETTLE	125.00	52.08
2 LITIGATE	115.00	47.92

Table 11.6
Part/Whole Percentages

	Trial Cost	Trial Benefits	Settle Cost	Settle Benefits	Good Neighbor	Finality
SETTLE	0.00	0.00	100.00	100.00	66.67	33.33
LITIGATE	100.00	100.00	0.00	0.00	33.33	66.67

Table 11.7
Weighted Part/Whole Percentages

	Trial Cost	Trial Benefits	Settle Cost	Settle Benefits	Good Neighbor	Finality
SETTLE	-0.00	0.00	-75.00	100.00	66.67	33.33
LITIGATE	-85.00	100.00	0.00	0.00	33.33	66.67

Table 11.8
Threshold Analysis

	Settle	Litigate	Weights
TRIAL COSTS	0.63	0.00	-0.750
TRIAL BENEFITS	-0.10	-0.00	1.100
SETTLE COSTS	-0.00	-0.12	-0.850
SETTLE BENEFITS	0.00	0.21	0.900
GOOD NEIGHBOR	3.22	2.49	0.700
FINALITY	1.58	5.06	1.300

are not statistically possible. Therefore, litigation would be as beneficial as settlement: (1) if the weight or probability of gaining settlement benefits is decreased to 90 percent; (2) if the neighbor value for settling decreased from 4 to 3.22, or if the neighbor value for litigating increased from 2 to 2.49; (3) if the weight of the neighbor relationship decreased to 70 percent, meaning that criterion is not as important as the others; or (4) if the finality score changed to 1.58 for settling or approximately 5 for litigation.

Factoring the probability of gain at settlement or trial into the criteria is done by changing the weights for them. One can show the expectation of winning the trial benefits is 50 percent and the settlement probability is 75 percent. If all the other values are the same, then the result shown in Table 11.9 does not change. Settling is still better than litigation. The threshold analysis indicates that litigation becomes as good as settlement: (1) if the trial benefits weight increases to 85 percent; (2) if the weight of settling benefits decreases to 40 percent; (3) if the neighbor relationship values change; or (4) if the lawyer's hourly rate for trial is $50/hour or $110/hour for settling (see Table 11.10). The trial weight can be helpful to show that any disagreement over the probability of winning in the 50 to 85 percent range would not change the outcome. The decrease in the probability of a successful settlement could occur with changing circumstances, and also shows that a wide margin of error exists before a change in the weight would affect the outcome. It would probably not be realistic to expect a better neighbor relationship from litigation than settlement. Also, the attorney threshold rates are unrealistic since settlement costs generally are much less than litigation costs.

Table 11.9
Total Scores with a New .50 Victory Probability

Alternative	Combined W P/W	%
1 SETTLE	100.00	60.61
2 LITIGATE	65.00	39.39

Table 11.10
Threshold Analysis with a New .50 Probability

	Settle	Litigate	Weights
TRIAL COSTS	2.59	0.00	-0.500
TRIAL BENEFITS	-0.52	-0.00	0.850
SETTLE COSTS	-0.00	-0.38	-1.100
SETTLE BENEFITS	0.00	1.22	0.400
GOOD NEIGHBOR	1.93	4.14	-.050
FINALITY	.75	10.63	2.050

A further variation on the analysis is dividing one alternative into two alternatives. In Table 11.11, the settlement alternative has been divided into arbitration and negotiation. See Table 11.12 for the scores of each alternative on the criteria. After analysis, negotiation is the best alternative, followed by arbitration, then litigation (see Table 11.13). A threshold analysis of the arbitration and negotiation alternatives on Table 11.14 suggest that if the relations for the criteria of settlement costs, settlement benefits, or a neighbor relationship were reversed, then the arbitration scores would tie the negotiation scores.

Another evaluation tool is to vary the measurement scales. The effect of measuring the trial benefits and settlement benefits in hundreds of dollars rather than a 1–5 scale is shown in Tables 11.15 through 11.18. If the estimated benefits are $2,000 each for litigation, arbitration, and negotiation, then negotiation remains preferable, with arbitration a close second and litigation a distant third. The threshold data interpretation is similar to the prior one. When currency values are used, the present value can be factored into the program by simply inputting an appropriate rate and time period. The appropriate rate can roughly be determined by subtracting the predicted inflation rate from the interest rates.[21] For instance, if the damages from trial would not be available for two years and the interest rate is approximately 10 percent with a 4 percent inflation rate, the $2,000 damages are actually worth only $1,780 in today's dollars.

When using the P/G% program during mediation, both the plaintiff's and the defendant's perspectives should be processed. In the property line dispute, the defendant's perspective is presented in Table 11.19. Additional facts are needed to quantify the defendant's perspective. The defendant was represented by an attorney at no cost through a legal clinic. Also, the plaintiff employed the defendant's son as part-time gardener. The alternatives are settling or litigating. The criteria used are the trial benefits, the proof and miscellaneous costs of litigation,

Table 11.11
New Alternatives

	Alternative	Budgets	
		Minimum	Actual
1	ARBITRATE	0.00	0.00
2	NEGOTIATE	0.00	0.00
3	LITIGATE	0.00	0.00

Table 11.12
New Relation Scores

Alternative/Criteria Scoring						
	Trial Cost	Trial Benefits	Settle Cost	Settle Benefits	Good Neighbor	Finality
ARBITRATE	0.00	0.00	5.00	3.00	3.00	4.00
NEGOTIATE	0.00	0.00	3.00	4.00	4.00	2.00
LITIGATE	10.00	2.00	0.00	0.00	2.00	3.00

Table 11.13
New Total Scores

	Alternative	Combined W P/W	%
1	ARBITRATE	63.05	38.21
2	NEGOTIATE	81.40	49.33
3	LITIGATE	20.56	12.46

Table 11.14
New Threshold Analysis

	Arbitrate	Negotiate	Weights
TRIAL COSTS	-1.78	2.75	??????
TRIAL BENEFITS	1.16	-0.54	??????
SETTLE COSTS	3.03	4.95	-.016
SETTLE BENEFITS	4.91	2.45	-.535
GOOD NEIGHBOR	4.78	2.46	-.652
FINALITY	6.78	.82	1.826

Table 11.15
New Measuring Units

Criterion	Measuring Unit	Weight
TRIAL COSTS	$100/HR	-.85
TRIAL BENEFITS	$100	.50
SETTLE COSTS	$100/HR	-.75
SETTLE BENEFITS	$100	.75
GOOD NEIGHBOR	1-5	1.00
FINALITY	1-5	1.00

Table 11.16
Relations with New Units

		Alternative/Criteria Scoring				
	Trial Cost	Trial Benefits	Settle Cost	Settle Benefits	Good Neighbor	Finality
ARBITRATE	0.00	0.00	5.00	20.00	3.00	4.00
SETTLE	0.00	0.00	3.00	20.00	4.00	2.00
LITIGATE	10.00	20.00	0.00	0.00	2.00	3.00

Table 11.17
Total Scores with New Units

Alternative	Combined W P/W	%
1 ARBITRATE	68.40	41.46
2 NEGOTIATE	76.04	46.09
3 LITIGATE	20.56	12.46

Table 11.18
Threshold Analysis with New Units

	Arbitrate	Negotiate	Weights
TRIAL COSTS	-0.82	0.99	??????
TRIAL BENEFITS	3.61	-2.65	??????
SETTLE COSTS	4.04	3.71	-.444
SETTLE BENEFITS	24.54	16.30	?????
GOOD NEIGHBOR	3.66	3.29	0.313
FINALITY	4.98	1.47	1.344

187

Table 11.19
Defendant's Perspective

Criterion	Measuring Unit	Weight
TRIAL BENEFITS	1-3	.80
MISC. COSTS	$100	-1.00
SETTLE BENEFITS	1-3	.50
GOOD NEIGHBOR	1-3	1.00
EMPLOY RELATIVE	1(N)/2(Y)	1.00

the settlement benefits, the neighbor relationship, and the continued employment of the defendant's relative by the plaintiff. The trial benefits are high because the defendant had an adverse possession claim to the four-foot strip of land, with about an 80 percent chance of winning that claim at trial. Proving that claim necessitates some costs, perhaps a survey cost of $100. The settlement benefits are slightly less than the trial benefits, with only a 50 percent chance of gaining those benefits. Settling is more conducive than litigating for neighborly relations and for employment of the defendant's son.

The P/G% analysis calculates settling as far more beneficial than litigating for the defendant. All data achieved from the threshold analysis is statistically impossible. Further experimentation with the alternatives, criteria, weights, and values would be necessary for thorough evaluation of the defendant's perspective.

SUBJECT-MATTER DECISION

Once a process decision has been made, subject-matter decisions can be processed through P/G%. Here the attorney should be creative in determining the possible alternatives and their criteria. By expansive thinking and consideration of multi-criteria, the mediator can often fashion a super-optimum solution at this stage. The property line dispute will illustrate the subject-matter decision process from the plaintiff's perspective. First, the alternatives should be fully explored. One alternative is the mediator awarding the land to the plaintiff. Another possibility is the mediator deciding damages are the appropriate remedy. A third possibility is the parties agreeing to split the four feet of land evenly and straighten the otherwise uneven property line (see Table 11.20).

Important criteria include the expense to the plaintiff, the effect on the plaintiff's property value, the probable compliance with the alternative, and the neighbor relation, as measured in Table 11.21. Using criteria scoring indicated in Table 11.22, altering the property line is the best choice. Awarding damages is slightly better than awarding the land. The threshold analysis first compares the determining land ownership alternative with the property line adjustment alternative. Then the property line adjustment is compared to awarding damages (see Tables 11.23 and 11.24). Both threshold analyses reveal that a shift in the neighborly relation criterion could make a difference, but other criteria and weights are impractical.

Table 11.20
Property Alternatives

| Alternative | Budgets | |
	Minimum	Actual
1 WIN LAND	0.00	0.00
2 PROPERTY LINE	0.00	0.00
3 DAMAGES	0.00	0.00

Table 11.21
Property Criteria

Criteria	Measuring Unit	Weight
EXPENSE	$100	-1.00
PROPERTY VALUE	1-3	1.00
COMPLIANCE	1-3	1.00
GOOD NEIGHBOR	1-3	1.00

Table 11.22
Property Relation Scores

	Expense	Property Value	Compliance	Good Neighbors
WIN LAND	2.00	3.00	1.00	1.00
PROPERTY LINE	2.00	2.00	2.00	3.00
DAMAGES	1.00	1.00	2.00	1.00

Table 11.23
Property Total Scores

Alternative	Combined W P/W	%
1 WIN LAND	50.00	25.00
2 PROPERTY LINE	93.33	46.67
3 DAMAGES	56.67	28.33

Table 11.24
Property Threshold Analysis

	WIN LAND	PROPERTY LINE	WEIGHTS
EXPENSE	.49	5.82	??????
PROPERTY VALUE	9.50	.37	3.600
COMPLIANCE	3.83	.24	-1.167
GOOD NEIGHBOR	3.24	.94	-0.083

	PROPERTY LINE	DAMAGES	WEIGHTS
EXPENSE	6.23	-0.17	-2.833
PROPERTY VALUE	.17	3.75	-1.200
COMPLIANCE	.6ε	4.89	???????
GOOD NEIGHBOR	1.10	2.77	0.083

PERCEIVED BENEFITS

Considering the general and specific information already presented, several benefits of using decision-aiding software like P/G% become apparent. When the decision-making process is more obvious, mediators and parties are forced to consider the alternatives, criteria, and weights that otherwise would involve gut reactions. The P/G% program can process criteria quantified in different measurement units through a percentaging technique, allowing subjective and non-monetary factors to be evaluated. P/G% can aid mediation on both a process selection level and on a subject-matter decision. The threshold analysis helps determine what a criterion's value or weight has on the outcome. Also threshold data can reduce the dispute issues where estimation of a probability or value may be the basis, since the disputed values may fall within the range that would not affect the outcome.

DECISION-AIDING SOFTWARE AND
LAWYERING ETHICALLY

Representational Conflicts

An attorney should consider the ethical implications of utilizing decision-aiding software. Generally, the use of an expert system, such as P/G%, encourages attorneys to use an explicit decision process rather than make implicit determinations. Explicit decision-making may make more explicit an ethical problem:

Being more explicit can generate an interesting ethical cost that Jim Sprowl (1986) has raised, namely that it forces lawyers to think more clearly about the goals they should be pursuing. That could be considered a benefit to improving the legal profession, even if it creates dilemmas for individual lawyers.[22]

A situation where P/G% clearly shows a potential ethical decision involves a representational conflict of interest when the client is better off settling and the attorney is better off litigating, or vice versa.[23] For example, suppose P/G% is used to determine whether to settle or to litigate from both the client's and the attorney's perspective in a damages case. Suppose that using a contingency fee basis, the lawyer receives 33 percent of any trial damages and 20 percent of any settlement. The relevant criteria would be the estimated trial damages, the estimated trial costs, the settlement offer, and the settlement costs. The criteria and their weights are also found in Table 11.25. If the estimated probability of winning is 65 percent, then the lawyer's probability of gain is 22 percent (.65 × .33) of the total damages. The client's damage recovery weight is .43 (.65 × .67). Assume that the lawyer charges $30 per hour for litigation, and $20 per hour for settlement. The −1 weight for the client's litigation and settlement costs indicates that these costs are figured as a lump sum as opposed to figuring by an hourly rate. For the settlement offer weights, the table shows that the client keeps 80 percent of the offer and the lawyer 20 percent. Table 11.25-C shows a predicted value of a $3,000 damage award, 20 hours of attorney time, and $400 of trial cost to the client. A settlement offer of $1,000 would involve 5 hours of attorney time and no additional client cost. From the lawyer's perspective, settling is better than litigating. The client, however, would prefer to litigate. Therefore, a representational conflict of interest becomes apparent.

Using threshold analysis on the criteria from the client's perspective results in determining what it would take to get the client to settle, which can lead to resolution of the conflict. Settling would be as beneficial to the client as litigating if: (1) the estimated damages from trial would decrease to $2,769.23; (2) the probability of receiving damages drops from 43 to 40 percent; (3) the litigation costs increase to $500; (4) the settlement offer increases to $1,125; or (5) the client would keep 90 percent of the settlement offer. Changing the weight for receiving damages could occur if the initial probability of winning is closer to 60 percent rather than 65 percent. Theoretically, the 40 percent damage multiplier could also be achieved if the client agreed to accept only 60 percent or less of the damages rather than 67 percent. It is unlikely, however, that the client will be receptive to accepting less than specified in the original contingency fee agreement. Similarly, it is unlikely that the lawyer will allow the client to keep 90 percent of the settlement offer when 80 percent was originally agreed upon. The realistic possibilities are narrowed to overestimating the probable damage award, underestimating the litigation costs, or increasing the settlement offer. The attorney should attempt to solve the conflict by attempting to get a settlement offer of at least $1,125.

From the attorney's perspective, litigating is better than settlement. The attorney would prefer settling if: (1) the damages estimate should be increased to $3,230.77; (2) the trial hours decrease to 18.33 or if the settlement hours increase to 7.5; (3) the settlement offer is reduced to $750; or (4) either the litigation multiplier is underestimated or if the attorney would accept only 15 percent

Table 11.25

Computer-Aided Negotiation: A Damages Case

A. The Alternatives of Trial versus Settlement

Alternative
1. Go to Trial
2. Settle

B. The Criteria and Weights of the Benefits and Costs

Criterion	Meas. Unit	Weight
1 (L)Dams.if Won	$	0.22
2 (C)Dams.if Won		0.43
3 (L)Lit.Hours		-30.00
4 (C)Lit.Costs		-1.00
5 (L)Set.Offer		0.20
6 (C)Set.Offer		0.80
7 (L)Set.Hours		-20.00
8 (C)Set.Costs		-1.00

C. Scoring the Alternatives on the Criteria for Trial

	(L)Dams.	(C)Dams.	(L)Lit.H	(C)Lit.C
Go To Trial	3000.00	3000.00	20.00	400.00
Settle	0.00	0.00	0.00	0.00

D. Scoring the Alternatives on the Criteria for Settlement

	(L)Set.O	(C)Set.O	(L)Set.H	(C)Set.C
Go to Trial	0.00	0.00	0.00	0.00
Settle	1000.00	1000.00	5.00	0.00

E. The Overall Results from the Lawyer's Perspective

	(L)Dams.	(L)Lit.H	(L)Set.O	(L)Set.H	Combined Rawscores
Go to Trial	650.00	-600.00	0.00	-0.00	50.00
Settle	0.00	-0.00	200.00	-100.00	100.00

F. The Overall Results from the Client's Perspective

	(C)Dams.	(C)Lit.C	(C)Set.O	(C)Set.C	Combined Rawscores
Go to Trial	1300.00	-400.00	0.00	-0.00	900.00
Settle	0.00	-0.00	800.00	-0.00	800.00

G. What It Would Take to Get the Client to Settle

	Go to Trial	Settle	Weight
(C)Dams. If Won	2769.23		0.400
(C)Lit.Costs	500.00		
(C)Set.Offer		1125.00	0.900
(C)Set.Costs		-100.00	

H. What It Would Take to Get the Lawyer to Trial

	Go to Trial	Settle	Weight
(L)Dams. If Won	3230.77		0.233
(L)Lit.Hours	18.33		-27.500
(L)Set.Offer		750.00	0.150
(L)Set.Hours		7.50	-30.000

---

of the settlement offer. If the damages have been underestimated, increasing the amount would solve the conflict. The option of changing the weights by changing the original contingency percent for the lawyer is again unlikely. If, instead, the probability of winning damages is at least 70 percent, then litigation is as attractive as settling. If possible, the attorney should strive to increase the probability of winning without adversely affecting other criteria to solve the conflict.[24] This may be unrealistic if a lawyer is asked to do more than possible with the facts of the case. However, P/G% analysis on a subject level may aid in deciding which specific aspect of the case, such as which issue should be emphasized, could result in increasing the trial win probability without great increase in litigation costs.[25]

Other solutions to the representational conflict are unacceptable or unrealistic. If the initial hour estimates are the best possible, then an attorney should not reallocate time based on personal profit. Instead, lawyers must represent their clients zealously,[26] which involves spending appropriate hours to adequately represent clients. If the lawyer's best estimate is 20 hours for trial, then agreeing to litigate and limiting the hours to approximately 18 would be unethical. Considering the hours spent is helpful, however, to quantify how much error in estimated hour allocation would change the attorney's preference. The attorney in this case may decide that the risk of error in estimating trial time correctly to within 1.5 to 2 hours is enough to pursue trial anyway. The attorney would not want to artificially increase settlement hours since that would reduce dollar per hour return, yet the information is again helpful to determine what threshold value would make a difference. Also, if an initial settlement offer has been made, an attorney would not pursue a lesser amount.

After the above analysis, one must ask if ethical considerations even allow an attorney to use decision-aiding software to determine if there is a representational conflict and quantify such a conflict. Model Rule 1.7(b): "A lawyer shall not represent a client if the representation of that client may be materially limited . . . by the lawyer's own interests, unless: (2) the client consents after consultation."[27] Therefore, if a conflict exists, the attorney may still represent the client after disclosure of the conflict.[28] Disciplinary Rule 5-101(A) echoes the Model Rule: "Except with the consent of his client after full disclosure, a lawyer shall not accept employment if the exercise of his professional judgment on behalf of his client will be or reasonably may be affected by his own financial, business, property, or personal interests."[29] Ethical Consideration 5-7 clarifies that contingency fee arrangements are not included in prohibited proprietary interests.[30] The actual decision whether to accept a settlement is the client's, so the lawyer can use decision-aiding analysis before accepting employment to determine if a conflict exists, and if so to inform the client of the extent and how it can be resolved.

Nagel further suggests that making the conflicts more visible by use of decision-aiding software may be good or bad, "depending upon what is done with that increased awareness."[31] After presenting an example similar to the one above, Nagel concludes:

1. If it is more profitable to the lawyer to go to trial, but it is more profitable to the client to settle or vice versa, then the lawyer should seek to increase the settlement to make settling more profitable to both of the[m]. The increase need only go as high as the threshold or tie-causing value of the settlement offer.

2. As an alternative, the lawyer should seek to increase the expected value of going [t]o trial in order to make going to trial more profitable to both of them. The increase need only go as high as making the trial even more profitable to the client than settling. The lawyer need not push for still more profit for the client when it means operating at a decreased profit to the lawyer or even an increased loss.

3. If in a rare situation, it is impossible to make settling or going to trial more profitable to both the client and the lawyer, then the lawyer should choose between settling and going to trial in light of the client's best interests.

4. Perhaps lawyers of the future should have an ethical obligation to systematically determine the relative profitability of settling and going to trial to the client and the lawyer at differing degrees of effort in order to be able to implement the above ethical principles to their mutual profit.[32]

OTHER ETHICAL ISSUES

Other ethical issues concerning attorneys' use of decision-aiding software are relatively unexplored. This technological advance should be shadowed by explicit ethical responsibilities. Liability for nonuse or misuse of computer programs can set a minimum legal standard of performance.[33] Ethics, however, addresses higher standards of conduct that are widely accepted in society.[34] Therefore, exploring questions of potential liability for a lawyer's nonuse or misuse of computer software is helpful, but inadequate to delineate the social expectations that can be embodied in an ethics code. Several organizations have developed ethical codes to regulate computer professionals.[35] The negligence laws and the computer ethics codes are geared to develop appropriate standards in the producer-user relationship and do not adequately address the ethical responsibilities involved in an attorney-client relationship or the mediator-client relationship. Well-defined ethics are needed to aid in creating and using appropriate expert systems.[36]

Ethical considerations specific to decision-aiding software use in alternate dispute resolution includes valuation, access, disclosure, and machine bias. Valuation refers to the weight given to computer capabilities. The user should perceive the computer as a tool and understand its capabilities and limitations. Otherwise society can become overly computer-dependent.[37] Perceiving the computer as error-free and with super-human knowledge could lead to improper weight given to the decision-aiding results. Also, learning of skills could be foregone if the user can rely on an expert system to provide the expertise needed.[38]

The ethical problem in all this is that those who sell and make use of computers emphasize what it can do and forget to tell people its limitations. . . . Until humans program the computer to match human capabilities, it is still a machine. This fact must be stressed to those of us who purchase and use them. We must not forget our capabilities just because the computer does many things faster than we can.[39]

Ethics regarding decision-aiding software use should stress that the computer is a tool and the ultimate decider is the user. To this end, an ethical standard holding the user responsible for understanding the system's capabilities and limitations should be established.

Another aspect of computer ethics in alternate dispute resolution is access to decision-aiding software. Many attorneys, mediators, and clients are not computer-literate, nor do they have access to decision-aiding software. Should both parties to a mediation have access to decision-aiding software? If only one party utilizes decision-aiding software, that party may have an advantage in the dispute resolution. For society in general, Robert Johnson states, "Providing people equal access to computers is an ethical and economic task the logistics of which have not been adequately explored."[40] Yet, disparities now exist in availability of other resources to lawyers and mediators. If the computer is truly viewed as a tool similar to research and expert human resources now available, equal access is either presumed or unnecessary. Instead, requirements of adequate representation and the market forces should spur lawyers and mediators to become computer-literate and utilize decision-aiding software, or employ a computer expert. However, regulations regarding disclosure of the expert system theory and operation are necessary to ensure adequate information transfer to evaluate the systems. Discovery and trial rules regarding expert systems should be established to provide guidance and reduce uncertainty.[41]

Disclosure of expert systems should be an ethical requirement in alternate dispute resolution. Then the question is: What information should be disclosed to whom? If a lawyer foresees using the decision-aiding software in a client's case, disclosure should be made to the client when the attorney-client relationship is entered into.[42] When specifying the obligations and duties of each party, generally in a contract, the attorney should inform the client that decision-aiding computer programs may be used to assist the attorney in evaluating and planning the case action. Further explanations regarding the expert system or how the attorney plans to use the resulting information may be appropriate at the relationship-building stage also. If a mediator uses the decision-aiding software, then all parties should be given information regarding the main underlying assumptions of the system, the limitations and capabilities of the system, the confidentiality of the information used, and the role the computer and its results play in the dispute resolution. By requiring broad disclosure of expert systems used for decision-aiding, the parties' bargaining power can be maintained.

Ethical considerations must also address machine bias. Since expert systems mimic expert analysis, underlying assumptions or biases may be programmed into the system.

That value assumptions are built into computerized systems seems unavoidable, but not necessarily a bad thing. . . . Problems arise, however, when the biases are built in unconsciously, and when those who use the system (or are affected by it) are not made aware of these biases.[43]

Ensuring that appropriate actions are taken to make the biases explicit involves both the previously discussed disclosure requirement and the realistic valuation concerns. If users of the system are required to understand the capabilities of the system, they must necessarily know the main underlying assumptions of the system. Some expert systems may allow these assumptions to be changed. Therefore, an ethical duty to disclose should include presenting the expert system's assumptions and biases.

THE FUTURE OF DECISION-AIDING SOFTWARE AND THE LAW

After exploring the underlying theory, the specific applications through examples, and the ethical considerations, the big question is: Is decision-aiding software a computer fad or is it going to change the practice of law and mediation significantly? A cost-benefit analysis suggests that decision-aiding software is generally worthwhile. Decision-aiding software can be purchased in the $100 to $200 range.[44] Some programs require the support of a word processor, such as Lotus 1-2-3.[45] The main cost is the time to learn the system. However, with user-friendliness advancements, the programs can be self-taught and more easily utilized.[46] The benefits are mentioned above. Once the P/G% system is mastered, it can be efficiently utilized. File shells that list the usual alternatives and criteria for certain cases, such as personal injury or divorce shells, that can be modified to fit the particular case also reduce cost per use.[47]

Rather than purchasing a decision-aiding program already on the market, attorneys can develop their own software. This would be profitable only if used in high volume. "One rule of thumb is that the volume in that transaction should be high enough to recover the front-end costs within two years.[48] Another alternative to purchasing the software is contracting experts to process certain cases through their own system.[49]

A large obstacle to decision-aiding software in mediation is attorney attitudes. Some feel that computers should not be replacing lawyers. The programs are decision-aiding, not decision-making, however, and require much user input and interpretation. The goal is not to replace lawyers or mediators, but only to make more explicit the decision process.[50] Actual use of computers has shown user acceptance: "The use of computers has been shown to improve manager decision making and to raise the level of confidence in decisions."[51] Evidence suggests that decision-aiding programs may be more readily accepted by legal scholars than practicing attorneys.[52] Indications of the future are clear. Since 1980, use of decision-aiding software has spread to virtually all fields.[53] "A 1986 survey of the nation's top 500 law firms disclosed that only 20 percent were using decision-aiding software. In 1987 the survey showed a jump up to 30 percent. This rapid increase indicates that the obstacles to the computer's use are diminishing."[54]

NOTES

1. S. Nagel, "Multi-Criteria Methods for Alternative Dispute Resolution: With Microcomputer Software Applications," (unpublished manuscript, Nov. 1989) pp. 30–34a.

2. P/G% was developed by Stuart S. Nagel and others. Nagel is a professor of political science at the University of Illinois. He served as a special master for computer-aided mediation for the United States District Court for the Northern District of Illinois. For more information, see "Multi-Criteria Methods," pp. 159–61.

3. For a discussion of other categories of decison-aiding software and a list of available programs corresponding to these types see S. Nagel, *Decision-Aiding Software and Legal Decision-Making: A Guide to Skills and Applications Throughout the Law* (Wesport, Conn.: Quorum Books, 1989).

4. "Multi-Criteria Methods," pp. g–h.

5. Ibid.

6. The example is based on facts from a negotiation wherein Stuart S. Nagel was special master in a federal case in Illinois. See ibid., pp. 25–26.

7. Ibid., pp. 31–33.

8. Ibid., pp. 31, 130.

9. Ibid., p. 131.

10. For an example of a super-optimum solution in a labor-management dispute between migrant farm workers and growers, see ibid., pp. 162–80.

11. *Decision-Aiding Software*, p. 53.

12. Ibid., pp. 53–54.

13. For a list of the actual and potential benefits of decision-aiding software, see ibid., pp. 22–23.

14. "Multi-Criteria Methods," p. 145.

15. Ibid., p. 23.

16. Ibid., pp. 148–49.

17. Ibid., p. 23.

18. Ibid., pp. 149–51.

19. Ibid., pp. 23–24.

20. *Decision-Aiding Software*, p. 16.

21. "Multi-Criteria Methods," pp. 91–92.

22. *Decision-Aiding Software*, p. 22.

23. Ibid., p. 210.

24. "Multi-Criteria Methods," pp. 10–14.

25. See, e.g., a product liability case involving fire insurance recovery mediated in the United States District Court for the Northern District of Illinois, "Multi-Criteria Methods," pp. 102b–i.

26. Model Code of Professional Responsibility DR 7-101 (1980).

27. Model Rules of Professional Conduct Rule 1.7(b) (1983).

28. Model Rules of Professional Conduct Rule 1.7(b) comment (1983).

29. Model Code of Professional Responsibility DR 5-101(A) (1980).

30. Model Code of Professional Responsibility EC 5–7 (1980).

31. *Decision-Aiding Software*, p. 212.

32. "Multi-Criteria Methods," pp. 196–97.

33. See, e.g., Gemignani, "Potential Liability for Use of Expert Systems," *IDEA: The Journal of Law and Technology* 29 (1988–89): 120–27.

34. Douglas Johnson, *Computer Ethics: A Guide for a New Age* (Gettysburg, Penn.: Brethren Press, 1984), pp. 37, 73–75 (hereinafter *A Guide for a New Age*).

35. For a discussion of computer codes of ethics promulgated by the Association for Computer Machinery, see Deborah Johnson, *Computer Ethics* (New York: Prentice-Hall, 1985).

36. Lynn Miller, "Teaching Computers to Think Like Lawyers," *Student Lawyer* 17 (May 1989): 22.

37. *A Guide for a New Age*, p. 63.

38. Richard Gruner, "Thinking Like a Lawyer: Expert Systems for Legal Analysis," *High Technology Law Journal* 1 (Fall 1986): 327.

39. *A Guide for a New Age*, p. 48.

40. Ibid., p. 85.

41. Alan Aldous, "Disclosure of Expert Computer Simulations," *Computer/Law Journal* 8 (Winter 1987): 51–72.

42. *Computer Ethics*, pp. 27–28.

43. Ibid., p. 80.

44. "Decision Pad: $195 Answer to Life's Most Challenging Questions," *Attorney's Computer Report* 6 (Feb. 1988): 4.

45. Ibid., p. 4.

46. *Decision-Aiding Software*, p. 23.

47. "Multi-Criteria Methods," pp. 82–97a.

48. Norv Brasch, "Expert Systems Promise to Have a Major Impact on Law Practices," *Attorney's Computer Report* 6 (Apr. 1988): 5–6.

49. Andrew Parker, David Johnson, and Paul Mode, "The Use of Computers in Damage and Settlement Analysis," in *Improving Law Firm Productivity by Encouraging Lawyers' Use of Personal Computers* (New York: Law and Business, 1985), p. 252.

50. Richard Brunelli, "Coin-Flip or Computer: Systemization of Legal Hunches Could be the Ultimate Litigation Tool," *Chicago Daily Law Bulletin* (Aug. 21, 1986) at 1, 13.

51. Susan Raridon, "The Practice of Law—The Next 50 Years," *Legal Economics* 36 (Apr. 1989).

52. Brunelli, "Coin-Flip or Computer," p. 13.

53. "Many Attorneys Don't Like the Idea of a Computer for Decision-Making," *Attorney's Computer Report* 5 (Dec. 1986): 5.

54. *Decision-Aiding Software*, p. 58.

CHAPTER 12

Sequential Arbitration Procedures: Dynamic versus Static Models of ADR

STEVEN J. BRAMS, D. MARC KILGOUR, AND SHLOMO WEBER

The sine qua non of arbitration, unlike mediation and other dispute-resolution procedures, is that an arbitrator's choice of a settlement is binding on the disputants. This is not to say that the arbitrator alone determines the settlement. Indeed, if the disputants are able to reach an agreement on their own—realizing that, if they do not, the arbitrator's judgment will come into play—then the arbitrator plays only a background role.

In most disputes, however, this background role is not inconsequential. It may crucially affect not only the bargaining process but also the nature of the settlement. For example, it may put pressure on the disputants to hammer out their own agreement rather than court the risk that the arbitrator will side with their adversary.

This risk would seem especially great under final-offer arbitration (FOA), in which two parties submit so-called final offers and the arbitrator is restricted to choosing one or the other. Unlike conventional arbitration, the arbitrator cannot "split the difference." Under FOA, the adversary's offer—rather than some compromise settlement selected by the arbitrator—is the only alternative to having one's own offer chosen.

It is for this reason, presumably, that of the 111 major-league baseball players who filed for arbitration under FOA in 1988, 93 (84 percent) negotiated contracts before FOA was actually implemented (Chass, 1988). As one baseball arbitrator put it, "I'm starting to feel like the atomic bomb. The deterrent effect of me as an arbitrator is enough" (Cronin, 1989, quoting Stephen B. Goldberg).

In this chapter, we shall show how the dichotomous choices under FOA can be rendered less stark by allowing the disputants to revise their initial offers. For example, one rule for sequential play specifies that the loser at any stage can make a counteroffer, which, if closer to the arbitrator's position than the winner's prior offer, allows the game to continue until one player loses twice in a row.

All the rules we shall propose induce the players—as they learn more about the arbitrator's position and the opponent's offers—to make progressively less extreme offers, converging toward the position of the arbitrator (and each other). These rules provide a natural extension of (single-stage) FOA, which is used not only in professional baseball but also to settle labor disputes involving certain classes of public employees in ten U.S. states (as of 1981; see Freeman, 1986) and in bidding on U.S. Defense Department contracts (Carrington, 1988; Halloran, 1988).

We shall discuss a model of FOA, and analyze its extension to two stages. We then generalize our results to procedures with any number of stages and also to procedures with no maximum length. We briefly consider a one-stage variant of FOA that has strong convergence properties. Originally proposed by Brams and Merrill (1986), this alternative nonsequential procedure and FOA will be compared with the sequential procedures.

We emphasize procedures because our main result characterizes the optimal strategies and convergence properties of a *class* of sequential procedures. Surprisingly, we find that one particular two-stage procedure leads to fewer extreme settlements than longer sequential procedures, including the one alluded to earlier in which offers and counteroffers alternate until one player loses twice in a row. Coupled with its practical advantages, this seems an especially strong commendation of this simple extension of FOA.

Like most previous models of FOA and its variants (reviewed in Brams, 1990, ch. 3; Brams, Kilgour, and Merrill, 1991), we postulate a noncooperative two-person, zero-sum game played between two disputants, who have incomplete information about the position of the arbitrator. The arbitrator is not an active player but rather a random variable, which is described by its probability distribution. To facilitate the analysis and numerical calculations, we assume this distribution is uniform. In principle, our model could be extended to nonuniform distributions, as has been done for FOA by Brams and Merrill (1983); we offer some conjectures on this matter later.

Although not a player in our model, the arbitrator nevertheless plays a critical role in conditioning the strategies of the players, as they learn more about the arbitrator's position over time and revise their bids accordingly. Gibbons (1988) proposes an alternative sequential model in which the arbitrator is a utility maximizer who learns from the offers of the two sides, making inferences about their private information (e.g., reservation prices).

It might be argued that the sequential procedures we propose give too much weight to the arbitrator. Why not simply let the arbitrator make the choice at the start, as under conventional arbitration? We shall consider this and other criticisms of sequential procedures when we compare them with FOA and Brams and Merrill's (1986) proposed one-stage alternative.

Before analyzing the sequential procedures, it is useful to recall the rationale of FOA. Proposed more than 20 years ago by Stevens (1966), this strikingly simple procedure had been discussed informally earlier (see Stern, et al., 1975: 113 n. 7) as a way of resolving disputes without imposing the arbitrator's judgment on the disputants:

If the arbitrator or panel was permitted to select only one or the other of the parties' final offers, with no power to make a choice anywhere in between, it was expected that the logic of the procedure would force negotiating parties to continue moving closer together in search of a position that would be most likely to receive neutral sympathy. Ultimately, so the argument went, they would come so close together that they would almost inevitably find their own settlement. (Rehmus, 1979: 218)

As we shall show, this convergence argument is not supported in theory. In practice, however, FOA seems to promote convergence by giving parties a strong incentive to bargain seriously and reach a settlement on their own, out of fear that the arbitrator might choose the relatively extreme offer of the other side.

Sequential procedures, by giving the parties a chance to respond to a decision against them, exorcise this fear to some extent. At the same time, they provide a formal mechanism for replicating the give-and-take of bargaining, but now in a context guided by an arbitrator.

RULES OF THE SEQUENTIAL ARBITRATION PROCEDURES

We begin by formulating a general model of sequential arbitration. This model subsumes all the procedures that we shall analyze in later sections.

Assume two players, A and B, play a game to determine a settlement amount s. A's sole objective is to minimize, and B's to maximize, s. A, for example, might be management, which wants to keep the wage scale as low as possible, and B labor, which wants higher wages. We make the simplifying assumption that the dispute involves no other parties and is over a single quantifiable issue, such as a wage scale, but models of FOA have been developed that allow for more than one issue (Wittman, 1986).

The value of s will depend in part on the arbitrator's judgment, which we model as a random variable X whose distribution is known to both players. While the distribution is common knowledge, the value of X, denoted by x, is unknown to A and B.

The different arbitration procedures to be modeled vary in length (i.e., maximum number of rounds allowed) and in the manner in which the settlement is determined. The detemination of a settlement may or may not occur in the last round allowed—if there is, indeed, a predetermined maximum number of rounds.

In the first round, A and B make simultaneous offers of a_1 and b_1, respectively. These offers are publicly announced, so they are known to both players and the arbitrator. If the length of the procedure is 1 (i.e., one stage), the arbitrator announces a settlement s; if the length is greater than 1, the arbitrator invites one player to make a new offer.

Similarly, on subsequent rounds the arbitrator may solicit new offers from the players, but only from one player at a time. Each stage ends either with a settlement, which depends on the arbitrator's judgment, or the arbitrator's invitation to one player to make a new offer.

Five rules govern all the sequential arbitration procedures we shall study. On the first round,

$$\text{If } a_1 \geq b_1, \ s = (a_1 + b_1)/2. \tag{1}$$

Thus, if the players' initial offers coincide or overlap, the settlement is the mean of the two offers, and play terminates.

If the offers do not coincide or overlap (in any stage), suppose that A's most recent offer is a and B's is b. Then

$$\text{If } a < b \leq x, \ s = b. \tag{2}$$

$$\text{If } x \leq a < b, \ s = a. \tag{3}$$

Rules 2 and 3 say that if the arbitrator's preferred settlement x is greater than or equal to B's "high" offer (and necessarily A's lower offer), or less than or equal to A's "low" offer (and necessarily B's higher offer), then these high and low offers, respectively, become the settlements.

In these cases, the arbitrator is at least as favorable to the high (rule 2) or low (rule 3) player's position as that player is to himself or herself, as indicated by the offers. With both players on one side of the arbitrator, the player who is closer "wins" by having his or her offer chosen. Notice that rules 1 to 3 together imply that a procedure cannot continue to a subsequent round unless $a < x < b$.

We postulate two more rules, to which we give names, which govern play after the first round under the sequential arbitration procedures:

4. *Second Chance*: Only the player whose most recent offer is farther from x is invited to make a revised offer.
5. *No Third Chance*: A player cannot make two revised offers in succession. If a player's revised offer (as defined by rule 4) remains farther from x than his or her adversary's last offer, then the adversary's last offer is the settlement, and play terminates.

Rules 4 and 5 are designed to speed the players' convergence toward the arbitrator's position. By permitting a player to learn that he or she is behind (i.e., farther from the arbitrator on any round), and giving that player exactly one chance to jump ahead (by moving closer to the arbitrator), that player will be motivated to try to recover immediately. After all, he or she does not get another chance.

By comparison, if the players were given a third chance (or even more), their optimal behavior would tend more toward inching than leaping toward the arbitrator (and the adversary), which would doom a rapid settlement. Although our goal is to give the players the opportunity to learn from the arbitrator that their offers are wanting, at the same time we desire to give the sequential procedures bite. Otherwise, the player who is behind at any stage will not have a strong incentive to make a significant concession, knowing that he or she might recoup at a later stage.

Because offers, and invitations by the arbitrator to make revised offers, are public, the players at each round acquire new information. This permits them to revise their estimates of the location of the arbitrator's position, x. In particular, the player farther from the arbitrator can deduce from the new information which revised offer is optimal, in a sense that we make precise later.

Call the interval within which the players can infer that x must fall the *current interval*. For example, suppose that the procedure permits more than one round and, at the conclusion of round 1, the current interval is (a_1, b_1). Next, suppose that the arbitrator announces that $a_1 < x < b_1$ and a_1 is closer to x than b_1, so B is permitted to make a second offer. Both players can now infer that the current interval is $[a_1, (a_1 + b_1)/2]$. (This interval includes its upper endpoint because we assume that if there is a tie, it is resolved in favor of A—an innocuous assumption if the distribution of X is continuous.) As the offers and revised offers continue, the process of interval-halving leads to the convergence of the current interval on x—unless one player overshoots x, in which case rule 2 or 3 will be operative and play will terminate.

The various sequential arbitration procedures differ in both length and *termination rule*. The latter determines the settlement if, given there is a last round, neither rule 2 nor rule 3 applies.

The greater the length of a procedure, the less likely that the number of rounds realized will equal the maximum. There are two reasons why a procedure might not play out to its full length: either a revised offer will not be closer to x than an adversary's last offer, invoking rule 5; or one player will overshoot x, invoking rule 2 or rule 3. Note that because all offers are public, a player's revised offer will never overshoot an opponent's last offer, which is the reason why rule 1 is moot in rounds after the first.

In the case of the sequential procedures, we assume that the arbitrator's judgment, as given by the random variable X, is uniformly distributed. This assumption implies that if the current interval is (a, b) in any round of play, then the conditional distribution of X is uniform on (a, b). For convenience, we take the (unconditional) distribution of X to be uniform on [0, 1]; a uniform distribution on any other interval can be obtained through a linear transformation.

FOA is a sequential arbitration procedure of length 1, in which the termination rule for determining final-round outcomes, if $a_1 < x < b_1$, is

$$s = \begin{cases} a_1 & \text{if } a_1 < x \le (a_1 + b_1)/2 & \text{(x at least as close to } a_1) \\ b_1 & \text{if } (a_1 + b_1)/2 < x < b_1 & \text{(x closer to } b_1) \end{cases} \qquad (1)$$

Given offers of a_1 and b_1, the expected settlement is

$$E(a_1, b_1) = \begin{cases} (a_1 + b_1)/2 & \text{if } a_1 \ge b_1 \\ a_1[(a_1 + b_1)/2 - 0] + b_1[1 - (a_1 + b_1)/2] & \text{if } a_1 < b_1 \end{cases} \qquad (2)$$

Simplifying the latter expression when $a_1 < b_1$,

$$E(a_1, b_1) = a_1^2/2 + b_1 - b_1^2/2 \qquad (3)$$

and differentiating,

$$\frac{\partial E}{\partial a_1} = a_1$$

it follows immediately that, for any b_1, A minimizes E by choosing $a_1 = 0$. Analogously, for any a_1, B maximizes E by choosing $b_1 = 1$. Because these strategies do not depend on the other player's choice, they are dominant.

Accordingly, $a_1 = 0$ and $b_1 = 1$ constitutes a dominant-strategy Nash equilibrium (saddlepoint) under FOA. Substituting into (1), the settlement that results from these optimal choices may be $s = 0$ or $s = 1$, each of which occurs with probability 1/2.

Now consider what happens when an additional stage is added to FOA. Under one version of FOA2, if rules 1 to 3 do not lead to a settlement after round 1, we allow the "loser" of this round to submit a revised offer. Then we apply the logic of FOA at the second stage.

Specifically, replace a_1 with a_2, or b_1 with b_2, in (3), depending on whether B or A, respectively, won on round 1. In other words, we apply the termination rule of FOA to round 2 of FOA2 to terminate play in the second stage, given that a settlement was not reached in the first stage according to rules 1 to 3. We refer to this version of FOA2 as *simple* FOA2.

To determine optimal strategies and possible outcomes under this procedure, suppose that $a_1 < x \le (a_1 + b_1)/2$. Because x is closer to a_1 than b_1, B is invited to submit a revised offer. The width of the current interval is the difference between these upper and lower bounds, or $(a_1 + b_1)/2 - a_1$. Applying the logic of FOA to this interval, the expected settlement is

$$E = a_1\left[\frac{(a_1 + b_2)/2 - a_1}{(a_1 + b_1)/2 - a_1}\right] + b_2\left[\frac{(a_1 + b_1)/2 - (a_1 + b_2)/2}{(a_1 + b_1)/2 - a_1}\right] \qquad (4)$$

Differentiating,

$$\frac{\partial E}{\partial b_2} = \frac{a_1 + b_1 - 2b_2}{b_1 - a_1} \begin{array}{c} > \\ = \\ < \end{array} 0 \text{ according as } b_2 \begin{array}{c} < \\ = \\ > \end{array} \frac{a_1 + b_1}{2}$$

Consequently, B maximizes E by choosing $b_2 = (a_1 + b_1)/2$. Analogously, if $(a_1 + b_1)/2 < x < b_1$, A's optimal revised offer would be $a_2 = (a_1 + b_1)/2$.

Substituting $b_2 = (a_1 + b_1)/2$ into (4), we obtain the following expression for the expected settlement in the first stage if $a_1 < b_1$:

$$\overline{E}(a_1, b_1) = a_1\left[\frac{3a_1 + b_1}{4}\right] + \left(\frac{a_1 + b_1}{2}\right)\left[\frac{b_1 - a_1}{2}\right] + b_1\left[1 - \frac{a_1 + 3b_1}{4}\right]$$

(5)

After simplification,

$$E(a_1, b_1) = a_1^2/2 + b_1 - b_1^2/2$$

But this is the same as (3) for FOA, so the optimal first-stage offers under simple FOA2 are identical to those for FOA (i.e., $a_1 = 0$ and $b_1 = 1$).

Given these values, the optimal second-stage offers found earlier can be evaluated: $a_2 = b_2 = (a_1 + b_1)/2 = 1/2$, whichever player is the loser and can revise his or her first-stage offer. Similarly, substituting these values into (5), the settlement that results from these optimal choices is $s = 0$ with probability 1/4, $s = 1/2$ with probability 1/2, and $s = 1$ with probability 1/4.

Under simple FOA2, we allowed only the loser at the first stage to revise his or her offer. But what if we allow the winner also to revise? Would this player have any incentive to move in from his or her extreme position (at 0 or 1)?

To answer this question, assume that $a_1 < x \le (a_1 + b_1)/2$, so B is permitted to revise as before. But now assume that A also is permitted to revise (by choosing $a_2 \ne a_1$). Then it is easy to show that it is not in A's interest to change his or her offer but instead to continue to select $a_2 = a_1$.

This result follows from the fact that simple FOA2 at the second stage is equivalent to FOA, wherein A has chosen the left endpoint, $a_1 = 0$, of the current interval [0, 1/2]. But under FOA this is A's dominant strategy, just as B's dominant strategy is to choose the right endpoint, $b_2 = 1/2$.

Generally speaking, rule 4, which permits only the player whose current offer is farther from x to revise, does not seem to be unduly restrictive—the closer player (i.e., the current winner) could not do better by changing his or her winning bid. Thus, although sequential arbitration procedures permit only the current loser to revise his or her offer in each round after the first, this feature in no way hurts the winner in this round, for whom it is optimal to stick to his or her prior offer.

It is noteworthy that under FOA, and in the first stage of simple FOA2, the players' optimal offers are the extremes of the current interval: $a_1 = 0$ and $b_1 = 1$ under both procedures. Hence, adding a stage to FOA has no effect on where the player start out. As we shall show later, it is always optimal for the players to commence with extreme offers, regardless of the number of stages.

Thus, sequential arbitration procedures do not deprive the players of the opportunity to do some initial posturing. In fact, they make it optimal to do so, which may be good for public relations purposes. Thereby players can demonstrate to their supporters that they will make stiff demands of an adversary, backing off only when compelled to do so by the arbitrator.

In the second stage of simple FOA2, if B loses because $0 < x \leq 1/2$, or A loses because $1/2 < x < 1$, each player's optimal response as loser is to choose the new implied endpoint, $1/2$. As we shall show, however, choosing an endpoint of the current interval is not in general optimal for sequential arbitration procedures of length greater than 2.

An alternative two-stage sequential arbitration procedure is one that involves averaging, which we call *modified* FOA2. Under this procedure, the termination rule for determining outcomes at the second (final) stage, if $a_1 < x < b_1$, is:

• the average of the current offers if the initial loser's (say, B's) revised offer b_2 is closer to x than a_1: $s = (a_1 + b_2)/2$.
• the initial winner's (say, A's) offer a_1 if a_1 remains closer to x at the second stage than b_2: $s = a_1$.

Modified FOA2 would appear to give an advantage over simple FOA2 to the initial winner. This is because if this winner (say, A) loses in the second stage, then B (the new winner) does not have his or her offer chosen outright; rather, B's offer is averaged with A's offer, diminishing the impact of A's losing at the second stage. This *seems* fair: if A does not prevail at the second stage, B's second offer, if winning, is devalued by being averaged with A's first offer—unless B is so accommodating as, by overshooting x, to offer more than the arbitrator thinks fair.

In this case, the arbitrator's choice is to the left or right of both current offers at the second stage. Then, according to rules 2 and 3, the settlement is the offer closer to x. Moreover, this settlement will necessarily be the revised offer of the initial loser (say, B). While this offer (b_2) may overshoot x at the second stage, it will never overshoot the offer of the initial winner (a_1) because the latter is known by the loser (B). Since the loser's knowledge ensures that his or her revised offer will always be closer to x, rule 3 or 2 may be applicable at the second stage, depending on whether B or A, respectively, was the initial winner.

The rules of modified FOA2 would seem to give both players an incentive to be competitive at the first stage. Thereby they increase their chances of winning initially—and, possibly, subsequently—without having to compromise. But if they give away too much trying to win initially, they may squander their pay-offs, whether they (1) win again at the second stage, (2) are forced to average, or (3) lose by drawing their adversary to their side of the arbitrator.

To evaluate the net effect of this subtle mix of incentives, consider modified FOA2 in the second stage. Suppose that it is B who loses initially and therefore submits a revised offer. The expected settlement is

$$E = a_1 \left[\frac{(a_1 + b_2)/2 - a_1}{(a_1 + b_1)/2 - a_1} \right] + \left(\frac{a_1 + b_2}{2} \right) \left[\frac{b_2 - (a_1 + b_2)/2}{(a_1 + b_1)/2 - a_1} \right]$$

$$+ b_2 \left[\frac{(a_1 + b_1)/2 - b_2}{(a_1 + b_1)/2 - a_1} \right] \tag{6}$$

$$= \frac{a_1(b_2 - a_1) + [(a_1 + b_2)/2](b_2 - a_1) + b_2(a_1 + b_1 - 2b_2)}{b_1 - a_1}$$

Observe that the first term of (6) is identical to the first term of (4) for simple FOA2; the second term reflects the averaging option under modified FOA2, and the third term the overshooting of x by B.

Differentiating (6),

$$\frac{\partial E}{\partial b_2} = \frac{2a_1 + b_1 - 3b_2}{b_1 - a_1} \overset{>}{\underset{<}{=}} 0 \text{ according as } b_2 \overset{<}{\underset{>}{=}} \frac{2a_1 + b_1}{3}$$

Thus, B's optimal revised offer is $b_2 = (2a_1 + b_1)/3$. Analogously, A's optimal revised offer is $a_2 = (a_1 + 2b_1)/3$.

Substituting $b_2 = (2a_1 + b_1)/3$ into (6) gives the following expected settlement in the first stage if $a_1 < b_1$:

$$E(a_1, b_1) = a_1[(5a_1 + b_1)/6] + [(5a_1 + b_1)/6](b_1 - a_1)/6$$

$$+ [(2a_1 + b_1)/3](b_1 - a_1)/6 + [(a_1 + 2b_1)/3](b_1 - a_1)/6$$

$$+ [(a_1 + 5b_1)/6](b_1 - a_1)/6 + b_1[1 - (a_1 + 5b_1)/6] \tag{7}$$

This yields, after some simplification,

$$E(a_1, b_1) = a_1^2/2 + b_1 - b_1^2/2$$

Once again, this is the same as (3) under FOA and implies optimal first-stage offers of $a_1 = 0$ and $b_1 = 1$.

Given these values, the optimal second-stage offers found earlier can be evaluated: $a_2 = 2/3$ and $b_2 = 1/3$. Similarly, substituting these values into (7), the settlement that results from these optimal choices is $s = 0$, $s = 1/6$, $s = 1/3$, $s = 2/3$, $s = 5/6$, or $s = 1$, each with probability $1/6$.

THE GENERAL THEOREM FOR OPTIMAL SEQUENTIAL PLAY

Prior to formulating and proving the theorem describing optimal play under general sequential arbitration procedures, we introduce some additional notation and define this class of procedures formally. Because we assume that the arbitrator's distribution function is uniform, bargaining on any interval can be treated as a linear transformation of bargaining on $(0, 1)$. The fact that the distribution function is uniform on every interval makes the situation homogeneous, which enables us to normalize strategies and outcomes relative to the current interval.

A simple convention will make the comparison of offers easier, thereby facilitating the determination of optimal strategies. All *revised* offers (i.e., those after the first round) will be expressed relative to the current interval and will be called *actions*. Specifically, if $i > 1$ under a procedure of length n, assume the interval is (a, b). Then A's action (if any) on round i, $\alpha_{i,n} \in [0, 1]$, corresponds to a revised offer of $a + (b - a)\alpha_{i,n}$; B's action (if any) on round i, $\beta_{i,n} \in [0, 1]$, corresponds to a revised offer of $b - (b - a)(1 - \beta_{i,n})$.

The parameters $\alpha_{i,n}$ and $(1 - \beta_{i,n})$ are the factors by which the current interval is changed—so as either to increase A's offer or decrease B's—thereby narrowing the current interval on round i. Put another way, if A is the player to make the revised offer, that offer is in the proportion $\alpha_{i,n}$ from the left endpoint of the current interval; if B makes the revised offer, that offer is in the proportion $\beta_{i,n}$ from the left endpoint of current interval, or $(1 - \beta_{i,n})$ from the right endpoint.

Assume that A makes the revised offer on round $i > 1$ under a procedure of length n. If the current interval is (a, b), then by homogeneity the expected settlement for A is

$$A_{i,n}(a, b) = a + (b - a)A_{i,n} \tag{8}$$

where $A_{i,n} = A_{i,n}(0, 1)$ is the expected settlement if the current interval were $(0, 1)$, with A to rebid in round i. Analogously, the expected settlement for B is

$$B_{i,n}(a, b) = b - (b - a)(1 - B_{i,n}) \tag{9}$$

where $B_{i,n} = B_{i,n}(0, 1)$ is the similar "normalized" expected outcome. In our notation, the dependence of $A_{i,n}$ and $B_{i,n}$ on x, $\alpha_{i,n}$, and $\beta_{i,n}$, all subsequent actions, and the termination rule is suppressed. An asterisk will denote optimal play.

We define a *sequential arbitration* (SA) procedure of length n to be one that satisfies rules 1 to 5 and has a termination rule that is *strategically symmetric* in the sense that

$$A^*_{n,n}(a, b) + B^*_{n,n}(a, b) = a + b \tag{10}$$

This condition means that if the player to make the revised offer in the last round is selected at random, then the expected settlement is *fair*: given optimal play by both players, it is the midpoint, $(a + b)/2$, of the current interval. This follows from the fact that the sum of the players' expected settlements is $(a + b)$ by (10), so each player on average will receive half this amount.

Both the termination rules used for FOA2—based on the simple and modified (i.e., averaging) procedures—satisfy (10). Although each of these procedures results in the selection of an initial winner, that winner is equally likely to be either player when both play optimally. This is equivalent to selecting at random either player to make the revised offer in the second stage, which will on average result in the midpoint of 1/2 if both players make optimal choices on each round. Other procedures also satisfy (10), such as making the settlement the arbitrator's position on the last round (if play goes to this point), which also has an expected value to each player of 1/2.

Theorem. Under an SA procedure of length n, with the arbitrator's distribution function uniform, there is a unique subgame perfect equilibrium satisfying

$$B_{i,n}^* = 1/(2 + B_{i+1,n}^*) \qquad A_{i,n}^* = 1 - B_{i,n}^*$$

$$\beta_{i,n}^* = 2/(2 + B_{i+1,n}^*) \qquad \alpha_{i,n}^* = 1 - \beta_{i,n}^*$$

where $1 < i < n$. Also, $\alpha_{1,n}^* = 0$, $\beta_{1,n}^* = 1$, and $E^* = 1/2$, which is the expected settlement for both A and B when they play optimally on the first round.

Proof. Assume that

$$A_{i+1,n}^* + B_{i+1,n}^* = 1$$

which is true if $i + 1 = n$ by (10). Suppose that B makes the revised offer in round i, and consider B's choice of $\beta = \beta_{i,n}$. By rules 2, 4, and 5,

$$B_{i,n}^* = \max_{\beta} \{(\beta/2)(0) + (\beta/2)A_{i+1,n}^*(\beta/2, \beta) + (1 - \beta)\beta\}$$

where the first term in the braces reflects B's losing twice in a row, (terminating play), the second term that B wins and the game continues, and the third term that B overshoots the arbitrator (also terminating play). But

$$A_{i+1,n}^*(\beta/2, \beta) = \beta/2 + (\beta/2)A_{i+1,n}^*$$

$$= \beta - (\beta/2)B_{i+1,n}^*$$

by (8) and the induction hypothesis. Simplfying,

$$B_{i,n}^* = \max_{\beta} \{\beta - \beta^2/2 - (\beta^2/4)B_{i+1,n}^*\}$$

It is straightforward to show that the maximum occurs at

$$\beta_{i,n}^* = 2/(2 + B_{i+1,n}^*)$$

and the maximum value is

$$B_{i,n}^* = 1/(2 + B_{i+1,n}^*)$$

Similarly, by rules 3 to 5, A's optimal choice $\alpha = \alpha_{i,n}^*$ must satisfy

$$A_{i,n}^* = \min_{\alpha} \{\alpha(\alpha) + [(1 - \alpha)/2]B_{i+1,n}^* + [(1 - \alpha)/2](1)\}$$

By analogous reasoning, the minimum occurs at

$$\alpha_{i,n}^* = B_{i+1,n}^*/(2 + B_{i+1,n}^*) = 1 - \beta_{i+1,n}^*$$

and the minimum value is

$$A_{i,n}^* = (1 + B_{i+1,n}^*)/(2 + B_{i+1,n}^*) = 1 - B_{i,n}^*$$

From the last equation it follows that

$$A_{i,n}^* + B_{i,n}^* = 1$$

completing the induction for round i, $1 < i \le n - 1$.

This inductive reasoning can be carried back from the next-to-last to the second stage. Hence, we need only determine the equilibrium in the first stage to prove the subgame perfectness of the equilibrium in the entire game (i.e., at all stages).

Consider the players' choices in round 1. If $\alpha_{1,1} = \alpha$ and $\beta_{1,1} = \beta$, $E_{1,n} = (\alpha + \beta)/2$ if $\alpha \ge \beta$. If $\alpha < \beta$

$$E_{1,n} = \alpha(\alpha) + [(\beta - \alpha)/2]B_{2,n}^*(\alpha, (\alpha + \beta)/2)$$

$$+ [(\beta - \alpha)/2]A_{2,n}^*((\alpha + \beta)/2, \beta) + (1 - \beta)\beta$$

$$= \alpha^2 + [(\beta - \alpha)/2]\{\alpha + [(\beta - \alpha)/2]B_{2,n}^*\}$$

$$+ [(\beta - \alpha)/2]\{(\alpha + \beta)/2 + [(\beta - \alpha)/2]A_{2,n}^*\}$$

$$= \alpha^2 + [(\alpha + \beta)/2][\alpha + (\beta - \alpha)/2] + \beta - \beta^2$$

$$+ [(\beta - \alpha)/2]^2[A_{2,n}^* + B_{2,n}^*]$$

But

$$A_{2,n}^* + B_{2,n}^* = 1$$

as shown earlier, so if $\alpha < \beta$,

$$E_{1,n}^* = \alpha^2/2 + \beta - \beta^2/2$$

which is analogous to (3). As shown for round 1 both FOA and FOA2 in section 3, $\alpha_{1,n}^* = 0$, $\beta_{1,n}^* = 1$, and $E_{1,n}^* = 1/2$.

Using the theorem, optimal offers under any SA procedure can be determined by iteration once a termination rule satisfying (10) is specified. For simple SA procedures of length n,

$$A_{n,n}^* = B_{n,n}^* = 1/2$$

which says that the expected settlement of each player on the last round is the midpoint of the current interval, based on each player's choosing his or her respective endpoint ($\alpha_{n,n}^* = 0$, $\beta_{n,n}^* = 1$). Numerical results for up to six rounds are shown in Table 12.1 for the simple procedure (i.e., without averaging on the last round), which we call FOAn.

Any other SA procedure that satisfies (10), such as determining the last round by conditional averaging—as under the modified procedure—also iterates, with numerical results shown in Table 12.2. In the case of the modified procedure,

$$A_{n,n}^* = 2/3 \qquad B_{n,n}^* = 1/3$$

which says that the expected settlement if A makes the revised offer on the last round will be 2/3 of the distance across the interval (from left to right), based on A's action of $\alpha_{n,n}^* = 1/3$. B's advantage is obvious.

To illustrate the calculation of optimal offers for A, based on the α^*s, consider the simple procedure for the case when $n = 3$ (i.e., FOA3). A's optimal initial offer is $a_{1,3}^* = 0$ because, when the current interval is $(a, b) = (0, 1)$, then

$$a_{1,3}^* = a + (b - a)\alpha_{1,3}^*$$

$$= 0 + (1 - 0)(0) = 0$$

from $\alpha_{1,3}^*$ in Table 12.1. On round 2, if B won on round 1 (with $b_{1,3}^* = 1$) and the current interval is therefore (1/2, 1), then

$$a_{2,3}^* = 1/2 + (1 - 1/2)(1/5) = 3/5$$

Table 12.1
Simple Sequential Arbitration Procedures

Maximum No. of Rounds n	Round i					
	1	2	3	4	5	6

Optimal Action $\alpha^*_{i,n}$ for Player A

	1	2	3	4	5	6
1	0					
2	0	0				
3	0	1/5	0			
4	0	1/6	1/5	0		
5	0	5/29	1/6	1/5	0	
6	0	6/35	5/29	1/6	1/5	0

Normalized Expected Settlement $A^*_{i,n}$ if Player A Bids in Round i

	1	2	3	4	5	6
1	1/2					
2	1/2	1/2				
3	1/2	3/5	1/2			
4	1/2	7/12	3/5	1/2		
5	1/2	17/29	7/12	3/5	1/2	
6	1/2	41/70	17/29	7/12	3/5	1/2

n	s/Pr	Probabilities (Pr) of Possible Settlements (s)							
1	s	0	1						
	Pr	1/2	1/2						
2	s	0	1/2	1					
	Pr	1/4	1/2	1/4					
3	s	0	1/5	2/5	3/5	4/5	1		
	Pr	1/5	1/10	1/5	1/5	1/10	1/5		
4	s	0	4/24	6/24	10/24	14/24	16/24	18/24	1
	Pr	5/24	2/24	1/24	4/24	4/24	1/24	2/24	5/24

Table 12.2
Modified Sequential Arbitration Procedures

Maximum No. of Rounds n	Round i					
	1	2	3	4	5	6

Optimal Action $\alpha^*_{i,n}$ for Player A

	1	2	3	4	5	6
1	0					
2	0	1/3				
3	0	1/7	1/3			
4	0	3/17	1/7	1/3		
5	0	7/41	3/17	1/7	1/3	
6	0	17/99	7/41	3/17	1/7	1/3

Normalized Expected Settlement $A^*_{i,n}$ if Player A Bids in Round i

	1	2	3	4	5	6
1	1/2					
2	1/2	2/3				
3	1/2	4/7	2/3			
4	1/2	10/17	4/7	2/3		
5	1/2	24/41	10/17	4/7	2/3	
6	1/2	58/99	24/41	10/17	4/7	2/3

n	s/Pr	Probabilities (Pr) of Possible Settlements (s)								
1	s	0	1							
	Pr	1/2	1/2							
2	s	0	1/6	1/3	2/3	5/6	1			
	Pr	1/6	1/6	1/6	1/6	1/6	1/6			
3	s	0	4/14	5/14	6/14	8/14	9/14	10/14	1	
	Pr	3/14	1/14	1/14	2/14	2/14	1/14	1/14	3/14	
4	s	0	8/34	9/34	10/34	14/34	20/34	24/34	25/34	26/34	1
	Pr	7/34	2/34	1/34	1/34	6/34	6/34	1/34	1/34	2/34	7/34

On round 3, if B won initially on round 2 (with $b_{2,3}^* = 2/5$) and the current interval is $(1/5, 2/5)$, then

$$a_{3,3}^* = 1/5 + (2/5 - 1/5)(0) = 1/5$$

Analogous calculations show B's optimal offers to be

$b_{1,3}^* = 1$ if $0 < x < 1$

$b_{2,3}^* = 2/5$ if $0 < x \le 1/2$

$b_{3,3}^* = 4/5$ if $3/5 < x \le 1$

Note that on round 2 the players do not make their revised offers equal to their preferred endpoints of the current interval, as they did under FOA2 on round 2, but instead move closer to their adversaries (B from 1/2 to 2/5; A from 1/2 to 3/5).

To continue this example, observe from Table 12.1 that A's expected settlement in the current interval first rises and then falls:

$$A_{1,3}^* = 1/2 \qquad A_{2,3}^* = 3/5 \qquad A_{3,3}^* = 1/2$$

To derive these values, use (12) and the theorem to obtain

$$B_{2,3}^* = 1/(2 + B_{3,3}^*) = 1/(2 + 1/2) = 2/5$$

and

$$A_{2,3}^* = 1 - B_{2,3}^* = 3/5$$

Then, in the first round,

$$A_{1,3}^* = B_{1,3}^* = E_{1,3}^* = 1/2$$

from the theorem.

The theorem does not describe explicitly the probability of different outcomes of optimal play, but as with FOA and FOA2, these probabilities can readily be calculated from the optimal strategies of the players at each stage. In our example, suppose that $0 < x \le 1/2$, so A wins on round 1. As noted earlier, B's optimal second-stage bid is $b_{2,3}^* = 2/5$. If $0 \le x \le 1/5$, A wins twice in a row; if $2/5 \le x \le 1/2$, B overshoots x, so $s = 2/5$. Finally, if $1/5 < x < 2/5$, A bids $a_{3,3}^* = 1/5$, and the settlement is $s = 1/5$ if $1/5 < x \le 3/10$ and $s = 2/5$ if $3/10 < x < 2/5$.

Combining these results and their analogues when $1/2 < x < 1$ (so B wins in the first round) yields the distribution of settlements summarized in Table 12.1:

s = 0 with probability 1/5; s = 1/5 with probability 1/10; s = 2/5 with probability 1/5; and so on. The cases in Table 12.2 can be calculated in similar fashion.

It is also possible to analyze the rounds of long games by finding limits, as n → ∞, of $A_{i,n}^*$ and $\alpha_{i,n}^*$. The results below apply to both the simple and modified procedures—indeed, any procedure that is strategically symmetrical. If i is fixed, one can show that

$$A_{i,n}^* \rightarrow A^* = 2 - \sqrt{2} \approx 0.5858 \qquad \text{as n} \rightarrow \infty$$

$$\alpha_{i,n}^* \rightarrow \alpha^* = 3 - 2\sqrt{2} \approx 0.1716 \qquad \text{as n} \rightarrow \infty$$

Similarly,

$$B_{i,n}^* \rightarrow B^* = \sqrt{2} - 1 \approx 0.4142 \qquad \text{as n} \rightarrow \infty$$

$$\beta_{i,n}^* \rightarrow \beta^* = 2\sqrt{2} - 2 \approx 0.8184 \qquad \text{as n} \rightarrow \infty$$

These limiting values can be obtained by equating $B_{i,n}^*$ and $B_{i+1,n}^*$ in the statement of the theorem and then solving the resulting quadratic equations. These values apply as n becomes very large and the distinction between the the ith and $(i + 1)^{st}$ rounds disappears (for fixed i).

The limit results say that the winner in each round of a long game will reap an expected settlement about 41 percent across the current interval from his or her preferred endpoint. Also, each player will submit a revised offer approximately 17 percent of the distance from this endpoint.

To illustrate this calculation, consider a game with large n (which we now suppress in our notation). On round 1, $a_1^* = 0$ and $b_1^* = 1$. If B wins on the first round, the current interval is (.5, 1), and A offers $a_2^* \approx .586$. If A wins on the second round, the current interval is (.586, .793), and B offers $b_3^* = .758$. If B wins on the third round, the current interval is (.672, .757), and A offers $a_4^* = .686$. If A wins on the fourth round, the current interval is (.686, .723), and B offers $b_5^* = .716$. And so the current interval is quickly narrowed, with the two offers approaching each other.

If the process continues indefinitely, the offers approach the limit of $1/\sqrt{2} \approx$ .707. This occurs when x equals exactly $1/\sqrt{2}$, which we call the *point of convergence* if B wins initially. If A wins initially, this point of convergence is $1 - 1/\sqrt{2} \approx .303$.

It is easy to show that if B chooses action β in some round, then the length of the current interval is reduced by a factor of $\beta/2$. Similarly, if A chooses action α, the length of the current interval is reduced by a factor of $(1 - \alpha)/2$. Comparison with the theorem shows that, if the game continues from round i to round i + 1, the length of the current interval is reduced by a factor of $B_{i,n}^*$ under optimal play.

Because $B_{i,n}^* \to \sqrt{2} - 1 \approx .4142$ as $n \to \infty$, the length of the current interval after $k \geq 3$ rounds will be reduced by a factor of approximately $(.4142)^{k-2}$. We require $k \geq 3$ because on round 1 the players make their simultaneous offers. On round 2 the loser responds by revising his or her offer, at which point there is a better than even chance $(.5858)$ that the initial loser will overshoot x, or the initial winner will be closer to x; in either case, the game will terminate. Hence, only as of round 3 does the question of whether the game terminated earlier arise.

The reduction in the length of the current interval also defines the probability that the game continues at least $k \geq 3$ rounds. It is not difficult to show that the probability that the game lasts at least k rounds is approximately

k =	3	4	5	6	7	8	12
Prob. =	.4142	.1718	.0711	.0294	.0122	.00505	.00015

Thus, with probability .4142 the game continues to round 3. Then there is only about one chance in 200 that the game goes to round 8, and one chance in 7,500 that the game reaches round 12. Patently, when the players make optimal choices, they have little to fear that the game will be interminable, or even close to it. The points of infinite convergence are a theoretical curiosity, not a practical reality.

Call an SA procedure with an indefinite termination rule FOA∞. Technically, FOA∞ really is an SA procedure with a fixed number of rounds, but this number is allowed to approach infinity. In the limit as $n \to \infty$, FOA∞ allows the players to continue until one player loses twice in a row.

In fact, Neale and Bazerman (1987) proposed this procedure, which they labeled "progressive approximation" FOA, as an alternative to FOA. In a series of experiments, they found that the disputants did tend to move toward each and reach a settlement more often than under FOA.

The speed of convergence of FOA∞ will depend on the number of rounds before one player loses twice in a row. The longer play continues, the closer on average the players will be to the arbitrator, as our earlier example carried to five rounds illustrated.

Even an SA procedure that sets the maximum at only a few rounds ensures that the players will not be too far from the arbitrator. Consider our earlier example of the simple procedure where $n = 3$:

Round 1: Simultaneous offers.

Round 2: Initial loser responds. If unsuccessful or overshoots, play terminates.

Round 3: Initial winner responds; play terminates regardless.

Thus, the initial loser is allowed exactly one revised offer; if successful, the initial winner is also allowed exactly one revised offer to try to regain winning status.

It follows from our earlier discussion of this procedure that the greatest distance that can separate the winning player from the arbitrator, if both players play optimally, is .20. This maximum will be approached if the arbitrator's position is, say, .19. Then A would win on round 1, and B would respond with a revised offer of $b^*_{2,3} = .40$. But $b^*_{2,3}$ is farther from .19 than $a^*_{1,3} = 0$, so A would win after two rounds, with the arbitrator a distance of .19 from the closer player's (i.e., A's) offer.

The maximum distance that can separate the arbitrator from a player is halved to .10 if the game terminates because of overshooting. For example, if the arbitrator's position is .49, again A would win on round 1, and B would respond with a revised offer of $b^*_{2,3} = .40$. This offer would place B (as well as A at 0) to the left of the arbitrator and, according to rule 2, terminate play. Observe that the settlement at .40 is slightly less than .10 from the arbitrator at .49.

Clearly, optimal play does not inexorably home in on the position of the arbitrator, especially when play terminates before the maximum number of rounds is reached. But, as we have illustrated, an upper bound can be placed on the distance that separates the winning offer from the arbitrator under any SA procedure.

A similar upper bound can be placed on the distance separating the two players from each other when play terminates. In our example, if x is, say, .01, then A will win initially and then subsequently when B revises downward his or her offer from 1 to .40. Yet a distance of nearly .40 separates the two players from each other, which is double the maximum distance of .20 that can separate the winning player from the arbitrator.

We emphasize that the maximum of .20 is a worst-case scenario. If the arbitrator's position were, say, .40 or .20—not to mention 0 or 1—convergence to this position would be absolute on round 2 by B and on round 3 by A, respectively. (Likewise, there would be absolute convergence to .60 and .80 by A and B, respectively, on rounds 2 and 3.) Thus, the degree of convergence of an SA procedure is sensitive to the particular position of the arbitrator.

On average, however, a procedure of greater length will narrow the gap between the arbitrator's position and the settlement. But even FOA∞ will not be helpful if the game terminates early.

In fact, the maximum distance that can separate the arbitrator from a player under FOA∞ is .207. For each player, this is also the probability that the initial loser's response, because it is farther from x than the initial winner's, ends the game on round 2. For example, if $x = .207 - \epsilon$, where ϵ is a small positive number, B's optimal response of .414 will terminate play since A's first offer will still be closer to x than B's second.

Perhaps surprising is the fact that the settlement under FOA∞, s = 0, is farther from the arbitrator than s = .40, which would occur under the simple procedure when n = 3 (i.e., FOA3, discussed earlier). FOA∞, therefore, does not ensure that a settlement will be closer to the arbitrator than does a procedure of fixed length.

IS CONVERGENCE DESIRABLE?

The question we raise in this concluding section would seem to have an obvious answer: insofar as the arbitrator is capable of choosing a fair settlement, convergence to this settlement seems unobjectionable. But then, one might ask, why not use conventional arbitration? This kind of arbitration would absolutely eliminate any discrepancy between the settlement and the arbitrator's position.

The ostensible reason for using an SA procedure is that it induces the players to converge on their own. Thereby the settlement is not imposed, although the players' convergence—or lack thereof—is very much driven by the position of the arbitrator. Neale and Bazerman (1987) found, nevertheless, that subjects in their experiment perceived such a resolution to be fair, at least in part because they had greater control over the outcome.

Compared with FOA, which induces no convergence at all in the uniform case, the settlement is certainly less likely to be one-sided. Even when limited to just two rounds, the modified procedure leads to a nonextreme settlement (i.e., not at 0 or 1) with probability .67—more than any other SA procedure. As we showed earlier, if there is no limit on the number of rounds, FOA∞ leads to a nonextreme settlement with probability .59.

All our results assume that the choice of the arbitrator is uniformly distributed. However, this assumption of maximum uncertainty may not be descriptive of many arbitration situations, wherein the arbitrator is more likely to take a centrist than an extreme position. We speculate that a unimodal distribution, with the mode at or near the mean or median, is likely to draw the players toward the center, both initially (Brams and Merrill, 1983) and subsequently, more quickly than does the uniform distribution. A "bonus" that the players derive from winning, independent of the value of a settlement, may also be helpful in moderating extreme offers at the start (Brams and Merrill, 1991).

The procedure with the greatest drawing power seems to be "combined arbitration" (Brams and Merrill, 1986; Brams, 1986), which combines FOA (if the arbitrator is between the two final offers) and conventional arbitration (if the arbitrator is outside the final offers); in the latter case, the arbitrator's choice becomes the settlement. If the arbitrator's distribution is unimodal and symmetric, the two players have dominant strategies of bidding the median of the arbitrator's distribution.

Compared with the sequential procedures, combined arbitration makes the players' perceptions of the arbitrator's distribution all-important. Like FOA, the players receive no feedback on the position of the arbitrator under this one-stage procedure, so they have no opportunity to update information on this position.

The proper choice between sequential procedures and combined arbitration will depend on how much weight one thinks should be accorded the arbitrator's actual position as a guideline for a settlement. If little or none—only the distribution matters—then combined arbitration would seem best. On the other hand, if one wishes the position of the arbitrator to be a magnet for the players, then one of the sequential procedures is superior.

But which one? To force a quick resolution and avoid what might be an inordinately long game, modified FOA2 seems best; it results in a nonextreme settlement in 67 percent of cases. Moreover, because a settlement is equally likely at 1/6 intervals across [0, 1]—except for the midpoint of 3/6 = 1/2—this version of FOA2 is not biased against outcomes anywhere on the unit interval except near 1/2.

By comparison, the simple version of FOA3 discussed earlier produces a nonextreme settlement in 60 percent of the cases, and FOA∞ does so in 59 percent. Also, under simple FOA3, outcomes at 1/5 and 4/5 are only half as likely as outcomes at 0, 2/5, 3/5, and 1, suggesting a bias against arbitrator positions near but not at the extremes.

Similarly, outcomes under FOA∞ are not equiprobable across the unit interval; the endpoints, 0 and 1, are most favored and have probabilities of .207 each, as we showed earlier. On the other hand, FOA∞ better replicates the give-and-take of bargaining and, if the process lasts more than a very few rounds, will bring the players extremely close to the arbitrator (and each other).

These are the trade-offs that need to be considered in selecting an arbitration scheme. Whereas a sequential procedure provides one possible way to mitigate the harshness of an extreme settlement, it should be remembered that the very lack of any procedural incentive to compromise under FOA may encourage the players to bargain on their own, without resorting to arbitration, to reach a settlement. Recently, however, Brams and Merrill (forthcoming) have shown how the possibility of compromise by players may be incorporated into both FOA and combined arbitration.

Sometimes, it appears, a formal mechanism may abet bargainers, especially when they have difficulty—for personal or other reasons—in making concessions in an unstructured setting. The leverage that an arbitrator exerts may help them cut through to the issues that separate them, leaving behind anger, pride, and other more subjective human feelings that often aggravate conflict and prolong disputes.

An understanding of the theoretical properties of sequential and other arbitration procedures should aid policy-makers in selecting the most appropriate one in particular situations. Among the SA procedures, we think modified FOA2 is the simplest and perhaps the most practical procedure to induce compromise. A nonextreme settlement is somewhat less likely under FOA∞ (59 versus 67 percent), but its saving grace is that after two rounds it permits greater learning of, and movement toward, the position of the arbitrator. This feature, along with its approximation of the give-and-take of bargaining (without an arbitrator), may be beneficial in many disputes.

NOTE

Steven J. Brams gratefully acknowledges the financial support of the United States Institute of Peace under grant USIP-362.

REFERENCES

Brams, Steven J. (1986). "New, Improved Final-Offer Arbitration." *New York Times*. Aug. 9, p. 22.

—— . (1990). *Negotiation Games: Applying Game Theory to Bargaining and Arbitration*. New York: Routledge.

Brams, Steven J., and Samuel Merrill, III. (1983). "Equilibrium Strategies for Final-Offer Arbitration: There Is No Median Convergence." *Management Science* 29, no. 8 (Aug.): 927–41.

—— . (1986). "Binding versus Final-Offer Arbitration: A Combination Is Best." *Management Science* 32, no. 10 (Oct.): 1346–55.

—— . (1991). "Final-Offer Arbitration with a Bonus." *European Journal of Political Economy* 7, forthcoming.

—— . "Arbitration Procedures with the Possibility of Compromise," forthcoming.

Brams, Steven J., D. Marc Kilgour, and Samuel Merrill, III. (1991). "Arbitration Procedures." In Peyton Young, ed., *Negotiation Analysis*. Ann Arbor: University of Michigan Press.

Carrington, Tim. (1988). "Pentagon Halts Multiple Submissions of 'Best and Final Offers' by Contractors." *Wall Street Journal*, July 26, p. 62.

Chass, Murray. (1988). "Arbitration: In Settlements, Size Counts." *New York Times*, Feb. 21, p. S7.

Cronin, Barry. (1989). "The Umpire Strikes Back." *Northwestern Perspective* 2, no. 3 (Spring): 2–7.

Freeman, Richard B. (1986). "Unionism Comes to the Public Sector." *Journal of Economic Literature* 24, no. 1: 41–86.

Gibbons, Robert. (1988). "Learning in Equilibrium Models of Arbitration." *American Economic Review* 78, no. 5 (Dec.): 896–912.

Halloran, Richard. (1988). "Honesty Called 'Impossible' in Pentagon Bidding System." *New York Times*, July 28, p. A20.

Neale, Margaret A., and Max H. Bazerman. (1987). "Progressive Approximation Final Offer Arbitration: Matching the Goals of a Conflict Domain." *International Journal of Management* 4, no. 1 (Mar.): 30–37.

Rehmus, Charles M. (1979). "Interest Arbitration." In Public Employment Relations Services, ed., *Portrait of a Process: Collective Negotiations in Public Employment*. Fort Washington, Pa.: Labor Relations Press, 209–33.

Stern, James L., et al. (1975). *Final-Offer Arbitration*. Lexington, Mass.: D. C. Heath.

Stevens, Carl M. (1966). "Is Compulsory Arbitration Compatible with Bargaining?" *Industrial Relations* 5, no. 2 (Feb.): 38–52.

Wittman, Donald. (1986). "Final-Offer Arbitration." *Management Science* 32, no. 12 (Dec.): 1551–61.

PART VII

Dispute Resolution in Economic and Political Theory

CHAPTER 13

Alternative Dispute Resolution in the United States: No Roses Without Thorns

STEPHAN PARMENTIER

In 1906 Roscoe Pound addressed the problems of the legal system in an article, "Causes of Popular Dissatisfaction with the Administration of Justice." Seventy years later, the Pound Follow-Up Conference was held, dealing with the same problems. It marked the beginning of the official reaction of contemporary legal professionals.

Former Chief Justice Burger has strongly supported the development of alternative means of dispute settlement. Congress and many state legislatures have witnessed legislative efforts to foster the development of nonjudicial remedies.

Meanwhile many concrete programs have mushroomed throughout the United States, in experimental or operational stage, dealing with an array of disputes of varying sizes and approaches.

All of these elements suggest the rise of a movement that justifies close attention. First, the phenomenon is a recent one, although related to previous innovations answering problems involved in the administration of justice. Second, it is of a pragmatic nature since it determines the opportunities and possibilities of various modes of dispute-processing. Rethinking and reorganizing the ways that conflicts are dealt with will affect not only the parties involved directly but will also have repercussions for the legal profession as a whole. Finally, the developments have caused new theories to burgeon.

This chapter will identify the major debate about alternative dispute resolution (ADR) by confronting and contrasting two main viewpoints. The first is the so-called common perspective that dominates in the media and the literature. Its authors, although coming from very different backgrounds, are united by their fervent enthusiasm for the alternative movement. The second, which lifts a warning finger against many aspects of alternative dispute resolution, is termed "critical." These writers hint at the cloud of rhetoric in which the common talk is immersed and link the alternatives to the expansion of state control in capitalist society. For this purpose, some of them refer to Marxist concepts.

My contribution is driven by two purposes. One is to view sociology as a questioning exercise yielding broad and interesting research agendas. The other is the relevance for practice because scholarly investigation has to offer more than ivory-tower knowledge for its own luxurious sake. Therefore, this chapter aims at inductivity, graduality, and an integrative view of the problems.

TRADITION AND INNOVATION

A Broad Selection

Mediation. Arbitration. Nonjudicial dispute settlement. Minitrial. Principled bargaining. Summary proceedings. Ombudsman. Delegalization. Informal justice. Alternative dispute resolution. The last decade has witnessed the emergence of a new vocabulary in the field of legal practice and organization. Numerous, even countless, are the programs, projects, proposals, organizations, centers, and publications that correspond to this novel terminology. The utmost diversity, and at times, divergence, suggests that the force uniting them is weak and largely undefined. Only some common interest in conflict and conflict resolution has brought them together.

In the American media and literature, ample attention is paid to the many new mediation programs in operation, the community mediators being trained, and the courses offered at law schools. Practices as different as court-annexed arbitration, victim-offender mediation, and public issue dispute resolution are frequently highlighted and discussed. The Society of Professionals in Dispute Resolution was established to advance the professional and educational interests of all those working in the field. And a good deal of academic and practitioner research time, energy, and money has taken dispute and dispute resolution as their focal point.

Theory of Conflict and Conflict Resolution

Conflicts and conflict theory are as old as humanity. A decade ago, Wehr charted the most important variables of conflict (Wehr, 1979). Felstiner, Abel, and Sarat (1981: 633–37) have recently tried to enhance scientific understanding by distinguishing several stages in the dynamic development of a dispute. They consider naming, blaming, and claiming as consecutive—but not automatic—steps in such a process.

If conflict theory is old, dispute theory is relatively new. In the last decade, sometimes excessive attention has been paid to the study of disputes and the various ways to handle, settle, or solve them. It is often argued that people have several options to deal with conflicts (Galanter, 1974). First, they can opt for inaction or action. Second, if they go for action, they can choose a one-party deed (avoidance); a two-party involvement (negotiation); or a three-party intervention (mediation, arbitration, or adjudication). Each of these techniques has a specific meaning and particular characteristics.

Furthermore, ADR has become one of the new focuses of the sociology of law. Blankenburg (1980: 7–8) has observed that legal sociology since the 1960s has gradually changed its main interest from research about the selectivity of the judicial process to the debate on access to judicial services. More attention was paid to reducing the barriers of the legal system in order to obtain adequate redress for the disadvantaged. Tomasic (1985: 55–58) signals the shift from the investigations on courts in general to the functioning of lower courts. Extensive research was devoted to the disputes these courts dealt with. Critiques of the legal system have spurred the quest for alternative ways to handle disputes.

Gessner (1983: 38–40) has pleaded for the expansion of legal sociology into a sociology of norms. He calls for an intermediary variable between action-based individual behavior and structure-based societal norms. Such variables can lie in the dynamic and continuous process of norm interpretation. At a certain point, this interpreting process hits the fact that norms in general, and legal norms in particular, represent power relations in society. Thus, when disputes are seen as conflicts between legal norms, they can contribute to a redefinition of them. Disputes may even directly be seen as conflicting power structures in society, which they can help redefine.

DESCRIPTION

It is often taken for granted that the description of a phenomenon is an innocent and neutral enterprise forming the base for what really matters—explanation. This contention turns out to be very weak. Describing an object is as important as explaining it and is even the first step in doing so. Therefore, I present different descriptions in their intimate connection with different explanations.

The Common Perspective:
A Description of the Present Situation

People from different backgrounds share common thoughts about the state of the official legal system in the United States. Here they are all subsumed under a single common perspective—not because their arguments always coincide but because of their unanimous enthusiasm for ADR. This talk has started pervading the media and thus has easily become the dominant view.

In this view, the legal system is ill-equipped to deal with the many problems it is facing. The fairly simple diagnosis rests, according to Trubek (1984), on the widespread assertion of the moral decline of contemporary American society. For evidence, the authors build on notions advanced earlier of "hyperlexis"

(Manning, 1977) and "legal pollution" (Ehrlich, 1976), allegedly corresponding to a threatening "litigation explosion" (Barton, 1975). Depending on their backgrounds and interests, the proponents of this thesis will view the major symptoms of this moral disease either as the severe congestion, or the adversarial character, or the extreme inefficiency of the present legal system.

Throughout the whole discussion, however, the treatment seems always at hand. According to all, a moral restoration can best be brought about by reducing society's level of legalization and formalization. The advocates either stress the anticipated positive results of a severely reduced case backlog (Burger, 1982: 277); or a far less adversarial procedure, enabling participants in a dispute to come to their own accommodating terms in a noncoercive setting (Folberg and Taylor, 1984: 7–15). One of the strongest and most powerful sources of inspiration for this latter ideal is found in the anthropological literature of small-scale societies in which parties do not resort to courts but solve their own problems with the facilitative help from others (Danzig, 1974; but see Fisher, 1975; Merry, 1982).

Finally, defending the deformalization trend goes hand in glove with the presentation of informality as an inherently good evolution. Schemes that depict the development from formality (courts) to informality (mediation) often imply that moving away from the court system provides far better and more promising programs (Sander, 1976: 114). However, as so many manifestations of the movement have popped up, the awareness has grown that reality is more complex than that. Therefore, distinctions were introduced between the new techniques (mainly mediation and arbitration) and the diverse settings (inside and outside the courts) they can be used in (Marks, Johnson, and Szanton, 1984: 42–50).

The Critical Perspective: Questioning the Previous Account

Total dissatisfaction with the superficial common talk has spurred a critical approach that goes beyond simple rhetoric. This questioning enterprise combines empirical research with a comparative, in-depth analysis. Here as well, the critical authors do not approach this problem in identical terms, but they certainly do agree on a critical, not-for-granted attitude.

First, the common diagnosis of the "litigation explosion" is severely questioned and ultimately discarded. Empirical research has revealed that only a small number of disputes end up in court, and that many of them are dealt with in many diverse forums that already exist (Miller and Sarat, 1981: 544). This model of the dispute pyramid has prompted the saying that "negotiation, arbitration, mediation, and summary proceedings are hardly alternatives: they are the norm for dispute resolution. Litigation in the form of trial held in courts is, in fact 'the alternative' when over 90% of all cases, civil and criminal, are settled before trial."[1] Moreover, court filings are not necessarily the end of the informal treatment but usually stimulate other ways of handling the dispute, now in the shadow of the court (Sarat, 1976: 342–43). In other words, litigation is not the only way for Americans to handle their conflicts.

Litigation has to be placed into comparative perspective. Recent studies have found a rise in litigation, but one that is not at odds with developments in other Western industrialized countries. Moreover, the increase is not a historically isolated phenomenon but has precedents (Galanter, 1983: 36–51). As Abel (1982b: 10–11) points out, the recent rise in court use can partly be seen as the legacy of the 1960s, when many legal newcomers (such as consumers, the elderly, the handicapped, and prisoners) started using the court system to have their rights enforced.

The combination of these data leads to rejection of the ''litigation explosion'' thesis and the connected categories of declining morality. Also, the common treatment is subjected to thorough criticism. Many common advocates emphasize the advantages of reduced adversariness in a less coercive context. Obviously this issue becomes a major focus of attention for the critics. For them, the ADR mechanisms that are somehow implicated in the state apparatus do not display a lesser degree of coercion but present it in a different way (Abel, 1982c: 270–72). All of the critical authors agree that these new informal forums receive their main reason for existence from their dependence upon the official court system. Figures indicate that the three officially set-up neighborhood justice centers get two-thirds to three-fourths of their caseload from the regular court system (Harrington, 1985: 113–21). This, of course, is not surprising for justice system models. But most of the programs that were started privately ultimately become caught in the realm of the courts as well. Their funding necessities make them very vulnerable to the pressures of the legal system. If surviving means guaranteeing minimal caseloads and sufficient impact on the court system, then seeking support from the courts is only a small but logical step (Wahrhaftig, 1982).

In addition to external coercion by reason of court referrals, the critics pay attention to the internal nature of the conflict-handling process. Abel (1982c) launches a vigorous attack against these sessions where allegedly the harsh reality of the justice system is substituted by the softness of accommodating procedures. In his view, the nature of these sessions remains equally coercive but their outlook has changed. New symbols ensure that manipulation is now relaxed and coercion disguised, to the extent of making calls for due process seem redundant.

Finally, the critics attack the common anthropological source of inspiration. Merry (1982: 28–40) has argued that in those small-scale societies characterized by cohesiveness, stability, and moral integration, the disputants and the dispute are not foreign to the environment they originate in. The mediators usually are highly ranked insiders who represent the common value system of the group and exert pressure on the parties. The mediated settlement mostly implies compensatory payment of damages and is done immediately after the agreement. Most of these features differ quite radically in the American context.

The aggregation of these mutually reinforcing research findings leaves the critics with a different description of reality. Abel (1980: 269–70) asserts that picturing the evolution from formality to informality as a progressive and good evolution does not hold at all. On the contrary, the critics want to elaborate a dynamic vision that does not eschew a dialectical-historical analysis to come to more serious terms with ADR. Spitzer (1982: 201) observes that it is very superficial and ideologically disguising to see ADR as the latest manifestation of the cyclical oscillation between the poles of formality and informality.

EXPLANATION

Like description, explanation is not a neutral enterprise. It depends on the angle adopted. This is very clear for the explanation of the rise of ADR.

The Common Perspective:
Explaining the Present Situation

One of the most puzzling aspects of this topic is the complex way in which arguments of various sorts and from very distinctive angles blend together in their advocacy of deformalization. In the quagmire, however, three major forces can be discerned, each of which attracts supporters from conservative and more liberal backgrounds.

At first glance, all arguments in favor of delegalization are pragmatic and thus seem convincing. They are all based on the tension between the ambitions and the pretentions of the legal system and its realizations. The enthusiastic advocates argue that the Weberian concepts of substantive legality and procedural legalization do not match anymore; they have even become contradictory (Harrington, 1982: 36).

Some of them locate many deficiencies in the traditional legal system. Following up on the contradiction between substantive justice and procedural formalism, some state the problem in terms of access to justice. The denial of justice, aggravated by the factors of cost, delay, and adversariness, allegedly add up to consumer dissatisfaction (Abel, 1980: 30–31). Others look at the legal system from a defensive point of view. They say that too much has been asked from the courts so as to push them beyond the reasonable limits of efficiency (Abel, 1980: 30; Galanter, 1980: 11). Helping to unburden the courts would have no effect without a far more radical effort to peel off several layers of regulation and legalism (Barton, 1975; Ehrlich, 1976).

A second group emphasizes the necessities and strengths of people's involvement. They argue that people are willing to break through the atomized and anonymous cast of adversarial litigiousness to start exploring other conflict-resolution ways. The zero-sum decision-making model is said to leave parties with an unbalanced and undesired process outcome (Alper and Nichols, 1981). New mechanisms would meet the people's demands to regain control over their own conflicts as an integral part of their lives. In strong wording, Christie (1977: 298–302) maintains that people could redevelop the sense of involvement that was lost when their conflicts were stolen from them by "professional thieves" (read "lawyers"), who transformed these into unrecognizable exterior things.

This empowerment is not confined to individuals or dyads, since increased independence would ultimately result in better community-building (Alper and Nichols, 1981). Wahrhaftig (1982: 95–97) even assigns ADR the task of educating people and empowering communities.

A third group of ADR advocates reasons in terms of efficiency. Organizations in general, and business in particular, express their overriding concern to get things done fast and cheaply, without external interference. For them, innovative dispute-handling is a matter of improved communication and better management (Green, 1982).

The Critical Perspective:
Challenging the Common Explanation

The critical authors look at arguments other than the efficiency of the legal system or people's dislike of adversariness. They approach ADR in terms of concrete interests molded by power relations and subject to identifiable underlying mechanisms in society. For that purpose they use methods that in a historical-dialectical move want to pierce to the core of the problem and link it back to a holistic perspective. For analytical purposes, I distinguish various steps in this process. Again, all authors do not necessarily agree on every argument, but they do share this critical attitude that goes beyond simple rhetoric.

Pointing at Greater Complexity: The Role of Ideology

A critical investigation already pointed to some serious flaws in the common description. First, this raises the question of causality. Trubek (1984: 826) argues that, because in the common view diagnosis and treatment are emerging at the same time, the push for alternatives was not the result of a careful consideration and consequent rejection of the litigation malaise. Rather the whole image of the litigation explosion was called into being to justify what was already going on.

Subsequently, it should be asked what the alternatives are actually an alternative to. If they are an alternative to the present legal system, how does one conceptualize previous historical experiments such as diversion or court reform (Harrington, 1982)? If they are an alternative to adjudication, how can this be related to the assertion that a good deal of the courts' activity already consists of routine processing (Friedman and Percival, 1976)? If they are an alternative to the formal system, how can this be linked to the long-term existence of commercial and labor arbitration (Harrington, 1982: 42), business negotiation, and mediation as "the second-oldest profession in the world" (Kolb, 1983: 1)? Finally, how can all these developments be grasped in the light of similar cross-temporal and cross-spatial experiences (Abel, 1982c: 267)? Probing these questions leads Abel to remark that the new thing about the "alternative movement" is not so much its existence as the talk about it (pp. 267–70). In other words, it is the critics' view that the attempts to explain why these experiments are emerging now can teach us a lot more about the nature and the future of ADR than investigating it from a deductive or logical point of view. By doing so, they point at the thick cloud of rhetoric and ideology hanging over the informal reality.

Locating the Nexus: Deformalization within Capitalism

Many authors share the so-called critical perspective. Some of them go further and eventually slip into Marxist categories. Unlike their European counterparts, however, American writers wander around quite freely in this field. Their framework is not built on fundamental political economy but remains confined to the usage of some key notions of Marxism. They link ADR with the capitalist environment and the pivotal role of the state. Although they see an expansion of state control through the "alternative" development, they differ in their specificity as to the mechanisms that generate it and in their appreciation about the extent and importance of this state control.

Smith (1981) has pointed out that within Marxism different routes can be taken. Two of these find support from the critical authors. Hofrichter (1982) leans toward the fundamentalist side. For him, the state is clearly subjected to the logic of capital but takes an external appearance and organization. To administer the wishes of capital, the state has to attempt to regulate social life and at the same time depoliticize it. Its chief function is the dispersal of an ever-recurrent set of contradictions arising from a capitalist economy. This happens through active intervention that may not always serve capital's interests in the short run but does preserve them in the long run. The state and the law provide the necessary control that capitalism needs for survival. Any threat forces the state to restore legitimacy and forces capital to assure control. Thus, the nature of the control that underlies the alternatives is more pervasive than ever. Hofrichter sees it as chaosmic, regulating the totality of social existence. Although he denies adhering to a theory of conspiracy, he seems very much caught in the view of the state intently pursuing the interests of capital.

The other interpretation of Marxism is overdetermination (Smith, 1981). For Abel (1980; 1982c: 301-4), the state is more than the mere executive branch of capital, although many state actions indirectly favor capital. The proclamation of liberalist ideas without the sufficient resources to enforce legal rights and the selective expansion of state control legitimate both state and capital. Abel also acknowledges the importance of specific groups—in this case the dynamic professional interest of all factions of the legal system—in shaping societal developments. Spitzer (1982: 190-200) shares his concern for a dynamic-historical perspective, but his story abut the Chinese cycles of formalism and informalism remains somewhat in the dark.

If the authors differ in envisaging the global world, they do focus their attention on the same problems of ADR. I will only discuss the most basic ones. One issue is coercion. For Abel (1982c: 270), the much acclaimed voluntary character of the alternatives is fake. There are too many connections with the official legal system, such as dependency on referrals for minimal caseloads and lawsuits pending while settlements are negotiated. Although the trappings and symbols of the formal system are absent, coercion continues in an accommodating environment.[2] In this context the role of a facilitating third party becomes crucial, but the outside means and guarantees for power-balancing are virtually eliminated. The alleged "haven from the formal system" (Abel, 1982c: 271) could turn out to be a labyrinth. Even more, Santos (1982: 258-59) sees the rhetoric of informal justice increasingly being infiltrated by bureaucracy and violence, the core ingredients of the legal system.

This is particularly relevant when related to the second topic, conflict neutralization. The alternatives are attacked for their goal, if not intent, to prevent fundamental critical questions about the present social order. Abel (1982c: 280-85) believes that many alternative programs play the same game as grievance procedures: they are created and controlled by those they are in fact directed against. Where compromise prevails, parties have to meet halfway. Thus, demands can be curtailed without questioning their justified character and the possible discriminatory and oppressive practices they originate from. Parties are asked to blame themselves, not structural social and economic conditions. For a very critical Hofrichter (1982: 240-43), there is no space left anymore for collective, class actions where precedents can be established. Disputes that would point at more general societal conflicts are dealt with on a case-by-case basis. Thus, individuals can get immediate redress, but groups as a whole lose in the long run.

This is intimately connected with the concept of increased state control, which forms the very core of all Marxist critiques. Conflict neutralization does not happen at random. The process selectively and intentionally focuses on the intraclass disputes of the economically and politically oppressed (Abel, 1982c: 274-75). Accordingly, many of the strong defenders of informalization only recommend it for others, reserving the at-times useful services of the formal legal system for themselves. This "legalistic delegalization" parallels the other trend of deregulation, which is strongly favored by business, especially in those areas where their opponents are strong (Abel, 1982c: 268-69).

The critics further describe the particular mechanisms that govern the expansion of state control. The legal system is only concerned with specific acts that violate the rules of law (*nullum crimen sine lege*). Informal justice, on the other hand, can screen a whole range of behavior, especially morally undesirable behavior, because of reduced visible coercion and lower expenditures. The advocates argue that delegalization can thus intervene in social relations before conflicts can erupt. For many critical authors, this is a double-edged sword. Hofrichter (1982: 237-40) points out that behavior now escaping state scrutiny will easily be taken in by informal institutions that are gradually regulating "the totality of social existence."

And there is more. The critics argue that the alternative programs do not live up to their promises. Many of them involve strangers, without ongoing relationship and with unequal resources. Therefore, the idea of dealing properly with the underlying causes of conflict can be considered mere ideology (Hofrichter, 1977: 169-70). Expectations are raised high but at the same time the due process rules, if not eliminated, are not guaranteed anymore and are certainly not apt to be checked (Abel, 1982c: 271).

The authors further indicate the existence of two concurrent trends to be viewed in dialectical unity. The decentralization and dispersal of control are countered by centralization of power (Spitzer, 1982: 87). Thus, Santos (1982: 261–63) opposes the Foucaultian view that chaosmic (atomized, mobile) power would substitute cosmic (centralized, physically located) power. Rather, it is their simultaneous, nonantagonistic appearance that characterizes the very nature of power exercise in late capitalism. Abel (1982c: 273) confirms that informal institutions are always planned as additive supplements to, and not as substitutes for, the existing legal system. This goes hand in glove with the increasing centralization of corporate power and calls to lift the restrictions on monopoly capitalism (Hofrichter, 1977: 169). For corroboration of these arguments, the authors establish linkages with the historical research on court reform in general (Harrington, 1982), and criminal justice reform—diversion and community corrections—in particular (Austin and Krisberg, 1981; Blomberg, 1977; Cohen, 1979). In the nonlegal field, there are heavy parallels with the expansion of control in workplace and community (Hofrichter, 1982: 228–35); Spitzer, 1982: 188–90). Spitzer (1982: 190) concludes that "widening the net while thinning the mesh" takes place in a very subtle way and is difficult to investigate—particularly since the corresponding language disguises rather than clarifies reality (Abel, 1982b: 9).

The Fundamental Contradiction: Delegalization and Legality

In their critique of informalization, the authors repeatedly refer to the characteristics of the formal legal system. Abel (1982c: 270–73) mentions that the law, in contrast to the alternatives, focuses only on specific rule-violating acts. In considering these offenses, a whole system of public due process variables has to be taken into account. For the critical authors, the degree of coerciveness of the legal system is not less, but its visibility is higher because of the formal trappings and the various policing forces.

Hofrichter's (1982: 232–43) arguments also imply that the legal system, even if not equipped to deal with broader underlying social causes, at least allows class and collective actions that can result in precedent-setting. The value that the general public attributes to the law is further illustrated by the fact that there is a simultaneous movement toward the courts, not only away from them. Each time some area of social life is deregulated and left to the parties for settlement, new problems and threats arise that push for legal recognition (Abel, 1980: 32–34).

Eventually authors confront a fundamental contradiction. In criticizing the alternatives they had to fall back on the alleged virtues of the existing legal system. However, all the earlier critiques voiced against the same legal system reemerge. Abel (1980: 40) acknowledges that legalization, in contrast with informalization, assumes parties to be unequal and therefore expects the legal system to make them equal. However, formal "blind" equality in an inherently unequal world is not a protective tool but rather serves the status quo (Abel, 1982c: 294). In other words, the law is not deemed a viable "alternative" to the alternative movement.

On the contrary, the critical authors argue that ADR has provided new legitimation for the legal system. Hofrichter (1977: 168–69) indicates how the crisis of the legal order pushes for new forms of social control to prevent social breakdown. The new alternatives not only restore social control but also appear as the solution to the problems of bias and inaccessibility of the legal system. Abel (1982c: 304–7) agrees that informalization restores and reinforces the legitimacy of the legal order by unburdening the courts and distracting attention from their problems. Furthermore, each time the alternative procedures are used, new faith is placed in the organisms that created them, which actually legitimizes the state and capital. He critically concludes that both systems—formal and informal—are mere myths, proclaiming rights but not providing the necessary structural and financial resources to make these enforceable.

The inevitable question arises concerning which route to take from here. Abel (1980: 38) reluctantly claims that in this context the choice is between informal and powerless institutions and powerful but formal ones. This leaves us with the ironic paradox that apparently nobody believes in law anymore. The common perspective embraces informalism, while the critics cautiously defend a legal system they actually distrust. Trubek (1984: 835) notes the lack of clarity in these critiques: apparently they imply a thorough transformation of the present system but they do not give any clues on how to bring that about.

PRESCRIPTION

A question about the future of the alternative movement contains two parts: what is likely to happen, and what is desirable?

What Can Happen in the Field?

In both major perspectives the predictions largely emanate from the descriptive and explanatory parts.

The common viewpoint sees an increased expansion of the informalization trends and embraces that evolution, for various reasons. Those arguing in terms of efficiency view a further unburdening of the courts as well as faster and cheaper decisions as likely and desirable. Those stressing the accessibility and nonadversariness are eager to pursue a better and swifter justice that can reduce society's global conflict level and empower participants.

The critical perspective also thinks of an expansion in the short run but is not so enthusiastic about it. It points to the issues of control, coercion, and conflict neutralization. The most striking fact, however, is that each of the critical authors claims to discern positive aspects in the alternative movement but no one grants it more than a catchy phrase in a small paragraph of a lengthy article, much less elaborates the remark. They talk in very general terms. Santos (1982: 264–65), for example, concludes that "there is no ideology without utopia," thus referring to the potential of community justice if built on the autonomous political movement of the dominated classes. Abel (1980: 309–10) follows suit by saying that the apparent lessons of the alternative mechanisms are that they only empower those who create them, not those who are its mere clients. Present institutions will not be able to keep on neutralizing conflict indefinitely since opposition of all kinds will grow and create new, genuine forums of community justice. Hofrichter (1977: 171) recognizes in this whole debate a unique opportunity to start a severely critical and broader questioning of the presently biased legal order. At the same time community residents learn new skills that can enhance their awareness of the inherent political character of law.

What Can Happen in the Study of the Field?

Having discussed two major perspectives at some length, I will now try to sketch a basis for future research and practice. I will therefore analyze and evaluate some propositions and advance some personal proposals from a perspective that is concerned with emancipatory action. Let us start with the critical paradigm, which provides some profound insights.

First, the critics argue in favor of a new description of the alternative trend. Their diagnosis attacks the myth of litigiousness. And indeed, empirical research suggests that the number of disputes ending up in court is only a tiny part of the totality of possible conflicts (Galanter, 1983; Miller and Sarat, 1981). However, in order to counterattack the litigation myth, further empirical research has to decompose the numerical litigation into content and context variables. Munger (1988), for example, has noted that in periods of crisis, litigation can increase dramatically because of a rise in interclass conflicts and disputes.

Marxist writers are also critical of the many proposals to establish alternatives for treatment. Their critique, however, displays severe terminological ambiguities. Hofrichter and Abel claim to analyze the nonjudicial, informal state-funded or organized neighborhood dispute forums (Hofrichter, 1982: 208) and the "institutions somehow implicated in the state apparatus" (Abel, 1982c: 270). Santos (1982: 249) even wants to deal with "alternatives to the traditional official court system and formal judicial procedures," whatever their name may be. However, they should more clearly and unambiguously elaborate their specific forum, for various reasons. First, it would entail clarity for the student of the phenomenon. Now it is unclear and very confusing how to conceptualize phenomena as different as no-fault divorce, plea-bargaining, business negotiation, intrainstitutional conflict, and dispute settlement within the Chinese community in the United States. It looks as if the critical authors lump all alternatives together in their analysis. When it comes to uttering critiques, however, they mainly criticize the mediation alternative. Second, classifying and differentiating these alternative forms would refine the authors' critique and evaluation in terms of future potential.

Much more new research will have to be conducted. Proponents of many programs implicitly refer to a past golden age or even present golden societies of informal and cooperative dispute settlement (see Adler, Lovaas, and Milner, 1988). Merry (1982) has pointed at the rhetoric related to anthropological research in this field. Historical analysis of earlier American history is most useful in its potential for generating alternative propositions as well as criticizing the exaggerated nostalgia (Auerbach, 1983).

The critics talk about external coercion as well. Indeed, the literature indicates the dependency of many programs on the judicial system for caseloads and referrals. But there is no direct link with funding. I checked one-hundred alternative programs of all sorts and origins throughout the United States[3] on the hypothesis that a close relationship with the official judicial system (i.e., percentage referrals by official organisms such as judges, police, and attorneys) would entail more financial means for the programs. However, the correlation between these two variables is only $r = 0.17$. This points to a larger complexity, taking into account the sources and conditions of funding, as well as expenditure costs and continuity of the programs.

Arguments about internal coercion, such as manipulation by accommodating techniques and false informalism, require other assessment procedures. They cannot be examined without direct participant observation and follow-up questionnaires to all participants in alternative (especially mediation) sessions. A start to this type of research was made by Silbey and Merry (1986) in their observations of different mediator styles. Following up on that, I have undertaken a small participant observation in a dispute-resolution center in St. Paul, Minnesota. Mediators do influence the final result to a great extent. But the notion of "coercion" does not describe this process in its various aspects adequately.

Finally, the alleged effects of the programs will have to be scrutinized. Empirical analysis should take on the claims of court relief, cost, and speed. Another issue is community involvement and community-building. Its various meanings should be analyzed (Wahrhaftig, 1982: 95–97), particularly when used as the magic stick to introduce new programs (Auerbach, 1983: 132–35). This can form the basis for a checklist to evaluate their progress.

This research agenda of description needs to be combined with other investigations in the field of explanation. The critics have stated that the major role of ideological rhetoric is clear when considering the simultaneous emergency of diagnosis and cure. Thus, explanations in terms of waves or cyclical movements can never reach the intellectual depth required to understand fully the contending forces of reality, because they neglect the role of interests and actors shaped by these. Part of this job is to make clear what exactly the alternatives are an alternative to.

More important is the location of informalism in capitalism, and the problem of conflict neutralization. A repeated warning for individualization of conflict and redress is not superfluous. It is obvious that face-to-face dispute settlements can be obstacles for collective actions through which broader concerns could emerge. Private party-to-party settings are not the best place to handle disputes about societal problems such as automobile safety standards, insurance contracts, or rent increases. These should be brought into the public arena. The issue is even more important at a time when the new dispute professionals have launched the idea to let the dispute-settlement process fit the specificity of the dispute. In other words, new procedures are developed corresponding to the concrete dispute at hand. A political analysis can point at how and when the alternatives' compromising attitudes do curtail the justified demands of individuals against mighty political and economic law-violating adversaries. Field observations should provide more insight into the possibilities to turn aside the dangers of "privatization."

The contention that courts push off "junk" cases to reserve their services for business also needs elaboration. Historical analysis about the early calls for out-of-court arbitration (Harrington, 1982: 42) suggests that business takes the pattern of using and reserving those mechanisms—including courts—that serve its interests best. Thus, the topic of expanded state control can benefit from comparative research on court reforms (Harrington, 1985) and diversion alternatives (Austin and Krisberg, 1981; Blomberg, 1977; Cohen, 1979).

A more complicated area is the general linkage of the alternatives to late capitalism. Comparative research shows that alternatives are found in many societies, including socialist and so-called nonindustrialized ones (Cain and Kulscar, 1984; Abel, 1982a; Koetz and Ottenhof, 1983). Further study is needed to conclude if this could do away with the common, extreme Weberian assertion that the distinctive characteristic of capitalism is formalism, while the distinctive feature of other societies is informalism. In fact, many, if not all, societies display a dynamic combination of the two trends in different historical periods. In other words, it is useful to conceptualize the alternatives not merely in terms of capitalist control but rather in terms of control in general, with special flavors according to the specific society. This focus can also teach us which reforms could be labeled progressive and which conservative (Spitzer, 1982: 190–200).

Finally, let me propose some ideas to help reduce the tension of the fundamental contradiction. Obviously, Marxist ideas have contributed to a demystification of the legal system, which is most valuable. However, more basic problems are lurking in the background. In an insightful and in-cite-ful article, Cain and Kulscar (1982: 377–94) attack the so-called deficiencies of a "dispute-focused approach." They argue that, because of the underlying assumptions, such an approach does not increase our knowledge, either of society or of the dispute concept itself. Instead, they defend a real sociological enterprise starting from a global conception of society and elaborating this in its various subdisciplines, of which disputes form only one. But the problems are not solved, even if this proposal would allow us to go beyond process and procedure to focus on outcomes. Indeed, one could argue that the Marxist authors have tried to let their dispute theory be thoroughly informed by a broader social theory, and yet they are caught in the fundamental contradiction. Being too concerned with the important legitimation function of law and the alternatives, they have overlooked a couple of terrains that can open up new ways for research and practice.

First, they have paid exclusive attention to the concrete analysis of present state-connected developments. This has happened at the expense of the inverse logic that first describes which disputes are suitable for alternative handling and then looks for the best mechanism. By doing this, they have neglected all those disputes that potentially could be settled alternatively but not in one of the state forums. As an example, the critics have rejected the working of neighborhood justice centers for several reasons. But their analysis still cannot answer the question of why it would be better that a dispute over a barking dog either goes to court or remains unresolved: in both cases it continues to create unnecessary tensions. To explore this idea is to look for dispute-processing that handles disputes positively without falling in the trap of expanded state control.

Second, in their exclusive focus on the state in capitalism, some authors have also downplayed the role of professional interests in shaping ADR. Abel (1982c: 302) has acknowledged the judges' concern to unclog overburdened courts and to increase their personal control. Lawyers are divided according to their status: elite lawyers do not care too much, but others who do approve of ADR try to make their expert services necessary. Last but not least, the movement has created its own professionals who have obvious interests in its expansion (Abel, 1982c: 301–4).

Finally, some comments on the prescriptive part of the critical authors. All end with some vague phrases that reflect a quiet pessimism. Far from offering a solution to the problem, additional research can engender more positive tones. Comparative studies have great potential. Spence (1982: 231–43) describes a community court in Chile. Although the idea originated in the government departments under Allende, the court was entirely operated by the local community of squatters. The experiment failed in the end because its activities were too small a part of the global political involvement of the people. Spence's investigation provides some clues for the argument that alternatives can work if under full control of a community that is at the same time politically aware and keeps an eye on bigger societal issues. This can be illustrated by the issues of domestic violence and drunkenness. In Western society, these problems rarely come to the attention of the courts and hence remain unaddressed. Such behavior, if brought to an alternative forum in the United States (e.g., community mediation), would be scrutinized very closely and lead to forced behavioral changes and follow-up behavioral control. The Chilean community court, on the other hand, was able to do two things: it observed the specific behavior between the parties, and also linked this behavior to the larger issue of unemployment in that community. Thus, by aggregating individual disputes, it proved the starting point for the transformation of society (Spence, 1982: 231–43).

Not every problem should be linked to fundamental political or economic issues. But the institutional framework should never exclude the possibility of these linkages and of the corresponding political process. This is a prerequisite for progressive alternative procedures.

But the trivial matters remain important because community or class unity will not come into existence between neighbors who are divided over petty problems. The fact that some existing alternatives do not function adequately should not lead us to leave problems simmering until the day of eruption. Thus, I want to revalidate the concerns of an "interpersonal perspective" but aim at placing it in a different context. Furthermore, the argument that some of those grass-roots programs have only small caseloads is not good enough a reason to jettison them. On the contrary, these projects still have potential as tools of empowerment for their users. More investigation will have to gather information on this issue.

Disputes occur at very different levels and of very different kinds (Kidder, 1981: 720–21). If this holds, mechanisms have to be found to do something about these conflicts at those different levels. Solution or settlement is not always the answer because disputes sometimes are mere symptoms of fundamental underlying social, political, and economic issues. That proves the fundamental weakness of the common approach that focuses on procedure, instead of context and outcome.

The distinctiveness of a critical viewpoint has benefited a lot from comparison and contrast with the so-called common stance that abounds in public. Such detailed analysis has revealed some serious gaps in the common and critical presentations.

In their vehement counterattacks, the critical authors have offered valuable insights into an important issue. They have addressed some questions of implementation, investigating how far the present observable effects of the alternatives relate to their goals and fulfill their initial promise. They have also studied the global environment of time, place, and manner in which this new tendency is developing and have drawn attention to the societal forces at work. Thus, they clearly have shifted the focus from process to outcome and the determinating variables of that outcome in a complex society. They have done so with a critical tool-kit containing historical and dialectical research procedures. Therefore, their work should be given foremost attention at a crucial moment when only rhetoric seems to prevail.

However, throughout the analysis, they have overlooked an important issue. Their obsession with the concrete historical movements has prevented them from inductive reasoning and resulted in a feeling of helpless pessimism. They have paid almost no attention to the viability of the movement's goals themselves and to the possibility of remedies other than the present alternatives. A rejection of the actual alternatives should not imply a denouncement of all possible alternatives. Indeed, a huge reservoir of petty and trivial problems is awaiting constructive handling. However, in order to avoid the danger of co-optation, it will have to be conceived differently. Only a bottom-up approach that also allows and encourages broader personal and political awareness can be a viable "alternative to the alternatives." But a capacious amount of creativity is needed to develop mechanisms that deal with both the barking dog and the unlawful rent increase, other than the ones available now.

Alternative Dispute Resolution   239

NOTES

1. Carrie Menkel-Meadow, *New York Mediator* 5, no. 1 (1986): 8.
2. For a more detailed elaboration of the role of the environment, see Richard Evarts, James Greenstone, Gary Kirkpatrick, and Sharon Leviton, *Winning Through Accommodation: The Mediator's Handbook* (Dubuque: Kendall/Hunt, 1983), pp. 33–38.
3. See the pool of 187 projects listed in Ray Larry, ed., *Directory of Dispute Resolution Programs* (Washington, D.C.: ABA, 1984). I have left out all those without precise numbers on referrals or funding, thus ending up with exactly 100 programs.

REFERENCES

Abel, Richard. (1980). "Delegalization: A Critical Review of Its Ideology, Manifestations, and Social Consequences." In Erhard Blankenburg, Ekkehard Klausa, and Hubert Rottleuthner, eds., *Alternative Rechtsformen und Alternativen zum Recht*. Opladen: Westdeutscher Verlag.
———, ed. (1982a). *The Politics of Informal Justice*, vol. 1, *The American Experience*; vol. 2, *Comparative Studies*. New York: Academic.
———. (1982b). Introduction. In Richard Abel, ed. *The Politics of Informal Justice*, vol. 1, *The American Experience*. New York: Academic.
———. (1982c). "The Contradictions of Informal Justice." In Richard Abel, ed., *The Politics of Informal Justice*, vol. 1, *The American Experience*. New York: Academic.
Adler, Peter, Karen Lovaas, and Neal Milner. (1988). "The Ideologies of Mediation: The Movement's Own Story." *Law and Policy* 10: 317.
Alper, Benedict, and Lawrence Nichols. (1981). *Beyond The Courtroom: Programs in Community Justice and Conflict Resolution*. Lexington, Mass.: D. C. Heath.
Auerbach, Jerold. (1983). *Justice Without Law? Resolving Disputes Without Lawyers*. Oxford: Oxford University Press.
Austin, James, and Barry Krisberg. (1981). "Wider, Stronger and Different Nets: The Dialectics of Criminal Justice Reform." *Journal of Research in Crime and Delinquency* 165.
Barton, John. (1975). "Behind the Legal Explosion." *Stanford Law Review* 27: 567.
Blankenburg, Erhard. (1980). "Recht als gradualisiertes Konzept—Begriffsdimensionen der Diskussion über Alternativen zur Justiz. In Erhard Blankenburg, Ekkehard Klausa, and Hubert Rottleuthner, eds., *Alternative Rechtsformen und Alternativen zum Recht*. Opladen: Westdeutscher Verlag.
Blomberg, Thomas. (1977). "Diversion and Accelerated Social Control." *Journal of Criminal Law and Criminology* 68: 274.
Burger, Warren. (1982). "Isn't There a Better Way?" *American Bar Association Journal* 68: 274.
Cain, Maureen, and Kalman Kulcsar. (1982). "Thinking Disputes: An Essay on the Origins of the Dispute Industry." *Law and Society Review* 16: 375.
———, eds. (1984). *Disputes and the Law*. Budapest: Akademiai Kiado.
Christie, Nils. (1977). "Conflicts as Property." *British Journal of Criminology* 17: 1.
Cohen, Stanley. (1979). "The Punitive City: Notes on the Dispersal of Social Control." *Contemporary Crises* 3: 339.

Danzig, Richard. (1974). "Toward the Creation of a Complementary, Decentralized System of Criminal Justice." *Stanford Law Review* 26: 1.

Ehrlich, Thomas. (1976). "Legal Pollution." *New York Times Magazine* Feb. 8, p. 17.

Felstiner, William, Richard Abel, and Austin Sarat. (1981). "The Emergence and Transformation of Disputes: Naming, Blaming, and Claiming." *Law and Society Review* (Special Issue on Dispute Processing and Civil Litigation) 15: 631.

Fisher, Eric. (1975). "Community Courts: An Alternative to Conventional Criminal Adjudication." *American University Law Review* 24: 1253.

Folberg, Jay, and Alison Taylor. (1984). *Mediation: A Comprehensive Guide to Resolving Disputes Without Litigation*. San Francisco: Jossey-Bass.

Friedman, Lawrence, and Robert Percival. (1976). "A Tale of Two Courts: Litigation in Alameda and San Benito Counties." *Law and Society Review* 10: 267.

Galanter, Marc. (1974). "Why the 'Haves' Come Out Ahead: Speculations on the Limits of Legal Change." *Law and Society Review* 9: 95.

———. (1980). "Legality and Its Discontents. A Preliminary Assessment of Current Theories of Legalization and Delegalization." In Erhard Blankenberg, Ekkehard Klausa, and Hubert Rottleuthner, eds., *Alternative Rechtsformen und Alternativen zum Recht*. Opladen: Westdeutscher Verlag.

———. (1983). "Reading the Landscape of Disputes: What We Know and Don't Know (and Think We Know) about Our Allegedly Contentious and Litigious Society." *UCLA Law Review* 31: 4.

Garth, Bryant. (1982). "The Movement toward Procedural Informalism in North America and Western Europe: A Critical Survey." In Richard Abel, ed., *The Politics of Informal Justice*, vol. 2, *Comparative Studies*. New York: Academic.

Gessner, Volkmar. (1983). Disputes. "The Concept and Its Relevance for Legal Sociology." In Maureen Cain and Kalman Kulcsar, eds., *Disputes and the Law*. Budapest: Adakemiai Kiado.

Green, Eric. (1982). "CPR Legal Program Mini-Trial Handbook." In Center for Public Resources, *Corporate Dispute Management 1982: A Manual of Innovative Corporate Strategies for the Avoidance and Resolution of Legal Disputes*. New York: Matthew Bender.

Harrington, Christine. (1982). "Delegalization Reform Movements: A Historical Analysis." In Richard Abel, ed., *The Politics of Informal Justice*, vol. 1, *The American Experience*. New York: Academic.

———. (1985). *Shadow Justice: The Ideology and Institutionalization of Alternatives to Court*. Westport, Conn.: Greenwood.

Hofrichter, Richard. (1977). "Justice Centers Raise Basic Questions." *New Directions in Legal Services* 2: 168.

———. (1982). "Neighborhood Justice and the Social Control Problems of American Capitalism: A Perspective." In Richard Abel, ed., *The Politics of Informal Justice*, vol. 1, *The American Experience*. New York: Academic.

Kidder, Robert. (1981). "The End of the Road? Problems in the Analysis of Disputes." *Law and Society Review* (Special Issue on Dispute Processing and Civil Litigation) 15: 717.

Koetz, Hein, and Reynald Ottenhof. (1983). *Les Conciliateurs: La Conciliation: Une Etude Comparative*. Paris: Economica.

Kolb, Deborah. (1983). *The Mediators*. Cambridge, Mass.: MIT.

Manning, Bayless. (1977). "Hyperlexis: Our National Disease." *Northwestern University Law Review* 71: 767.

Marks, Jonathan, Earl Johnson, Jr., and Peter Szanton. (1984). *Dispute Resolution in America: Processes in Evolution*. Washington, D.C.: National Institute for Dispute Resolution.

Merry, Sally Engle. (1982). "The Social Organization of Mediation in Non-industrial Societies: Implications for Informal Community Justice in America." In Richard Abel, ed., *The Politics of Informal Justice*, vol. 2, *Comparative Studies*. New York: Academic.

Miller, Richard, and Austin Sarat. (1981). "Grievances, Claims, and Disputes: Assessing the Adversary Culture." *Law and Society Review* (Special Issue on Dispute Processing and Civil Litigation), 15: 525.

Munger, Frank. (1988). "Law, Change and Litigation: A Critical Examination of an Empirical Research Tradition." *Law and Society Review*, 22: 57.

Sander, Frank. (1976). "Varieties of Dispute Processing." *Federal Rules Decisions* (Pound Follow-Up Conference) 70: 111.

Santos, Boaventoura de Sousa. (1982). "Law and Community: The Changing Nature of State Power in Late Capitalism." In Richard Abel, ed., *The Politics of Informal Justice*, vol. 1, *The American Experience*. New York: Academic.

Sarat, Austin. (1976). "Alternatives in Dispute Processing: Litigation in a Small Claims Court." *Law and Society Review*, 10: 339.

Silbey, Susan, and Sally Merry. (1986). "Mediator Settlement Strategies." *Law and Policy* 8: 7.

Smith, Steven. (1981). "Considerations on Marx's Base and Superstructure." *Social Sciences Quarterly*, 65: 940.

Spence, Jack. (1982). "Institutionalizing Neighborhood Courts: Two Chilean Experiences." In Richard Abel, ed., *The Politics of Informal Justice*, vol. 2, *Comparative Studies*. New York: Academic.

Spitzer, Steven. (1982). "The Dialectics of Formal and Informal Control." In Richard Abel, ed., *The Politics of Informal Justice*, vol. 1, *The American Experience*. New York: Academic.

Tomasic, Romano. (1985). *The Sociology of Law*. London: Sage.

Trubek, David. (1984). "Turning away from Law?" *Michigan Law Review* 82: 824.

Wahrhaftig, Paul. (1982). "An Overview of Community-Oriented Citizen Dispute Resolution Programs in the United States." In Richard Abel, ed., *The Politics of Informal Justice*, vol. 1, *The American Experience*. New York: Academic.

Wehr, Paul. (1979). *Conflict Regulation*. Boulder, Colo.: Westview.

CHAPTER 14

Dispute Resolution and Democratic Theory

CHARLES ELLISON

This chapter seeks to provide a theoretical overview of dispute resolution and its applications in the legal system and public policy processes. The central claim is that dispute resolution is a form of political theory and public policy that: (1) inadequately analyzes the problems of democracy; (2) embodies processes that are generally not consistent with democratic principles; and (3) may, therefore, contribute to, rather than lessen, the legitimation problems of American democracy. In pursuing this theme, we explore the problems dispute resolution poses for democratic theory in existing programs in state and local government, in its diagnosis of the problems of democratic governance, as a form of pluralist political theory, as a means of bureaucratizing and privatizing public policy conflicts and processes, and in its political uses. We then suggest a more democratic approach to public policy conflicts and their resolution.

DISPUTE RESOLUTION IN STATE AND LOCAL GOVERNMENT

Dispute resolution programs and processes in the legal system extend its dominant norms of negotiation and settlement (Edwards, 1986; Menkel-Meadow,1985). There are nearly 500 programs in state trial courts, one-half located in cities of more than 500,000 and concentrated in six or seven states, and at least 182 community dispute resolution programs (Pipkin and Rifkin, 1984; Keilitz, et al., 1988; McGillis, 1986). Yet the evidence that the programs improve the efficiency and quality of justice and legal processes is equivocal and ambiguous, certainly not persuasive. They may process cases more quickly or inexpensively only when comparatively fewer cases are handled. Their informality may lessen judicial and attorney involvement, but this poses problems for the quality of justice (Brunet, 1987). Nor do we know that dispute resolution creates new public norms in lieu of substantive law or increases public access to legal services or support for the justice system. Caseloads are generally not large or growing, programs are underutilized, and mediator supply has outstripped demand, although caseload may increase with an agency's age and market size (Pipkin and Rifkin, 1984). Community programs have "failed quite flagrantly to reduce court caseloads and court costs" (McGillis, 1986: 14). They do not seem to enhance leadership development, reduce tension or resolve conflict, or achieve superior resolutions and more lasting agreements. They have no appreciable impact on recidivist behavior (Tomasic, 1982), although programs may reduce feelings of "fear of revenge and anger" (McGillis, 1986: 68).

Dispute resolution is a relatively recent feature of state and local government policy processes. Its spread to subnational governments, intergovernmental relations, and many substantive policy areas in the past decade can be explained, in part, by the ubiquity of negotiation in the legal system; changing approaches to federalism; the propensity toward bargaining as a style of policy-making; and its diverse methods, constituencies, and goals. State legislation has expanded its use in numerous substantive policy areas (Brodigan, et al., 1988). Twenty-two states are pursuing and considering a broad range of programs and initiatives. Six have established offices to help public officials manage and facilitate more effective, satisfactory, and timely resolutions of public policy disputes, with less cost and divisiveness.

Assessments of these offices define indices of success, but suggest that a negotiation-based approach to public policy conflicts is a problematic tool for democratic governance. Political requirements include sponsorship of a powerful state politician and leadership by a dispute resolution professional. The agency should have "long-term state-funding commitments" and control of the "state's main sources of advocacy, referral, and oversight" for all dispute resolution activities (Susskind, 1987: 13; Szanton, 1988: 5). "Successful case work" and resolution of visible policy disputes attract favorable public comment (Susskind, 1987: 15). Providing training and technical services and placing mediators in state departments build clientele and agency support and stimulate demand for services (Susskind, 1987; Szanton, 1988). However, state programs can minimize public knowledge about public policy, involve more coercion and less voluntarism, and shift attention toward the very fact of policy decision and away from its impacts and effectiveness.

First, public knowledge of and support for dispute resolution seem weak:

Mediation and other forms of dispute resolution are best institutionalized through an almost invisible, behind-the-scenes, set of interactions among policymakers, state officials, and various disputants. . . . This behind-the-scenes approach, . . . consulting with state officials who want advice on how best to handle difficult disputes . . . build[s] good working relationships which, in turn, have enhanced the reputation of the mediation offices within state government. While the public in each of the states may as yet have almost no inkling of what has been accomplished thus far, the prospects for institutionalization have been boosted by this strategy. (Susskind, 1987: 13–14).

Second, "voluntary mediation does not attract sizable numbers of disputants [and] is, perhaps as a consequence, more expensive per case." Thus, "legislating the demand" is a key strategy for political survival (Edelman, 1984: 143, 137). Automatic diversion of disputes can assure long-term success: "The offices need to find ways to enlarge the number of matters routinely brought to ADR." Since "the most promising source of supply is the court system, . . . the ultimate goal should be automatic referral processes made part of standard court procedures" (Szanton, 1988: 13). Third, offices have not yet demonstrated the impacts and consequences, and costs and benefits, of their activities. Program documentation and evaluation are essential, because "it is likely that, if closely examined by the press or political opponents, at least some of those numbers [currently used to suggest the value of office successes] will become liabilities" (Susskind, 1986; Szanton, 1988:12).

The severe barriers to and conceptual difficulties in evaluation underscore our concern about the compatibility of dispute resolution and democratic politics. Confidential ad hoc processes, without written records or audience, in the interstices of public organizations limit access to data. Mediators may be more concerned with processes than outcomes. Participants may attach different meanings to the same outcome, and one cannot accept their comments without further inquiry. Impacts may not be observable or immediately known. When they are, linking a specific outcome directly to a particular form of intervention may prove difficult (Bercovitch, 1984).

Evaluations of negotiation-based approaches to policy formulation and implementation have common problems. They rarely assign responsibility for the current state of affairs or offer significant analysis of the consequences of agreements months and years later. Most employ inadequate measures—participant satisfaction, process, or bureaucratic criteria—to assess outcomes. "What counts most in evaluating the fairness of a negotiated outcome are the perceptions of the participants [and the community]," presumably shortly after agreement has been reached (Susskind, 1987: 21). People may like the fairness, comprehensibility, and even the outcomes, but there is little empirical evidence that they choose negotiation over more traditional adjudicatory processes (Edelman, 1984; Harrington, 1984; Merry and Silbey, 1984; McGillis, 1986). Process measures determine whether parties present the facts and best evidence, comply with the process, agree voluntarily and efficiently on future behavior, and keep future relations stable, as well as whether similar cases are treated in like fashion (McGillis, 1986; Susskind, 1987). Promulgation of regulations on schedule, clientele support for an agency's position, and lack of conflict and litigation over regulation are taken as measures of successful regulatory negotiation. Rarely do evaluations examine dispute resolution as a political phenomenon, that is, how "disputes are displaced, rephrased, or simply repressed" (Sarat, 1988: 711). Additionally, the desire of some parties to reduce the risk and uncertainty associated with policy conflict is an important incentive for successful dispute resolution. Evaluations do not consider the appropriateness of this flight from politics—the fear of the costs of potential policy decisions made by formal government bodies—as a basis for public policy processes.

DISPUTE RESOLUTION AS POLITICAL THEORY

The Problem of Democratic Governance

Dispute resolution programs and processes embody a form of political theory that identifies problems of democratic governance and proposes to solve them in ways that weaken democracy. It is political, because it identifies a problem of formal government institutions, adopts informalism as a guiding ideology, and justifies use of the social technologies of negotiation to supplement those institutions (Adler, 1987). First, it defines excessive levels of social and political conflict—that overload public institutions, impair authoritative decision-making and policy implementation, and pose legitimation problems—as the problem of democratic governance. It tends to treat all public policy conflicts as distributional disputes where "the focus is on the distribution of tangible gains and losses" (Susskind and Cruikshank, 1987: 17). However, conflict has multiple sources. Distinctions between distributive policies and matters of constitutional law, right, and principle are not made quite so easily. In policy conflicts, different parties attach distinct meanings and values to the issues at hand, and these may change as the process of conflict itself transforms the nature of disputes (Schattschneider, 1959; Dinell, 1988).

This simplified view of political conflict and public policy is rooted in frustration with uncertainty and the ease with which democratic politics allows and encourages appeals to other political arenas. The emphasis is on the limits of government—the costs of use, problems associated with too much participation and delay, and insufficient expertise. Traditional political institutions are overburdened, inefficient, and unable to resolve conflicts finally and satisfactorily. Litigation is an undesirable public policy tool, courts are clogged, legislative compromises unravel, and implementation generates rather than resolves conflict. Impasse or gridlock spreads, while public dissatisfaction mounts. Unresolved conflict represents a failure of the political process and creates disillusion with government if left unresolved. The inevitable result is legitimation crisis. In sum, conflict paralyzes and endangers American democracy.

Second, dispute resolution rests on an ideology of informalism—critical of law, lawyers and litigation, courts, and formal political institutions—although its processes are part of public bureaucracy (Adler, 1987; Amy, 1987; Cormick, 1987;

Harrington, 1985a; Hofrichter, 1987). The informal state is those activities and modes of public action in which formal government bodies share and/or transfer their authority to make and/or implement public policy to third parties (Salamon, 1981). Its "statements of public purpose" articulate and mobilize a profound disaffection with and withdrawal from political discourse and modes of participation (Milner, et al., 1987: 3). This "vision [that] denigrates the use of formal public institutions" nonetheless extends the domain and forms of political life, alters the terms of participation, affects the working of formal political institutions, and reallocates public goods and resources (Amy, 1987; Milner, et al., 1987: 2). The informalism of dispute resolution extends the power of the state while decreasing its public accessibility, visibility, and accountability.

Third, a bundle of negotiation-based techniques is designed to supplement political institutions (Adler, 1987). For example, mediation is portrayed as a voluntary and participatory process where parties explore mutual interests, cooperate, and create "opportunities for productive bargaining" generally not available in formal processes (Adler, 1987: 61). Negotiation processes offer consensus and mutual gains bargaining to political institutions increasingly unable to "process" and implement solutions to complex multiparty conflicts. "The limits of representative action" are one source of discontent with democratic institutions (Kunde and Rudd, 1988: 36).

There is a growing frustration with the ability of the traditional policy-making apparatus to effectively include the multiple perspectives in public policy conflicts and to secure commitment to a solution that can be implemented. The existing traditional approaches often do not allow the parties to engage each other simultaneously or participate directly in generating solutions that are both technically and politically feasible. (Ehrmann and Lesnick, 1988: 96).

Thus, political officials could resolve a multiparty annexation and public infrastructure dispute in metropolitan Denver once "a critical mass of the public" recognized that a problem had to be solved. Presumably, political officials and public-spirited civic elites could shore up legitimacy by negotiating an agreement to solve this specific problem. The public might be symbolically reassured; however, we still wonder about the outcomes of agreements and the question of accountability: "The solution would be unlikely to satisfy everyone, but, to most of the public, it would provide a sense that sufficient action had been taken" (Kunde and Rudd, 1988: 38).

Seen as an efficient approach to solving "problems of management and uncoordinated decision making in urban areas," dispute resolution is in the tradition of applying private sector management strategies to government (Bradley, 1988: 46). It is a "parallel organizational structure," one of the "informal structures and the new communication and decision making processes . . . applied to community decision making and coordinated management of urban resources" (Bradley, 1988: 48–49). Fragmented government jurisdictions that once reduced political conflict and placed the fundamental issues of politics beyond their scope

have themselves become problematic. Dispute resolution offers a new government decision-making tool, resembling those employed in suburban jurisdictions
where political conflict is expressed "informally, secretly, and without the sanc-
tion of law" (Newton, 1978; Wood, 1958: 196–97).

Dispute resolution is a form of managerialist political theory in rebellion against
itself. Although it embraces the positivist epistemology and utilitarian ethics of
managerialism, it weakens—and, some might argue, ultimately rejects—the
managerialist commitment to the public interest, professionalism, and a politics
above conflict and negotiation (Steinberger, 1985). It maintains an image of
government as a problem-solving apparatus, but doubts that public institutions
alone can play this role effectively. It combines a managerialist diagnosis of the
problems of American democracy with remedies that, ironically, may compound
those problems. It theorizes that the problem of American democracy is that there
is too much of it.

DISPUTE RESOLUTION AS PLURALIST THEORY

Dispute resolution—in legal and public policy processes—embodies the political
theory of pluralism. It proposes that negotiation of social and political conflicts
can be the basis of public policy formulation and implementation. Proponents
have a bureaucratic, rather than a political, conception of courts and legal processes as society's foremost dispute-processing mechanisms. Dispute resolution
is a pluralist response to the assertion (not always well substantiated) that legal
institutions are overloaded and inaccessible. It appears as a form of public policy,
when courts confer a "bargaining endowment" on parties that simultaneously
meet their bureaucratic needs (Galanter, 1986: 220).

Critics emphasize the public values associated with the judiciary, that courts
make law and are key actors in "complex policy debates" (Trubek, 1980–81:
41). Courts are an important forum for those seeking the realization of value commitments and public policy goals (Galanter, 1986). Adjudication's public purpose is to articulate and interpret the rights, principles, and rules that help to
protect individuals and groups (McEwen, 1987). Rights can enable suppressed
voices and conflicts to surface and can restrain and compel state justification of
acts of power. Rights discourse enables members of a political community to live
together with conflict (Minow, 1987). The public nature of the legal process,
of the duties of its officials, and of the values of law may be displaced, when
dispute resolution inappropriately extends the bargaining process:

Adjudication uses public resources. . . . Public officials [are] chosen democratical-
ly. . . . [Their] power [is] conferred by public law, not by private agreement. Their job
is not to maximize the ends of private parties, nor simply to secure the peace, but to ex-
plicate and give force to the values embodied in authoritative texts such as the Constitution and statutes; to interpret those values and to bring reality into accord with them. (Fiss,
1984: 1085)

Thus, critics believe that negotiation processes reduce law to "just another way of ordering private relations" (Silbey and Sarat, 1988: 67). Through settlement, the state fails to articulate legal principles, shape the conduct of citizens, offer opportunities for remedy, and act "as a public resource for defining rules and rights" (McEwen, 1987: 252). Law, thus, becomes more a process of "resolving private disputes" "in an arena of distributive bargaining and therapeutic negotiation" and less an exercise "of authoritative decisionmaking allocating socially sanctioned values" (Fiss, 1984: 1085; Silbey and Sarat, 1988: 85).

Dispute resolution in public policy processes also embodies a pluralist theory of the state (Amy, 1987). The state organizes forums, structures participation, and facilitates and enforces the resolution of agreements between private parties (Harrington, 1985b). This is "an indifferent state" in that all parties are presumed to possess equally meritorious claims (Merry, 1987: 2069). Mediation ideology still maintains its pluralist flavor: "The ideology of mediation . . . assumes that disputing constitutes a process whereby individuals advance wants within an equilibrium model of the system which stresses accommodation and consensus . . . based on avoidance of values" (Harrington, 1985b: 37). Politics and policy are not about normative issues; rather, they are about resolving distributional disputes by bargaining over who gets how much of what. Politics, is, thus, a process of settling disputes, rather than of formulating and enforcing public rules. The actors establish a consensus on the values and purposes of the game and bargain as necessary to adjust incrementally their relative positions. Consensus based on mutual gains is invariably the best solution to most disputes.

Participants in negotiation-based resolution of public policy disputes are specially chosen representatives of all "stakeholding" groups. The fiction is that these groups are a surrogate public, representing all relevant and affected interests. Stakeholders—a term generally used in analyses of strategic management in the private sector—are those organized groups, elites, and interests that are most directly affected by and have significant expertise concerning the dispute as it has been framed (Freeman, 1984). Representation of public interest and citizen constituencies is a widely recognized problem whose solution can be prohibited by stakeholders: "Although there is usually no shortage of volunteers to represent the public interest, for some issues it is unlikely that there will be widespread acceptance of the legitimacy of any small group of such representatives" (Haygood, 1988a: 84). By contrast, those stakeholders with the power to block or assist in the implementation of a settlement must surely be included. Indeed, dispute resolution processes provide " 'stakeholding interests' with the control they seek" (Susskind and Ozawa, 1984: 5). That these interests should have control or that others, equally affected but less powerful or organized, can be reasonably excluded is rarely questioned. Negotiated rule-making and policy dialogue are two negotiation processes that involve interested, expert, and influential parties. The former is a policy formation process whereby a regulatory agency forms an "advisory committee composed of representatives of groups with an identifiable stake in a regulation to develop a proposed regulation through face-to-face negotiations'' (Haygood, 1988a: 78). Policy dialogues—''complex, multiparty discussions aimed at clarifying policy questions and developing agreements relating to broad public issues''—also enable stakeholder control of policy formulation (Ehrmann and Lesnick, 1988: 94).

A good agreement or settlement is one that satisfies those parties in the negotiations. All have the right to come away happy, or at least less unhappy than they would be with no settlement or the prospect of continuation of the dispute (Lindblom, 1959; Luban, 1985). Dispute resolution literature generally assumes that settlements are necessarily in the public interest. It "simply redefine[s] the public interest to be any policy that satisfies the interests participating in the decision-making process" (Amy, 1987: 139). These interests, taken together, are equated with the public interest. When parties jointly define their problem and mutual interests, it is assumed that this is not inconsistent with the public good.

The public interest may not be well served by dispute resolution processes for many reasons. Thinking about policy primarily or solely in distributive terms may compromise rights and principles. Important segments of the public may be left out or underrepresented. Mediators may be unable or unwilling to represent those who are excluded and to reduce power imbalances (Susskind and Cruikshank, 1987). That stakeholders "might *intentionally* conspire to violate the interest of those who are left out" or that outcomes may be substantively incompatible with the public good may seem obvious, but these problems have not yet been addressed satisfactorily (Amy, 1987: 137). Finally, we should take dispute resolution processes at face value: the public interest surely is embedded in the fact of settlement itself. Thus, dispute resolution is not simply an extension of pluralist politics, because it represents informal, yet bureaucratic, processes designed to manage conflict. The goal of dispute termination, the use of negotiation to achieve bureaucratic ends, and the concept of stakeholder as a constituency that needs to be managed reflect managerial interests that exist in tension with the pluralist character of dispute resolution processes.

BEYOND PLURALISM: BUREAUCRACY TRANSFORMS CONFLICTS INTO DISPUTES

Dispute resolution generally serves bureaucratic purposes and only rarely the needs of democracy. It denies the heterogeneity and complexity of social and political conflict and transforms it into the bureaucratic and professional category of dispute. It offers no adequate account for its origins and nature as relations among individuals, groups and organizations, and/or classes that concern the degree of innovation and indicate the avenues of change in a society (Cain and Kulcsar, 1981–82; Coser, 1956). All states—from their constitutions to their most minor policies and services—mediate social conflicts, shape access to the polity, and transform social conflicts (to a greater or lesser degree) into political conflicts. Democratic politics is a never-ending struggle over the scope of, parties to, and organization of conflict. The political organization of conflict shapes the respective capacities of social and political actors, the socialization and privatization of conflict, and the bias of political outcomes (Schattschneider, 1959).

A particular image of society and social conflict is embedded in the concept of dispute resolution. "Society is by definition ordered" (Cain and Kulcsar, 1981–82: 379). Social life appears or tends to be harmonious, approaching a normative consensus. Conflict is generally undesirable and certainly much too pervasive; settlement is preferable to excessive conflict. Conflict is viewed as an evil to be avoided, absorbed, resolved, and/or repressed—all within the prevailing order. Rarely mentioning the positive values of conflict (Coser, 1956; Sennett, 1970), it represents a negative attitude toward conflict and a positive attitude toward government action in response to it.

The concept of dispute is a social construct that transforms social relations and conflicts into pieces of bureaucratic and legal culture (Adler, 1987). Disputes are treated as if they are isolated phenomena or events abstracted from social relations and unrelated to a theory of society or social action (Cain and Kulcsar, 1981–82). Conceived in empirical rather than normative or legal terms, its behavioral bias individuates and depoliticizes social conflict and shifts attention from social structure and organization to groups, individuals, and dispute processes. Disputes have been defined in terms of the perception of injuries received or threatened, the need for remedies, and the public articulation and denial of grievances as claims (Felstiner, et al., 1980–81). A dispute between two parties is voiced publicly, before a third party (Merry, 1987; Silbey and Sarat, 1988). But this is too heavily influenced by legal metaphors for our purposes. Nor is it clear that the legal requirement for victim status is or should be at the heart of all public policy conflicts. Dispute-processing transforms conflict, removes it from its social context, eliminates the relevance of its history, and freezes the action as in a photograph. A dispute is then understood as a trouble case, an episode or blip, rather than a manifestation of normally problematic social relations. Dispute resolution institutionalizes conflict "within a particular conception of social order" in order to manage and, if possible, prevent the continuation of social and political conflict (Hofrichter, 1987: 109).

Public officials can possess both positive and negative attitudes toward political action and social and political conflict. The result is four categories of political response, as indicated in Figure 14.1. The lower half of the figure represents cases in which public officials take no overt action with respect to conflict. They do not intervene, but avoid action on the basis of insufficient resources, indifference, fear, or the need to monitor and gather information. The upper left quadrant suggests they can also act as organizers, advocates, or lobbyists to expand the intensity and scope of conflict. This can be purposive action, but it is also a product of the unintended consequences of prior action. Finally, dispute resolution clearly sits in the upper right quadrant. Its processes and techniques organize and transform some (but not other) social and political conflicts into disputes. In this sense, it is never neutral, because it influences and organizes the future course of conflict (Bercovitch, 1984).

Figure 14.1
Public Officials' Responses to Conflict

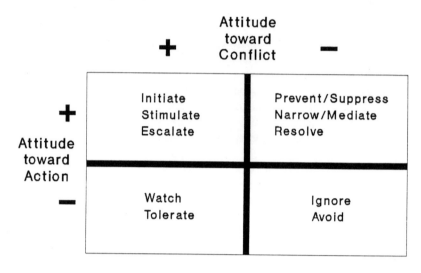

Bureaucracies and professionals process social and political conflicts in order to control them. Management and mediation of social and political conflicts redefine them as disputes between parties. A conflict is a social reality. It is a fight, a kind of clash or warfare, where antagonistic parties compete and oppose one another. A dispute is a bureaucratic category, characterized by a kind of debate or linguistic exchange. Labeling a conflict as a dispute is the first step toward institutionalizing it and limiting its scope as a prelude to dispute resolution. A dispute is merely a controlled "moment of disorder" that disrupts the normal, smoothly functioning patterns of social and political life (Cain and Kulcsar, 1981–82: 379). Such imbalances tend to be idiosyncratic, not inherent in the social order, yet are "unthinkable as a permanent condition" (Cain and Kulcsar, 1981–82: 379). Thus, "the need for resolution"—to process conflicts and manage and contain disputes as a means of restoring order—"is integral to the concept [of dispute]" (Cain and Kulcsar, 1981–82: 379). Accommodation and avoidance of serious conflict are taken to be desirable goals. Dispute resolution, then, does not resolve social differences and may not resolve political conflicts. It is a process for accommodation and settlement of disputes (Cormick, 1987). A willingness to deal with discrete and current issues, rather than structural bases of conflict, can enable parties to settle their disputes, even as the broad contours of conflict remain intact.

If disputes occur on the terrain of bureaucracy, dispute-processing is a pattern of bureaucratic activity that transforms them over time (Prottas, 1979). Dispute-processing entails both techniques and structures. We are more familiar with the dispute-processing techniques. It may be that "disputes are more often processed than resolved," that the techniques are more than a means to the restoration of order (Sarat, 1988: 708). In this sense, dispute resolution is not "merely a technical and individual problem of correlating available means to essential needs," or "a technocratic activity . . . defined as the creation or design of pragmatic solutions to problems" (Silbey and Sarat, 1988: 117). It is rather a process that displaces, rephrases, and represses both social and political conflicts and bureaucratic disputes (Sarat, 1988).

Thus, dispute resolution is more than a shared bundle of negotiation techniques; it also becomes the social relations and ad hoc organizational structures scattered throughout the world of public policy and intergovernmental relations. These organizational structures—some situated deep within or in the interstices between bureaucratic agencies and others sponsored by government but voluntary and quasi-governmental—constitute part of the growing informal state. Dispute resolution is likely to occur in temporary forums "protect[ed] from pressures to play directly to courts and constituencies" (Laue, et al., 1988: 7). These ambiguous enclaves in the world of politics, political forums with no or a very limited audience, relegate disputes to these private spaces in public life.

PUBLIC AND PRIVATE IN MEDIATION CULTURE

Mediation is one widely used dispute resolution process. The literature on mediation in government and public policy contains at least two distinct and largely contrary conceptions of the mediation process, the parties and their rationality, and the role of the mediator. These are the rational actor or choice and cultural perspectives. One fundamental difference between them is that the dominant rational actor model tends to treat mediation as an essentially private process, while the cultural perspective views mediation in more public terms.

The rational actor approach holds that disputants are or should be rational actors maximizing their interests in a normless, apolitical, technocratic problem-solving process. This view presumes a methodological individualism, that society can be understood in terms of individual actions. Disputes are discrete and individual, radically abstracted from social action, and thus unrelated to the historical context and patterns of social life that give it meaning. The concept of dispute itself—where calculating individuals and groups engage in decision-making—assumes that parties make self-interested choices about the cost, speed, anticipated outcomes, and other factors of settlement. Individualistic behavior, generally associated with economic transactions, is reflected in the rhetoric of costs and benefits, stakes and risk, anticipated outcome, and exchange. Mediation—a problem-solving process in which "conflicts of interest [are] pursued by rational actors making choices between sets of instrumental goals"—then resembles bureaucratic processes that encourage instrumentally rational behavior (Merry and Silbey, 1984: 154).

The rational model envisions persons or parties essentially in behavioral terms. Individuals bear a unique set of desires, preferences, and wants formed as a result of the "ever changing experiences, stimuli and responses" in their world (Silbey and Sarat, 1988: 110). Persons are not citizens with rights; they are subjects with needs and problems separate from the "moral context which gives them meaning and value" (Silbey and Sarat, 1988: 110). They can compromise and exchange their preferences for new opportunities, but one has no "legitimate claim to look behind or beyond the articulated preferences of the disputants" (Silbey and Sarat, 1988: 110). This is clearly an antinormative account of disputing, not least because it replaces rights (that must be taken seriously) with an uncritical acceptance of each party's self-account of wants and interests. The private interests of private parties, without seeming relationship to a broader social context, create a culture of mediation without public purpose.

Negotiation-based approaches to the resolution of public policy disputes apply an "economic metaphor" linking assumptions about the distributive nature of public policy and the instrumental rationality of disputants (Shapiro, 1988: 37). Public policy is primarily, even solely, distributive, involving resource allocation decisions. Developed as a means of allaying public opposition, some forms of "negotiation and mediation . . . are derived from a type of economic theory often referred to as the economic theory of compensation" (Portney, 1987: 3). This economic approach to public policy and "the distribution of society's legalities and illegalities" starts with the insight that the rational, self-interested behavior of different parties leads them to value certainty, risk, money, peace, policy outcomes, and other "goods" differently (Shapiro, 1988: 37). When the policy agenda is crowded and parties possess and rank preferences differently, there is the possibility of trades that "include compensation, contingent promises, or other creative 'side payments' through which all sides can benefit" (Susskind and Madigan, 1984: 186). These solutions—where one is relatively indifferent to the gains of others—leave the less powerful dependent upon the new gains of the powerful, while both maneuver to externalize the costs to parties not participating or represented in the process. Thus, Portney notes that, in the siting of hazardous facilities, this approach can disadvantage citizens whose communities already bear high health risks. Fiss (1984: 1085) also warns that the public may pay the price, since "when the parties settle, society gets less than what appears, and for a price it does not know it is paying." The metaphors of the rational actor approach make clear that mediated agreements generate privatized forms of public policy.

A cultural interpretation holds that one must understand mediation in its cultural and political context. This more public conception of mediation recognizes the social and historical context of policy conflicts, the social embeddedness of the parties themselves, and the public principles central to the conflict. It holds that the rational conception of persons is flawed, because it overlooks "the role of cultural norms and values for the substance and process of dispute behavior" (Merry and Silbey, 1984: 157). Thus, it "does not describe the way people behave" (Merry, 1987: 2063). Disputes are not mere bureaucratic episodes or constructs unrelated to the social world and "the moral, affective, and habitual aspects of action" (Merry and Silbey 1984: 160). They are "social event[s], embedded within a structure of social relationships and a cultural world of rules, practices of handling conflict, and normative principles within which positions are phrased in the course of disputing" (Merry, 1987: 2060). People have their own customs and beliefs, developed in social groups and cultures, about "what is worth fighting for, what is the normal or moral way to fight, what kind of wrongs warrant action, and what kinds of remedies are acceptable" (Merry and Silbey 1984: 157). Disputants have their own habits and beliefs about virtuous behavior, living with others, and dealing with insults and grievances (Merry and Silbey, 1987). When they seek redress in the courts, they generally have a "principled grievance" (Merry and Silbey, 1987: 154), defining the dispute in terms of values and principles and seeking a just and legally binding resolution that conforms to their notions of right and justice. In sum, disputants may want to maximize an interest or achieve a particular goal, but they also enter disputes to uphold principles and to enhance their power as democratic citizens: "Ordinary people go to court because they have an understanding of themselves as endowed with rights and entitled to the protection of the state" (Merry, 1987: 2072).

These two views are repeated in analyses of mediation processes, concepts of rationality, and the role of the mediator. The cultural perspective sees mediation as a highly structured, yet informal, rule-governed process in which third parties manage disputes (Hofrichter, 1987), rather than as the political equivalent of "free market transactions." Professional literature offers detailed models and guidelines for processing disputes. State and local agencies, courts, and mediators design public policy applications. Mediation has its own rules and rituals, "a general vocabulary of symbols, myths, discourse, and codewords" (Adler, 1987: 69). Mediators stage a process whose rules and practices establish a firm basis for political decisions (Hofrichter, 1987: 120). "Each guideline allows mediators to narrow the range of possible discourses and outcomes, obscuring and delegitimating alternative agendas. . . . What appears as a spontaneous process is thus a precisely rationalized procedure" where control is "constituted in the roles, rules, rhetoric, and individuation of the process" (Hofrichter, 1987: 123, 126).

Mediation processes are cultures with multiple standards of rationality, but they often socialize and even pressure participants toward forms of reasonableness more consistent with the rational actor model. Parties generally have conflicting, different, and common interests (Amy, 1987). When a mediator exposes them to "direct and undistorted communication processes" and they show a willingness to respond to new information, he hopes that they will deal with conflict without need for law or other formal public rules. They can develop new perceptions and understandings of conflict, learn new values, and accept the need to modify their behavior. When parties reassess their interests, negotiations are a learning experience. Alternatives to mediated agreement may then seem irrational, uncivilized, and unworkable, as well as increasingly costly. Accommodation comes to be seen as the only reasonable course. However, dispute resolution is not always amicable and cooperative. Power and threat, pressure and adversary relations, can be very much a part of negotiation processes (Amy, 1987; Cormick, 1987). Parties are not always involved in long-term relationships and need not always like or trust one another to reach agreement (Cormick, 1987: 308). In these cases, too, mediators encourage parties to understand their own best interests rationally, that is, to avoid the costs of prolonged dispute and failure to reach lasting outcomes free of unproductive conflicts in the future.

Mediators help create that culture by working on and with the terms of rationality and emotion in ways that increasingly privatize what is, in fact, a public policy process. This dialectic can be ambiguous when the parties do not share dispute termination as their paramount goal (Brunet, 1987; Merry and Silbey, 1984). Mediators frequently focus on cognitive and conceptual, as well as on the social and interpersonal, dimensions of disputes in order to facilitate resolution. One of a mediator's early tasks is to set the manner and tone of the process, to stimulate a shared belief system among the parties that reduces the urgency of distinctions between them and displaces the culture in which they normally find themselves. Language, the currency of dispute resolution processes, can be used to define and treat shared problems and create new policy options (Volkema, 1988). Mediation techniques "enabl[e] the parties to meet and experience each other as real human beings" and get to know one another (Amy, 1987: 50).

Mediators emphasize interpersonal and emotional dimensions of disputes, that they "are often rooted in personality conflicts, misunderstandings, and data disagreements" (Amy, 1987: 66). Misperceptions, irrationality, and emotions can drive conflicting parties. Disputants may need to overcome stereotypes accentuated by distance, hostility, and lack of communication. In such cases, mediation takes on a therapeutic character, personalizing relations between the parties. Mediators utilize techniques to "discredit or dissipate supposedly counterproductive emotions" and misperceptions (Amy, 1987: 114). Thus, mediation privatizes policy processes, when it artificially creates a unique culture of its own or identifies the origins of disputes in and emphasizes "the emotional and psychological problems of the participants" (Amy, 1987: 113).

One of the major functions of the mediator is the privatization of the dispute, that is, to limit the diversity and number of participants, issues, and audience associated with the mediation process. Agenda-setting, problem formulation, and, later, joint fact-finding are all designed to compress the range of diverse views and problems to be considered. The use of language is central to efforts to determine the scope of deliberations, frame the issues at hand, and define the problems to be negotiated (Volkema, 1988). Determination of the scope and definition of a dispute simultaneously defines the expertise and participants most relevant to dispute resolution. Issue-reframing is, in a sense, the reduction of the number of participants and simplification of the meaning of the dispute. When possible, mediators seek to pyramid interests or organize "cohesive and non-redundant negotiating teams" to limit participation to key "stakeholding" groups (Susskind and Cruikshank, 1987; Susskind and Madigan, 1984: 184). Indeed, all aspects of the process are designed to make the dispute more manageable and resolvable.

The ambiguity of the mediator role rests on its rhetoric of impartiality and portrayal as a neutral, while the mediator is simultaneously a partisan of the mediation process. Mediators are often experienced professionals who play an authoritative and directive role, channeling the dispute, using techniques of influence and persuasion, and moving the process toward an acceptable form of settlement (Silbey and Sarat, 1988). They may be officials in, adjunct to, or under contract with public agencies and/or court bureaucracies. Indeed, courts or other political actors may impose or threaten deadlines as a bargaining incentive. Referrals from justice and other agencies provide evidence that the sanctions and incentives are not simply within the relationship of the parties. However neutral mediators are toward the parties and their dispute, mediation and other negotiation-based approaches to the resolution of public policy disputes are a form of politics that tends to privatize public policy conflicts and their resolution. Indeed, the shrewdest politics is that in which one successfully persuades others that politics is the furthest thing from his mind.

THE POLITICAL USES OF DISPUTE RESOLUTION

Dispute resolution, as a means to resolve problems of democratic governance, is simply a wager that the fact of settlement will enhance legitimacy. Generally, dispute resolution privatizes public policy conflicts and processes. Thus, we think it more plausible to suggest that its uses and consequences (unintended and otherwise) will either not affect or add to those legitimation problems. We begin with the uses of dispute resolution in the legal order, especially as it relates to individuals, public agencies, systemic concerns, and the quality of public life.

Perhaps the strongest claim dispute resolution advances for individuals is that they gain a measure of justice by having available a broader range of remedies: "What settlement offers is a substantive justice that may be more [flexible and] responsive to the parties' needs than adjudication. Settlement can be particularized to the needs of the parties, it can . . . provide richer remedies than the commodification or monetarization of all claims, and achieve legitimacy through consent" (Menkel-Meadow, 1985: 504). Critics reply that although negotiation processes offer participatory forms that might heighten one's sense of control and importance, their forms of self-regulation induce citizens to set aside "political grievances," accept inadequate representation, and overlook and forfeit legal rights and protections (Hofrichter, 1987: xxix).

Dispute resolution programs are firmly rooted in the bureaucratic requirements of the state and the bureaucratic and political power of judges. They serve organizational interests by preserving the institutional capacity to reach settlements, even at the expense of the protection of rights (Harrington, 1985a). This administrative and technocratic rationale for managing and "resolving internal organizational problems of courts" functionally differentiates the judicial system according to types of disputes to be processed (Harrington, 1984: 203–4). New approaches to case management, screening, diversion, and processing—with new roles for dispute resolvers and disputants and more flexible decision rules—channel disputes in order to reduce bureaucratic inefficiency, processing costs, and overcrowding (Adler, 1987; McGillis, 1986). In the name of "technocratic concerns for efficiency, adaptability, and cost effectiveness," they "limit, transform, or avoid courts and adjudication" (Silbey and Sarat, 1988: 14). Informalism is designed to expand judicial power and legitimize its authority (Harrington, 1985a).

Dispute resolution may compromise the quality of justice as it serves the bureaucratic needs of the state, creating a two-class system, with minor criminal, neighborhood, and family disputes in public agencies and business disputes accorded a central place in formal legal processes (Pipkin and Rifkin, 1984; Marks, et al., 1984; Silbey and Sarat, 1988). Its processes expand justice system bureaucracies and preserve existing relationships, rather than transform ongoing relationships or rights (Harrington, 1985a; Tomasic, 1982). They are "political mechanisms that produce a system of meanings and practices connected to management" of the system in ways that perpetuate inequalities and advantage "those already in entrenched positions" (Hofrichter, 1987: 3; Merry, 1987: 2073). The quality of outcomes and implementation suffers, because dispute resolution processes discourage full discovery and sharing of information (Abel, 1987; Brunet, 1987). They may meet the bureaucratic needs of the legal system only by sacrificing the political and legal rights of the people: "Working-class Americans are being discouraged from using the very institutions they now see as their own, perhaps because their problems seem insolvable or unrewarding to the courts" (Merry, 1987: 2073).

Dispute resolution—both its processes and outcomes—may also play a systemic function: the maintenance of social order through the management of social conflicts (Cain and Kulcsar, 1981–82; Hofrichter, 1987). Negotiation is an informal administrative extension of the state that manages political conflict (Hofrichter, 1987: xxv). Informalism enables dispute resolution to appear helping, consensual, and noncoercive, but it is a more thorough form of social control: "Because coercion is less extreme and less visible in these informal institutions, the reach of control can be wider [and] less resistance is generated" (Silbey and Sarat, 1988: 37). Its processes regulate the social lives of citizens, expropriating their conflicts and troubles (Abel, 1982; Merry, 1987). They expand the "areas of social life [that] become coordinated objects of public policy" and enable earlier interventions less constrained by "jurisdictional boundaries or legal categories" (Hofrichter, 1987; 58; Silbey and Sarat, 1988: 37). They also simplify and neutralize social conflicts in order to reduce disorder. Class and other social conflicts are redefined as intraclass and/or interpersonal disputes. The systemic uses of dispute resolution—displacing the structural, public interest, and equity dimensions of social conflict—frustrate democratic principles. On the one hand, they reflect the state's increasing need for ad hoc, strategic, and crisis management forms of intervention to maintain the social order and serve the interests of capital (Hofrichter, 1987). On the other hand, as a form of state action, dispute resolution introduces its own contradictory dynamics and generates its own legitimation problems:

Constitutional governments . . . create and recognize new rights even while they relinquish their ability to guarantee and enforce them. The courts join in proliferating symbols of entitlement, enlivening consciousness of rights and heightening our expectations of vindication. As adjudication becomes more elaborated and more prone to decompose into bargaining, the promise of full and decisive vindication that it holds out beckons and recedes before us. (Galanter, 1986: 229)

Nothing destroys the quality of public life more than the tendency of dispute resolution to privatize judicial and public policy processes. Hofrichter (1987: 74) summarizes the claim that it privatizes politics and impoverishes public life: "Transform[ing] . . . the public sphere into the private sphere and social issues into interpersonal problems . . . , the informal state limits the space of the public sphere." Equally applicable to judicial and other government processes, this means that dispute resolution denies the cultural and normative, legal, and public interest dimensions of political life.

Negotiation not only ignores and obscures the normative dimensions of conflict, it also weakens the cultural and political significance of judicial processes. Through adjudication citizens tell their stories to the public. Court procedures have expressive qualities that enable citizens to convey cultural values that are significant for political life (Resnick, 1987). Dispute resolution processes deflect attention from the public values associated with the history of conflicts and the impacts of settlement. The lack of records and suppression of information weaken the prospect of judicial review and political accountability, as they deny any meaningful role to the public (Brunet, 1987; Resnick, 1987).

Dispute resolution weakens the law as a component of public life. Law guides public norms and conduct, but dispute resolution may weaken or compromise it in several ways. Law and public policy may actually be made by private groups (Brunet, 1987; Lowi, 1979). Informal processes may retard the development of law in areas where powerful private interests seek continued underdevelopment. The public value of law can, thus, be sacrificed, as can its use as a means to challenge government or corporate abuses of power (Edwards, 1986; Minow, 1987). Dispute resolution offers powerful private interests what they most seek from government—evasion of the costs and uncertainties associated with a decision by courts and other government bodies to apply public law and norms to their activities (Newton, 1978; Schattschneider, 1959).

It may also contribute to inequality. Its agreements have been characterized as lawless justice (Fiss, 1984; Marks, et al., 1984). Can dispute resolution, systematically or otherwise, degrade justice? Critics hold that its processes fail to take rights seriously, reject substantive claims for justice out of hand, and allocate benefits in ways that ignore the interests of larger social groups. The fate of third parties is a special area of concern (Weckstein, 1988). Privatization harms their interests in many unknown ways, as a result of denials of information and failures to test legal principle. One logical outcome of dispute settlements is efforts by parties to pass costs on to those not represented in the process (Fiss,

1984: 1076). Finally, dispute resolution obscures the public dimension by sustaining the myth that "power disappears in the absence of hierarchy" (Silbey and Sarat, 1988: 37). The fiction that negotiation processes overcome power grants new advantages to the powerful. Thus, it seems that dispute resolution reproduces and perhaps enhances power imbalances and disparities and that its proponents have yet to offer defensible standards of fairness and justice.

Many of these arguments apply with equal force to negotiation-based resolution of public policy disputes. Susskind and Cruikshank (1987) hold that the application of mediated negotiation and other techniques actually reduces inequalities. A mediator is obligated to defend the public interest and a shared resource pool can lessen resource inequalities. Further, participation provides disadvantaged groups greater access and more information and, hence, improves their bargaining position and opportunity to influence outcomes. Mediation need not threaten the authority of public officials; they retain responsibility for making public decisions. Amy (1987) responds that institutionalization of dispute resolution tends to increase coercion and "raises serious questions about the democratic nature of the process" (Amy, 1987: 150). He concludes that mediation tends to be an unrepresentative, unfair, and involuntary process whose biases legitimize unequal agreements that necessarily reproduce inequalities between the parties. The most important bias may well be the privatized character of dispute resolution processes. However, no one has demonstrated empirically that such outcomes are any more unequal than those of other existing policy processes.

We can, nonetheless, summarize the claim that mediated approaches to policy disputes tend to advantage political and economic elites and disadvantage relatively powerless and less organized groups. First, policy conflicts often have structural roots and represent fundamental value conflicts. When parties and processes deny basic value differences, then we are symbolically reassured that no important public values are threatened and need not feel compelled to participate. The denial of this normative dimension reduces the size of the political audience, with obvious political consequences. As Amy (1987) notes, when environmentalists give on this initial point, they surrender the strategic moral high ground and their most important resource in the defense of environmental values.

Second, mediation defines and narrows conflicts in ways that address particular, localized incidents and personalities and evade "underlying systemic issues" and major social problems (Amy, 1987: 193). This depoliticization of public policy disputes, along with the exclusion of citizen groups, tends to benefit business and bureaucratic interests (Amy, 1987; Stever, 1983). Parties may agree on the nature of their joint problem, but that is no guarantee that that understanding reflects the public interest.

Third, formal institutions often protect participants and provide due process guarantees, but dispute resolution offers no such procedural safeguards against exploitation of the less experienced. Ad hoc processes, rather than legal guidelines, produce good outcomes: "No one would want the rules of the game to get in the way of an ingenious solution'' (Susskind and Cruikshank, 1987: 22). But these outcomes are shaped by informal processes that may not be equitable.

Fourth, the powerful social and psychological pressures of small group relations can ''work to produce consensus even when it does not actually exist'' (Amy, 1987: 113). The lack of citizen experience with negotiations, the cooling out of their anger, and the tendency to be too trusting can also disadvantage less powerful groups.

Fifth, negotiated approaches to public policy disputes, such as regulatory negotiation, often require substantial resources and, thus, benefit those with more resources. Inequalities between parties extend to staff, technical information and expertise, organizational resources, capital, control of the means of production, and the availability of options outside mediation. Negotiation may accept and not inquire into these inequalities. Although their actions may precipitate a dispute, business interests often appear creative, seeking to make an investment to provide a service or solve a problem. Opponents are often put in the position of unrealistic and negative amateurs trying to block a project and yet having no positive course to suggest. This mismatch inclines the less powerful toward concessions, so that they gain something from an agreement, even if they are the weaker party.

Sixth, negotiated approaches to public policy disputes weaken the authority and public interest commitment of public officials (Stever, 1988). It may be that policy development and formulation benefit from deliberation, debate, bargaining, and consensus-building. However, when bargaining becomes ''an essential part of the implementation and administration of public policy,'' public officials must bargain to achieve previously articulated public values (Stever, 1988: 134). In this case, they are simply another group of stakeholders, bargaining for values that are no more legitimate than those of any other. This lends itself to self-interested bureaucratic behavior, likely to benefit bureaucrats and powerful constituencies, but lacking any relation to the public purposes of government.

Finally, negotiation-based approaches also tend to reinforce existing inequalities, when the primary goal is settlement and order. Consensual agreement rests on a shared ''formulation of a problem and its solution because everyone knows the settlement is the best available under the circumstances, and because it attends to each party's most important concerns'' (Susskind and Cruikshank, 1987: 77). This will tend to be an incrementalist ''solution'' to policy problems, ''consistent with preexisting practices'' and pluralist political theory (Lindblom, 1959; Sullivan, 1984: 203). Mediated agreements may, therefore, simply postpone conflicts to other times and arenas or suppress them completely. Negotiated approaches work when they successfully reduce the scope of conflict by limiting access to at least one political arena, the courts. If the practice mirrors the literature of dispute resolution, we can conclude that issues of equity and the distributive character of dispute resolution processes and settlements are not matters of great concern. Here lies one of the great ironies of negotiation-based approaches to public policy conflicts: although disputes are viewed in distributive terms, one of negotiation's primary uses is to shift attention toward the process itself and away from the tendency of negotiation processes and outcomes to have and reproduce unequal outcomes and impacts.

DEMOCRATIZING DISPUTE RESOLUTION

We do not conclude that all is right with traditional political institutions or that dispute resolution can never be an appropriate public policy tool. We do claim that dispute resolution: (1) has not accomplished its purposes; (2) fails to analyze adequately the problems of democratic governance; (3) embodies a form of pluralist political theory that lacks a viable concept of public interest; (4) is generally a technique to meet bureaucratic needs; (5) tends to privatize public policy conflicts and their processes; and (6) tends to reproduce inequality in ways that do not strengthen, and may indeed undermine, the legitimacy of democratic political order.

The challenge is to make social and political conflicts serve democratic purposes. To do this, we believe that advocates of negotiation-based approaches to the resolution of public policy conflicts must develop:

1. broader understandings of conflict, policy processes, and the outcomes and impacts of settlement
2. a concept of politics and recognition of the political uses of various approaches
3. a reformulated theory of democracy to minimize their bureaucratic uses
4. reconstituted processes that enhance rather than attack public life

We must recognize and accept the need for diverse social and political conflicts in a democratic society and take multiple stances toward them. Some conflicts should perhaps be suppressed or settled, while others might be initiated and expanded. At times we will need to "design[ing] social processes that facilitate or encourage disputes that are all too rarely articulated" (Sarat, 1988: 708). The appropriateness and timing of third-party intervention for different types of conflicts need more study, for the claim that a conflict must be "ripe" for resolution says little. We must also recognize the distinct meanings of intervention in diverse settings. There are stages in the policy process, and negotiated settlements have different significance in policy formulation than in policy implementation processes (Stever, 1988). Finally, the fetish of process cannot continue. Responsible public officials and professionals cannot avoid careful study of the outcomes and impacts of their work, especially on third parties and the public, over time. Order—that is, dispute termination or settlement—is not a satisfactory substitute for evaluation.

The field must develop an adequate concept of politics:

Politics is not simply about communication, it is also about power struggles. It is not only about common interests, but about conflicting interests as well. And it not only involves

horse-trading, but competition between conflicting values and different moral visions. . . . .
Inescapable struggles over power and visions of the good society still lie at the center of the
important political battles taking place in America. (Amy, 1987: 228)

Proponents cannot maintain the fiction that dispute resolution is not political. We
cannot remain blind to its political uses and the political context in which it has
developed. Its ideological roots are consistently antipolitical. It tends to emphasize
depoliticized definitions of politics and public policy and to obscure power and its
exercise. And, can we believe that this movement in no way symbolizes—along
with similar institutional and policy changes in the last fifteen to twenty years—a
continuation of steady efforts to make our political institutions less accessible to
and representative of citizens seeking to exercise new political rights in ways that
threaten economic power?

Dispute resolution has all the earmarks of a weapon of bureaucracy, rather than
a tool of democracy. We have seen how mediation, for example, is one of many
social mechanisms that tends to eliminate difference in the name of efficiency, order,
and making things manageable. Why, we should ask, does society not provide adequately for the function of conflict resolution? Why must state bureaucracies organize
this social function? A democratic dispute resolution does not deny conflict and even
values disorder. It accepts the difficulties associated with democratic participation
and fair representation, rather than resort to a concept of stakeholder that inadequately simulates the public. Most important, it realizes that democracy needs an
audience.

Democratic dispute resolution does not attack public life, but it affirms it in four
ways. First, it advances a concept of democratic citizenship that respects the cultural
life and political rights of citizens. Court bureaucracies send us a message about
the exercise of rights, when they hand out longer sentences to those who to go to
trial and shorter ones to those who utilize plea-bargaining mechanisms. We should
not forget that the legal and political rights of citizens are among the most basic
preconditions of democracy. Conceptions of citizens as stakeholders or groups who
bear certain preferences in a political marketplace discredit democracy and its normative meanings.

Second, dispute resolution processes must reverse the tendency to secrecy and
confidentiality. Negotiations cannot always be held in a fishbowl; however, documentation of dispute-processing, maintenance and availability of records, full public
disclosure, public access and visibility, frequent monitoring by responsible public
officials, and more are necessary to prevent an accelerated descent into Kafka's
bureaucratic world. Evaluation of dispute resolution activities and knowledge of
third-party and public impacts of settlements are otherwise impossible.

Third, dispute resolution processes should not encourage parties to understand
issues of public policy and social structure in private—that is, psychological, emotional, and group process—terms. If conflicts can have ''irrational'' dimensions that
settlement must overcome, they also can have a legitimate structural dimension that
should be clarified, not obscured, by third party interventions.

Fourth, a democratic dispute resolution does not cultivate images of moribund political institutions or compromise the law and its public values. It rejects the privatization of politics and recognizes that the public interest is not well served by processes that vest control of policy in the hands of a few powerful stakeholders. Most important, it recognizes that dispute resolution is likely to become a vehicle for the exemption of powerful private interests like firms and multinational corporations from public rules and the exclusion of citizens from the essential political arenas of democracy. This is unacceptable on principle. And, it raises issues of political accountability, policy impacts, and political legitimacy.

However, conflict resolution potentially embodies a usable form of public life. Its purpose would be to enable citizens to imagine and remake authority through participation in productive conflicts (Sennett, 1980). The experience of conflict can make power visible and provide opportunities for challenge and change. Conflicts offer us the chance to confront difference face-to-face. The powerful must come out of hiding in these processes, while the less powerful must engage the more powerful other. We all take risks in this situation for it requires recognition of and discourse with one's opponents. For the less powerful, it places them close to those with power and enables them to see the humanity of and constraints on the powerful. This experience might shatter illusions about the omnipotence of the powerful and enable the imagination of new forms of authority. These new forms would be based on principles of power-sharing and restraining the power of the powerful. Perhaps these processes could persuade the powerful to break out of their self-imposed need to expand their power and to agree to exercise more humane forms of power. Conflict processes and resolution can be a visible discourse about the public terms, categories, and rules of politics, rather than transactions based on private preferences. This alternative rests on the conviction that we already suppress too much conflict, that we ought to be committed to the constructive experience of conflict as both the basis for conflict resolution and a democratic public life.

REFERENCES

Abel, Richard L. (1982). "The Contradictions of Informal Justice." In Richard L. Abel, ed., *The Politics of Informal Justice*. New York: Academic.

Adler, Peter S. (1987). "Is ADR a Social Movement?" *Negotiation Journal* 3:59–71.

Alford, Robert R., and Roger Friedland. (1985). *Powers of Theory: Capitalism, the State, and Democracy*. New York: Cambridge University Press.

Amy, Douglas J. (1987). *The Politics of Environmental Mediation*. New York: Columbia University Press.

Bercovitch, Jacob. (1984). *Social Conflict and Third Parties: Strategies of Conflict Resolution*. Boulder: Westview.

Bradley, Richard H. (1988). "Managing Major Metropolitan Areas: Applying Collaborative Planning and Negotiation Techniques." *Mediation Quarterly* 20:45–56.

Broderick, Raymond J. (1989). "Court-Annexed Compulsory Arbitration: It Works." *Judicature* 72:217–25.

Brodigan, Bruce, et al. (1988). *State Legislation on Dispute Resolution*. Chicago: American Bar Association.

Brunet, Edward. (1987). "Questioning the Quality of Alternative Dispute Resolution." *Tulane Law Review* 62:1–56.

Cain, Maureen, and Kalman Kulcsar. (1981–82). "Thinking Disputes: An Essay on the Origins of the Dispute Industry." *Law and Society Review* 16:375–402.

Cormick, Gerald W. (1987). "The Myth, the Reality, and the Future of Environmental Mediation." In R.W. Lake, ed., *Resolving Locational Conflict*. New Brunswick: Center for Urban Policy Research.

Coser, Lewis A. (1956). *The Functions of Social Conflict*. New York: Free Press.

Dinell, Tom. (1988). "Some Thoughts on Public Disputes." *PCR Update* 3:5.

Edelman, Peter B. (1984). "Institutionalizing Dispute Resolution Alternatives." *Justice System Journal* 9:134–50.

Edwards, Harry T. (1986). "Alternative Dispute Resolution: Panacea or Anathema?" *Harvard Law Review* 99:668–84.

Ehrmann, John R., and Michael T. Lesnick, (1988). "The Policy Dialogue: Applying Mediation to the Policy-Making Process." *Mediation Quarterly* 20:93–99.

Executive Office for Administration and Finance. (1988). *Massachusetts Mediation Service: Annual Report (July 1987–June 1988)*. Boston: Commonwealth of Massachusetts.

Felstiner, William L. F., Richard L. Abel, and Austin Sarat. (1980–81). "The Emergence and Transformation of Disputes: Naming, Blaming, Claiming" *Law and Society Review* 15:631–54.

Fiss, Owen M. (1984). "Against Settlement." *Yale Law Journal* 93:1073–90.

Forester, John. (1987). "Planning in the Face of Conflict: Negotiation and Mediation Strategies in Local Land Use Regulation." *APA Journal* 58:303–14.

Freeman, R. Edward. (1984). *Strategic Management: A Stakeholder Approach*. Boston: Pitman.

Galanter, Marc. (1986). "Adjudication, Litigation, and Related Phenomena." In Leon Lipson and Stanton Wheeler, eds., *Law and the Social Sciences*. New York: Russell Sage Foundation.

Gladwin, Thomas N. (1987). "Patterns of Environmental Conflict over Industrial Facilities in the United States, 1970–78." In R. W. Lake, ed., *Resolving Locational Conflict*. New Brunswick: Center for Urban Policy Research.

Harrington, Christine B. (1984). "The Politics of Participation and Nonparticipation in Dispute Processes." *Law and Policy* 6:203–30.

———. (1985a). *Shadow Justice*. Westport, Conn.: Greenwood.

———. (1985b). "Socio-Legal Concepts in Mediation Ideology." *Legal Studies Forum* 11:33–38.

Haygood, Leah V. (1988a). "Negotiated Rule Making: Challenges for Mediators and Participants." *Mediation Quarterly* 20:77–91.

———. (1988b). "Opportunities and Challenges in Providing State-Level Support for the Mediation of Public Disputes." *Resolve* 19:1, 3–10.

Hofrichter, Richard. (1987). *Neighborhood Justice in Capitalist Society*. New York: Greenwood.

Keilitz, Susan, Geoff Gallas, and Roger Hanson. (1988). "State Adoption of Alternative Dispute Resolution: Where Is It Today?" *State Court Journal* 12:4–11.

Kidder, Robert L. (1980–81). "The End of the Road? Problems in the Analysis of Disputes." *Law and Society Review* 15:717–25.

Kunde, James E., and Jill E. Rudd. (1988). "The Role of Citizens Groups in Policy Conflicts." *Mediation Quarterly* 20:33–44.

Laue, James H., et al. (1988). "Getting to the Table: Three Paths." *Mediation Quarterly* 20:7–21.

Lindblom, Charles E. (1959). "The Science of Muddling Through." *Public Administration Review* 19:79–88.

Lipsky, Michael. (1980). *Street-Level Bureaucracy*. New York: Russell Sage Foundation.

Lowi, Theodore J. (1964). "American Business, Public Policy, Case-Studies, and Political Theory." *World Politics* 16:677–715.

——— . (1972). "Four Systems of Policy, Politics, and Choice." *Public Administration Review* 32:298–310.

——— . (1979). *The End of Liberalism: The Second Republic of the United States*. New York: W. W. Norton.

Lowry, Kem. (N.d.). "Mediation of Complex and Public Interest Cases: An Evaluation Report to the Judiciary." Program on Conflict Resolution, University of Hawaii.

Luban, David. (1985). "Bargaining and Compromise: Recent Work on Negotiation and Informal Justice." *Philosophy and Public Affairs* 14:397–416.

McEwen, Craig A. (1987). "Differing Visions of Alternative Dispute Resolution and Formal Law." *Justice System Journal* 12:247–59.

McGillis, Daniel. (1986). *Community Dispute Resolution Programs and Public Policy: Issues and Practices*. Washington, D.C.: National Institute of Justice.

Mansbridge, Jane J. (1980). *Beyond Adversary Democracy*. New York: Basic Books.

Marks, Jonathan B., Earl Johnson, Jr., and Peter L. Szanton. (1984). *Dispute Resolution in America: Processes in Evolution*. Washington, D.C.: National Institute for Dispute Resolution.

Meeks, Gordon, Jr. (1988). "Negotiating a State Environmental Quality Act: The Arizona Groundwater Case." *Mediation Quarterly* 20:57–73.

Menkel-Meadow, Carrie. (1985). "For and Against Settlement: Uses and Abuses of the Mandatory Settlement Conference." *UCLA Law Review* 33:485–514.

Merry, Sally E. (1979). "Going to Court: Strategies of Dispute Management in an American Urban Neighborhood." *Law and Society* 13:891–925.

——— . (1987). "Disputing Without Culture." *Harvard Law Review* 100:2053–73.

Merry, Sally E., and Susan S. Silbey. (1984). "What Do Plaintiffs Want? Reexamining the Concept of Dispute." *Justice System Journal* 9:151–78.

Milner, Neal, Karen Lovaas, and Peter Adler. (1987). "The Public and the Private in Mediation Ideology." Working Paper, Program on Conflict Resolution, University of Hawaii.

Minow, Martha. (1987). "Interpreting Rights: An Essay for Robert Cover." *Yale Law Journal* 96:1860–1913.

Newton, Kenneth. (1978). "Conflict Avoidance and Conflict Suppression: The Case of Urban Politics in the United States." In Kevin R. Cox, ed., *Urbanization and Conflict in Market Societies*. Chicago: Maaroufa.

Peterson, Paul E. (1981). *City Limits*. Chicago: University of Chicago Press.

Pipkin, Ronald M., and Janet Rifkin. (1984). "The Social Organization in Alternative Dispute Resolution: Implications for Professionalization of Mediation." *Justice System Journal* 9:204–27.

Portney, Kent E. (1987). "The Dilemma of Democracy in State and Local Environmental Regulation: The Case of Citizen Participation in Local Hazardous Waste Treatment Facility Siting." Paper presented at the annual meeting of the Midwest Political Science Association, Chicago.

Prottas, Jeffrey M. (1979). *People-Processing*. Lexington, Mass.: D. C. Heath.

Ray, Larry, and Emerson Bruns. (1988). "Statewide Dispute Resolution Initiatives Directory." Washington, D.C.: American Bar Association. Typescript.

Resnick, Judith. (1987). "Due Process: A Public Dimension." *University of Florida Law Review* 39:405-31.

Salamon, Lester M. (1981). "Rethinking Public Management:Third-Party Government and the Changing Forms of Government Action." *Public Policy* 29:255-75.

Sarat, Austin. (1988). "The New Formalism in Disputing and Dispute Processing." *Law and Society Review* 21:705-15.

Schattschneider, E. E. (1959). *The Semisovereign People: A Realist's View of Democracy in America*. Hinsdale, Ill.: Dryden.

Selva, Lance H., and Robert M. Bohm. (1987). "A Critical Examination of the Informalism Experiment in the Administration of Justice." *Crime and Social Justice* 29:43-57.

Sennett, Richard. (1970). *The Uses of Disorder: Personal Identity and City Life*. New York: Random House.

———. (1980). *Authority*. New York: Alfred A. Knopf.

Shapiro, Michael J. (1988). *The Politics of Representation: Writing Practice in Biography, Photography, and Policy Analysis*. Madison: University of Wisconsin Press.

Silbey, Susan, and Austin Sarat. (1988). "Dispute Processing in Law and Legal Scholarship: From Institutional Critique to the Reconstitution of the Judicial Subject." Madison: Institute for Legal Studies.

"Statewide Offices—The Directors Speak." (1987). *Dispute Resolution FORUM*, Dec.

"Statewide Offices—The Experts' Views." (1987). *Dispute Resolution FORUM*, Dec.

Steinberger, Peter J. (1985). *Ideology and the Urban Crisis*. Albany: State University of New York Press.

Stever, James A. (1983). "Citizen Participation in Negotiated Investment Strategy." *Journal of Urban Affairs* 3:231-40.

———. (1988). *The End of Public Administration: Problems of the Profession in the Post-Progressive Era*. New York: Transnational.

Sullivan, Timothy J. (1984). *Resolving Development Disputes Through Negotiations*. New York: Plenum.

Susskind, Lawrence E. (1986). "Evaluating Dispute Resolution Experiments." *Negotiation Journal* 2:135-39.

———. (1987). "Experiments in Statewide Offices of Mediation." *Dispute Resolution FORUM*, Dec.

Susskind, Lawrence E., and Jeffrey Cruikshank. (1987). *Breaking the Impasse*. New York: Basic Books.

Susskind, Lawrence E., and Denise Madigan. (1984). "New Approaches to Resolving Disputes in the Public Sector." *Justice System Journal* 9:179-203.

Susskind, Lawrence E., and Connie Ozawa. (1984). "Mediated Negotiation in the Public Sector: The Planner as Mediator." *Journal of Planning Education and Research* 4:5-15.

——— . (1985). "Mediating Public Disputes: Obstacles and Possibilities." *Journal of Social Issues* 41:145–59.

Swanson, Peter J. Bryan. (1988). "State and Federal Initiatives in the Use of Mediation." *Mediation Quarterly* 20:101–12.

Szanton, Peter L. (1988). "Four State Offices of Dispute Resolution: A Report to the National Institute for Dispute Resolution." Washington, D.C. Typescript.

Tomasic, Roman. (1982). "Mediation as an Alternative: Rhetoric and Reality in the Neighborhood Justice Movement." In Roman Tomasic and Malcolm M. Feeley, eds., *Neighborhood Justice: Assessment of an Emerging Idea.* New York: Longman.

Trubek, David M. (1980–81). "The Construction and Deconstruction of a Disputes-Focused Approach: An Afterword." *Law and Society Review* 15:727–47.

Volkema, Roger J. (1988). "Problem Statement in Negotiation and Policy Formation." *Mediation Quarterly* 20:23–30.

Weckstein, Donald T. (1988). "The Purposes of Dispute Resolution: Comparative Concepts of Justice." *American Business Law Journal* 26:605–24.

Wood, Robert C. (1958). *Suburbia: The People and Their Politics.* Boston: Houghton-Mifflin.

Select Bibliography

Abel, Richard, ed. *The Politics of Informal Justice*, vol. 1, *The American Experience*. New York: Academic, 1982.

——. *The Politics of Informal Justice*, vol. 2, *Comparative Studies*. New York: Academic, 1982.

Agranoff, R. *Intergovernmental Management*. Albany: State University of New York Press, 1986.

Alford, Robert, and Roger Friedland. *Powers of Theory: Capitalism, the State, and Democracy*. New York: Cambridge University Press, 1985.

Alper, Benedict, and Lawrence Nichols. *Beyond the Courtroom: Programs in Community Justice and Conflict Resolution*. Lexington, Mass.: D. C. Heath, 1981.

American Bar Association. *Dispute Resolution Program Directory 1986–1987*. Washington, D.C.: ABA Special Committee on Dispute Resolution, 1986.

Amy, Douglas. *The Politics of Environmental Mediation*. New York: Columbia University Press, 1987.

Auerbach, Jerold. *Justice Without Law: Resolving Disputes Without Lawyers*. Oxford: Oxford University Press, 1983.

Axelrod, Robert. *The Evolution of Cooperation*. New York: Basic, 1984.

Bacow, L., and M. Wheeler. *Environmental Dispute Resolution*. New York: Plenum, 1984.

Bard, M. *Family Crisis Intervention: From Concept to Implementation*. Washington, D.C.: U.S. Department of Justice, 1973.

——. *The Function of the Police in Crisis Intervention and Conflict Management*. Washington, D.C.: U.S. Department of Justice, 1975.

Barry, Brian. *Political Argument*. London: Routledge and Kegan Paul, 1965.

Becker, Gary. *Human Capital*. New York: Columbia University Press, 1975.

——. *Treatise on the Family*. New York: Columbia University Press, 1981.

Bellow, G., and B. Moulton. *The Lawyering Process*. New York: Foundation, 1981.

270   Select Bibliography

Bercovitch, Jacob. *Social Conflict and Third Parties: Strategies of Conflict Resolution.* Boulder: Westview, 1984.

Bidol, P., et al. *Alternative Environmental Conflict Management: A Citizen's Manual.* Ann Arbor: University of Michigan Environmental Conflict Project, 1986.

Bingham, Gail. *Resolving Environmental Disputes: A Decade of Experience.* Washington, D.C.: Conservation Foundation, 1986.

Blankenburg, Erhard, Ekkehard Klausa, and Hubert Rottleuthner, eds. *Alternative Rechtsformen und Alternativen zum Recht.* Opladen: Westdeutscher Verlag, 1980.

Brodigan, Bruce, et al. *State Legislation on Dispute Resolution.* Chicago: American Bar Association, 1988.

Cain, Maureen, and Kalman Kulcsar, eds. *Disputes and the Law.* Budapest: Akademia Kiado, 1984.

Carpenter, Susan L., and W. Kennedy. *Managing Public Disputes: A Practical Guide to Handling Conflict and Reaching Agreements.* San Francisco: Jossey-Bass, 1988.

Center for Public Resources. *Corporate Dispute Management 1982: A Manual of Innovative Corporate Strategies for the Avoidance and Resolution of Legal Disputes.* New York: Matthew Bender, 1982.

Chanda, Nayan. *Brother Enemy.* New York: Simon and Schuster, 1986.

Chodorow, Nancy. *The Reproduction of Mothering.* Berkeley: University of California Press, 1986.

Clausewitz, Carl. *On War.* Ed. and trans. Michael Howard and Peter Paret. Princeton, N.J.: Princeton University Press, 1976.

Cooley, J. *Appellate Advocacy Manual.* Deerfield, Ill.: Callaghan, 1989.

Coser, Lewis. *The Functions of Social Conflict.* New York: Free, 1956.

Coulson, Robert. *Business Arbitration: What You Need to Know.* New York: American Arbitration Association, 1987.

Cox, Kevin, ed. *Urbanization and Conflict in Market Societies.* Chicago: Maaroufa, 1978.

de Bono, E. *Lateral Thinking: Creativity Step by Step.* New York: Harper and Row, 1970.

Despontin, M., P. Nijkamp, and J. Spronk, eds. *Macro-Economic Planning with Conflicting Goals.* Berlin: Springer Verlag, 1984.

Evan, William, ed. *The Sociology of Law: A Social-Structural Perspective.* New York: Free, 1980.

Evarts, Richard, James Greenstone, Gary Kirkpatrick, and Sharon Leviton. *Winning Through Accommodation: The Mediator's Handbook.* Dubuque: Kendall/Hunt, 1983.

Executive Office for Administration and Finance. *Massachusetts Mediation Service: Annual Report, July 1987-June 1988.* Boston: Commonwealth of Massachusetts, 1988.

Filey, Alan. *Interpersonal Conflict Resolution.* New York: Scott, Foresman, 1975.

Fisher, Roger, and William Ury. *Getting to Yes: Negotiating Agreement Without Giving In.* New York: Houghton-Mifflin, 1981.

Folberg, Jay, and Alison Taylor. *Mediation: A Comprehensive Guide to Resolving Disputes Without Litigation.* San Francisco: Jossey-Bass, 1984.

Ford Foundation. *New Approaches to Conflict Resolution.* New York: Ford Foundation, 1978.

Freedman, J. *Crisis and Legitimacy.* New York: Cambridge University Press, 1978.

Freedman, L. *State Legislation on Dispute Resolution.* Washington, D.C.: ABA Special Committee on Dispute Resolution, 1984.

Freeman, Edward. *Strategic Management: A Stakeholder Approach.* Boston: Pitman, 1984.

Friedman, James. *Game Theory with Applications for Economics*. New York: Oxford University Press, 1986.

Fuller, L. *The Morality of Law*. New Haven: Yale University Press, 1964.

Gass, S. *Impacts of Microcomputers on Operations Research*. Amsterdam: North Holland, 1986.

Gilmore, G. *The Ages of American Law*. New Haven: Yale University Press, 1977.

Glendon, Mary Ann. *The New Family and the New Property*. 1981.

Goldberg, Stephen, Eric Green, and Frank Sander, eds. *Dispute Resolution*. Boston: Little, Brown, 1985.

Guetzkow, Harold, et al. *Simulation in International Relations: Developments for Research and Teaching*. Englewood Cliffs, N.J.: Prentice-Hall, 1963.

Hadden, Susan, ed. *Risk Analysis, Institutions, and Public Policy*. Port Washington, N.Y.: Associated Faculty, 1984.

Hafkamp, W. A. *Economic-Environmental Modelling in a National-Regional System*. Amsterdam: North Holland, 1984.

Haims, Y., and V. Chankong, eds. *Decision-Making with Multiple Objectives*. Berlin: Springer Verlag, 1985.

Hall, D. *A History of South-East Asia*. 3d ed. London: Macmillan, 1968.

Harrington, Christine. *Shadow Justice: The Ideology and Institutionalization of Alternatives to Court*. Westport, Conn.: Greenwood, 1985.

Herrman, M. *Mediation in a Regional Setting*. Washington, D.C.: National Association of Regional Councils, 1987.

Hofrichter, Richard. *Neighborhood Justice in Capitalist Society*. New York: Greenwood, 1987.

Horwitz, M. *The Transformation of American Law*. 1780–1860. Cambridge: Harvard University Press, 1977.

Huelsberg, N., and W. Lincoln, eds. *Successful Negotiating in Local Government*. Washington, D.C.: International City Management Association, 1985.

Humphreys, P., and A. Wisudha. *Methods and Tools for Structuring and Analyzing Decision Problems*. London: London School of Economics and Political Science, 1987.

Isard, W., and C. Smith. *Conflict Analysis and Practical Conflict Management Procedures*. Cambridge: Ballinger, 1982.

Janssen, R. *Evaluatiemethoden ten behoeve van het Milieubeleid enbeheer*. Amsterdam: Free University, 1984.

Koetz, Hein, and Reynald Ottenhof. *Les Conciliateurs, La Conciliation, Une Etude Comparative*. Paris: Economica, 1983.

Kolb, Deborah. *The Mediators*. Cambridge, Mass.: MIT, 1983.

Kressel, Kenneth, and Dean Pruitt, eds. *Mediation Research: The Process and Effectiveness of Third-Party Intervention*. San Francisco: Jossey-Bass, 1989.

Lake, R., ed. *Resolving Locational Conflict*. New Brunswick, N.J.: Rutgers University Press, 1987.

Laponce, J., and Paul Smoker, eds. *Experimentation and Simulation in Political Science*. Toronto: University of Toronto Press, 1972.

Laue, James, ed. *Using Mediation to Shape Public Policy*. San Francisco: Jossey-Bass, 1988.

Lax, D., and J. Sebenius. *The Manager as Negotiator*. New York: Free Press, 1986.

Lichfield, N., P. Kettle, and M. Whitebread. *Evaluation in the Planning Process*. Oxford: Pergamon, 1985.

Lipsky, Michael. *Street-Level Bureaucracy*. New York: Russell Sage Foundation, 1980.

Lipston, Leon, and Stanton Wheeler, eds. *Law and the Social Sciences*. New York: Russell Sage Foundation, 1986.

Lowi, Theodore. *The End of Liberalism: The Second Republic of the United States*. New York: W. W. Norton, 1979.

Lowrance, William. *Of Acceptable Risk*. Los Altos, Calif.: William Kaufmann, 1976.

McGillis, Daniel. *Community Dispute Resolution Programs and Public Policy: Issues and Practices*. National Institute of Justice, 1986.

Mansbridge, Jane. *Beyond Adversary Democracy*. New York: Basic, 1980.

Marks, Jonathan, Earl Johnson, Jr., and Peter Szanton. *Dispute Resolution in America: Processes in Evolution*. Washington, D.C.: National Institute for Dispute Resolution, 1984.

Mayers, Lewis. *The American Legal System: The Administration of Justice in the United States by Judicial, Administrative, Military, and Arbitral Tribunals*. New York: Harper, 1955.

Meeks, G. *Managing Environmental and Public Policy Conflicts: A Legislator's Guide*. Denver: National Conference of State Legislators, 1985.

Mermin, Samuel. *Law and the Legal System: An Introduction*. Boston: Little, Brown, 1982.

Mills, Miriam, ed. *Alternative Dispute Resolution and Public Policy*. Westport, Conn.: Greenwood, 1990.

Minnery, J. *Conflict Management in Urban Planning*. Brookfield, Vt.: Gower, 1986.

Moore, Christopher. *The Mediation Process: Practical Strategies for Resolving Conflict*. San Francisco: Jossey-Bass, 1986.

Moore, C., and C. Carlson. *Public Decision Making: Using the Negotiated Investment Strategy*. Dayton, Ohio: Kettering Foundation, 1984.

Nagel, S. *Decision-Aiding Software and Legal Decision-Making: A Guide to Skills and Applications Throughout the Law*. New York: Greenwood-Quorum, 1989.

——— . *Multi-Criteria Dispute Resolution and Decision-Aiding Software*. New York: Greenwood-Quorum, 1990.

——— . *Teach Yourself Computer-Aided Mediation*. Champaign, Ill.: Decision Aids, 1989.

Neustadt, Richard. *Alliance Politics*. New York: Columbia University Press, 1970.

Nicolson, Sir Harold. *Diplomacy*. 3d ed. London: Oxford University Press, 1963.

Nijkamp, P. *Environmental Policy Analysis*. New York: Wiley, 1980.

O'Hare, M., L. Bacow, and D. Sanderson. *Facility Siting and Public Opposition*. New York: Van Nostrand Reinhold, 1983.

Peterson, Paul. *City Limits*. Chicago: University of Chicago Press, 1981.

Prottas, Jeffrey. *People-Processing*. Lexington, Mass.: D. C. Heath, 1979.

Raiffa, Howard. *The Art and Science of Negotiation: How to Resolve Conflicts and Get the Best out of Bargaining*. Cambridge: Harvard University Press, 1982.

Rapoport, Anatol, and Albert Chammah. *Prisoner's Dilemma: Study in Conflict and Cooperation*. Ann Arbor, Mich.: University of Michigan Press, 1965.

Rawls, J. *A Theory of Justice*. Cambridge, Mass.: Harvard University Press, 1971.

Ray, Larry, ed. *Directory of Dispute Resolution Programs*. Washington, D.C.: American Bar Association, 1984.

Richman, R., et al. *Intergovernmental Mediation: Negotiations in Local Government Disputes*. Boulder: Westview, 1986.

Rietveld, P. *Multiple Objective Decision Methods and Regional Planning*. Amsterdam: North Holland, 1980.

Riskin, L., and J. Westbrook. *Dispute Resolution and Lawyers*. Minneapolis: West, 1987.

Robert, Henry. *Robert's Rules of Order Revised*. New York: William Morrow, 1915, reprint. 1971.

Rogers, N., and R. Salem. *A Student's Guide to Mediation and the Law*. New York: Matthew Bender, 1987.

Rosenau, James, ed. *International Politics and Foreign Policy*. New York: Free, 1961.

Rushefsky, Mark. *Making Cancer Policy*. Albany, N.Y.: State University Press of New York, 1986.

Sacarto, D. *Economic Development Conflicts: Model Programs for Dispute Resolution*. Denver: National Conference of State Legislatures, 1985.

Schattschneider, E. *The Semisovereign People: A Realist's View of Democracy in America*. Hinsdale, Ill.: Dryden, 1959.

Shapiro, Michael. *The Politics of Representation: Writing Practice in Biography, Photography, and Policy Analysis*. Madison: University of Wisconsin Press, 1988.

Shawcross, William. *Sideshow*. New York: Simon and Schuster, 1979.

Steinberger, Peter. *Ideology and the Urban Crisis*. Albany: State University of New York Press, 1985.

Stever, James. *The End of Public Administration: Problems of the Profession in the Post-Progressive Era*. New York: Transnational, 1988.

Sullivan, Timothy. *Resolving Development Disputes Through Negotiations*. New York: Plenum, 1984.

Susskind, Lawrence, and Jeffrey Cruikshank. *Breaking the Impasse: Consensual Approaches to Resolving Public Disputes*. New York: Basic, 1987.

Talbot, A. *Settling Things*. Washington, D.C.: Conservation Foundation, 1983.

Tomasic, Roman. *The Sociology of Law*. London: Sage, 1985.

Tomasic, Roman, and Malcolm Feeley, eds. *Neighborhood Justice: Assessment of an Emerging Idea*. New York: Longman, 1982.

Umbreit, M. *Crime and Reconciliation: Creative Options for Victims and Offenders*. Nashville: Abingdon, 1985.

———. *Victim Offender Mediation: Conflict Resolution and Restitution*. Indiana: PACT Institute of Justice, 1985.

Ury, William. *Beyond the Hotline: How Crisis Control Can Prevent Nuclear War*. New York: Houghton-Mifflin, 1985.

Ury, William, Jean Brett, and Stephen Goldberg. *Getting Disputes Resolved: Designing Systems to Cut the Costs of Conflict*. San Francisco: Jossey-Bass, 1989.

U.S. Senate, Select Committee on Small Business and Subcommittee on Oversight of Government Management of the Committee on Governmental Affairs. *Hearings on Regulatory Negotiation*. Washington, D.C.: U.S. Government Printing Office, 96th Cong.

Von Neumann, John, and Oskar Morgenstern. *Theory of Games and Economic Behaviour*. 2d ed. Princeton, N.J.: Princeton University Press, 1947.

Voogd, H. *Multicriteria Evaluation for Urban and Regional Planning*. London: Pion, 1983.

Wehr, Paul. *Conflict Regulation*. Boulder: Westview, 1979.

Weitzman, Lenore. *The Divorce Revolution*. New York: Free Press, 1985.

Williams, G. *Legal Negotiation and Settlement*. Minneapolis: West, 1983.

Wood, Robert. *Suburbia: The People and Their Politics*. Boston: Houghton-Mifflin, 1958.

Name Index

Subject Index

About the Editors
and Contributors

STUART S. NAGEL is Professor of Political Science at the University of Illinois and a member of the Illinois bar. He is the secretary-treasurer and publications coordinator of the Policy Studies Organization. He is the author or editor of such relevant books as *Multi-Criteria Methods in Alternative Dispute Resolution: With Software Applications* (Quorum, 1990) and *Decision-Aiding Software and Legal Decision-Making* (Quorum, 1989). He has been a special master to the federal courts for doing computer-aided mediation.

MIRIAM K. MILLS is Professor of Organizational Science at the School of Industrial Management of the New Jersey Institute of Technology. Previously, she was the Director of Manpower and Labor Relations of Jersey City Medical Center, New Jersey, and Director of Personnel at the Jewish Home and Hospital for the Aged in New York. A frequent contributor to various journals, she coauthored *Evaluation Analysis with Microcomputers* and coedited *Biomedical Technology and Public Policy*. Dr. Mills is also an arbitrator with the Federal Mediation and Conciliation Service and other labor panels.

MICHAEL V. ALEXEEV was born in Moscow, and received degrees in Economics and Mathematics from Moscow University. His Ph.D. in Economics is from Duke University. Currently he is an Assistant Professor in the Department of Economics, George Mason University, and specializes in Microeconomic Theory and Soviet Economics. He has published numerous articles in economics journals and also acts as consultant to the W.E.F.A. group.

DAVID J. ALLOR is Associate Professor and Director of the School of Planning and Fellow of the Center for the Study of Dispute Resolution, University of Cincinnati. His research, teaching and service interests are in qualitative analysis, organizational development, decision-making, and mediation. He is the author of *The Planning Commissioners Guide: Processes for Reasoning Together*.

STEVEN J. BRAMS is Professor of Politics at New York University and author of *Negotiation Games: Applying Game Theory to Bargaining and Arbitration*. He is the author or coauthor of nine other books, which involve applications of game theory or social choice to a variety of subjects, including superpower conflict, voting and elections, and biblical analysis and theology. He was a Guggenheim Fellow and is currently president of the Peace Science Society (International).

MARGARET F. BRINIG is Associate Professor of Law at George Mason University, where she specializes in Domestic Relations and also teaches Alternative Dispute Resolution and Insurance. She is currently in the Ph.D. program at George Mason and has published extensively in the field of family law.

JOHN W. COOLEY was formerly Assistant United States Attorney, United States Magistrate, and Senior Staff Attorney for the United States Court of Appeals for the Seventh Circuit, and the immediate past Chairman of the Chicago Bar Association's Arbitration and ADR Committee. An adjunct professor at Loyola University of Chicago School of Law, he co-designed and co-taught an innovative course on Alternatives to Litigation.

CHARLES ELLISON is an Associate Professor in the School of Planning and a Fellow in the Center for the Study of Dispute Resolution in the College of Law, University of Cincinnati. His research interests in dispute resolution focus on democratic theory and public policy. His current work includes studies of the public policy conflicts associated with the Feed Materials Production Center at Fernald, Ohio, a Department of Energy nuclear materials facility, and of tax base sharing among local governments.

DANIEL J. FIORINO is Associate Director of the Office of Policy Analysis at the U.S. Environmental Protection Agency, where he is involved in a variety of water, pesticides, and toxics policy issues. His recent articles have appeared in *Public Administration Review, Risk Analysis, Columbia Journal of Environmental Law*, and *Science, Technology, and Human Values*. He holds a Ph.D. in Political Science from Johns Hopkins University.

MICHAEL HAAS is Professor of Political Science at the University of Hawaii at Manoa. He also taught at the University of London in 1990. He is the author of three recent books published by Praeger—*Korean Reunification*, *The Pacific Way*, and *The Asian Way to Peace*. His current research on Cambodia will culminate in *After the Killing Fields*, to be published by Praeger in 1991.

RON JANSSEN studied regional economics at the Free University in Amsterdam. Formally a researcher at the National Institute for Forestry and Landscape Research in Wageningen, he joined the Ministry of the Environment in 1984. Since 1986 he has been employed at the Institute for Environmental Studies and his main topic of research is the evaluation and development of decision support systems in relation to environmental policy making.

D. MARC KILGOUR is Professor of Mathematics at Wilfrid Laurier University in Waterloo, Ontario, Canada, and Adjunct Professor of Systems Design Engineering at the University of Waterloo. His research interests and consulting activities are concentrated in mathematical modeling, especially conflict modeling and game theory. His current research areas include verification and enforcement in arms control and other contexts, international deterrence, conflict analysis methodology, bargaining and arbitration, and the classification of strategic conflicts. He has recently published *Game Theory and National Security* (co-authored with Steven J. Brams), along with numerous papers in political science, operations research, mathematics, systems engineering, biology, economics, and philosophy journals.

LINDA M. V. LISK obtained a Bachelor of Arts degree in Business Administration from Calvin College in Grand Rapids, Michigan. At the Southern Illinois University School of Law in Carbondale, Illinois, she earned her Jurist Doctorate and was active in the women's law forum and Phi Alpha Delta. Presently, Ms. Lisk is a naval officer training for duty in the Judge Advocate General Corps at the Naval Education and Training Center in Newport, Rhode Island.

PETER NIJKAMP holds a Chair in Regional and Urban Economics at the Free University, Amsterdam, and is a fellow of the Royal Dutch Academy of Science. He has a deep interest in quantitative methods for decision analysis and has widely published in the field of environmental management models, resource models, information systems, and non-market transactions.

STEPHAN PARMENTIER is Assistant Professor of Sociology Law at the Faculty of Law of the Katholieke University Leuven, Belgium. At present he is preparing his Ph.D. dissertation about the effective access to the international procedures for the enforcement of human rights. He has written several articles in the areas of sociology of law, dispute resolution, and human rights.

MARK E. RUSHEFSKY is a Professor of Political Science and Director of the Master's in Public Administration Program at Southwest Missouri State University. He is the author of *Making Cancer Policy* and *Public Policy in the United*

States: Toward the Twenty-First Century. He has also written numerous articles and chapters on health, energy, and environmental policy.

MARIA R. VOLPE is an Associate Professor of Sociology and Coordinator of the Dispute Resolution Program at John Jay College of Criminal Justice, City University of New York. She teaches dispute resolution courses at the undergraduate and graduate levels; conducts dispute resolution skills training for a wide range of groups, and is on the editorial board of *Mediation Quarterly* and the *Journal of Contemporary Criminal Justice*. She is Second Vice President of the Society of Professionals in Dispute Resolution and has lectured and written extensively about dispute resolution processes, particularly mediation and the criminal justice system.

SHLOMO WEBER is Professor of Economics at York University, Toronto, Canada. He received his master's degree in mathematics and mechanics from Moscow State University, and a Ph.D. in mathematical economics and game theory from the Hebrew University of Jerusalem, Israel. His research interests are primarily in game theory and its applications to various areas of economics and political science. He has published articles in *Econometrica*, *American Political Science Review*, *Journal of Economic Theory*, and the *Journal of Mathematical Economics*, among others.

GILBERT R. WINHAM is Professor in the Department of Political Science at Dalhousie University in Halifax, Nova Scotia, Canada. His research has been in the area of international diplomacy and negotiation, particularly commercial negotiation, and his most prominent work is *International Trade and the Tokyo Round Negotiation*. Since 1980, Dr. Winham has conducted semi-annual trade negotiation simulation exercises at the GATT in Geneva, for the purpose of training trade officers from developing countries. Dr. Winham is currently serving as a member of dispute settlement panels established under the Canada-U.S. Free Trade Agreement.